THE BRONTËS AND EDUCATION

All the seven Brontë novels are concerned with education in both senses, that of upbringing as well as that of learning. The Brontë sisters all worked as teachers before they became published novelists. In spite of the prevalence of education in the sisters' lives and fiction, however, this is the first full-length book on the subject. Marianne Thormählen explores how their representations of fictional teachers and schools engage with the intense debates on education in the nineteenth century, drawing on a wealth of documentary evidence about educational theory and practice in the lifetime of the Brontës. This study offers much new information both about the Brontës and their books and about the most urgent issue in early-nineteenth-century British social politics: the education of the people, of all classes and both sexes.

MARIANNE THORMÄHLEN is Professor of English Literature at Lund University, Sweden. She is the author of *The Brontës and Religion* (Cambridge, 1999), as well as of books on T. S. Eliot and the Earl of Rochester, and the editor of *Rethinking Modernism* (2003).

THE BRONTËS AND EDUCATION

MARIANNE THORMÄHLEN

CAMBRIDGE
UNIVERSITY PRESS

CAMBRIDGE UNIVERSITY PRESS

Cambridge, New York, Melbourne, Madrid, Cape Town, Singapore, São Paulo

Cambridge University Press
The Edinburgh Building, Cambridge CB2 8RU, UK

Published in the United States of America by Cambridge University Press, New York

www.cambridge.org
Information on this title: www.cambridge.org/9780521832892

© Marianne Thormählen 2007

First published 2007

Printed in the United Kingdom at the University Press, Cambridge

A catalogue record for this publication is available from the British Library

ISBN 978-0-521-83289-2 hardback

Contents

Acknowledgements

Among the institutions that assisted the writing of this book, the Swedish Research Council played an especially prominent role. By giving me a grant entailing 50 per cent research on a long-term basis from 2005 onwards, the Council enabled me not only to finish the book ahead of the deadline in the contract, but to work away without feeling even slightly guilty towards my department and colleagues: a rare privilege which added significantly to the happiness that this book project has given me.

Before the Research Council liberated me from worries about how I was going to fund my many research trips, the following organisations did much to ease the burden: the Royal Society of Letters in Lund, the Magn. Bergvall Foundation, the Craford Foundation, the Elisabeth Rausing Memorial Fund and the New Society of Letters in Lund. Without their generous assistance, the book would never have got off the ground.

The Bodleian Library and the English Faculty Library in Oxford were my standbys when I began the book and have remained so, more recently joined by the British Library, including the latter's newspaper division in Colindale. In all these libraries my requirements have met with understanding and flexibility, attitudes which enabled me to make the most of the limited periods of time I was able to spend there, and I am extremely grateful to them.

The Research Library in the Brontë Parsonage Museum in Haworth has been my haven on a number of visits over the years, and *The Brontës and Education* relies heavily on its unique collections. Curators have come and gone, but the Librarian Ann Dinsdale was always there, helpful, supportive and immensely knowledgeable. The opportunity to consult her, and Rachel Terry and Leanne Eskdale, has been a tremendous advantage throughout.

The Armstrong Browning Library in Waco, Texas, gave me a happy and productive month as a grant-funded visiting scholar, in the course of which I was able to study important materials which I would otherwise never have seen. I am most grateful to its Director Professor Stephen Prickett and his friendly, efficient staff, who ensured that my weeks on the Baylor campus were as pleasant as they were profitable.

I owe a special debt to Dr Linda Bree of the Cambridge University Press, who called this book into being by persuading me to leave the paths of modernism and return to the nineteenth century. When she commissioned the book from me, neither of us could have known that it would give me greater pleasure than anything else I have written; but my gratitude to her encompasses that pleasure, too.

Every writer who ever had a perceptive, constructive, enthusiastic but level-headed reader, who seized each new chapter the moment it came off the printer, prioritised the reading of it before other urgent jobs and promptly delivered insightful comments, tactful criticism and heaps of encouragement, will understand how fortunate I was in having two such helpers by my side throughout the project. My heartfelt thanks go to my colleague Dr Birgitta Berglund and my daughter Imke Thormählen for making this a better book than I could have produced on my own, and for seasoning their criticism and advice with humour of a kind that made rewriting easy, even enjoyable. The latter also gave up a precious holiday week to scrutinise the final manuscript, picking up a number of errors and infelicities. All remaining inadequacies are of course entirely my own responsibility.

Other people at work and at home gave me the reliable assistance and encouragement that any long-term project needs. I am grateful to my loyal professorial *Kameradin* Beatrice Warren for her generosity in all things and her sanity when mine was insufficient, to my trusty assistant Kiki Lindell whose swift and yet scrupulous services have made my life a great deal easier, to my life-long mentor Professor Claes Schaar for making me promise, twenty years ago, not to let anything stand in the way of my research and to my unfailingly supportive husband Axel and daughter Åsa for never allowing me to forget that promise and for doing everything in their power to enable me to keep it. At a late stage, I ventured to put a third of the manuscript before the English Literature Research Seminar at Lund and was rewarded by a host of illuminating observations and astute suggestions. Warm thanks to Dr Birgitta Berglund (again), Stefan Ekman, Dr Sara Håkansson, Staffan Johansson, Anneli Källerö, Lisa Larsson, Kiki Lindell, Anna Lindhé, Dr Jane Mattisson, Karolina Rey and Dr Annika Sylén Lagerholm, and to the two much-appreciated honorary members of the seminar during the spring term of 2006, Professor Susan McCabe and Kate Chandler.

Working on *The Brontës and Education* I became aware of another debt which had accumulated for years without my realising it. I am the daughter of teachers and grew up in a home where education was always a major concern, but it took this book to make me aware of how much my parents taught me about it. My late father was a legendary sports teacher who was as pleased with the modest progress of clumsy and disabled boys, for whom he devised individual training programmes carefully adapted to their abilities, as with the prizes won by his crack athletes. My mother made the natural sciences fascinating and comprehensible even for me, managing her school laboratories with gentle firmness and rock-solid professional competence, inspiring some of her pupils to choose her beloved chemistry as a career. This book is a late daughterly tribute to Curt and Ella Wahlberg, the best of parents and teachers.

Lund, Sweden, in August 2006
Marianne Thormählen

Abbreviations and editions

References to the seven Brontë novels are made parenthetically in the running text. Upper-case Roman numerals refer to volume numbers (wherever appropriate), lower-case ones to chapters and Arabic figures to page numbers in the Oxford World's Classics editions listed below:

CHARLOTTE BRONTË

The Professor, ed. Margaret Smith and Herbert Rosengarten, with an introduction by Margaret Smith (Clarendon edition in 1987; issued as a World's Classics paperback in 1991)

Jane Eyre, ed. Margaret Smith, with an introduction and revised notes by Sally Shuttleworth (Clarendon edition in 1975; new World's Classics paperback edition in 2000)

Shirley, ed. Herbert Rosengarten and Margaret Smith, with an introduction by Margaret Smith (Clarendon edition in 1979; issued as a World's Classics paperback in 1981)

Villette, ed. Margaret Smith and Herbert Rosengarten, with an introduction and notes by Tim Dolin (Clarendon edition in 1984; new World's Classics paperback edition in 2000)

EMILY BRONTË

Wuthering Heights, ed. Ian Jack, with an introduction and notes by Patsy Stoneman (Clarendon edition in 1976; new World's Classics paperback in 1998)

ANNE BRONTË

Agnes Grey, ed. Robert Inglesfield and Hilda Marsden, with an introduction and notes by Robert Inglesfield (Clarendon edition in 1988; issued as a World's Classics paperback in 1991)

The Tenant of Wildfell Hall, ed. Herbert Rosengarten with an introduction by Margaret Smith (Clarendon edition in 1992; issued as a World's Classics paperback in 1993)

The abbreviation 'Smith, *Letters*', supplemented by the relevant volume number (Roman numerals), refers to Margaret Smith's three-volume edition, published by Oxford University Press, of *The Letters of Charlotte Brontë with a selection of letters by family and friends.* The respective volumes appeared in 1995 (1829–1847), 2000 (1848–1851) and 2004 (1852–1855).

The abbreviation *BST* refers to the *Brontë Society Transactions.*

In the endnotes and bibliography, publishers' names are omitted in respect of books published before 1900.

Introduction

The Brontës and Education is the first published full-length investigation of the topic stated by its title, as *The Brontës and Religion* (1999) was of Christianity in the Brontë novels.[1] Like its predecessor, *The Brontës and Education* aims to enrich the reading experience of present-day audiences by increasing their understanding of dimensions in the Brontë fiction that are otherwise easily overlooked. That is not all it attempts to do, however. To a greater extent than *The Brontës and Religion*, this new book looks beyond the works of the Brontës to the wider social context in which those works were created.

All the seven Brontë novels are seriously and variously concerned with education in both its main senses, that of upbringing and that of knowledge acquisition. They were written by professionals in the field: the four of Patrick Brontë's children who survived adolescence all taught for a living. Education was the foremost issue in societal debate throughout their lives, and their lives were constantly touched by education. For that reason, biography plays a more prominent role in this study than in the earlier volume. Fortunately, the last fifteen years have witnessed the publication of first-class biographical research which has done away with many of the myths surrounding the Brontës and laid the foundation for fresh critical scholarship with biographical references.[2]

While *The Brontës and Education* seeks to provide deeper insights into the fabric of the Brontë novels, it has another purpose as well: that of alerting twenty-first-century readers to the fascinating drama of education in nineteenth-century Britain, a drama in which the Brontë family were actors. Throughout the research of which this book is the outcome, two statements by experts on the history of education acquired ever-increasing validity: 'It is a common mistake to regard the history of education as steady uninterrupted progress from the earliest beginnings to the present system';[3] and 'We are fumbling around in education because we know so little about the future and do not bother to know enough about the past'.[4] Studying the

Brontë fiction alongside early-nineteenth-century educational materials, from policy statements to teacher manuals and schoolbooks, is a powerful corrective against the notion that current methods and practices represent the pinnacle of enlightened thinking where education is concerned.

Those who grappled with educational issues in the nineteenth century would have little reason to be overawed by the achievements of their successors in the twenty-first. For one thing, their problems are still with us, unresolved. The difficulty of imparting adequate instruction to each member of a group in which individual capabilities vary wildly is as great and pressing now as it was 200 years ago.[5] The current debates on faith schools and the teaching of 'creationism' raise the same arguments as nineteenth-century disputes over the religious element in education. Even when it comes to the question of what pupils should learn, there are similarities: educationists then and now have often maintained that the possession of factual knowledge matters less than the ability to pursue and locate it when needed, a stance by no means uncontroversial among practitioners (and parents). These resemblances do not mean that there has been no essential progress in education over the past 150 years; but progress has been connected to general developments in society, rather than to the emergence of new and significant educational wisdom.

This book joins the historically contextualising line in Brontë studies that has seen several weighty contributions over the past few decades;[6] but its approach to the historical context diverges from the predominating mindset in modern Brontë scholarship. For one thing, as is clear from the preceding paragraphs, it is not based on an *a priori* assumption that the present is inherently superior to the past. In addition, the focus is not on the 'Victorian' period but on the first half of the nineteenth century, with frequent shifts back into the eighteenth. The traditional idea that the Brontë fiction is an expression of protest against 'Victorian conventions' fails to recognise that Queen Victoria was only about eight months older than Anne Brontë. While the Brontë writings are certainly coloured by a strong libertarian pathos that sometimes manifests itself in criticism of repressive and unjust social phenomena, the forces they attack were formed long before British society under Victoria could be said to have acquired anything like a configuration of values (insofar as it ever did). The ideals, norms and practices with which the Brontë fiction engages – by no means always in terms of disagreement – were to a great extent rooted in the eighteenth century, as ensuing chapters will show.

Another problem with the notion of 'Victorian conventionalism' is that it obscures the realisation that the views, beliefs and principles of nineteenth-century people were as varied and complex, not to say contradictory, as ours. When venturing into print, or attempting to persuade recipients of letters, our predecessors trod as warily as we do in order not to offend what they saw as the prevailing sensibilities of the time. Not only was it as difficult to distinguish between genuine conviction and mere mastery of shibboleths then as it is now; the same persons spoke and acted in ways we would naturally regard as forward-looking at one time, only to come across as reactionaries at another. The Brontës, father and children, are excellent illustrations.[7] 'Judgementalism' is frowned on in our own supposedly tolerant age, but condemning – or at least patronising – the people of the past who shaped our present has usually been a fairly safe occupation in literary scholarship. The desire to promote understanding is a more constructive approach.[8]

The absence of a censorious attitude to the materials it engages with sets *The Brontës and Education* apart from a good deal of late-twentieth-century Brontë criticism in another respect as well. Like *The Brontës and Religion*, this book does not read the Brontës' works, records of their lives and historical/contextual texts against the grain. To quote the earlier volume, 'I found so much *in* the "grain" . . . that the wish to introduce new perspectives by reading *against* it never arose' (p. 5). The inculcation of 'suspicious reading' in the second half of the twentieth century brought great benefits, training critics to pick up manipulative and conflicting dimensions in texts and thus enhancing awareness of complexity and variety. Occasionally, though, the urge to uncover surreptitious contradictions in a text in a manner somehow hostile to what was perceived as its ostensible 'message' has sent readers rather too far away from its manifest concerns. As the twentieth century progressed, D. H. Lawrence's 'Never trust the teller, trust the tale' was transformed into an exhortation not to trust the tale either. But those who disseminated such teachings were themselves tellers of tales, and it is not immediately obvious why we should trust them more than others. Where tales have not emitted the characteristic odour of insincerity (as happened often enough), I have, by and large, trusted them.

The Brontës and Education is the outcome of the study of a very large number of tales, whose tellers were sometimes mere names and occasionally not even that ('A Lady', 'A Clergyman in the Church of England'). Their 'messages' varied as widely as their tones, registers, scopes and positions, but in one respect they formed a contrapuntal structure without dissonances: they proclaimed the duty of human beings to endeavour to make themselves better people. The self-improvement ethos that was such a strong force in nineteenth-century Britain expressed itself in many different ways, including projects geared to inspiring the young with 'the necessity of self-culture' and meetings of local 'Mental Improvement Societies'.[9] The Brontë fiction forms part of this great moral structure.

One of the seven novels deviates markedly from the other six in this regard, however. While *Wuthering Heights* makes it clear that Heathcliff's educational backsliding contributes to the rupture of his childhood alliance with Catherine, and that an illiterate Hareton was not an acceptable husband for young Cathy, self-education is never held up as a moral obligation.[10] When people read books and learn things, it is because they want to. In Charlotte and Anne Brontë's novels, by contrast, persons of all ages and stations, and both sexes, are depicted as being aware of the duty to improve themselves through (self-)education. Those who do not feel it, or choose to disregard it, are seen to be ethically flawed, at times even villainous.

In view of the importance of education in the Brontë fiction, it might have seemed natural to discuss these works as *Bildungsromane*, and *Jane Eyre* has often been cited as an example of that genre.[11] However, none of the terms offered by the relevant conceptual arsenal fits even the majority of the novels well enough to form a useful terminological implement. While *Bildung*, *Entwicklung* and *Erziehung* are highly relevant to them all, the process of maturation is not the core issue in them.[12] Self-education projects in the works of the Brontës do not stop with well-adjusted adulthood, nor are they limited to successful socialisation in this world. The end towards which storylines tend is not an adult in harmony with society, but an adult in harmony with herself as part of the Creation, including its spiritual and imaginative-creative aspects.[13] For a Brontë protagonist to lead a successful life, he or she must have an answer to the question posed by the apprehensive teenager Helen Lawrence on the brink of a disastrous marriage: 'What shall I do with the serious part of myself?' (*The Tenant of Wildfell Hall* XXII.190).

Nineteenth-century definitions of 'education' usually invoke the Latin origin of the word, speaking of how education 'calls forth' or 'draws out' the faculties of the learner.[14] As used in this book, the concept stands for the development of knowledge, skills, abilities and/or character by means of teaching, training, study and experience, including the formation of a young person's personality under the influence of his or her elders, parents as well as instructors.[15] In other words, it is an extremely variegated phenomenon; and the more multifarious the subject, the more helpful a simple organisational rationale is apt to be. Consequently, the outline of

The Brontës and Education was determined by a plain set of interrogatives: when and why; who and where; what; and how.

The first section, 'Education and society', sketches the broad context of the study. Starting out from the *Jane Eyre* passage where the narrator praises the virtues of the British peasantry, it maps the contentious area of popular education in the first half of the nineteenth century. Adult (self-)education is also discussed, with reference to Mechanics' Institutes, phrenology and the mental-improvement culture of the late eighteenth and early nineteenth centuries. The last few pages of the section consider ethical and epistemological tensions in the context of the persistent, and persistently troubled, valorisation of truth in the time of the Brontës.

The second chapter in Section II, 'Home and school', also addresses the importance and elusiveness of truth, albeit from a different angle. This chapter, the most extensive discussion of child-rearing – and of relations between parents and children – in the book, brings up the early-nineteenth-century horror of childish mendacity. Another issue raised in it is (male) children's cruelty to animals. The upbringing of boys in *The Professor* and *The Tenant of Wildfell Hall* is considered against educationists' constant pleading with parents to foster compassion and kindness in their sons. Subsequent chapters deal with professional instructors in homes and schools, placing the Brontës' own experiences and those of their fictional teachers in the context of the low social status, and the incipient professionalisation, of educators.

The third section, 'Subjects and skills', is by far the longest, as is natural in that it attempts to answer the question of what a good education in the time of the Brontës actually contained. Its five chapters deal, in turn, with the 'academic' subjects studied by girls in the Brontë fiction, and by the Brontës themselves; the so-called accomplishments, on the one hand highly prestigious and on the other attended by a pervasive uneasiness; the place of religion in education; the differences between male and female education in association with the lives and works of the Brontës; and the substance of the sisters' self-study and reading outside the schoolroom. Among the matters addressed in this section are the places of geography and history in the contemporary curriculum, the furore over natural history in the early and mid-nineteenth century, the learning of foreign and Classical languages and the distinction between reading and study.

Pedagogy is the chief topic of Section IV, 'Strategies and methods'. It proceeds from the preoccupation with how children and young people should be taught that generated so much discussion and experimentation in late-eighteenth-century and early-nineteenth-century Europe. Continental pioneers inspired British educationists, but the domestic tradition from Locke onwards was also strong. The first of the two chapters ends with a review of the pedagogical principles and practices of M. Constantin Heger. The second chapter looks at what makes a teacher succeed or fail, inter-weaving contemporary works on pedagogical matters and the experiences of pedagogues in the Brontë fiction.

The fifth, concluding section of *The Brontës and Education* raises issues that were touched on in the preceding ones, but never examined at length. Called 'Originality and freedom', it analyses the responsibility of individuals for their selves, both in this world and the next. The connections between originality, creativity and genius are explored, leading up to a discussion of how Charlotte Brontë fashioned her sisters' literary reputations for posterity. That topic, much debated in recent years, has a direct bearing on the subject of the book in that Charlotte's statement that her sisters were not 'learned' has been regarded as a key factor in the context. Finally, the section reviews the importance of mental and spiritual liberty to the individual's pursuit of self-improvement. Once again, *Jane Eyre* supplies the point of departure; and it is shown that the balancing of reason and feeling, as well as the schooling of principle and judgement, can only be successfully undertaken by a free spirit fully aware of what she owes her own integrity.

I

Education and society

Introductory Remarks to Section I

Books about Britain in the early nineteenth century characteristically refer to the period as one of progress and reform. The title of Asa Briggs's classic *The Age of Improvement 1783–1867* sums up a fundamental belief held by British people at all levels of society during the life-span of Patrick Brontë (1777–1861): the belief that human beings could become better and make their world better by labouring with and for one another.[1] The impulses that guided them and the policies they evolved were diverse, conditioned by social factors as well as by individual inclinations; the latter aspect is important, not least because this was a time when individuality asserted itself vigorously in all walks of life and in members of both sexes. The student of the nineteenth century who attempts to map out consistent lines of development, attaching them to representatives of political parties and philosophical schools of thought, soon becomes thoroughly bewildered. Terms such as 'conservative', 'progressive' and 'radical' fail to do justice to the complexity of movements and people. Reformers are seen to have made common cause across class and party lines.[2] Similarly, causes that posterity regards as enlightened were sometimes opposed by persons whose reforming zeal manifested itself in other contexts. One thing, however, was clear then and is equally so now: in the words of an 1828 review of a schoolbook, '[t]his is truly the age of intellectual improvement, and in every form and manner exertions are multiplied to advance it'.[3]

The Brontë family was part of all this social mobility and variety, as well as of the efforts to improve the 'condition of England', another key concept in histories of the period. As a man and a clergyman, Patrick Brontë had a larger scope for action and debate than his daughters, a scope encompassing political, religious and scientific matters as well as public-health issues. To all the Brontës, however, as to so many of their contemporaries, one sphere was of paramount importance: the sphere of education. It impinged on their lives at every turn, and their writings touch on every conceivable aspect of it.

This first section of *The Brontës and Education* engages with education as a matter of general societal concern, drawing on the Brontë fiction and on circumstances in the Brontës' lives. Gradually moving from the public to the private sphere, from social to personal improvement, the discussion takes account of educational policies, practices and ideals, ending in a consideration of the ideal of ideals to educators during the age of improvement: the supremacy of truth.

CHAPTER I

The education of the people

ELEMENTARY EDUCATION: 'BEHIND THE NEEDS OF THE TIME'[1]

Brontë scholars and *Jane Eyre* critics have devoted far more attention to Lowood than to the village school for girls where Jane Eyre teaches after running away from Thornfield. That is understandable – the Lowood section is much more extensive, and Jane's experiences there are formative in several ways – but to anyone who wants to explore the interaction between Charlotte Brontë's fiction and the educational issues of her time, Morton school is of peculiar interest. The self-congratulatory tone of the narrator-teacher, closing the premises where she has achieved remarkable results in a matter of months, has a patriotic overtone which is easily overlooked by a modern reader. It would not, however, have been lost on a participant in mid-nineteenth-century debates on education for the people:

I stood with the key in my hand, exchanging a few words of special farewell with some half-dozen of my best scholars: as decent, respectable, modest, and well-informed young women as could be found in the ranks of the British peasantry. And that is saying a great deal; for after all, the British peasantry are the best taught, best mannered, most self-respecting of any in Europe: since those days I have seen paysannes and Bäuerinnen; and the best of them seemed to me ignorant, coarse, and besotted, compared with my Morton girls. (*Jane Eyre* III.viii.389)[2]

With Charlotte Brontë, extradiegetic narratorial commentary – that is, comments that halt the flow of the narrative to make a statement with no bearing on the actual story – usually signals deep personal concern on the author's part. Consequently, one may wonder why the superiority of the 'British peasantry' mattered so much to her. The answer is found in the dispute on elementary education for the lower orders that dominated socio-political debates all over England during the writing of *Jane Eyre*.

Throughout the early and mid-nineteenth century, reformers tried to persuade Parliament to introduce schemes of compulsory primary education on a national basis, but without success. The reason for the repeated failures lay in the conflict between Church of England adherents and Dissenters. In the early nineteenth century, such formal education as was provided for the children of the lower classes was usually organised either by 'The National Society for promoting the Education of the Poor in the Principles of the Established Church throughout England and Wales' – which was of course Church of England – or by 'The British and Foreign School Society', the corresponding Dissenter body.[3] From 1833 onwards, their activities were supported by government grants. Neither side was prepared to make any concessions when it came to controlling the religious content of education.[4] The result was that while Continental European countries operated national schemes of compulsory education for children of all faiths, Britain remained mired in religious dispute until the Education Act of 1870 finally effected a compromise.[5]

Frustrated advocates of national education would lament over '[t]he sectarian spirit which is the curse of English society' and invoke the examples of other countries, thereby touching another raw nerve.[6] British patriotism could ill endure the notion that things might be better handled abroad. In addition, the element of compulsion in the proposed national-education schemes offended those to whom the ancient British liberties were what made their country great. On this point opponents to the compulsory schemes agreed, whichever camp – religious or political – they came from. For instance, the arch-Liberal William Cobbett called the 1833 'attempt to force education' on the people 'a French, . . . a *doctrinaire* plan', to which he would always remain hostile.[7]

It was bad enough for a patriotic Briton to be told that the German states, especially Prussia, and Holland were more successful than England when it came to educating the lower orders.[8] The suggestion that Napoleonic France, and countries left with the legacy of French occupation, had anything to teach Britain was obviously even more offensive. Nevertheless, the great British educationist James Kay-Shuttleworth's brother Joseph Kay did not scruple to call Napoleon 'the deliverer' of the poor in occupied territories. The implication that the British peasantry might have done less badly under a Napoleonic régime than under their own masters was not a million miles away.[9]

Such unpatriotic sentiments were anathema to the staunch British patriot Charlotte Brontë, and this is where Jane Eyre's 'paysannes and Bäuerinnen' are coming from. The repeated 'British peasantry' and the translation, twice over, of 'peasant woman' rubbed the mid-1800s readership's collective nose in the contention that the rural population of Great Britain – especially its womenfolk – were doing very well as they were. Not only were the supposedly better-off Germans and Frenchwomen no better educated; they were socially, morally and intellectually inferior.

Readers of *Jane Eyre* who had belonged to the readership of *Blackwood's Edinburgh Magazine* in the 1830s – the magazine kept a remarkably low profile in the 1846–47 dispute on state education – would be quick to pick up that message. Throughout the 1830s, *Blackwood's* conducted a vociferous campaign against compulsory national education. In the pastoral care of the Anglican clergy, it argued, the peasantry would come to no harm, especially in view of the diligence that was theirs by virtue of their British nationality: whereas national schemes of elementary education might be necessary in France, whose 'great mass of population has ever been a *dormant* population', all of England hums like 'a great busy hive'. Consequently, the education of the people could, and should in *Blackwood's* view, 'be left *free*'.[10]

So much for 'paysannes', according to *Blackwood's*. 'Bäuerinnen' had done rather better as a result of the extension of literacy in German-speaking countries, but only thanks to the efforts of the clergy, especially in Protestant areas. The main problem with popular education in France, argued *Blackwood's*, was that it was secular: the centralised, state-controlled system was run by men who never ventured into those corners of their minds where their religion might be deposited. Hence, the instruction disseminated by their system was fundamentally flawed.[11]

In the year before Charlotte Brontë wrote the 'paysannes and Bäuerinnen' passage in *Jane Eyre*, the Vicar of Leeds, Dr Walter Farquhar Hook, put forward a proposal which tended in the same direction as the efforts made by John Russell's new Whig government to launch a scheme of national education. Hook's solution to the problem of religious instruction was simple: the teaching administered by schoolteachers should be secular, and religious education would be supplied by Anglican clergymen and Dissenter ministers to their respective flocks on premises set apart for that purpose.[12]

Another Yorkshire clergyman who pinned his hopes on the 1846 plan for national education was Patrick Brontë. At precisely the time when his daughter Charlotte placed the case for the opposition in Jane Eyre's mouth, he wrote a letter to the *Leeds Intelligencer* warmly supporting 'the best plan ever devised . . . for the universal spread of divine knowledge, and useful science'.[13]

There would have been little point in sending such a letter to the *Leeds Mercury* whose editor, the Whig Dissenter Edward Baines, did his best to convince Russell that Hook's plans were misguided. A hint of local patriotism adheres to his argument: quoting a Government Inspector's report, Baines averred that 'the further we go to the North, . . . the greater is the interest taken in education, and the better its quality'.[14] In other words, no national scheme of compulsory education was necessary, at least not in Baines's part of the country. Baines was certain that a voluntary system was sufficient, having declared a few years earlier, 'In the meantime we will hold fast our Liberties. We will not be dragooned into a State Religion'.[15] Here, patriotic sentiment is allied to non-Anglican fears in resisting a foreign-style coercive scheme unsuitable for the children of free-born Englishmen.[16]

From the late summer of 1846 to the late spring of 1847, the period during which Charlotte Brontë wrote most of *Jane Eyre*, no subject was as eagerly discussed by the two local Leeds weeklies as the government's proposals on national education. Baines's writings on the subject, including his leaders and lengthy 'Letters' to the new Prime Minister Lord John Russell, would fill a substantial volume. His basic argument may be illustrated by a quotation from the *Leeds Mercury*:

It is no more the duty of the Government to educate the people, or to assist in educating them, than it is to *feed* the people, or to *assist* in feeding them. Government was instituted for no such purpose. It is for *parents* to educate their children, and for the rich to assist the poor. And let the advocates of State education remember, that *you cannot inflict a greater injury on a people than by doing for them that which they ought to do for themselves.* Is not this truth now preached daily in Parliament with regard to Ireland? [Both the *Mercury* and the *Intelligencer* for this period reported and commented extensively on Ireland's distress.] Did not LORD JOHN RUSSELL proclaim the great lesson, that 'Heaven helps those who help themselves'? It is the proud distinction of freemen, that they think and act for themselves; and it is the disgrace and curse of slaves, that their masters think and act for them.[17]

Baines's patriotism comes out in near-hysterical accusations against ministers, who would be 'criminal . . . to persevere' with the national-education plans (27 March 1847, 4), and tirades against anyone who ventured to suggest that the poor of other nations were better educated, including the 'wild and extravagant' Joseph Kay (19 September 1846, 4), brother of that 'educational dictator', James Kay-Shuttleworth (20 March 1847, 4).

The alleged dictator wrote for the opposition, contributing to the *Leeds Intelligencer* and receiving that weekly's unstinting praise and support.[18] The *Leeds Intelligencer* also defended Joseph Kay's position on the merits of popular education on the Continent, ridiculing Baines's ideas about France as sunk in 'an unnatural apathy' and stoutly proclaiming, 'There is no nation in Europe which is making such rapid moral and intellectual strides' (3 October 1846, 4).

The narratorial comment in *Jane Eyre* hence forms part of a raging nationwide dispute, a dispute in which Yorkshire combatants played active roles and which reverberated within the walls of Haworth Parsonage. Any reader who took even a passing interest in the debate on national education will have interpreted the passage on the Morton schoolgirls taught by Jane Eyre under St John Rivers' inspection, and at his initiative, as an expression of support for the idea that the education of the British peasantry did not require the imposition of a national, compulsory scheme: sound at heart and safe in the hands of good Churchmen, the simple people of the countryside would still flourish in liberty. The tone of Jane's comment is very close to the *Leeds Mercury* idiom. It is hard to believe that Charlotte made her heroine-narrator articulate a stance on the most pressing social question of the day which she did not share. She knew it was a stance diametrically opposed to her father's, and to that of close friends and colleagues of his.[19]

The difference between father and daughter is one of personality as well as of social position. Patrick Brontë, who was used to being in charge and knowing best, would not be greatly concerned about the state scheme inevitably resulting in the governments' gaining control of popular education – especially as most of that control would, in practice, be exercised by men like Brontë himself. Charlotte's libertarian stance was that of a woman with limited opportunity to control her own life, let alone the lives of others. It is not surprising that the man with an instinct to rule and the woman whose overall ambition was personal liberty found themselves on opposing sides on this contentious issue.

When Charlotte Brontë made her narrator articulate the *Leeds Mercury* attitude on national education in defiance of her father's *Leeds Intelligencer* view, she made use of the freedom of opinion that always existed in the home of the Brontës. Freedom of opinion was one thing, however; freedom to reject an occupation that was one's obvious duty was another. Whatever the four young Brontës felt about it, they could not escape teaching in the Sunday school established by their father in 1832.

Originally created in the late eighteenth century with a view to teaching the children of the lower orders to read their Bible and develop good habits and manners, Sunday schools in Britain were a variegated phenomenon during the half-century that preceded the opening of the Haworth school.[20] Up and down the country, Sunday schools flourished and declined. Some were open all day on Sunday and some extended their hours to weekdays, evenings included. In some places tuition was given to adults as well as children, as it was recognised that untaught parents could soon undo what had been achieved at school. Academic standards varied greatly, as did the proportion of secular instruction.[21] Before the Factory Act of 1833, a Sunday school was often the only chance for the child of poor parents, who were dependent on the labour of their offspring during the week, to receive any kind of schooling.[22]

Every effort to extend literacy among the lower classes was likely to breed fears of social unrest in a country where the horror of anything that smacked of revolution remained potent for decades, and Sunday schools were affected by such anxieties as well. The frequent reluctance among Sunday-school organisers to teach the poor to write belongs in that context – if they should read they should read the Bible, which was easily available thanks to the non-denominational Bible Society (to which Patrick Brontë belonged) and to Bibles being exempt from the tax on paper.[23] Writing was a different matter, and not one that the early reformers found necessary.[24]

In view of the protean nature of Sunday-school education, one can only speculate about the actual content of the Sunday-school classes taught by the Brontës. One thing is certain, though: as part of the all-important instruction in reading, pupils read aloud in class. A characteristic account of Branwell Brontë's impatience with a pupil's stumbling progress through a text has been preserved by the latter's brother. Provoked by Branwell's exhortation to 'get on, or I'll turn you out of the class', the incensed lad retorted, 'Tha' willn't, tha' old Irish –' and left.'[25]

The only Brontë heroine who serves as a Sunday-school teacher is Caroline Helstone, who sacrifices both mental and physical comfort in the interests of the young women in the 'first class' which is her special province (*Shirley* II.v.293, III.xi.589–90).[26] The reader of *Shirley* learns nothing of what she teaches; the narrator's interest in her relations with her pupils focuses on her shyness and their good-natured sympathy for her (II.vi.312–13).

Nor does the reader of *Jane Eyre* find out much about the narrator's two years of teaching at Lowood. By contrast, Jane's work in her village school takes up about two pages in the novel (III.v.358–9 and III.vi.365–6). In the context of general attitudes to popular education in the early and mid-nineteenth century, Jane's descriptions of her Morton pupils, their families and her own influence in the neighbourhood are interesting for a number of reasons.

One of them is the narrator's recognition of the intrinsic worth of girls whose ignorance and rough manners initially overwhelmed her. She reminds herself that 'these coarsely-clad little peasants are of flesh and blood as good as the scions of gentlest genealogy; and that the germs of native excellence, refinement, intelligence, kind feeling, are as likely to exist in their hearts as in those of the best-born', adding, 'My duty will be develop these germs' (III.v.359). This amounts to an acknowledgement that low social status does not in itself entail moral, cultural and intellectual inferiority. That is a decided step away from the view prevalent in the eighteenth century, even among people involved in benevolent schemes among the poor, according to which the lowest classes were especially prone to immorality.[27] It is also a plain statement to the effect that the remedy for the disadvantages of poverty is education, and that it is the educated person's obligation to assist that process. Even in the nineteenth century these sentiments will have seemed radical to some, including those *Blackwood's* writers who mourned the demise of Old England's virtues – 'its loyalty, its devotion, its charity, and its unobtrusive industry' – lost for ever owing to the 'prodigious efforts to force on the education of the people'.[28]

To some readers of *Jane Eyre*, however, Jane's opinions must have seemed familiar. It is significant that she speaks of the 'germs of native excellence, refinement, intelligence, kind feeling' as residing in the pupils' *hearts*. The word Charlotte Brontë chose for her narrator invokes the classic Evangelical privileging of the heart as the site of innate good feeling before any other human faculty. More than that, it ties in with early-nineteenth-century efforts to improve the nation by strengthening the domestic affections. Promoting a virtuous national identity by such means was a patriotic duty that educated women owed their country.

An example of this nation-building labour is Elizabeth Hamilton's *The Cottagers of Glenburnie: A Tale for the Farmer's Ingle-Nook* (1808). In that story by a well-known writer on education, a village schoolmistress civilises a whole Scots ('North British') community in much the same way as Jane Eyre does at Morton.[29] Her success goes by way of the education of the heart in the domestic sphere, which produces girls improved in personal neatness as well as in understanding. Hamilton's theoretical basis was supplied by the Scottish Enlightenment philosophers of the Common-Sense school, who were in their turn indebted to Locke.[30] Her emphasis on the domestic affections is paralleled in *Jane Eyre*: the heroine calls those 'domestic endearments and household joys' from which St John Rivers unsuccessfully tries to wean her '[t]he best things the world has' (III.viii.390) and refuses to back down from that triumphant claim.

These similarities between the ideas of patriotic women educationists of preceding generations and opinions voiced in Charlotte Brontë's novel serve as a warning against viewing *Jane Eyre* as a more ideologically radical work than it is. Even so, the proclamation of inherent equality is noteworthy. So is the insistence on 'natural politeness, and innate self-respect' (III.vi.366) as qualities that win Jane's admiration as well as her sympathy. Similarly, *Shirley* pays tribute to the rustic schoolgirl's sense of what she owes her dignity: 'the poverty which reduces an Irish girl to rags is impotent to rob the English girl of the neat wardrobe she knows necessary to her self-respect', wrote the granddaughter of Irish peasants (*Shirley* II.v.296).[31] The implication is that education under the aegis of the Church of England fosters a healthy pride associated with national strength and independence (the relevant *Shirley* chapter is the one where 'Rule, Britannia!' vanquishes the sad hymn of the Dissenters who vainly attempt to halt the march of the Church of England schools; II.vi.304).

The denigration of Continental pupils and teachers that has irritated readers of *The Professor* and *Villette* for generations should be seen in this context. Charlotte Brontë was a patriotic Englishwoman at a time when patriotism was not considered suspect, the daughter of a man whose life-trajectory proved that intrinsic merit, judiciously assisted, could raise a member of the Irish peasantry to English middle-class rank thanks to education. Charlotte Brontë's sensitivity to suggestions that foreigners were better at educating the lower orders becomes easier to understand when one realises how recently her own family had acquired both Englishness and a social position above those lower orders, and how precarious that position was.

ADULT EDUCATION: PURSUITS OF IMPROVEMENT

While Patrick Brontë was undeniably of humble origins, the Pruntys were not paupers, and their eldest son was able to acquire some schooling.[32] He also received instruction from local clergymen who recognised his promise and did what they could to help. His chief teacher, however, was Patrick Brontë himself. Not only did he manage to master the Classics well enough to be admitted to Cambridge at the age of 25; he took a lively interest in the arts and sciences throughout his life, buying such books as he could afford and studying them during his few hours of leisure.[33] The late eighteenth and early nineteenth century was a good time for autodidacts, provided they were able to lay their hands on educational literature. In addition to the many schoolbooks adapted 'For the Use of such grown Persons as have neglected this useful Study in their Youth' (from the title-page of Abbé Lenglet du Fresnoy's *Geography for Youth*, published in Dublin in 1795), compilations of information on all sorts of subjects appeared under such titles as *The Universal Preceptor* and *Systematic Education*.[34] The latter work was expressly aimed at readers aged 16 to 25, a period when young people, 'freed from the restraint of school-discipline', may 'fall into the habits of desultory and baneful reading' (Advertisement, iii). It is worth observing that the authors hoped it would 'be of eminent service to those young persons in the process of whose early education the Classics have been almost the exclusive subject of attention' (iv). It sounds like an attempt to throw in some useful knowledge after a childhood and youth spent struggling with Homer and Virgil.[35]

The phrase 'useful knowledge' is another of those concepts that have a particular connection with the early nineteenth century. Operating from 1827 onwards, the Society for the Diffusion of Useful Knowledge (S.D.U.K.) issued large amounts of scientific/utilitarian works published in fortnightly parts. Along with the S.D.U.K.'s *Penny Magazine*, these publications were intended to provide the newly literate members of the lower classes with alternatives to the 'seditious' literature feared by those who had their doubts about the benefits of universal literacy. In addition, the S.D.U.K. encouraged the publication of similar reading matter by others.[36]

A reference to the S.D.U.K. will usually be accompanied by a mention of that other extensive endeavour to help the lower classes educate themselves, the Mechanics' Institutes.[37] Created by George Birkbeck and supported, like the S.D.U.K., by Henry Brougham, the Mechanics' Institutes movement began in Glasgow and quickly spread southwards, the London Mechanics' Institute opening in 1824. The next few years saw the founding of a number of Mechanics' Institutes in Yorkshire, including the large institution in Leeds and the Keighley Mechanics' Institute. By 1851 there were over 700 Mechanics' Institutes in Britain.[38]

The purposes of the Mechanics' Institutes were to promote scientific knowledge and spread useful general information among the upwardly mobile members of the lower and lower-middle classes, especially skilled artisans. An additional aim was to provide 'intellectual pleasures and refined amusements, tending to the general elevation of character'.[39] Some Institutes also ran schools for the young, both boys and girls, offering both primary and secondary education which often seems to have been of a comparatively high standard.[40] Each Institute was managed by local people, however, which means that the content of activities varied a good deal.

So did the attending clientèle. It is often pointed out that the Mechanics' Institutes were gradually taken over by the middle classes in pursuit of rational entertainment outside the home, the *cachet* of science and technology being part of the attraction for them.[41] This failure of the Mechanics Institutes' original object was regretted at the time, the pro-state-education lobby connecting it with the lack of 'a national elementary education, capable of awakening, not only a desire, but a capacity for the higher species of knowledge'.[42] Women were admitted but were usually a relatively small minority, with restricted access to the lending libraries attached to the Institutes.[43] As Charlotte Yonge's *Abbeychurch* (1844) implies, the participation of a vicar's daughters in Mechanics' Institute activities was by no means universally approved of.

Nobody seems to have had any such scruples where the Brontë sisters were concerned, though, and the appeal of the Mechanics' Institutes for the entire family is apparent. The extent to which the Keighley Mechanics' Institute (the corresponding institution in Haworth opened in 1848) provided the family with reading matter has been debated, but their continual involvement in its activities is amply documented.[44] Those activities included concerts sponsored by the Institute as well as lectures, some by Patrick Brontë himself and his curate William Weightman.[45]

In addition to lectures and reading matter, the Mechanics' Institutes provided opportunities to attend public debates on issues of current interest. Among the topics suggested in a contemporary (1839) source are such perennially relevant matters as 'Is it sound policy in any Government to impose restraint on the importation of Foreign Goods, with the view of protecting Home Production?' and 'Is War justifiable?' Other noteworthy questions for debate concern the mental capacity of women: 'Are Literary and Scientific Pursuits adapted to the Female Character?' and 'Are Females endowed by Nature with Intellectual Abilities equal to those of the other Sex?' Recommendations for subjects and occupations to be addressed during Institute meetings include items relevant to Brontë interests, among others bread-making, railway travel, 'Poetry, Moralizing Effects of' and phrenology.[46]

The recommendation to discuss phrenology was a natural one for a Mechanics' Institute. The Institutes and other organisations for mutual instruction by artisans were active proponents of phrenology, and their libraries contained George Combe's immensely popular *Constitution of Man* as well as other phrenological works.[47] The Brontës may well have made their first serious acquaintance with the new science through the Keighley Mechanics' Institute, but reflections on and reactions to it were everywhere.[48]

The impact of phrenology in the nineteenth century is hard to understand for those who have only come across it as an obsolete pseudo-science. Combe's *Constitution of Man* was not only a best-seller in the 1830s and 1840s; it remained in print throughout the century.[49] Those to whom their first encounter with it was a life-defining moment were not primarily

concerned with interpreting other people's characters by looking at bumps
on their heads. They were told, for the first time, that their bodies and minds
had evolved in accordance with natural laws and could be kept strong and
sane by study of and adherence to those laws. This did not amount to
an advocacy of narrow-minded materialism, let alone hedonism: on the
contrary, phrenology supplied a systematic approach to self-improvement
based on control of the lower, 'animal propensities'. The means of fostering one's moral and intellectual faculties, thereby keeping the animal
propensities in check, were available to everybody. It was a self-help ideology promoted by men who were convinced of the rightness of their views
and possessed the ability to express them with authority.[50]

Not surprisingly, some of the most hostile reactions came from religious
spokesmen who were deeply troubled by the transfer of power and agency
from God to the individual human being as a creature of Nature.[51] A
clergyman named J. S. Hodgson who attacked phrenology in 1839 pointed
out that native peoples should, according to the teachings of phrenologists,
have been insensible to the Christian religion but had in fact embraced
it. He went on to present arguments against phrenology articulated by
the scientists of the day (who, as he emphasised, tended to disassociate
themselves from it). For instance, Hodgson contested the idea that the
'energetic action' of any organ depends on its size, suggesting that fineness
of texture might be just as important.[52]

Other Christians responded differently to the teachings of phrenologists.
Some attempted to reconcile phrenology with Christianity, stressing every
human being's duty to understand his or her constitution, to control its
weaknesses and to improve its strengths while calling on God's help and
trusting in his mercy.[53] To a Christian in whose theology Nature was sub-
jugated under, or seen as an emanation of, God's will, natural laws posed
no threat to faith. Combe himself pronounced that '[t]he laws of health,
industry, and morality, are . . . enacted by the Creator, and are universally
prevalent'.[54]

The Brontës were aware of the opposition to phrenology; for one thing,
Blackwood's and *Fraser's* attacked it, sometimes with virulence.[55] However,
Charlotte and Anne appropriated its assumptions without apparent unease
and handled its terminology with assurance. In this they were no different
from other women in their time. Indeed, phrenology was sometimes held
up as a liberator of women.[56] One book which presented it in that light
appeared from Aylott and Jones, the publishers of the Brontës' poetry, in the
same year as the poems of the 'Bells' (1846). Called *The Science of Phrenology,
as applicable to Education, Friendship, Love, Courtship, and Matrimony, Etc.,*

this book was dedicated to 'the ladies'. The author, J. C. Lyons, insisted that '[a] female should be indulged in every attempt to learn the nature and uses of all useful things':

A little consideration, with any sensible person, could not fail to convince even the most obstinate, of the necessity of a female being conversant with knowledge of every description; and if the stupid etiquette of society has hitherto prevented it, let phrenology exercise its potent power, in opposition to all rules contrary to nature and reason. If it be fashionable to be sickly, sentimental, to eat little, to read the last new novel, to waste valuable time in flirting with the masculine portion of society; away with it, as a vice eating up the intellect, blinding the reason with lustful temptations, enervating the system with a languid, abject, and melancholy [sic], bordering upon hypochondria. (pp. 9–10)

It was natural for Hodgson's hostile and Lyons' favourable work to address phrenology in the context of education. Combe's influence on education took time to assert itself in practice, but school editions of the *Constitution* were available from the 1830s onwards, and leading educationists espoused its views.[57]

One explanation for the readiness with which many early-nineteenth-century reformers in education embraced Combe's teachings was that they constituted a system that could form the basis of a practical method. During the lifetime of the Brontës, father and children, 'system' and 'method' were key concepts in education. For instance, Andrew Bell's monitorial instruction scheme was the 'Madras system', and Johann Heinrich Pestalozzi's pedagogy was referred to as 'the system of Pestalozzi' and 'Pestalozzi's method'.[58] The titles of textbooks would often incorporate the word 'grammar' or even 'catechism', even if the subjects they dealt with were far removed from the fields of language or theology, implying a rigorously constructed approach in carefully worked-out detail.[59]

While Maria and Richard Lovell Edgeworth had no problem with admitting that they had 'no peculiar system to support', they did feel the need to reassure their readers that their 'plan' was not committed to paper without 'method'.[60] A few decades later, Mary Maurice declared that whereas her maternal paragon Mrs Eustace did not teach 'according to the systems usually laid down', '[m]ethodical teaching is of the first importance'.[61] Even these champions of practicality in education hence felt obliged to state that there was nothing haphazard about the pedagogical advice they supplied.

The lives and works of the Brontës show that this dedication to careful organisation in educational matters touched them as well. Anne Brontë's system of markings in her Bible, Latin primer and volume of devotional poems is the most striking example.[62] Nevertheless, the Brontë student sometimes catches a hint of impatience with exaggerated rigour in the acquisition of knowledge. The soundly and repeatedly ridiculed pedagogy of Hortense Moore in *Shirley* is that of a preceptress who boasts that she is able to impart 'a system, a method of thought' and that she commands a 'superior method of teaching' (I.v.68 and I.vi.76). The reader's sympathy is entirely with her unfortunate pupil – a self-confessed ignoramus who still turns out to possess a few very real attainments, above all an unusually acute literary sensibility developed in a desultory fashion and according to her own tastes.[63]

The first records of the three eldest Brontë girls' intellectual capabilities, the reports on Maria, Elizabeth and Charlotte's 'Acquirements' on entering the Clergy Daughters' School at Cowan Bridge, speak of an absence of 'Grammar' and 'systematic knowledge'.[64] Whatever benefits in that line Cowan Bridge might have been able to provide, the children did not stay there long enough to experience them. At Roe Head Charlotte Brontë had to cram herself with pre-packaged knowledge to get into the advanced class and maintain a position at the top of it, and there is no reason to assume that it was anything but a chore for her (albeit not a chore against which she rebelled).[65] Initially, neither she nor Emily was impressed by Monsieur Heger's method of teaching them French.[66] Insofar as members of the Brontë family were comfortable with systematic studies, the methodology had to be of their own devising and the execution left to their own discretion. In resisting pressure to become assimilated to systems imposed from outside, they were true bearers of the Romantic legacy.[67]

CHAPTER 2

The improvement of the mind

Although there were occasional reservations against the extension of literacy from quarters where it was feared that the possession of reading skills might incite the masses to rebellion, the Brontë girls grew to adulthood in a social context where the education of the poor was regarded as a means of promoting peace and prosperity in Britain.[1] It was the duty of every educated individual who had the means to do so – money, influence, teaching ability, and so on – to support it. On no segment of the population did this duty weigh more heavily than on Anglican clergymen and Dissenter ministers and on their families. Hence the participation of the four young Brontës in Sunday-school activities. However, another obligation was also keenly felt by at least two of them: the obligation to improve their minds by means of constant independent study.[2]

The title of this chapter was borrowed from Isaac Watts's classic of 1741, a copy of which was given to sixteen-year-old Anne Brontë as a school prize (for good conduct). In recent times it has been assumed that a sprightly teenage girl would not have been pleased to receive Watts's *The Improvement of the Mind* as a gift, but in fact it is a much more enjoyable read than one might expect.[3] It remained in print throughout the early 1800s and was often recommended by writers on education, including those who wrote primarily for women.[4]

Another work with a similar title also repeatedly appeared in new editions during the early nineteenth century: Mrs Hester Chapone's *Letters on the Improvement of the Mind*. It has often been stated as fact that the Roe Head curriculum rested on this book (originally published in 1773), a copy of which had been given to Miss Margaret Wooler when she was twelve.[5] Conceived as advice to a niece of that age, Chapone's *Letters* soon became a staple of female education and remained so up to the mid-nineteenth century. Its exalted status was invoked by writers of fiction as well as of manuals on education; the opening pages of *Vanity Fair* refer to Miss Pinkerton's acquaintance with 'Mrs Chapone' as one of that lady's two great claims to distinction in the world of education (the other being her association with Dr Johnson). Several of the historical and literary works recommended in it also appear in Charlotte Brontë's suggestions-for-reading letter to Ellen Nussey of 4 July 1834.[6] In other words, it seems highly likely that Chapone's work was familiar to educators of the Brontës.

Both these books, as well as others whose titles also include the operational word 'improvement', were written for the perusal of independent individuals seeking advice on how to make the most of their own faculties, as well as those of younger persons for whom they were responsible.[7] While individual authors of courtesy literature placed their emphases differently, and there is considerable variety when it comes to such matters as recommended reading, the consensus regarding the underlying reasons for pursuing mental improvement is striking. The cultivation of the mind is held up as a religious duty, partly because a trained intellect is serviceable in the work of the world, partly because it helps a person form sound habits and partly because it enables the owner better to perceive the glory of God and his Creation. The thorough-going fusion of reason, feeling and morality is apparent, and so is the fact that this fusion occurs in 'improving' literature for both male and female readers. The preface to an 1827 abridged edition of Robert Burton's *The Anatomy of Melancholy*, a book owned by the Brontës, is a case in point:

[The work is] intended to convince youth of both sexes, that a life abandoned to an intemperate pursuit of pleasure . . . destroys the sense of rational enjoyment, deadens the faculties of the mind, weakens the functions of the body, corrupts both the moral and intellectual system, creates a disgusting apathy and languor, and ends at last in Habitual Melancholy[.]

Another similarity between conduct books intended for a general readership and works specifically directed to women is the emphasis on thought. Books like *Systematic Education*, which encouraged women to pursue learning as well as men do, characteristically stressed the need to further the cognitive capacity. According to its authors, the study of history should be regarded in that light:

Historical facts ought to be considered as materials for thinking. If properly estimated, they serve, not simply to amuse the imagination, but to exercise the nobler faculties of the human mind, to strengthen the understanding, and to amend the heart. To this topic may be justly applied the observation of President Montesquieu, '*Il ne s'agit de faire lire, mais de faire penser*'. (p. 248)

Women writers on educational matters were equally explicit about the desirability of sharpening the powers of the independent intellect. Study,

said Elizabeth Sandford, 'is subservient to two important purposes: it furnishes the mind with matter to reflect on, and habituates it to think'.[8]
Praising Thomas Arnold both as (would-be) Church reformer and as educator, Harriet Martineau wrote that his pupils '[owed] to him the power
and the conscience to think for themselves, and the earnest habit of mind
which makes their conviction a part of their life'.[9]

The mention of Martineau should, however, serve as a warning against
taking the notion of consensus too far. After all, her thinking led her away
from (Unitarian) Christianity to agnosticism, unlike other extollers of mental improvement whose grapplings with the reconciliation of mind, heart
and spirit were conducted from, and moved them towards, very dissimilar
positions.[10] An ever-growing literate population pursuing mental improvement on an individual basis bred a disputatiousness which is apt to surprise
the present-day student, himself/herself no stranger to diversity of opinion.

These tensions are discernible within many authors of the period, and
Charlotte Brontë is one of them.[11] Both her correspondence and her fiction contain logically inconsistent views, conflicting values and anxious,
inconclusive probings. This middle-class Tory woman with her roots in
Evangelical Christianity could express sentiments and opinions that would
have suited a clubbable Whig male of comfortable means and tepid beliefs
or an ardent Radical working man. The range of her tone is similarly
wide, shifting from glowing eulogy to mordant accusation and jovial self-
deprecation (and many other shades besides) in a manner that holds the
reader captive at every turn.

Emily and Anne Brontë, as different from Charlotte as from each other,
do not display their sister's diversity – but it must of course be borne in mind
that we have far fewer records of their personal lives and a much smaller body
of writing by them both. Where Emily is concerned, any attempt to trace a
consistent set of values and beliefs, evolved in obvious connection with the
contemporary intellectual milieu and expressed in her writings, is vain. Her
plots, settings and characters have few perceptible interfaces with conditions
in the world she lived in: she created her own worlds. Anne's didactic vein,
fed by acute observation of her surroundings, coexisted with warmth and
humour, seasoned with an engaging self-irony and a gift for dialogue. All
these qualities coalesce in the forming of narratives which manage to be
complex without conveying a sense of forces pulling in different directions.

In one respect, however, the three Brontës are alike and in tune with the
variegated climate of opinion in the early and mid-nineteenth century: a
dedication to truth and a concomitant horror of deception, especially the
kinds of deception people practise on themselves.

All the Brontë novels are engaged with self-deception. *Agnes Grey's* initial faith in her ability as a teacher and Helen Lawrence's belief that she will make a virtuous man out of an irreligious wastrel may be 'very natural error[s]' in young girls.[12] The consequences they are forced to endure, however – Helen particularly – demonstrate that however 'natural' the errors may have been, they were not slight.[13] Catherine Earnshaw's idea that she will be able to marry Edgar Linton without losing or injuring Heathcliff, whom she regards as an inalienable part of herself, has dire results, and Isabella Linton and young Cathy are of course also victims of their own illusions. In all these cases the self-deceivers, bent on having their own way, were warned by wiser and/or more experienced counsellors whose advice they chose to ignore. In the case of Lucy Snowe an avowed dedication to truth, the 'Titaness among deities' (*Villette* XXXIX.465), does not prevent her from deceiving herself – but here the self-deluder pursues what torments her rather than seeking self-gratification.[14] Male Brontë characters also create misery for themselves and others by failing to face facts; the bigamy-plotting Mr Rochester and the self-confessed emotional coward Mr Lockwood are the most notable examples.

Similarly, major Brontë characters struggle to endure and enounce the truth, above all, of course, the fearless truth-teller Jane Eyre. An expression used with reference to another Brontë heroine who tries to avoid romantic delusions is significant: Caroline Helstone's 'earnest wish was to see things as they are' (*Shirley* I.x.172). Her desire – considerably more modest than Lucy Snowe's ambition to seek the goddess in her temple, lift her veil and meet her 'dread glance' – is said to be rewarded by 'a glimpse of the light of truth here and there'.[15]

In the troubled decades following the French Revolution, whose dust did not settle for generations on either side of the Channel, British intellectuals kept voicing their concern with the human ability to perceive 'things as they are'. For instance, the full title of William Godwin's novel *Caleb Williams*, which problematises the relationship between an individual's obligations to the concepts of truth and justice and to his fellow humans, was *Things As They Are, or The Adventures of Caleb Williams*.[16] The preoccupation with the idea of seeing things as they were betrays an anxiety about the opposite, as much earnest talk about a desideratum normally does. To many Brontë readers, the phrase 'things as they are' thus carried implications of doubt on several planes – implications which served to remind them of the pregnability of any claim to possess the truth. A few years after the appearance of the Brontë novels, John Stuart Mill wrote in a letter that sounds remarkably 'modern', 'the multitude of thoughts only breeds increase of uncertainty. Those who would be the guides of the rest, see too many sides to every question . . . they feel no assurance of the truth of anything'.[17]

Nevertheless, however aware the early Victorians were of the dangers and prevalence of relativity and subjectivity, those concepts had not yet taken possession of people's minds.[18] In Houghton's words, they 'might be, and often were, uncertain about what theory to accept or what faculty of the mind to rely on; but it never occurred to them to doubt their capacity to arrive at truth'.[19] In *Culture and Anarchy* (1869) Matthew Arnold could still speak of 'things as they [really] are', just as Sarah Ellis had done 25 years earlier when she urged young women to cultivate a love of truth, as it would teach them 'to see every object as it is, and to see it clearly'.[20]

In this unstable mental climate, it was particularly vital for the educators of the young to teach their charges to guard against the perils of illusion, deception and error. Such vigilance was thought to be even more crucial for girls, who were traditionally protected from the teachings of personal experience to a greater extent than boys (as 'Helen Graham' reminds Gilbert Markham at the beginning of *The Tenant of Wildfell Hall*, III.30–31). They had to be guided by an incorruptible sense of what was right which would not be swayed by delusive words or visions. It was the duty of their instructors to foster that capacity in them, and contemporary writers on the education of girls never wearied of insisting that an allegiance to the truth is the mainstay of all mental and spiritual endeavour. The ideal governess Miss Porson in Catherine Sinclair's *Modern Accomplishments, or The March of the Intellect* is said to believe that 'the first object in education should be to inculcate a love of truth without disguise or embellishment'.[21] The chapter on 'Mental Training' in Bessie Rayner Belloc's *Remarks on the Education of Girls* emphasises the importance of a commitment to truth, and Elizabeth Sandford enquired why there should be so much reluctance to impart knowledge to women: 'Why should they not be trained in the path of true wisdom, and rendered not merely the recipients of a little learning, but the lovers of knowledge and truth?'[22]

In a manner characteristic of the period, early-nineteenth-century British commentators on the nature of truth in the context of education fused epistemological and ethical dimensions.[23] A love of truth keeps the pursuer of mental improvement from the lure of specious reasoning dressed in fake elegance.[24] Genuine knowledge schools the judgement and enables its owner to distinguish between good and evil, whatever blandishments the latter may evince. An allegiance to the truth is not only the best guide in this world; it also leads human beings to salvation in the next.[25]

The Brontë fiction is part of this combined valorisation of the truth and awareness of the many pitfalls in the path of those who pursue it. Charlotte Brontë's writings – letters as well as fiction – bear especially eloquent testimony to both aspects, but Emily's scorn for the opinions of benighted reviewers and Anne's refusal to compromise with prevailing tastes may also be considered in this context. The Brontës might, like the narrator of *Shirley*, grant that only glimpses of the truth can be afforded to human beings; but the idea of deliberately disregarding such glimpses for any reason whatsoever was one they could not possibly entertain.

In the Brontës' fiction as well as in their lives, this devotion to the truth is seen to coexist with a determination to uphold one's integrity at all costs. A telling passage from one of Charlotte Brontë's letters illustrates that combination. The recipient, Mr Williams of Smith, Elder to whom Charlotte Brontë addressed a large number of important letters, had apparently suggested that she widen her scope to include more in the way of 'condition-of-England' issues:[26]

Details – Situations 'which' I do not understand, and cannot personally inspect, I would not for the world meddle with . . . – besides – not one feeling, on any subject – public or private, will I ever affect that I do not really experience – yet though I must limit my sympathies – though my observation cannot penetrate where the very deepest political and social truths are to be learnt – though many doors of knowledge which are open for you, are for ever shut for me – though I must guess, and calculate, and grope my way in the dark and come to uncertain conclusions unaided and alone – where such writers as Dickens and Thackeray having access to the shrine and image of Truth, have only to go into the temple, lift the veil a moment and come out and say what they have seen – yet with every disadvantage, I mean still, in my own contracted way to do my best. Imperfect my best will be, and poor – and compared with the works of the true Masters – of that greatest modern Master, Thackeray, in especial . . . it will be trifling – but I trust not affected or counterfeit.

Like Jane Austen a couple of decades earlier, Charlotte Brontë thus expressed her resolve to stick with what she knew; but her letter is interesting for other than professional reasons. Given well-meant advice by a man whose access to sources of knowledge unavailable to her she does not question, she does not allow that advice to modify her position in the slightest, nor does her statement of that position contain even a hint of apology. The circumstances that prevent her from walking into the temple of Truth are not of her making, nor can she do anything to alter them. Within the confines of the sphere that is hers, however, she moves with complete freedom and tolerates no interference.

The unbending manner in which the Brontës pursued their respective self-improvement projects is paralleled in the actions and attitudes of their main female characters, however flawed and ignorant they may be. Even when they recognise greater educational attainments in the men who attempt to assert authority over them, they retain their moral sovereignty: no Brontë heroine ever yields to a man's judgement in ethical matters. Never deluded into overlooking moral faults in men, they retain the ability to speak and act on principle, even when their words and actions clash with the views and desires of male would-be directors of their fate; and they never resign the responsibility for their moral selves to any outside agent. Part of this resolute assertion of their integrity as independent moral subjects rests on the circumstance, demonstrated all over the Brontë fiction, that men's wider knowledge of the world does not invest them with superior insights into things as they are.

II

Home and school

CHAPTER 3

Household education versus school training

'Are you book-learned?' she inquired, presently.
'Yes, very.'
'But you've never been to boarding-school?'
'I was at a boarding-school eight years.'
She opened her eyes wide. 'Whatever cannot ye keep yourseln for, then?'
'I have kept myself; and, I trust, shall keep myself again.'

(Jane Eyre III.iii.341)

Though Moor House servant Hannah's faculties were never 'loosened or fertilized by education' (*Jane Eyre* III.iii.340), she knows what schooling is for. Having registered the destitute but well-spoken Jane's claim to respectable social rank, Hannah immediately identifies the sole area in which a middle-class woman without 'brass' can support herself: education. As the servant of two governesses (on temporary leave to bury a father), she is aware that formal education at a boarding school is an essential qualification for any woman who aspires to live by teaching.

Hannah's creator had possessed that knowledge since childhood. Charlotte Brontë's own schooling was a family investment in her future ability to earn a living as a teacher, with the added bonus of her being able to pass on what she had learnt to Emily and Anne. Even the period at Cowan Bridge was part of a scheme to educate the Brontë girls (except Elizabeth, who clearly was not held to be the academic type) for teaching posts. The original advertisement for the Clergy Daughters' School in the *Leeds Intelligencer* spoke of pupils' being fitted 'to return with Respectability and Advantage to their own Homes, or to maintain themselves in the different Stations of Life to which Providence may call them'. It went on to mention an extra fee for girls who required 'a more liberal Education' owing to their aspiring to become 'Teachers and Governesses'.[1] The natural future occupation of pupils was hence defined from the outset, and that consideration will have added to the school's attractions for the harassed widower Patrick Brontë.

The only son of the Brontë family was a different case. A strikingly gifted boy, Branwell could be expected to do better for himself and his family than his sisters, for whom the only other obvious option apart from teaching was marriage. Branwell's literary ambitions were in evidence from an early age, and considerable effort and expense were invested in his artistic pursuits. Nevertheless, spells of tutoring would have been seen as natural means of earning his keep while a more profitable and prestigious career got under way; and in the Brontë family Branwell's two posts as tutor were regarded as opportunities rather than backslidings – especially the first, with the Postlethwaites of Broughton-on-Furness, when he was 22. The Brontë children had reason to respect the possibilities offered by successful tutoring, as their father's career had taken off from just such a post.

Patrick Brontë taught the Tighe children for four years, on the basis of whatever local schooling had been available to him and years of laborious self-education. Before that, he had actually, and not least in view of his extreme youth amazingly, run his own school, apparently with a degree of success.[2] His post as tutor was the bridge to Cambridge, ordination and a career in the Church of England. Having mastered the Classics with some coaching but mostly on his own, he was living proof that a young man could acquire respectable academic knowledge without ever having attended grammar or boarding school.[3] Of course, financial considerations played a part where Branwell's education was concerned: at no time could Patrick Brontë have afforded to send him to a reputable boarding school for middle- and upper-class boys. However, there were other reasons why a devoted and well-educated father might prefer a home education for his cherished only son.

Home or school was a question which had been debated for generations when Patrick Brontë was faced with having to make decisions on the education of his children. Any modern reader to whom the notion of domestic education seems reactionary will be surprised at the many distinguished names found on the side of 'home'.[4] The Edgeworths were in favour of it, as was Harriet Martineau decades later (in *Household Education*). Even closer to home from Patrick Brontë's point of view, Hannah More, Legh Richmond and the Brontë family friend John Buckworth backed domestic education in print.[5]

A number of factors combined to make the home seem the best place to educate a child. First of all, it allowed parents complete control of what and how their child was taught. At a time when intellectual attainments and artistic skills were held to be far less important than morality, and morality rested on religious principles, parents and guardians felt the need to supervise every formative influence to which a young person was exposed.[6] Second, as the many tales of horror schools in nineteenth-century literature remind us, badly run schools posed dangers to children's physical and mental health, sometimes to their lives. It was hard for parents to ascertain just how well managed a school was; pupils were discouraged and often prevented from communicating complaints to their families, whose lack of opportunities for informed inspection made them liable to persuasion by unscrupulous school directors and other interested parties. Third, the society of other adolescents and older teenagers might introduce a young person – particularly a young male – to downright vice. The preface to Richmond's *Domestic Portraiture* does not gloss over Richmond's aversion to schools and the painful cause of his repugnance:

[Richmond] never spoke without emotion when he recollected the vices which his eldest son had contracted by a public education, and the sad influence of bad connections formed under those circumstances; and which, counteracting the good effects of early instruction at home, caused the ruin, as he used to say, 'of his poor wanderer'.[7]

A book owned by the Brontës (apparently after belonging to the Fennell family), George Wright's *Thoughts in Younger Life on Interesting Subjects*, summarises the anti-boarding-school case in the late eighteenth century in vehement terms: a 'sensible and judicious parent', Wright avers, will feel a 'just abhorrence of the impropriety of the methods made use of in our modern boarding-schools, both with respect to their advancement in learning, and prevention from imbibing ill habits from one another'. This abhorrence, says Wright, will induce a father to 'keep [his young offspring] under his own inspection, and take the management of their education into his own hands'.[8]

After the school-related deaths of his two eldest daughters, that is what Patrick Brontë did. It was not until Charlotte was 14 that he sent a child of his to school again, and this time he had taken particular care to ensure her safety.[9] Under the circumstances, schooling for Charlotte represented the optimal outlay of scanty funds: not only would it qualify her for future teaching posts; by enabling her to help educate her sisters, it gave Patrick more time to instruct his son. At that point in time, with Branwell's personality well established, paternal tuition rather than school attendance may have seemed advisable for the boy quite apart from the financial aspect: the possibility that the temperamental, imaginative and impressionable Branwell might become a school casualty, like Richmond's 'poor wanderer', may well have occurred to Patrick Brontë.[10] The boy's small stature and slender build would also have been disadvantages in an institution where bullies – among pupils and staff – implemented various tyrannical practices. An early Angria poem by Charlotte Brontë testifies to family awareness of the miseries of public schools, depicting the young Charles Wellesley at Eton as afflicted by 'the pompous tutor's voice' and 'the hated school-boy's groan'.[11]

In view of all the vigorous and widespread support for domestic education, one may well wonder what kept boarding schools in business. Again, the family at the Parsonage illustrates the pros as well as the cons of formal schooling in institutions. First, not all homes contained parents willing and able to teach their children for hours every day over a period of several years. For instance – though this is not a circumstance of relevance to the motherless Brontës – the rapid extension of the middle class meant that many parents, mothers especially, were simply too ignorant to be able to teach children for whom they harboured worldly ambitions. Second, school-time offered opportunities to create social contacts that would prove useful in later life, as certainly happened with Charlotte Brontë. Third, collective instruction offered inspiration in the form of emulation and competition, which might put a naturally stolid pupil on his or her mettle while affording an intelligent and ambitious one, such as Charlotte Brontë, gratifying rewards. And then, there is the consideration that impels the Crimsworths in *The Professor* to send their one precious boy to Eton: precisely because school is not home, it entails enforced adaptation to the outside world in which the young adult will sooner or later be obliged to make his or her way, unaided and unprotected by solicitous parents.[12]

This section of *The Brontës and Education* relates all these concerns to the Brontës and their novels. Moving from the domestic sphere by way of home education at the hands of professionals to schools and schoolteachers, it places the Brontë fiction in the context of educational principles, activities and conditions in the lifetime of Patrick Brontë and his children.

CHAPTER 4

Parents and children

Apart from the desirability of formal schooling experience for any woman who wished to go on to teach professionally, there was another powerful reason why the Brontë girls could not be educated exclusively at home: there was no mother in it. Time and again, writers on education in the early and mid-nineteenth century pointed out that the mother was the natural teacher of her children. Above all, they were to receive their decisive early religious instruction at her hands.[1]

Even if the Brontë children's mother had survived, it is hard to see how she could have found time to teach her daughters, at different ages and stages, on a regular basis. Her sister, whose educational attainments are likely to have resembled hers, taught young Anne and gave all the girls some instruction in sewing. Even those undertakings seem extensive in view of her responsibilities in the household. Though neither unintelligent nor uneducated, Aunt Branwell could never have assumed the role of main teacher to the intellectually ambitious adolescent girls. As their father was busy with his manifold professional duties and with Branwell's education, the resources of their home were plainly insufficient for them. Self-study and occasional attendance at lectures could not fill the gap: some sort of schooling was the obvious answer.

PRINCIPLES IN THE REARING OF CHILDREN

Education, however, is more than the acquisition of knowledge and skills, and all writers on education in the late eighteenth and early nineteenth century emphasised that a child's character was formed at home. No school could compensate for the failure of parents and guardians to instil the fundamental childish virtues of truthfulness, obedience, piety and kindness to all created beings. Evangelical homes were particularly vigilant towards any early manifestations of 'evil propensities';[2] but High Church people and Dissenters also regarded falsehood and disobedience as serious transgressions, even in small children. Lying was seen as an indirect rebellion against parental authority and hence akin to, and owing to its covert nature even more vicious than, open defiance. Both amounted to a challenge not only against your elders but against God, who had placed you under their control and entrusted them with the responsibility of educating you 'for Heaven', as Helen Huntingdon quite orthodoxly describes the essence of motherhood (*The Tenant of Wildfell Hall* XXVIII.228).

No wonder Mr Brocklehurst claims that 'the Evil One had already found a servant and agent' in young Jane Eyre. Her rebelliousness against her guardian is not in doubt; her scheme for avoiding hellfire and the fact that she found the Psalms boring confirm her impiety; and, worst of all, she is, according to Mrs Reed and Mr Brocklehurst, a liar. It is as a liar she is shamed in front of the entire school, and it is her alleged mendacity that causes the Misses Brocklehurst to whisper, 'How shocking!' (*Jane Eyre* I.vii.66). Correspondingly, all opprobrium vanishes once Miss Temple has obtained corroboration of Jane's own story (I.viii.74). Nelly Dean in *Wuthering Heights* also has a horror of mendacity, telling fibbing Cathy that she would 'rather be three months ill, than hear you frame a deliberate lie' (II.x.217). Lucy Snowe is appalled at the nonchalance with which young Labassecouriennes admit to having 'menti plusieurs fois', a confession which 'the priest heard unshocked, and absolved unreluctant' (*Villette* IX.82); and Agnes Grey's realisation that young Tom's vaunted veracity ('He seems to scorn deception', said his mamma; *Agnes Grey* II.15) was 'by means unimpeachable' (III.25) adds to her distress.

Deceitfulness, especially in the young, was hence generally thought to be a most grievous failing in the early nineteenth century, an idea affirmed by the Brontë fiction. In this respect British educationists disagreed explicitly with Rousseau, even though they might agree with him on other matters. For example, Catharine Macaulay (later Graham) devoted an entire 'Letter' to 'the Vice of Lying', challenging Rousseau's notion that children should, in Macaulay's words, be kept 'in ignorance on the subject of truth and falsehood'.[3] Similarly, Maria Edgeworth accused Rousseau of giving 'very dangerous counsel' in advising parents 'to teach truth by falsehood'.[4] She did, however, approve of Rousseau's idea 'that children should never be questioned about any circumstances in which it could be their interest to deceive'.[5]

The notion that parents should help their children to be truthful by removing any temptation to deceit provides an interesting context in which to revisit the classic Brontë anecdote of 'the cover of the mask'. Often pondered by Brontë biographers, the story was told by Patrick Brontë to

Elizabeth Gaskell in a letter, some 30 years after the incident. His avowed intention was to make his children, whom he thought more knowledgeable 'than [he] had yet discover'd', 'speak with less timidity' than they would otherwise do. '[H]appening to have a mask in the house, I told them all to stand, and speak boldly from under /cover of/ the mask'.[6] The unoriginality of the precocious replies to the paternal interrogator dispels any idea that the purpose was to elicit bold statements that the child would not otherwise have dared to make. Instead, Patrick Brontë's idea that his children knew things he might not have been able to make them articulate by other means was confirmed: stimulated by the patent dimension of game-playing, they showed him how conversant they were with current notions on education in a wide sense. Whether they agreed with or even understood these notions is immaterial: this was a game, the first piece of recorded fantasy in the lives of the singularly imaginative young Brontës, and it was their father who invited them to play. It may be an exaggeration to regard the incident as an early parental authorisation of playful make-believe – occasioned by the presence in the house of the prime symbol of theatrical representation – as distinct from the strict obligation to tell the truth in everyday life. However, Patrick Brontë obviously knew the difference between untruthfulness and harmless fantasy, and he would certainly never have told Mrs Gaskell a deliberate lie.[7] At the very least, the episode will have encouraged the young Brontës to explore the construction and representation of human thoughts, views and actions beyond the boundary of literality without fearing the disapproval of a wrathful and uncomprehending parent.

In fact, as many Brontë scholars have observed, Patrick Brontë seems to have respected his children's right not only to allow their imaginations to roam freely, but also to evolve their own views on life, to an unusual extent. To call him unique in this respect would be wrong, though. Several early-nineteenth-century writers on child-rearing pointed out that parents should listen to their offspring and even be prepared to be guided by them in situations where young people knew best. For instance, the well-known Mrs Ann Taylor spoke of the respect due to the young, showing great sensitivity to changing habits and mindsets.[8]

Naturally, the idea of tiny children lisping Psalm verses at their mothers' knee and evincing George Washington standards of veracity when barely out of nappies was always an illusion.[9] Early-nineteenth-century authors of works on the care of children were perfectly aware of that, and some were explicit on the subject. Another widely known and respected writer, Mrs Jane West, freely admitted that the 'task of teaching "the young idea how to shoot" [is not] always delightful', speaking of '[s]leepless nights, and anxious days'.[10] Patrick Brontë's friend and colleague John Buckworth was even more outspoken:

And even in the earliest stage of youth, how common is it for children to give pert and impudent answers, to manifest impatience, self-will, and stubbornness; and to be noisy, contradictory, and passionate, in spite of all the authority which a parent can enforce![11]

The children of Yorkshire families with recently acquired wealth were apparently especially likely to be obnoxious. According to a mid-twentieth-century descendant of the Inghams at Blake Hall, where Anne Brontë had some of the experiences she later fictionalised in *Agnes Grey*, the accounts of the young Bloomfields' naughtiness are perfectly realistic.[12]

Whether the most upsetting childish misbehaviour in *Agnes Grey*, young Tom's tormenting of birds, is a fictional account based on real-life experience is a matter of speculation. Judging from the frequency of expostulations against actions of this kind in contemporary manuals on education, cruelty to animals seems to have been – or at least was thought to be – common among early-nineteenth-century British boys.[13] Kindness to all created beings is constantly enjoined, as in the following 'lines addressed to a LADY on the Education of her child' by James Jennings:

> Teach him a sympathy to feel
> For *Nature* – for the *general weal*.
> . . .
> 'BE KIND TO ALL – TO MAN – TO BEAST, –
> BIRD – FISH – WORM – INSECT' – Thus a feast
> Of *Happiness* will he partake,
> And happy other beings make.
> Teach him – ALL VIOLENCE IS WRONG!
> A Truth as useful as it's strong. –
> THERE'S NO EFFECT WITHOUT A CAUSE: –
> This one of Nature's wisest Laws.[14]

Like Agnes Grey (V.46), writers on the upbringing of children are apt to quote Proverbs 12:10, 'the merciful man shews mercy to his beast', when dealing with 'the barbarity of tormenting poor dumb creatures'.[15] The aligning of cruelty to animals with the bullying of younger siblings keeps occurring in compilations of advice to parents, too, along much the same lines as in *Agnes Grey*.

So what measures did manual writers suggest that parents adopt to succeed as rearers of the young? Again, the picture is strikingly uniform across political and religious divides and over several decades.

First, parents are urged to evince a combination of affectionate guidance and absolute intolerance of disobedience. A judicious combination of mildness and firmness in curbing the self-will of children, even from the very beginning, is constantly recommended. A moment's peace obtained by giving in to an importunate child 'may be purchased with years of anarchy and sorrow', in the words of Ann Taylor.[16] She affirms – with a Biblical phrase also used by other manual writers in similar contexts – that 'parents must bear rule in their own houses . . . [this should be] as irrevocable as the laws of the Medes and Persians'.[17] Second, parents have to pull in tandem. Not only must they 'learn to act together, and each one to strengthen the authority of the other';[18] they must take care to avoid domestic disharmony, as parental discord is an important reason for misbehaviour among children.[19] Third, children should not be left to 'the mercenary services of ignorant domestics'; the hand that rocks the cradle should be that of 'the intelligent christian [sic] mother'.[20] Fourth, parents must ensure the virtuousness of their child 'by shewing a good example'.[21] Self-discipline, method and consistency in a parent are far more effective than mere exhortation.[22] Finally, parents are warned not to frighten, intimidate and indoctrinate their offspring. A wise mother gives children a choice when she can, but when she cannot they must submit at once.[23]

Some of this advice seems as pertinent today as it did two centuries ago. The most striking difference is the emphasis on the early detection and eradication of evil tendencies, manifested as defiance or disobedience, for the good of the child's immortal soul. Strictly interpreted, that principle calls for incessant surveillance and a concomitant loss of freedom – on the part of both children and parents – that is hard to imagine today. The Brontë sisters were extremely lucky to be spared this régime: their elders had neither the time nor the inclination to try to impose it.

DYSFUNCTIONAL FAMILIES, DOMESTIC TYRANTS AND ENDANGERED SONS

Though the Brontë girls were fortunate in their own upbringing, their writings contain numerous examples of parental inadequacy. For instance, Mrs Reed, who boasts of her 'consistency in all things' (*Jane Eyre* I.iv.34), prides herself on a characteristic in which she is peculiarly deficient as a parent, although her ill-treatment of Jane is consistent enough. The mothers of the Murray girls in *Agnes Grey* and Esther Hargrave in *The Tenant of Wildfell Hall* are little better than slave-traders in their own flesh and blood.[24] Old Mr Earnshaw, though essentially a jovial and in Nelly Dean's eyes 'good' man, works the destruction of his family by bringing the child Heath-cliff into it. Hindley's subsequent persecution of Heathcliff and the latter's revenge are rooted in Earnshaw's undisguised preference for the swarthy foundling to whom he gave the name of a dead son – a preference which naturally breeds hatred in the surviving son whose nose is so suddenly put out of joint.[25] Hindley himself comes close to accidentally killing his small boy. Another ogreish action of his is to demand caresses from little Hareton and curse him when the terrified child fails to comply. Heath-cliff's treatment of his wretched son Linton hastens, if not causes, the boy's death.

One circumstance that is bound to strike anyone who looks at parents in the Brontë novels is the scarcity of ordinary two-parent families in their books. All main characters have lost or lose one or both parents in childhood or on the threshold of adulthood. Another notable circumstance is that even the few intact nuclear families described in some detail in the Brontë fiction are less than idyllic. Briarmains, the home of the Yorkes in *Shirley*, is a site of domestic disharmony, open and covert.[26] Even the parsonage that is home to the Grey family only qualifies as a happy home thanks to Mrs Grey's incessant campaigning against her husband's self-pity. Parental incompatibility is seen to undermine or preclude domestic peace; again, the Yorkes are a carefully worked-out example.[27]

Anne Brontë devoted a whole page of her short novel to a dispute between the Bloomfield parents, in the course of which Mr Bloomfield accuses his wife of inept housekeeping in front of their children and the governess (*Agnes Grey* III.22–3). Agnes 'never felt so ashamed and uncomfortable in [her] life, for anything that was not [her] fault' (III.24); but anyone who contemplates the scene from the wife and mother's point of view realises that the victim here is the humiliated Mrs Bloomfield. Pronounced a failure at her chief job, that of running the household, by the person who wields absolute power in it, she suffers a loss in dignity and authority that cannot but affect her standing with the children and governess who witness it. The graphic little scene thus illustrates the dangers of parental disharmony described by conduct-book writers. (It also shows that the corporate psychologists of the twentieth century were not the first to realise that discord at the top breeds trouble in the ranks.)[28]

Mr Bloomfield is a bully whose only son is seen to follow in his foot-steps. Male domestic tyrants young and old are another notable feature in the Brontë novels. Edward Crimsworth, John Reed, Hindley Earnshaw, Heathcliff and Arthur Huntingdon are a dismal set who actively enjoy the use of their power to make other members of their households wretched.

A lack of good paternal examples may be seen as an explanatory factor; in two cases (John Reed and Huntingdon) maternal over-indulgence is also said (and in Reed's case shown) to contribute to the making of vicious household despots.

The exhortations to foster kindness in boys that advisers on child-rearing kept repeating should be seen in relation to the opportunities for inflicting domestic misery that the nineteenth-century male possessed. Unrestrained by law and unchecked by social networks (in that disapproving friends and relations could be dropped if he so chose), he was also in complete control of the material assets on which everybody's survival depended. The only hope of counteracting tyranny lay in establishing such a large store of compassion for all living things in the growing boy that the man's authority would be powerless to corrupt it. Time and again, the readers of books on child-rearing were reminded of Solomon's exhortation to '[t]rain up a child in the way he should go; and when he is old, he will not depart from it' (Proverbs 22:6).

Kindness to those whom one has the power to hurt was thus not only an expression of considerateness to fellow creatures of God. It was training in the quality of mercy, on which the Christian life itself depended, and tyranny was an offence against God's design for humankind. Accordingly, conduct-book writers told their readers that while the husband and father was the head of the family and commanded everybody's obedience in that function, there was a higher authority than his. In John Buckworth's words, 'When the commands of the husband, are *contrary* to the commands of God, it is the duty of the wife to obey God rather than man'.[29]

That is what Helen Huntingdon does when leaving her husband. Anne Brontë took care to make her motives impregnable: Arthur Huntingdon's own example to his little boy could not be more horrific, and he effectively neutralised the mother's influence. In addition, he positively encouraged those childhood sins that all dispensers of published advice to families identified as especially dreadful, disobedience and profanity.

The extent to which Huntingdon has already managed to corrupt his son when Helen decides to run away with him makes her task particularly demanding. All she has on her side is the child's affection for her (established in the infancy during which his father neglected him), as well as the Divine assistance she invokes. The debates on childcare in Linden-Car (in the third chapter, called 'A Controversy'), discussed by many Brontë scholars, should be contemplated in connection with the very real danger that young Arthur is in. While still at Grassdale Manor, his mother summed it up in the following terms:

If I, for his good, deny him some trifling indulgence, he goes to his father, and the latter, in spite of his selfish indolence, will even give himself some trouble to meet the child's desires: if I attempt to curb his will, or look gravely on him for some act of childish disobedience, he knows his other parent will smile and take his part against me. Thus, not only have I the father's spirit in the son to contend against, the germs of his evil tendencies to search out and eradicate, and his corrupting intercourse and example in after life to counteract, but already *he* counteracts my arduous labour for the child's advantage, destroys my influence over his tender mind, and robs me of his very love[.] (*The Tenant of Wildfell Hall* XXXVI.312)

It is an interesting passage not least in that it contains so many of the central concepts and phrases found in contemporaneous works on child-rearing, such as 'curb [the child's] will', 'disobedience', 'evil tendencies', 'eradicate' and 'corrupting . . . example'. Helen's gentle attempts to discipline by means of grave looks are also in complete agreement with the recommendations of late-eighteenth- and early-nineteenth-century childcare advisers.

A child who has 'learnt to tipple wine like papa, to swear like Mr. Hattersley, and to have his own way like a man, and [send] mamma to the devil when she tried to prevent him' (XXXIX.335) would do well if he became 'the veriest milksop that ever was sopped' (III.28) – but that is not of course a fact that the Markhams and their friends can appreciate. Young Arthur's only hope is his mother, and her sole purpose in life is to save the soul God has sent her 'to educate for Heaven' (XXVIII.228). Her anxiety is hence entirely understandable and indeed justified, as the reader of *The Tenant of Wildfell Hall* comes to realise more than half-way through the book. Given the circumstances, it is a mark of Anne Brontë's skill as a writer that she managed to present both the pros and cons of having the boy educated solely by his mother so persuasively, investing the arguments against it with cogency and some eloquence.[30]

No amount of maternal solicitude can remove all obstacles in a young person's path, as both disputants acknowledge. Indeed, Helen expects her son to be tempted and tested often enough even if she uses 'all the means in [her] power to ensure . . . a smoother and a safer passage' for him (III.29). By shifting the issue to the education of girls, Helen goes on the offensive: if a girl should have the kind of protection and preparation that Gilbert thinks inappropriate for a boy, does that not amount to believing women congenitally frail or even vicious? As Gilbert emphatically denies this logical inference, Helen does 'have the last word' (III.32).[31]

The dangers of over-protection in the sense of physical mollycoddling were frequently brought out in early-nineteenth-century advice books for parents. For example, Ann Taylor warned mothers that 'superabundant care would prove highly injurious both to body and mind, and must expose [sons] to the ridicule of their associates'. However, boys should be taught 'a taste and relish for domestic life'; that will 'render them more cautious than they might otherwise be in the choice of their connexions'.[32] An explicit attempt to align boys with girls as feeling, thinking beings was made by another woman writer. Having deplored contempt for women, Elizabeth Hamilton wrote:

Why should not boys be inspired with the feelings of delicacy as well as girls? Why should the early corruption of their imagination be deemed a matter of light importance? What do we gain by attaching ideas of manliness and spirit to depravity of heart and manners? Alas, many and fatal are the errors, which may be traced to this unfortunate association![33]

Hamilton thus dignified the male sex by extending moral virtues usually associated with women to them – a move in the opposite direction from that of 'Mrs Graham', but with the same result: where the most important education is concerned, the education of minds and hearts, both sexes should be taught along the same lines.

One of the reasons why Helen and Gilbert's discussion is so fascinating is that it connects with the perennial debate on the moral worth of women in relation to that of men. Time and again, participants have argued that far from being the weaker sex where virtue is concerned, women are in fact intrinsically superior. The implications for the nature and sphere of female activity have varied enormously throughout the centuries, some upholders of women's inherent moral superiority arguing that the exercise of womanly virtues should be restricted to the domestic sphere.[34] It is significant that Anne Brontë made Helen suggest that Gilbert holds the opposite view – that women are morally frailer than men – and that he instantly recoils from the idea.

Gilbert Markham's mother calls Helen's determination to educate young Arthur herself a 'fatal error' which she will 'bitterly repent' – strong words for this easygoing woman (*The Tenant of Wildfell Hall*, III.29). However, she rejects Helen's description of the alternative option: 'I am to send him to school, I suppose, to learn to despise his mother's authority and affection!' Such a sad outcome of school training is not envisaged by another parent of a carefully home-educated young boy in the Brontë fiction, though the thought of his future schooling causes his parents great uneasiness.

The dangers that threatened the boy Arthur are briefly outlined in Charlotte Brontë's *The Professor*, but only as something the narrator does not see in his son Victor: 'I found . . . few elements of the "good fellow" or the "fine fellow" in him; scant sparkles of the spirit which loves to flash over the wine-cup, or which kindles the passions to a destroying fire' (XXV.244). The reason why William Crimsworth perceives a greater risk to his son in continued home education than in going to Eton is related to another kind of (over-)protection: both parents fear that the boy's temper will get him into trouble later in life if he does not learn to curb it while still young. Manifested in sudden outbursts of resentment, 'the leaven of the offending Adam' must be brought under Victor's own control. The world will not apply his parents' modes of persuasion, reason and love, to cool his wrath when its 'electrical ardour . . . emits . . . ominous sparks' (XXV.245). The discipline of an institution will, his father trusts, impose an 'ordeal of merited and salutary suffering' on Victor, who will emerge from it 'a wiser and a better man' (Coleridge's 'sadder' reverberates in the phrase).

Two gifted young boys whose personalities contain potential hindrances to their achieving well-balanced maturity, in books written by two sisters who were being forced to witness the degradation of a talented and temperamental brother – the biographical dimension is impossible to ignore.[35] The differences between the two fictional portrayals are as interesting as the similarities: Anne Brontë represented constant maternal solicitousness as the endangered boy's best hope; Charlotte Brontë outlined the imposition of an external system of discipline, very far removed from the forgiving love of home, as the preferred option. Branwell Brontë had neither. Bereft of his mother and her substitute, his eldest sister Maria, he never knew the hour-by-hour, day-to-day attentions of a loving mother. Nor was his waywardness brought under the control of an impersonal establishment whose rules, formal and informal, brooked no disobedience. Anne and Charlotte did not depict their fictional boys in situations even remotely resembling Branwell's: most importantly, Arthur and Victor are the only children of devoted mothers. Nevertheless, the reader of *The Tenant of Wildfell Hall* and *The Professor* who knows something about the lives of the Brontës cannot help thinking of Branwell's tragedy – if only to reflect that the freedom from surveillance, restraint and tight collective discipline that was such a boon to Patrick Brontë's daughters may have been a factor in the wreck of his son.

'TO ARM AND STRENGTHEN YOUR HERO':[36] FAMILY VALUES AND ADULT STRUGGLES

The Professor makes it clear that not even two loving parents in a blissfully contented home may be enough to fortify a boy for adult life. In *Agnes Grey* another happy home, run by a resourceful and high-principled mother, likewise turns out to have given a daughter insufficient preparation for life in the outside world. The doting father and able instructor Edgar Linton does not manage to protect his one ewe lamb from falling into Heathcliff's claws. The only adult Brontë character of any importance who, having been raised by an admirable parent, navigates past the reefs of early adulthood with ease and soon finds port after none-too-stormy seas is John Graham Bretton in *Villette* – and he had attended a day school (III.19). That circumstance is interesting in view of the fact that day schooling was often held up as an acceptable compromise, allowing both for parental vigilance and for adaptation to peers outside the home.[37]

Most of the contented and complete nuclear families in the Brontë fiction are part of briefly outlined happily-ever-after endings, where children are still young (though the reader of *The Tenant of Wildfell Hall* is reassured that Arthur grows into a fine young man in due course). The comparative lack of harmonious 'normal' family backgrounds seen to equip young adults for untroubled success in life might be taken to suggest a degree of aloofness on the Brontës' part from the conduct-book idea of the good home, created by loving parents, as the source of all essential human virtues.

There is no need to envisage such implicit dissent, however. Not only did the authors live in an age where death disrupted family life everywhere, as happened in their own case. Many heroes and heroines of contemporary literature were orphans, father- or motherless or the products of unhappy or illicit unions. It is enough to think of Dickens, Thackeray and Gaskell for examples, not to mention the Brontë favourites Byron and Scott, to whom the many people with unorthodox family backgrounds in the Brontë juvenilia owe a good deal. Abnormal familial patterns and relations were always the stuff of mystery and drama.

Confronted with the exigencies of independent adult life, Brontë protagonists struggle to adapt while holding on to principles rooted in their early years. Among those principles, a dedication to truth, obedience to God's laws and the curbing of self-will play prominent roles. The operation of these classic nursery virtues in the labour to develop the individual personality, safeguarding its integrity while grappling with the trials of young adulthood, is a significant element in the mature Brontë fiction.

CHAPTER 5

Professional educators in the home

GOVERNESSES IN FACT . . .

Those Brontë characters who must earn their living by undertaking the job that parents were unable or unwilling to do, educate children in their own homes, face many obstacles in their attempts to develop the faculties of others while at least retaining their own. The biographical connection is apparent: all the Brontë children except Emily had resident posts as governesses or tutor at one time or another, and all experienced varying degrees of unhappiness in their jobs.

In this, of course, they were not alone. Throughout the nineteenth century, the tribulations of governesses filled thousands of pages of print, in the form of manuals for governesses, advice to parents, articles and letters in journals and newspapers and, finally, fictional tales numerous enough to form a genre of their own.[1]

All discussions of Victorian governesses in fact and fiction dwell on their difficult social position. Neither 'family' nor servants, they were often despised downstairs as well as upstairs. Their charges, sensing the poor status of the women who tried to control them, would cheerfully rebel against attempts to enforce obedience. The children's mothers, jealous of any affection a governess might manage to win from their offspring, would constantly undermine her efforts. The fact that many parents who employed governesses were themselves badly educated *parvenus* made matters worse, especially as some of them were uncomfortably aware of their inferiority in this respect.[2]

In addition, the tacit consensus that nothing but material need would induce a respectable woman to seek paid employment stamped the governess as impecunious by definition. This circumstance made her particularly sensitive to perceived slights, increasing the uncomfortableness of the whole situation both for the governess and for the parents who employed her.

48

Where Charlotte and Anne Brontë are concerned, lack of self-confidence and aplomb seems to have constituted a painful disadvantage in their governess posts. Out of their depth in the homes of people with whom they had nothing in common, they must have exuded a constant air of being ill at ease. In an entertaining attempt to view the situation from the point of view of their employers, the writer of an early article in the *Brontë Society Transactions*, Lady Barbara Wilson, admitted, 'The more I study Charlotte Brontë as a governess, the more I realize that I would have hated her to fill the role in my own household'.[3] Anne apparently had a slight stammer, a real affliction in a person required to exercise authority over children.[4] Wilson's reflections are worth quoting at somewhat greater length:

I cannot help feeling . . . a grain of pity for those unfortunate ladies who chartered a Brontë for service in their schoolrooms. They cannot all have been the superfiends they were depicted. The Brontës must have been kittle cattle to handle. Always trailing their threadbare but neatly-darned cloaks, in quest of real or fancied insults; out of sympathy with their charges, devoid or almost devoid of the saving grace of humour, filled with a nostalgic desire for their own home, they must have . . . been a severe trial to their employers. (231–2)

A somewhat later article in the *Brontë Society Transactions*, Susan Brooke's discussion of Anne Brontë at Blake Hall, summarises the most fundamental reason why Charlotte and Anne could never have been happy as governesses except in the most exceptional families: 'A governess was expected to be intellectually subservient; to express opinions of any kind was a break of etiquette, and to utter sentiments which ran counter to those of her employers was an unpardonable offence'.[5] This description is amply borne out by governess manuals: the law of absolute parental rule did not just extend to the children in a family but also to any person who was hired to teach them.

For two extremely astute, intellectually orientated, artistically skilled and ethically sensitive young women, trained to educate themselves with no other higher guide than their own consciences, 'subservience' of the kind outlined by Brooke is not only intolerable – it is impossible. The dislike that Charlotte expressed for the mothers of her young charges, Mrs Sidgwick and Mrs White, testifies to her resentment at having to submit to régimes conducted by women she despised.[6] Anne's unhappiness at Blake Hall is mediated by one of Charlotte's letters to Ellen Nussey, in which Charlotte quotes from a letter Anne had written to her.[7] That Anne was no more contented at Thorp Green in her early days there is clear from her diary paper of 1841 and her sisters' references to Anne as being 'harassed' and in 'Bondage'.[8] The point made by Wilson (and later by others, notably Barker) about the difficulty of having a Brontë on one's staff is well made.[9] However, it must be said in their defence that everything they had learnt militated against their suppressing their personalities so as not to deviate from mental, spiritual and emotional climates established by people they could not but regard as their inferiors in every non-material respect.

If the freedom-loving Brontës could never have been comfortable living and working in circumstances they were powerless to control, other women confronted the necessity of coming to terms with the governess' lack of space and liberty with determined optimism. The first requirement was to accept, once and for all, that a governess is in a subordinate position. 'Does not the same apply to every profession?' asked Mary Maurice, herself an experienced instructor, in 1849, failing to mention that few 'professions' would require their practitioners to spend practically every hour of every day as outsiders on the employers' home ground.[10] Having internalised this unalterable law, a governess should try to put herself in the position of both children and parents.[11] In other words, she must teach herself to show empathy and tact. That is a tall order at the best of times, and especially when the person expected to be simultaneously submissive and empathetic is a penniless young woman in her twenties.

Age is a factor in relation to parents, too, however. Many nineteenth-century commentators realised that going to live in the house of strangers in order to raise their children was a hard task for a girl barely out of her teens – but nor was it easy for a young mother struggling to find her materfamilial feet to manage a governess with kindness and good humour.[12] All sorts of jealousies might flourish in such a volatile situation.[13] Nor were mothers and governesses the only categories involved; nurses and nursery-maids were also part of the female rivalry scenario.[14]

Charlotte and Anne Brontë were doubtless aware of these tensions, irrespective of the degree to which one may suppose them to have had experiences of that kind themselves. Mrs Gaskell tells the story of how one of Charlotte's charges said 'I love 'ou, Miss Brontë', only to hear his mother exclaim, 'Love the *governess*, my dear!'.[15] As for Anne, it is clear that the Robinson girls she taught – especially two of them, Bessy and Mary – were devoted to her. Charlotte's description of the two young women 'clinging round [Anne] like two children' when visiting Haworth in 1848 makes touching reading.[16] What Mrs Robinson felt about their enduring affection for their former governess we cannot know; but the vignette of the 'overjoyed' girls 'clinging' to their governess could be taken to suggest that

Miss Brontë was closer to them than their own mother. Whatever Anne's pedagogical ability may have been, she had obviously succeeded in the all-important struggle to win the hearts of her pupils.

. . . AND FICTION

It is an intriguing fact that the only one of the Brontë sisters who attained any appreciable degree of success as a governess wrote the book which paints that occupation in the darkest colours. True, *Jane Eyre* refers to the unhappiness of the Rivers sisters in families unworthy of them, as well as to the torture inflicted on the Ingram governesses by heartless charges; and Shirley Keeldar, on being informed of Caroline Helstone's wish to be a governess, exclaims, 'What an idea! Be a governess! Better be a slave at once' (*Shirley* II.ii.241). But among the Brontë novels, only *Agnes Grey* details the vexations of a governess' life: obstreperous children, parents whose folly undermines what little progress has been made, insolent servants, obnoxious relatives, perpetual anxiety, lack of privacy, the pangs of conscience at achieving less than she should, the awareness of gradually losing hard-won intellectual and moral ground herself, recurrent humiliations due to her uncomfortable social position and domestic drudgery curtailing her few moments of leisure.

Many Brontë scholars have stressed the didactic aspect of *Agnes Grey*, regarding the novel as at least in part a contribution to the ongoing debate about the role of the governess.[17] While the autobiographical dimension is not denied, recent critics have pointed to similarities between circumstances depicted in *Agnes Grey* and contemporaneous works on female education in general and governess instruction in particular.

As a result, Anne Brontë's first novel can now be seen to play a part in a highly dynamic historical context. In addition to the relevancies indicated by others, some passages from the anonymous *Advice to Governesses*, published in 1827, are worth quoting; they almost read like a blueprint for *Agnes Grey*:

The first vexation a governess meets with, frequently arises from a mother's want of confidence, and from her interference in the school-room; from her great tenderness to her children, not suffering their instructress to use her own discretion; from indulgence breaking in upon hours devoted to study; and from her not permitting necessary discipline, but counteracting useful regulations.

Governesses may, much to their misfortune, be requested to teach 'a little urchin, the tyrant of the nursery', and to take him along on walks:

She complies; and he is for ever running into mischief, and involving [his sisters] in it. She remonstrates, and he spurns her authority; for all boys are alike in rebellion against female government, unless it be backed by power. . . . [A governess should have nothing to do with boys] if she can possibly help it; at any rate, [she should] stipulate for the full permission of punishing, as well as rewarding; for, when the young delinquent is carried to his mother for correction, she takes his part, or does not listen dispassionately[.][18]

All these instances of agreement between governess manuals and the like on the one hand and *Agnes Grey* on the other should not blind us to the relevance of Lamonica's observation that '*Agnes Grey* is not primarily a critique of the unhappy condition of the Victorian governess in the private home. Rather, it is a commentary on the upper- and rising middle-class Victorian family – the context in which the governess was becoming a "standard furnishing"'.[19] The portrayals of the Bloomfield and Murray families are not so much condemnations of unkind employers as explorations of human behaviour that impedes character formation. The narrator of *Agnes Grey* does not say that parents should not rule; she shows that when they rule inadequately, not even the most dedicated professional educator can succeed in what is every preceptor's chief duty, that of raising good human beings.

A radical way of excluding harmful parental interference is to dispense with parents altogether, which is what Charlotte Brontë did in her fictional accounts of two successful governesses, Jane Eyre and Mrs Pryor in *Shirley*. In the former's case, the governess is given complete freedom to mould her pupil's character; in the latter, the grown-up pupil is seen to watch over her own character development.

Consequently, Jane Eyre's 'new servitude' (*Jane Eyre* I.x.85) at Thornfield before Mr Rochester's arrival is in one sense her first taste of autonomy. Realising that the elderly lady who welcomed her with such warmth ('the kindness . . . so frankly offered . . . before it was earned'; I.xi.98) is her social equal, Jane is relieved: 'my position was all the freer' (I.xi.100).[20] It is a significant choice of word, expressing the narrator's awareness that the 'new servitude' comprises an element of unexpected personal liberty. On her way to Thornfield, Jane had thought much more about her forthcoming relationship with Mrs Fairfax than about her imminent and intimate association with a little girl. Unlike Agnes Grey before she is robbed of her illusions, Jane has not attempted to envisage what it will mean to take charge of a child.

It is natural to relate this difference between Agnes and Jane to their personal circumstances. The youngest member of a loving family comes from an emotional climate that could hardly be more dissimilar to that inhabited by the child and girl Jane Eyre. The ten-year-old who had told her aunt that she could not live 'without one bit of love or kindness' (I.iv.36) has had precious little of either at eighteen. Apart from what Lowood offered in that line – from Miss Temple and Helen Burns, and occasionally from some of the other teachers and pupils – the only kindness she has known, and that not unmixed with harshness, came from the Gateshead servant Bessie. The extent of Jane's emotional destitution comes out on the eve of her departure from Lowood, when Bessie calls to see her (I.xi.90). The appearance of the simple woman who once showed her some warmth is enough to transform the outwardly sober and reserved young schoolteacher into a jubilant little girl. It is a moving scene, and it is the last we see of the child Jane Eyre: from the next day onward, she is an adult who has taken her life into her own hands.

It is all the more interesting that this passionate teenager does not develop any intense affection for Mrs Fairfax or Adèle. Jane Eyre, so sensitive to the painful aspects of social hierarchy, is no egalitarian where non-material qualities and abilities are concerned. She certainly likes both the house-keeper and the child; but they are mentally inferior to her, and adult Jane's love is reserved for people she recognises as her peers: the Rivers sisters and, of course, Mr Rochester. Here spirit calls out to spirit, and social rank is irrelevant.

The pages in *Jane Eyre* where the narrator dwells on her discontent before Rochester comes to Thornfield are usually discussed from the point of view of gender – 'Women are supposed to be very calm generally: but women feel just as men feel', and so on (I.xii.109).[21] Those are certainly noteworthy expressions of a libertarian pathos that rebels against conventional ideas of the woman's sphere, like Caroline Helstone's impassioned address to 'Men of England!' (*Shirley* II.xi).[22] However, what is peculiarly striking about Jane's sentiments is that they coexist with a lot that may be described as a governess' dream. The work is easy and sufficiently if not generously paid;[23] and she is treated with respect, even affection – but those patent blessings are not enough. 'Action', 'practical experience' in 'the busy world', being denied her, she has recourse to her imagination (the 'bright visions' before her 'mind's eye' and the never-ending tale sounding in her 'inward ear', I.xii.109). Eager to experience 'more vivid kinds of goodness' than those offered by Mrs Fairfax and Adèle, she walks the grounds and climbs the stairs to look beyond the sphere to which she is confined. In other words, she is bored.

This dimension in *Jane Eyre* is more profoundly radical than the attacks on governess abusers in chapters II.ii (alternatively chapter 17; the Ingrams) and III.iv (30; the posts of the Rivers sisters). Charlotte Brontë was obviously aware that it would surprise and might offend readers. Having let Jane describe her lukewarm feelings for Mrs Fairfax and Adèle, she added the following comment:

> This, *par parenthèse*, will be thought cool language by persons who entertain solemn doctrines about the angelic nature of children, and the duty of those charged with their education to conceive for them an idolatrous devotion: but I am not writing to flatter parental egotism, to echo cant, or prop up humbug; I am merely telling the truth. (I.xii.108)

That is a brusque, and somewhat exaggerated, recapitulation of much early-nineteenth-century writing on education by a disgruntled observer with plenty of personal experience.[24] Over the next few paragraphs, Charlotte Brontë repeatedly made Jane express her anticipation of blame for being discontented in a post that holds everything a governess could wish for. The pages on Jane Eyre's restlessness remind us that this book is not a 'governess novel' in the sense defined by Lecaros.[25] It is not a piece of domestic realism but the story of a questing spirit seeking self-improvement by arduous routes that test her unusual faculties and inner strength to the utmost. Freedom is a necessity in that pursuit, and the narrator's innate resistance to subjugation is vigorously expressed throughout the book; but it is a condition, not the impetus itself.[26]

Jane Eyre ultimately finds fulfilment in marriage to her master, another unrealistic touch from the point of view of governess-manual writers. Governesses, actual and presumptive, were repeatedly warned not to entertain the notion of marrying a member of 'the family' or a family friend.[27] In this respect, too, *Agnes Grey* is much closer to the picture of governess life transmitted by manual writers and authors of 'realistic' tales: she marries a curate, a man in her father's line of work and of similar social status.

Both the marriages of these former governesses are represented as blissfully happy, and both are preceded by a brief period of successful schoolteaching. The case of the third prominent governess in the Brontë fiction, 'Mrs Pryor' in *Shirley*, is different: escaping from misery as a governess into matrimony, she was obliged to return to governessing after fleeing from a hellish marriage. Charlotte Brontë's revenge on Elizabeth Rigby (Lady Eastlake) for her hostile review of *Jane Eyre* was a counter-attack on several levels. First, as is well known, she quoted extensively from Rigby's text, placing the snippets in the mouths of two characters chiefly remarkable for their pharisaism and humbug. Second, she made the character Mrs Pryor, who reproduces these phrases as accusations against herself in her earlier life, into an abject advocate of 'submission to authorities, scrupulous deference to our betters' (II.x.377) – in other words, a complete negation of the Chartist rebelliousness which Rigby had seen in *Jane Eyre*. Third, she turned Rigby's accusation according to which 'Currer Bell' had harmed the governess cause (by creating such a reprehensible representative of that class as Jane Eyre) against the critic, casting the Rigby mouthpieces as governess-tormentors.

Mrs Pryor's High Toryism and deference to the upper strata of society are hence ingredients in a piece of rancorous satire. However, Charlotte Brontë also made skilful use of these characteristics in her rendition of the relationship between Shirley and the woman who, in Shirley's own words, 'was my governess, and is still my friend' (I.xi.196).

As a former preceptress who is now a motherly companion, Mrs Pryor is chiefly concerned with manners rather than morals. With the diffident disposition and pessimistic outlook on life that Charlotte Brontë gave her, Mrs Pryor would not have been convincing as an authoritative ethical and spiritual guide for vigorous, self-confident Shirley. Her very virtues seem negative, in the original sense of the word.

This, however, is precisely where she becomes important in the moral education of Shirley, herself so positive. The girl is shown to be sensitive and perspicacious enough to be aware of Mrs Pryor's essential goodness and dedication to duty, as well as sufficiently well-principled to respect those qualities in her governess/companion. Shirley's nature is seen to be too buoyant and forceful to bend under external pressure, and any instructor who would try to impose his or her views and values on such a person must fail; but Mrs Pryor's very inability to assert herself forces the young woman to be considerate, compassionate and kind. The aftermath of the Hollow incident is a case in point; Shirley heartily repents of her wrath:

'I have behaved very shamefully, very ungenerously, very ungratefully to her . . . How insolent in me to turn on her thus, for what after all was no fault, only an excess of conscientiousness on her part. . . . I regret my error most sincerely: tell her so, and ask if she will forgive me.' (II.x.364)

When it comes to intellectual accomplishments, Shirley acknowledges Louis Moore's superiority, but the only person who can teach this strong young woman to be good is herself. Strength, truth and goodness are the supreme qualities in Charlotte Brontë's fiction, and the quoted lines suggest the way in which Mrs Pryor fosters them in Shirley.

A GENTLEMAN TUTOR

Shirley's ultimate union with her former tutor has caused varying degrees of uneasiness among Brontë scholars. Many of them have expressed their disapproval of Louis Moore in terms that amount to charging Charlotte Brontë with poor workmanship.[28]

One thing Charlotte Brontë cannot be accused of is a lack of deliberation over the qualities which she gave to this fictional character. As some critics have observed, he is a carefully constructed complement to Shirley. There is an androgynous element in his nature, as there is in that of 'Captain Keeldar', his headstrong bride with the masculine first name.[29] While making him a gentle, patient and skilful 'nurse' to his pupil Henry (III.xiii.629), Charlotte Brontë took care to equip him with physical courage and strength (evinced in connection with a burglary; III.xiii.628). In other words, Charlotte Brontë attributed masculine force to her gentleman scholar-tutor as well as mental strength; indeed, she even made him arrogant, not to say overbearing, at times.[30] However difficult it may be for a present-day reader to treat a heroine's express wish to be 'improved' by her mate with equanimity (III.xiii.619), the provision of a masterful husband for a strong personality like Shirley is not unnatural in itself. Why, then, is this character so problematic?

Part of the answer lies in Charlotte Brontë's having transmitted so much of what the reader is told about Louis Moore through his own musings and his notes, the pointlessness of which was criticised from the start.[31] Neither his commendable conduct at the time of the burglary nor his consummate nursing is shown to the reader by the narrator; Louis Moore describes them himself. The man presented by the narrator is a withdrawn 'satellite' (III.iii.455) whose protracted dialogues with Henry and Shirley do not always show him in a prepossessing light. Above all, he suffers from a fatal drawback: he has no sense of humour. Unlike, for instance, the obviously flawed Brontë heroes Mr Rochester and Gilbert Markham, he never says or writes anything remotely funny, let alone self-ironic. If Charlotte Brontë wanted to assign every conceivable virtue to him, it seems a pity that she omitted that one. The fact that the two incorruptible discerners of true worth in the novel, the perfect clergyman Mr Hall and the noble labourer William Farren, are impressed by him does not mean that the reader is. In other words, the imputation of artistic failure seems just.

Another factor that tends to undermine the reader's satisfaction with Shirley's choice is the novel's treatment of his profession. The repeated reminders that Louis Moore is of good, if impoverished, family, the brother of the millowner who was generally regarded as a suitable husband for the mistress of Fieldhead, do not neutralise the connotations of inferiority that cling to the word 'tutor'. Even when used by Shirley and Louis themselves, it is a term of disparagement. Having realised that Shirley 'must be scared to be won', Louis declares, 'for the first time I stand before you *myself*. I have flung off the tutor, and beg to introduce you to the man: and, remember, he is a gentleman' (III.xiii.621).

The implication that a tutor is by definition an inferior being is obvious, and it comes out even more clearly in the subsequent exchange between Louis' employer Mr Sympson and his newly affianced niece. Informed by Louis that he will from now on 'protect, watch over, serve' Shirley, Mr Sympson expostulates, 'You, sir? – you, the tutor?' only to receive implicit confirmation that his taunt has hit home in Shirley's swiftly interposed 'Not one word of insult, sir . . . not one syllable of disrespect to Mr. Moore, in this house' (III.xiii.627). It is the term 'tutor' that is the bearer of the offensive connotations. As was the case with 'governess', the word 'only' invites itself as a prelude to 'the tutor'.[32]

However, the inferiority inherent in 'tutor' is one of social position and, by implication, material fortune, not of personal capabilities nor even of birth, as Louis' case demonstrates (though he is made to stress it so that the point is not lost). For a worshipper of worldly advancement, as Shirley accuses her uncle of being (III.viii.557–8), poverty would disqualify any man from marriage to the rich Shirley Keeldar. In their heated exchange over her rejection of the wealthy but less than assertive Sir Philip Nunnely, Shirley states that the man she marries must be her master: she will 'accept no hand which cannot hold [her] in check' (III.viii.551).

As her former tutor, Louis was in precisely that position when the pair first became acquainted. The teenage girl may have been an heiress, but she was also a pupil. Much has been written about the pupil-master relationship in Charlotte Brontë's fiction, but only one pair of lovers corresponds to the original matrix of adult male teaching adolescent girl in a schoolroom. Frances Henri may be William Crimsworth's pupil, but she is also a teacher in her own right; Lucy Snowe is the English mistress in Madame Beck's school and hence M. Paul's colleague. Jane Eyre is never taught by Rochester; he is her 'master' in the sense of 'employer', not a dispenser of academic knowledge. Only Shirley is shown to have spent considerable periods of time under the control of a man who shaped and influenced her faculties by virtue of superior educational attainments and a commanding presence.

Perhaps one of the reasons for the general dissatisfaction of *Shirley* critics with the Keeldar–Moore match is that it offers a juvenile-wish-fulfilment

resolution to a relationship experienced by many people, most of whom
regard it as a passing phase: a girlhood crush on a compelling male teacher –
and here it leads on to marriage. The romantic dimensions of such relationships are well known; they are also normally felt to be the man's responsibility to keep in check. Louis Moore may occasionally express his conviction
that he has no hope of marrying Shirley, but he never suggests that he is not
inherently worthy of her. On the contrary, he delights in her faults, because
they 'are the steps by which I mount to ascendancy over her' (III.vi.522).[33]
The reader gradually realises that the free-and-easy Shirley has never been
entirely at liberty, being bound by a secret love in which her subjugation
was an original constituent.[34] As she agonises over the imminent surren-
der of her freedom to the man whose initial superiority was in one sense
simply a factor of her youth, it is not unnatural for a reader to wish that
Charlotte Brontë had not made her go through with it. The ending of
Shirley has always been felt to be less than unequivocally happy;[35] and a
reader who accepts the author's challenge to 'look for the moral' may well
be troubled by the circumstances in which Louis becomes the leopardess'
keeper (III.xiii.623–4).

In marrying his former pupil, the tutor gains the freedom for which he
yearned with a personalised ardour that seems at least as great as his love for
Shirley.[36] The man who was content to contemplate celibacy as long as he
could embrace Liberty thus ends up having it all, including the autonomy
his wife surrenders to him. A tutor could only be 'an appendage of a family'
(III.xiii.614), not the head of a household, and hence by definition confined
by his profession. He would be far better paid than a governess; in 1844,
an article in *Fraser's Magazine* pointed to the glaring discrepancy between
the salary of a male teacher in a private family, who could receive as much
as £300 a year, and that of a governess, who would consider herself well
paid with £40.[37] Nevertheless, his existence was a kind of bondage. No
difficulty we may have with *Shirley's* tutor should prevent us from seeing
that Louis Moore is yet another manifestation of the link between servitude
and teaching that is so prominent in the Brontës' lives and works.

THE QUALIFICATIONS OF PROFESSIONAL INSTRUCTORS IN THE HOME

Charlotte Brontë took care to give her tutor the impeccable morals that
were so signally lacking in her brother, who was dismissed from two
tutoring posts because of sexual misconduct.[38] Louis' responsible gravity is
often emphasised, as in Mr Yorke's observation that 'you tutors are such

solemn chaps: it is almost like speaking to a parson to consult with you'
(III.iv.478). It is interesting to compare this sentence with Branwell's own
description of his outwardly 'calm, sedate, sober, abstemious' conduct at
the Postlethwaites'.[39] Regardless of whether Branwell's account exaggerated
either his virtuous behaviour or the immoral desires it concealed or both,
one thing is certain: a tutor's reputation for good conduct was an indispensable job qualification. Just as no mother would hire a governess on
whose character the slightest stain was discernible, no father would entrust
his son's upbringing to a young man of dubious morality.

Where other qualifications were concerned, the second quarter of the
nineteenth century presents a very varied picture indeed. The earnestness
with which Anne Brontë attempted to increase her store of knowledge and
skills for her pupils' benefit is a Brontë-related indication of the increasing
professionalisation of governesses. Anne, however, was obliged to teach herself. In the year of her death, the first institution specifically geared towards
raising the academic standards of governesses was established with Queen's
College in London. Initially associated with the Governesses' Benevolent
Institution (GBI) and owing much to the efforts of Mary and F. D. Maurice,
Queen's College became independent of the GBI in 1853.[40] The need for
some sort of formal qualification for governesses had become apparent during the 1840s debate on the 'plight of governesses', a class whose members
often existed in what has been called a 'cycle of destitution-subsistence-
destitution':[41] salaries were far too low to permit any appreciable saving,
and a governess out of work would sometimes live in penury.[42]

If so many influential and well-intentioned people felt that the answer
was to be found in another type of cycle (or rather trajectory), formal
education-examination-certificate-decent salary, one would have expected
Charlotte Brontë to have agreed with them. However, a letter of hers written
in May 1848 expresses a sceptical attitude:

> The Governesse's Institution may be an excellent thing in some points of view –
> but it is both absurd and cruel to attempt to raise still higher the standard of
> acquirements. Already Governesses are not half nor a quarter paid for what they
> teach – nor in most instances <are> 'is' half or a quarter of their attainments
> required by their pupils. The young Teacher's chief anxiety, when she sets out
> in life, always is, to know a great deal; her chief fear that she should not know
> enough; brief experience will, in most instances, shew her that this anxiety has
> been misdirected.[43]

Charlotte Brontë made a clear distinction between the GBI, of whose efforts
to relieve the distress of old, sick and unemployed governesses she apparently
approved, and the ambition to raise the level of academic attainment. In this

letter she goes on to maintain that a sanguine, flexible temperament, sturdy health and good strong nerves are infinitely more serviceable to anyone who would teach children than 'a brilliant list of accomplishments'.[44] That does not, however, amount to a disparagement of higher education for a woman. In a later letter to the same recipient, her publisher's reader W. S. Williams, she welcomed his daughter's opportunity to study at Queen's College: 'Come what may afterwards, an education secured is an advantage gained – a priceless advantage', continuing, characteristically, 'it is a step towards independency – and one great curse of a single female life is its dependency'.[45] What Charlotte rejected was the idea that formal education would help a governess in the sense that it would make her more capable of coping with the job and enduring the life.

It is hence not surprising that none of those who dissuade Caroline Helstone from going out as a governess points out that her self-acknowledged ignorance would be an obstacle. Mrs Pryor's reiterated objection is that Caroline's constitution is not sufficiently robust (II.ii.241 and II.x.377–8), and that the work would break her health and spirits.[46]

However, Charlotte Brontë's awareness that the late 1840s expected a wider range of knowledge and skills than the early nineteenth century is evident in *Jane Eyre*. Jane's advertisement that leads to the Thornfield post describes the applicant as 'qualified to teach the usual branches of a good English education, together with French, Drawing, and Music', on which list Jane comments, '(in those days, reader, this now narrow catalogue of accomplishments, would have been held tolerably comprehensive)' (I.x.87).

By contrast, Agnes Grey offers a very respectable set of qualifications, as her mother points out: 'Music, Singing, Drawing, French, Latin, and German . . . are no mean assemblage; many will be glad to have so much in one instructor' (VI.52). During the correspondence that precedes Agnes' departure for Horton Lodge, Mrs Murray turns out not to be very interested in Agnes' acquirements; living close to a large town 'she could get masters to supply any deficiencies in that respect'. This less than courteous observation was followed by the employer's ominous insistence that 'a mild and cheerful temper and obliging disposition were the most essential requisites' (apart from the obligatory 'unimpeachable morality'; VI.53).

As it turns out, Rosalie Murray is indeed taught music and singing by 'the best master the country afforded' (VII.62), besides receiving 'occasional instruction' from Agnes. There is nothing unusual about this arrangement. Special masters for the accomplishments were commonplace, especially in towns and cities. Keighley was large enough to supply such tuition for the benefit of the young Brontës, who had lessons in art and music from the best teachers Patrick Brontë could afford.[47]

In remote rural areas well-qualified instruction of any kind was of course harder to obtain, but as long as the remuneration was sufficient it was to be had. A fictional example of such an arrangement is supplied by the only reference to home education provided by a professional teacher in *Wuthering Heights*: Heathcliff's boast to Nelly that he has engaged a tutor 'to come three times a week, from twenty miles [sic] distance, to teach [Linton] what he pleases to learn' (II.vi.184). It is an unrealistic-sounding scheme, though, in that the distance alone would take the best part of a day to travel, and nothing more is heard of this man in the novel.

Another casual reference to a professional instructor saddled with a tough job occurs towards the end of *Agnes Grey*, where Matilda Murray's manners are said to be 'considerably improved' by a 'fashionable governess' (XXII:178). Such so-called 'finishing governesses' were a special sort, frowned on by serious writers on female education.[48] The reader who remembers Matilda in *Agnes Grey*'s schoolroom cannot help wondering what it took to civilise the girl whose chief talent seemed to consist in her being 'as good a judge of horseflesh' as her father and his friends (IX.75).

THE DANGERS OF DOMESTIC DISHARMONY

Whatever a governess might do in a case like Matilda's, *Agnes Grey* makes it clear that the key to success is the attitude of parents. What little 'amelioration' Agnes Grey manages to effect is achieved outside the parental scheme of things, and perforce severely limited.[49] A notable circumstance when it comes to Agnes' relation to her pupils' parents is that both educator and parents are shown to be aware of the children's and young people's faults, but that no common ground for attacking them is ever established: instead of joining forces, the two parties blame each other. The Bloomfield parents signal their dissatisfaction with their children's unruly behaviour, but Agnes does not take up what might be seen as an invitation to discuss the problems (III.30–1). She can hardly be blamed for responding to the implicit reproach rather than to the merest possibility of a dialogue with people by whom she feels 'censured and misjudged' (IV.33) – but to an outside viewer, it does look like an opportunity lost.

Similarly, Mrs Murray is aware that Rosalie needs careful watching and Matilda a firm hand; but when she communicates these insights to Agnes (see, for instance, *Agnes Grey* XIV.113–14), all the governess can see is that she is being criticised by the person on whom she herself puts all the blame.

While any reader's sympathy is bound to be with Agnes, a cold look at the situation so skilfully described by Anne Brontë leads to the realisation that a home where there is tension between the adults involved in the children's upbringing cannot but fail as a place of education.[50]

In a letter to Emily, written when she was just settling into her first governess post, Charlotte Brontë articulated the reason why so many governesses found it impossible to reach an understanding with their charges' parents: 'Mrs. Sidgwick expects me to do things that I cannot do – to love her children and be entirely devoted to them'.[51] In the eyes of the rebellious Miss Brontë, the employer's precious offspring were a set of 'riotous, perverse, unmanageable cubs' (191). The over-indulgence of mothers, and general lack of parental discipline, is an obbligato throughout masses of texts relating to the situation of governesses; *Agnes Grey* is an obvious example.

In these texts, parental indulgence is not only seen to thwart the governess' efforts to teach children manners as well as knowledge; it is decried as a danger to their happiness in this world and their eternal bliss in the next.[52] It is hard to see how professional educators who perceived such dangers could shrug them off in the interests of give-and-take, especially as they knew that all the giving would have to be done by them. Likewise, however, it is difficult to imagine parents putting up with their children being subjected to what they saw as uncalled-for strictness, especially if they sensed that it was meted out by someone who anticipated fire and brimstone as the ultimate alternative. In view of all the conflicting emotions swirling around in any home where the mother had handed over the job of educating her children to an outsider, with all the guilt, envy and jealousy that this involved, one wonders how domestic harmony could ever be achieved under these circumstances.[53]

CHAPTER 6

Schools and schooling

The great advantage of a boarding school from the professional educator's point of view is that it allows parental interference to be kept to a manageable minimum. It is a mark of professionalism in Madame Beck that she, alone among the parents in the Brontë fiction who employ staff to teach their children in their homes, is seen to respect the nursery-governess' sphere of authority.[1] In Madame Beck's home and school, an unsatisfactory employee is not censured but sacked. Madame retains overall control, not least thanks to her extensive intelligence policy; but as long as a person she has hired gives reasonable satisfaction, he or she is allowed to get on with the job.

Lucy Snowe is compelled to admit that Madame Beck's school is a model where the physical welfare of pupils is concerned:

No minds were overtasked; the lessons were well distributed and made incomparably easy to the learner; there was a liberty of amusement, and a provision for exercise which kept the girls healthy; the food was abundant and good: neither pale nor puny faces were anywhere to be seen in the Rue Fossette. She never grudged a holiday; she allowed plenty of time for sleeping, dressing, washing, eating; her method in all these matters was easy, liberal, salutary, and rational: many an austere English school-mistress would do vastly well to imitate it – and I believe many would be glad to do so, if exacting English parents would let them. (*Villette* VIII.73)

The remarkable concluding sentence amounts to accusing English parents of demanding that their children's schools submit their young ones to physical hardship. If one wishes to disregard the implication of downright parental sadism, an alternative interpretation is parental parsimony: good food was costly, as everybody knew, and skimping on food and kitchen staff was always an obvious way to cut costs in any institution. In any case, what Lucy Snowe is saying is that the harsh régimes found in English schools are at least partly the fault of parents – a striking allegation, irrespective of how one reads it. Even allowing for the fact that it is the narrator who speaks, not Charlotte Brontë, it gives the reader pause, not least because it is known to have been written by someone who blamed an 'austere' school for the deaths of two much-loved elder sisters.

Cowan Bridge, or the Clergy Daughters' School, to which Patrick Brontë sent his daughters, was to cost him the lives of his two eldest children. The subject of heated discussion after the publication of *Jane Eyre* and, later, Gaskell's *Life* – defenders of the school and its founder William Carus Wilson crossing swords with witnesses whose memories agreed with the fictionalised picture drawn by Charlotte Brontë – Cowan Bridge attracted a good deal of attention from Brontë scholars throughout the twentieth century. For instance, a number of articles on it have appeared in the *Brontë Society Transactions* over the years.[2]

Juliet Barker's sifting of the evidence in the case has resulted in a set of judicious conclusions: the food and cooking at Cowan Bridge were substandard even by the low standards of the time; many girls fell ill from epidemic disease which killed a sizeable proportion of sufferers, at school or (as happened with Maria and Elizabeth Brontë) subsequently at home; staff and rules were strict and living conditions hard (even in comparison with what the Brontë children, who were far from spoilt, were used to), and the pupils were not in a position to complain to their families;[3] and the girls were obliged to wear uniforms signalling their 'charity-child' status.[4]

What appals a modern reader of Barker's account is that the Clergy Daughters' School was apparently no worse, and in some respects actually better, than other comparable institutions at the time. It is difficult to stomach the notion that 'English parents' were guilty of so much misery in demanding that schools expose their children to hardships entailing dangers to their physical and mental health. Nor is it easy to accept the idea that these demands conflicted with the better instincts of teachers. If any category of adults could be expected to harbour merciful inclinations, one would have thought that it would be the parents, not the people who relieved them of their responsibilities to their defenceless offspring.

An attempt to assess the historical accuracy of these pictures falls outside the scope of this book, but one thing may be said with certainty: there were schools of all sorts and standards in early-nineteenth-century England, ranging from the horrific to the excellent. In their teens the Brontës experienced one of the better ones, the Wooler sisters' school at Roe Head, Mirfield, later transferred to Heald's House at Dewsbury Moor. An entirely different establishment from Cowan Bridge, it only took a small number of older girls who were taught and looked after by well-intentioned women of some academic ability.[5] The unhappiness that all three Brontë girls suffered there was not due to any shortcomings on the part of the school or those who ran it; Roe Head may not have been a first-class establishment, but it was a good-enough small school and most of its pupils seem to have been reasonably happy there.

Any school away from home would have been an affliction to the Brontës. Homesick for Haworth, the only place where 'the Gondals' and Angria could really flourish, they found the constant company of others irksome almost beyond endurance. Charlotte's Roe Head Journal depicts a passionately imaginative young woman who bitterly resents having her brief spells of creative reverie broken into.[6] Anne's poetry bears eloquent witness to the homesickness she endured during her long years at Thorp Green, the most sustained period of professional employment on the part of a young Brontë. Emily's one experience of schoolteaching on her own was short in comparison, though it may well have seemed painfully protracted to her.[7] Irrespective of whether her six months at Miss Patchett's school Law Hill near Halifax (in 1838–39) actually merited Charlotte's designation 'slavery', there was a pattern to Emily Brontë's absences from home.[8] Regardless of the nature of the surroundings, and of whether she was alone or accompanied by her sister Charlotte, being away from Haworth eroded Emily's physical strength to the point where her health was endangered. It took all her determination, and Charlotte's mitigating and mediating efforts, for her to be able to endure nine months in Brussels. Her suffering was not brought on by stifled creativity; as Brontë scholars have shown, the period at Law Hill yielded some fine early poems.[9] What only Haworth offered, however, was opportunities to withdraw into her imagination for comparatively long and uninterrupted periods of time, combined with freedom from enforced communication with other people.

As all three Brontë sisters experienced varying degrees of misery in schools, ranging from melancholy to acute wretchedness in mind and body, the fact that they decided to start a school of their own might seem strange. It was, however, the only option that would, had the plan been realised, have allowed them to earn a living without being obliged to submit to a régime set up and operated by others. As various possibilities that would have required them to live away from Haworth were rejected, the lack of capital being an obvious drawback, another scheme emerged that would have permitted them to live together at home: running their own school in the Parsonage.[10]

Plans to take a small number of boarders were made and a prospectus printed. As several people consulted about the project had feared, however, the location clearly told against it, and no pupils materialised. The disappointment was not so acute as it might have been, in that conditions in the Parsonage were hardly ideal for admitting a group of resident young girls: Patrick Brontë was in poor health and half-blind, and Branwell was drinking heavily. Emily could only have greeted the realisation that she was not to lose her precious privacy with relief. Nevertheless, regarded against the background of all the hopes and hard work that had gone into the scheme, to say nothing of the expense (most of which had been borne by Aunt Branwell, now dead), it was still a failure.

Failures of that kind were experienced by many others at the time (Charles Dickens' mother included). Education for girls, especially small boarding schools of the Roe Head type, was a buyer's market. It is not surprising that parents chose more attractive locations for the establishments they entrusted their daughters to than grimy Haworth. Besides, as Juliet Barker has pointed out, the fees quoted by the projected 'Misses Brontë's Establishment' were on the expensive side.[11]

The eagerness to launch ventures of this kind was deplored by Mary Maurice in *Governess Life* of 1849. Maurice argued that governessing was the better option in that it meant freedom from domestic cares and financial risk:

[T]hose who have the care of schools . . . have indeed, a house of their own, but if they have no independent capital, and no other resources, the work is one of extreme risk, and of constant anxiety. . . . Too many fancy that if they can save enough to commence a school, they shall be much happier; and not unfrequently they lose all they have earned . . . Many are nevertheless doing this, and the competition is so great, that, without an excellent connexion, few have a chance of success. (Pages 40–1)

These particular warnings came too late for the Brontës, but they certainly knew of a number of establishments that meant hard work and considerable anxiety for owners.[12] While their yearning for the combination of home life and an income was strong enough to override all objections while the project was still on the drawing-board, their awareness of the concomitant hazards must have made the collapse of the scheme easier to bear.

SCHOOLS IN THE BRONTË NOVELS

The miscarriage of the Brontës' own school project was in a sense compensated for in the sphere of fiction, by the successful schools run by some of their protagonists. While the first school that will occur to anybody in the context of the Brontë novels is pre-reformation Lowood, that is in fact the only bad school in the mature work of the Brontës. Even then, its badness only extends to matters non-academic; *Jane Eyre* does not voice any criticism against the curriculum.[13] By contrast, the moderate academic aims and attainments of Continental schools directed by French and Belgian people (in *The Professor* and *Villette*) are disapproved of by the narrators, though they admit that the institutions promote the physical well-being of pupils, are capably managed and do well as business enterprises. In addition to these flawed establishments, the Brontë fiction contains three model educational institutions for middle- and upper-class girls that are seen to thrive commercially: Mrs Crimsworth's school in *The Professor*, Mrs Grey's in *Agnes Grey* and Mademoiselle Lucy Snowe's 'Externat de demoiselles' in *Villette*.[14]

All these schools start out from humble proportions (as did Madame Beck's flourishing establishment, according to Lucy Snowe) and keep growing as a result of good management. Ability is not the only factor, however: Charlotte Brontë's experience of schools at home and abroad comes out in her narrators' acknowledging the importance of influential contacts and good will ('connexion', as Mary Maurice called it; the word occurs in the same sense in *The Professor*, XXV.230). Recommendations from friends produce the first pupils in all three establishments (see also *Agnes Grey* XIX.160 and XXIV.187), and success with them lays the foundations for expansion. Not only the number of initial scholars is humble in Charlotte Brontë's two novels; these girls' social background is comparatively modest, too. More aristocratic pupils follow as the schools move up-market; 'burghers at first – a higher class ere long', as Lucy Snowe puts it. William Crimsworth is less succinct:

As to Julia and Georgiana G– daughters of an English baronet – as to Mdle. [sic] Mathilde de – heiress of a Belgian Count, and sundry other children of patrician race, the Directress was careful of them as of the others, anxious for their progress, as for that of the rest – but it never seemed to enter her head to distinguish them by a mark of preference – one girl of noble blood she loved dearly, a young Irish baroness, Lady Catherine –, but it was for her enthusiastic heart and clever head – for her generosity and her genius – the title and rank went for nothing. (XXV.232)

This reads like a piece of inverted social snobbery, consistent with Crimsworth's amply documented complexes in that line. However, a whiff of authorial self-indulgence can be felt in the passage, too – a moment of wish-fulfilment in fictional form, seasoned with Charlotte Brontë's characteristic class anxiety.[15]

What Charlotte does not gloss over is the immense effort involved in running a school. The portrayals of those very different directresses Frances Crimsworth, Madame Beck and Lucy Snowe all stress the combination of everyday hard slog, permanent vigilance (Frances, too – see *The Professor* XXV.231), unslackened attention to business opportunities and incessant care for the good reputation of their schools. *Agnes Grey* also emphasises Mrs Grey's hard work in terms that leave the reader in no doubt that it takes unusual capabilities to prosper in her trade.

According to Agnes, her mother's success is to a great extent due to Mrs Grey's energetic and cheerful disposition, which makes light of difficulties and treats the most irksome duties as 'only [serving] to exercise [her] patience' (XXI.171). That Charlotte Brontë also realised the importance of a positive frame of mind in a school directress is clear from this passage in the last chapter of *Villette*:

The secret of my success did not lie so much in myself, in any endowment, any power of mine, as in a new state of circumstances, a wonderfully changed life, a relieved heart. The spring which moved my energies lay far away beyond seas, in an Indian isle. At parting, I had been left a legacy; such a thought for the present, such a hope for the future, such a motive for a persevering, a laborious, an enterprising, a patient and a brave course – I *could* not flag. Few things shook me now; few things had importance to vex, intimidate, or depress me: most things pleased – mere trifles had a charm. (XLII.494)

This is a Lucy whom the reader has not encountered before, and in respect of whose long-term survival he or she has scant grounds for optimism; but the fact that Charlotte Brontë took care to describe Lucy's 'relieved heart' at such length signals an awareness that a lugubrious person cannot hope to succeed as a school directress. Not only must teachers and pupils feel comfortable in her establishment; parents must like and trust her, too. In other words, the operation of this 'genial flame' is a realistic touch.

The kind of school that Mrs Grey starts, and the Brontës themselves planned to have, is also Jane Eyre's highest aim in life. Asked about her hopes for the future by Mr Rochester disguised as a gypsy woman, she says, 'The utmost I hope is, to save money enough out of my earnings to set up a school some day in a little house rented by myself' (II.iv.198). Rochester mocks that modest ambition as a 'mean nutriment for the spirit to exist on'. It shows, however, how entrenched the school dream was in the mind of a writer to whom teaching, never a congenial pursuit, could only be borne if accompanied by some degree of personal freedom.

The possibility of combining the servitude of teaching with some sort of private sphere is taken up from a different angle in *Villette*. When Lucy Snowe declines the offer of being Paulina's companion, she prefers an occupation which she does not much enjoy in itself, but knows she can perform adequately and earn a modest living by, to becoming a member of a household controlled by others on whose personal approval she would be totally dependent:

> I could teach; I could give lessons; but to be either a private governess or a companion was unnatural to me. Rather than fill the former post in any great house, I would deliberately have taken a house-maid's place, bought a strong pair of gloves, swept bed-rooms and staircases, and cleaned stoves and locks, in peace and independence . . . Madame Beck and I, without assimilating, understood each other well. I was not *her* companion, nor her children's governess; she left me free[.] (XXVI.298)[16]

Previously, questioned by Paulina, Lucy had admitted to being a teacher 'for the sake of the money I get', a roof over her head and the knowledge that she was not a burden to anybody. The Bassompierres had hoped to find her inspired by 'motives of pure philanthropy' (XXV.285), but she loses no time in disabusing them of that notion. Lucy's comment on her relationship with Madame Beck amounts to an acknowledgement that her employer has understood her deepest need, the need for personal liberty, and taken care to satisfy it as far as possible. This is a mark of unusual favour, and Lucy shows her gratitude by 'taking double pains with the pupils she committed to my charge' (XXVI.299).[17]

The school Jane Eyre eventually finds herself running is a very different place from the one she dreamt of while still a governess at Thornfield. Charged with teaching twenty ignorant peasant girls whom she can barely understand (III.v.358), she still possesses her precious liberty. It is better, she reminds herself, to be a village schoolmistress, 'free and honest, in a breezy mountain nook in the healthy heart of England' (III.v.359), than a kept woman in the south of France.

The village school at Morton is a particularly interesting educational institution in that it encapsulates much of the ongoing debate on popular education in early- and mid-nineteenth-century England.[18] Started by the local clergyman as a complement to an already existing boys' school, financially supported by rich people in the neighbourhood, it represents the kind of schooling for the lower orders in which those who opposed national schemes of compulsory education placed their trust. Indeed, its striking success could be viewed as a piece of anti-national-compulsory-education propaganda. The subjects taught there are mentioned elsewhere in this book;[19] the ensuing pages are concerned with the situation of the teacher.

'ARE YOU A TEACHER?' CRIED SHE[20]

If the social standing of governesses and tutors was difficult to define and even more difficult to cope with in practice for all concerned, the only comparative advantage of the status of schoolteachers was that it was at least unambiguous – that is to say, unambiguously low. Naturally, there were differences of degree within the profession; a master or mistress at a respectable school for the middle or upper market was in a much more prestigious position than a village schoolteacher.[21] Nevertheless, Mary Maurice's warnings to those who thought of quitting governess jobs in order to work in schools contained an observation whose justness seems unchallengeable: 'There is a strong feeling amongst those employed in education, that the teacher in a school is in a much lower position than that of a private Governess'.[22] Whatever distress a governess might experience, from the point of view of social standing the presumption of gentility was on her side.[23] By contrast, a schoolteacher was a member of the 'out-there' workforce, and not a highly respected one either – even in the mid-1800s, when a good deal had been done to raise the status of the teaching profession.

Many of those efforts had been invested in attempts to give schoolteachers some kind of training. 'Model' or 'normal' schools, including the pioneering institutions launched by Joseph Lancaster's British and Foreign School Society, offered opportunities for future teachers to learn on the job before taking up their first regular post.[24] In the many experimental schools set up by educationists with philanthropist support, attention was paid to teacher training. Even in quarters solidly opposed to national schemes for popular education, the realisation that teachers needed preparation for their work was in evidence.[25] The system of school inspection that got under way in the late 1840s was of course geared to raising the standards of teachers as well as pupils. The long-term inadequacy of monitorial teaching having become obvious to all, the pupil-teacher system was initiated at the same time and furnished with a set of regulations for the testing and certifying of this new formal category of teachers.[26] Even so, Mary Maurice's view of the schoolteachers' prestige is paralleled in many mid-nineteenth-century texts. An example from 1855 serves as a reminder that it applied to both sexes:

What . . . the teacher desires is, that his 'calling' shall rank as a 'profession', that the name of 'schoolmaster' shall ring as grandly on the ear as that of 'clergy-man' or 'solicitor': that he shall feel no more that awful chill and 'stony British stare' which follows the explanation that 'that interesting young man' is only the 'schoolmaster'.[27]

If that was how a young man might feel half a century after formal teacher training began, it is easy to imagine how village schoolteachers were regarded at the time where Charlotte Brontë placed the main action of *Jane Eyre*. A contemporaneous description goes some way towards confirming Florence Nightingale's anecdote of the old man who was made parochial schoolmaster because he was past minding the pigs:

The master of the parish school was admitted, 'if more than usually respectable, to the hospitality of the clergyman's kitchen', but was 'looked down upon with sovereign contempt by the domestics'. He was pitied and despised by the farmer and shopkeeper.[28]

The low status of schoolteachers in the mid-nineteenth century was often and regretfully commented on in the papers that found their way to Haworth Parsonage. For instance, the *Leeds Intelligencer* of 17 April 1847 quotes (on p. 7) an excerpt from a publication called *National Education* by a clergyman named J. Dufton, in which a man is said to have set up a superannuated servant as a schoolmaster, though the old man was 'noto-riously unfit for any such employment'. The man 'holds the place at this present hour', and the writer regrets that this is far from being an isolated example. A few years earlier, a teacher's manual had frankly admitted that the teaching profession was too often '*the last hope of the unfortunate*'.[29] The salaries paid to teachers were commensurate with the dismal status of their profession. As late as 1851, Mann's *Census* stated that the average pay of a schoolmaster and -mistress was £55 and £31 sterling respectively, the latter sum being barely enough – even with accommodation thrown in – to keep body and soul together.[30] Such poverty did nothing to raise the esteem for schoolteachers in the eyes of parents, whose disinclination to send their children to school was universally lamented by commentators on popular education.[31]

Jane Eyre's initial feeling of degradation in her post as mistress of Mor-ton school should be regarded in this context. Having accepted it, albeit 'humble' and 'plodding', partly because 'it was independent; and the fear of servitude with strangers entered [her] soul like iron' (*Jane Eyre* III.iv.355), Jane looks back on her first day in a state of desolation:

I felt – yes, idiot that I am – I felt degraded. I doubted I had taken a step which sank instead of raising me in the scale of social existence. I was weakly dismayed at the ignorance, the poverty, the coarseness of all I heard and saw round me. But let me not hate and despise myself too much for these feelings: I know them to be wrong – that is a great step gained; I shall strive to overcome them. To-morrow, I trust, I shall get the better of them partially; and in a few weeks, perhaps, they will be quite subdued. In a few months, it is possible, the happiness of seeing progress, and a change for the better in my scholars, may substitute gratification for disgust. (III.v.359)

In due course Jane Eyre discovers 'estimable characters' among the girls and comes to form the nucleus of a civilisation-disseminating project in the rural community where she works. Visiting the rustic homes of her best pupils, she is 'loaded with attention' and comments:

There was an enjoyment in accepting their simple kindness, and in repaying it by a consideration – a scrupulous regard to their feelings – to which they were not, perhaps, at all times accustomed, and which both charmed and benefited them; because, while it elevated them in their own eyes, it made them emulous to merit the deferential treatment they received.

I felt I became a favourite in the neighbourhood. Whenever I went out, I heard on all sides cordial salutations, and was welcomed with friendly smiles. To live amidst general regard, though it be but the regard of working-people, is like 'sitting in sunshine, calm and sweet': serene inward feelings bud and bloom under the ray. (III.vi.366)

To a twenty-first-century reader, this might seem offensively patronising; but the first readers of *Jane Eyre* are more likely to have reacted against Charlotte Brontë's repeated suggestions that given a chance to develop, fine feeling is as likely to exist among the lower orders as in the upper strata of society (if not more; as is the case with so many of her contemporaries among nineteenth-century novelists, Charlotte Brontë's adult fiction rarely has a good word to say about the aristocracy – except Wellington, of course). Charlotte's depiction of the simple people of the countryside thus does not echo the nostalgia for the forelock-tugging yeoman that is sometimes sensed in the pages of such Tory publications as *Blackwood's*.[32] It is significant that even St John Rivers, who has his own sights set on a prominent position in the next life, states that he started his village schools on finding that 'the children of the poor [in his new parish] were excluded from every hope of progress' (*Jane Eyre* III.iv.354).

The word 'progress' used in connection with the lower classes connotes social advancement, even when used by someone with predominantly otherworldly ambitions, and the aspect of social mobility is important here.

Both Jane Eyre and St John Rivers articulate their conviction that education will help the poor improve their lot, and as we have seen Jane leaves her reader in no doubt of her belief in the essential equality of rustics and aristocrats.[33] This attitude marks a change from the view, widely held in the first half of the nineteenth century, that stations in life are God-given and that the poor should not harbour ambitions to rise in society.[34]

When Charlotte Brontë made Jane Eyre and St John Rivers, the purveyors of civilising education to the children of farmers and farm labourers, represent their function as a moral obligation, she fused the social ambitions of an earlier generation – the one that bred her self-reliant father – and the improvement ethos that permeated her own. It is a move in the direction of social mobility; but it is worth observing that she took care to equip both Jane and St John themselves with an impeccable 'gentlefolk' pedigree.

CLASS AND EDUCATION IN THE BRONTË NOVELS

The class sensitivity that is so marked in Charlotte Brontë's novels keeps manifesting itself in connection with education, the Morton-school passages in *Jane Eyre* forming a particularly noteworthy example. It is when she encounters a disposition for 'improvement' (see III.vi.366) that Jane Eyre brings her civilising influence to bear, warmed and strengthened by the response she receives. What is played out before the reader is thus a simultaneous development of minds, manners and feelings, where the teacher is also a beneficiary. Similarly, Caroline Helstone in *Shirley* benefits from her Sunday school girls' good feelings and respect.[35]

Though it would be both an exaggeration and a simplification to call the Brontë novels 'progressive' or 'radical' where the issue of class is concerned, they are anything but stereotyped.[36] The Old Etonian scion (admittedly on the distaff side) of a blue-blooded family marries a penniless lacemender and names his son after the Flemish tradesman who did him a good turn; Jane Eyre regards herself as Rochester's equal even while she is 'only the governess'; the tutor gets the heiress in *Shirley*; John Graham Bretton marries above himself, and his lack of wealth is one thing his reluctant father-in-law does not hold against him; in *Agnes Grey* the daughter of a rich and aristocratic man chooses love and independence in comparative poverty rather than bending to her father's wishes and values, preferring to maintain herself by teaching after she has been widowed; the gentleman farmer in *The Tenant of Wildfell Hall* marries a far richer woman who is also above him socially; and what would 'degrade' Catherine were she to marry Healthcliff is that he has been 'brought . . . so low' (*Wuthering Heights* I.ix.71) by Hindley, whose main crime against Heathcliff consisted in withdrawing 'the bene-fit of [Heathcliff's] early education', leaving an almost wilfully uncivilised young man in a state of 'mental deterioration' (I.viii.60). When Heathcliff returns with the bearing of an educated gentleman, looking 'intelligent' and with 'no marks of [his] former degradation' (I.x.84), Catherine wounds her husband's feelings to the quick when insisting that her former foster brother is 'now worthy of any one's regard' (I.x.87).

Money and formal rank are irrelevant when it comes to determining the worth of a person; 'good family' matters when seen to coexist with sound inclinations and worthy conduct; but the all-important quality in a Brontë character is the will to improve by seeking out and undergoing an education of mind and heart. Those to whom such opportunities are denied are not castigated for deficiencies that are not their fault. Robert Gérard Moore, whose acquisition of a social conscience is rarely dwelt on by critics, delivers the following oration towards the end of *Shirley*:

I went where there was want of food, of fuel, of clothing; where there was no occupation and no hope. I saw some, with naturally elevated tendencies and good feelings, kept down amongst sordid privations and harassing griefs. I saw many originally low, and to whom lack of education left scarcely anything but animal wants, ahungered, athirst, and desperate as famished animals: I saw what taught my brain a new lesson, and filled my breast with fresh feelings. (III.vii.542)

In other words, Robert admits to having been both mentally and emotion-ally schooled by experiencing the results of withholding education from the people.

Robert Moore's account has points in common with James Kay-Shuttleworth's attitude to the poor and to the responsibilities of their social superiors. Kay-Shuttleworth was repelled by the 'depravity' of paupers, and Robert speaks of 'many' who were 'originally low'; but belief in the civilising powers of education even in factory-dominated communities is common to the great reformer and to Charlotte Brontë's fictional industrialist.[37]

Whatever makes those who should know better deny less fortunate peo-ple the chance to improve by study is implicitly and explicitly criticised throughout the Brontë fiction. So is the failure to make use of such chances when they are offered. However, misapplied educational attainments are also presented in terms of stern disapproval. Any conceitedness based on the possession of such attainments is roundly condemned, as in Gilbert Markham's accounts of the accomplished Jane Wilson:

[The Wilson brothers'] sister Jane was a young lady of some talents and more ambition. She had at her own desire, received a regular boarding-school education, superior to what any member of the family had obtained before. She had taken the polish well, acquired considerable elegance of manners, quite lost her provincial accent, and could boast of more accomplishments than the vicar's daughters. She was considered a beauty besides; but never for a moment could she number me amongst her admirers. . . . She had, or might have had many suitors in her own rank of life, but scornfully repulsed or rejected them all; for none but a gentleman could please her refined taste, and none but a rich one could satisfy her soaring ambition. (*The Tenant of Wildfell Hall* I.18)

At the end of the novel, Jane Wilson's ambitions are still unfulfilled:

[S]he . . . lives . . . in a kind of closefisted, cold, uncomfortable gentility, doing no good to others and but little to herself; spending her days in fancy-work and scandal; referring frequently to her 'brother the vicar' and her 'sister the vicar's lady,' but never to her brother the farmer and her sister the farmer's wife; seeing as much company as she can without too much expense, but loving no one and beloved by none – a cold-hearted, supercilious, keenly, insidiously censorious old maid. (XLVIII.421)

The trouble with Jane Wilson is not that she has been educated above her station;[38] it is that her education has been vitiated by being made to serve as a basis for the worst kind of pride. Although Anne Brontë gave her narrator personal reasons to dislike this minor character, the vehemence of the hatchet job he performs on her is striking. No reader can fail to realise that this is a person whom education has not improved. On the contrary, it has made the sister of two useful men worse than useless. Neither home nor school is blamed: as happens repeatedly in the Brontë fiction, a person is shown to have fostered vicious tendencies in her own character instead of disciplining them. Whatever the responsibilities of educators in families and educational establishments – and the Brontë novels repeatedly emphasise the seriousness and importance of those responsibilities – they cannot achieve anything of real value where the sense of individual responsibility is lacking. Self-improvement is not only a duty, it is the driving force of the life-project itself.

III

Subjects and skills

Introductory Remarks to Section III

As she grew up, a sound English education corrected in a great measure
her French defects; and when she left school, I found in her a pleasing
and obliging companion: docile, good-tempered, and well-principled.
Jane Eyre III.xii.450

Jane Eyre's recapitulation of the benefits that an English school bestowed
on young Adèle is revealing for three reasons: it postulates that foreign birth
is a misfortune only partially remediable by being educated in England; it
suggests that docility is a high-ranking moral virtue, comparable to a good
temper and high principles;[1] and it implies that the character-building
properties of a young woman's education are more important than any
academic attainments or occupational skills it may impart. The last two
views were prevalent among early-nineteenth-century commentators on
education, and the first was, as Chapter 1 showed, shared by many.

Soundness and Englishness form the basis of the patent assumption of
superiority which underlies Jane's words on the education of Adèle Varens.
By the early nineteenth century, the phrase 'a sound English education' had
acquired connotations beyond the literal meaning of the words: it summed
up the essence of the knowledge-orientated part of the female curriculum.
Whatever the scope of the tuition, under whatever circumstances it was
offered and whatever the qualifications and ambitions of the instructor, 'a
sound English education' was one part of what a girl was sure to encounter
in the schoolroom. The other, skills-orientated part was 'the usual accomplishments' – music, drawing, dancing, and modern languages – which
was largely reserved for the middle and upper classes.[2] The chapters in this
section look at the content of both parts, a consideration of the role of
religion in the early-nineteenth-century curriculum serving as an interlude
between them. That 'sound English education' of whose virtue-enhancing
properties Charlotte Brontë made Jane Eyre express such a high opinion
forms a natural starting-point.

CHAPTER 7

A sound English education

An establishment or a governess that offered pupils 'a sound English educa-tion' taught English grammar and literature, geography, history and a little arithmetic. The rudiments of natural science might be imparted, too, with a heavy emphasis on 'natural history'. In addition, any girl who received any kind of organised education would be taught needlework commensurate with her social status.[1] All these subjects were what the Brontë sisters learnt, taught and proposed to teach, and all of them feature in their fiction.

GEOGRAPHY

One of the sound-English-education subjects stands out in Charlotte Brontë's novels because of the seniority of those who teach it. Geogra-phy is the province of the directresses at Lowood and in Madame Beck's pensionnat (*Jane Eyre* I.v.47–8, *Villette* XV.153 and XXXV.398), and this is no accident. In the early nineteenth century geography was, in the words of a contemporary manual called *The Complete Governess*, felt to constitute 'a sort of connecting link for all our knowledge'.[2] At best, geography instruc-tion supplied knowledge of the parts of the world and their interrelations; the various European countries and their distinctive characteristics and boundaries; geological facts and conditions; different climates all over the world and the factors that influence them; and the branches of industry and agriculture that created the wealth of individual nations. At worst, geography consisted in the rote-learning of 'facts' the significance of which was completely incomprehensible to the learner, as well as of lists of rivers, towns, bays and so on whose essential characteristics, including location and relative importance, remained unknown.

A circumstance associated with the high standing that this subject enjoyed in the nineteenth century was 'the use of the globes'. In an early article on the Brontës and education, Sir William Henry Hadow explains the phrase:

Geography . . . still chiefly meant that mysterious subject, 'The use of the globes', which I can still dimly recall to memory. There were two large, moveable globes in wooden frames; one . . . terrestrial, and the other astronomical. The teacher turned them round and round, and pointed out that here was France and there America, here the Pole Star and there the Southern Cross; but it did not attain to any standard that modern geographical teaching would recognise even as a poor relation.[3]

The first time Jane Eyre sees Miss Temple in the schoolroom, she gazes at the superintendent with 'admiring awe'. Her veneration is not lessened when the lady whose mere appearance instantly causes everyone to rise to their feet 'takes her seat before [the] pair of globes' fetched for her by monitors. The ability to use the globes conferred a certain prestige on a teacher.[4] It is hence a compliment to the future governess that Adèle's 'schoolroom', the library at Thornfield, has been equipped with a pair of globes (*Jane Eyre* I.xi.103).

Hadow's sketch from memory does not do justice to the skills of a knowledgeable globe-user. The 1823 edition of the Rev. J. Goldsmith's *A Grammar of General Geography*, an often-praised book demonstrably used by the Brontë children, explains how to find latitudes and longitudes on the terrestrial globe and poses some far from easy practice questions. Goldsmith's introduction to the celestial globe is even more of a challenge, with practice questions such as 'If a comet appears in that part of the heavens whose longitude is 125°, and latitude 64°, to what constellation must I look for it?'[5]

Goldsmith's book was familiar enough to the Parsonage children for them to insert fictitious names (for instance 'Gaaldine' and 'Gondal'), with explanations, in the 'Vocabulary of Proper Names' that Goldsmith supplied at the back of his book. Another geography primer they knew was the English translation of Abbé Lenglet du Fresnoy's *Geography for Youth*, which originally belonged to an Irish uncle.[6] The fact that it is a translation from the French lends a certain piquancy to some of its statements on other nations. Otherwise clearly adapted to current English notions (of the French, too), it mentions that Corsica's acquisition by France extended 'the benefits of the new [French] constitution' to the islanders – surely a covert expression of admiration for the legislators of Revolutionary France.[7]

Two centuries ago, no book on geography was without characterisations of the peoples and races that inhabited other parts of the globe. It is easy to see how 'facts' such as the following ones may have encouraged ethnocentric notions in studious children:

Europe is the most powerful quarter of the world, and Africa the weakest.

The most tyrannic and despotic governments are those of Morocco, Turkey, and Russia.

The freest people, under civil government, are those of England, and of the United States of America.

In commerce, the English stand at the head of all nations, and in shipping and intercourse transcend all other nations put together.

The most civilized and intelligent quarter of the world is Europe; the most barbarous is Africa.

The most barbarous nations, known to the polished nations of antiquity, are become the most polished among the moderns; as Albion, Gallia, Belgium, and Helvetia; now Britain, France, Netherlands, and Switzerland.[8]

However, there is no shortage of warnings against unfounded chauvinism in this educational literature. Goldsmith, for instance, reminded his readers that 'all men are the offspring of *one common parent*' and that 'the swarthy negro and the delicate European are brethren, descended from the same ancestor'.[9] An older geography book which Charlotte Brontë used at Roe Head is eloquent in its insistence that no race should consider itself inherently better than any other:

As I am a citizen of the world, I look upon all men as my brethren; and have long endeavoured to set them right in their notions of one another.

I am extremely concerned to see almost every people representing the inhabitants of distant nations as barbarians, and treating them as such.

For my part, I have met with people as polite, ingenious, and humane, whom we have been taught to look upon as cannibals, as ever I conversed with in Europe; and from my own experience, am convinced, that human nature is every where the same[.][10]

Similarly heart-lifting passages occur in one of the classics of English education, Maria and R. L. Edgeworth's *Practical Education*, first published in 1798 and repeatedly reprinted. Maria Edgeworth expressed her disapproval of the many generalisations on national character in geography books, reminding her readers that '[t]he patriotism of an enlarged and generous mind cannot . . . depend upon the early contempt inspired for foreign nations'.[11]

The fostering of such enlarged and generous minds was one of the chief aims of geography according to another schoolbook owned by Charlotte Brontë, the *Grammatical Exercises, English and French* by a long-established textbook author, 'Mr. Porny, French-master at Eton College'.[12] Porny supplied the following short essay as a suitable basis for practising translation into French:

Geography is a science no longer esteemed a fine accomplishment only, but a necessary part of education; for no study seems better calculated for the entertainment and instruction of young persons than this. Geography gives them a perfect idea of the exterior surface of the globe, of its natural and political divisions, and of the produce of every part of it; hence it is justly called the eye of History, the Soldier's companion, the Merchant's director, and the Traveller's guide. It is also a study of the first consideration among those qualities requisite for forming the scholar; for it is adapted not only to satisfy our curiosity, but also to enlarge our mind, to banish prejudices, and make us acquainted with our real advantages, and those of our fellow-creatures.[13]

The metaphor according to which geography is 'the eye of History' forms an apt point of transition to that other staple of the 'sound English education' curriculum. Geography and history were often thought of as belonging together, the former being regarded as the duller and worthier of the two.[14]

A third school headmistress in Charlotte Brontë's fiction, Mrs Frances Crimsworth, née Henri, teaches both geography and history, often waxing 'genuinely eloquent' in her exposition of their finer points (*The Professor*, XXV.231). The 'elements of . . . geography [and] history' were also among the things Jane Eyre taught her most advanced pupils at Morton school (*Jane Eyre* III.vi.366).

Like Frances in *The Professor*, writers on female education in the eighteenth and nineteenth centuries found themselves inspired to eloquence when reflecting on the desirability of a young girl's studying history. To Hester Chapone, history was '[t]he principal study I would recommend'.[15] Later writers on education for women, such as Sarah Stickney Ellis and Margaret Thornley, agreed.[16] The opening paragraphs of the latter's first chapter on history summarise the reasons for the importance attached to it at the time:

History holds a high pre-eminence among the candidates for employment in building up human intelligence. It consists in a statement of all that has been devised and adopted over the whole world for the regulation of human confederations, with the casualties to which such regulations are subject. It comprehends all the treasures which experience has acquired at a most costly sacrifice, and accumulated for the use of the present generation. It exhibits mankind in all the diverse conditions of existence . . . It traces the progress of national advancement and deterioration, and reveals the impulses, upward or downward, by the power of which they have been effected. It states, in the indisputable language of fact, what are the secondary causes of human perversion and misery, what the means of human improvement and happiness; and it bears clear, decided, and ample testimony to the truths respecting human nature which the Scriptures reveal. (53)

Actual schoolroom practice did not always live up to Thornley's exalted view of the subject. Much of the 'history' taught to early-nineteenth-century children consisted in the memorising of dates and the transmission of anecdotes with moral implications and dubious historical accuracy. Some of the history-books for young readers failed to exploit the inherent excitingness of the subject, erring on the side of blandness. Impatience with the exaggerated gentility of women writers in the field was one of the reasons that prompted Dickens to write his own *A Child's History of England*, serialised in 1851–53.[17]

The unsatisfactoriness of historical study in homes and schools was well known to contemporary commentators on education. Margaret Thornley, for instance, allowed that a grasp of chronology was essential, but warned instructors against making it the sole object of history lessons.[18] Sarah Ellis, to mention another example, admitted that the various devices by which dates could be impressed upon the recollection of young ladies were

no less ingenious than commendable; but could any plan be adapted for enabling them to draw conclusions from such facts, to compare historical events with each other, to trace the progress of civilization, and to ascertain what circumstances have most invariably led to the rise or the fall of different empires – instead of being confined to isolated facts, their conversation would then be fraught with the richer burden of those important truths, for which history supplies nothing more than illustration.[19]

The 'repetitions in history' at Lowood clearly consist in learning dates and summaries of events by heart.[20] This brief reference is a trace of one of the two chief modes of trivialising history that flourished even in the better girls' schools. The other is suggested by what William Crimsworth, who teaches English relying on historical texts, calls 'the trite little anecdote of Alfred tending cakes' (*The Professor* XVI.121). It is the subject of Frances Henri's remarkable English *devoir*; another girl, by contrast, had 'copied the anecdote out fair' from 'an abridged history of England'. It is difficult to imagine that any post-1800s history of England, abridged or not, would devote enough space to such a story for it to make up an entire school essay.[21]

One of the things William admires in Frances' *devoir* is the picture she draws of 'the crownless king' himself. In the Brontës' time, insightful writers on historical education realised that what later ages have called the human-interest angle is a powerful stimulus for young minds – and not only for them. Having recommended the careful study of facts, with attention to chronology, maps and tables, Anna Laetitia Barbauld acknowledged that women are more interested in human behaviour and feelings than in details of battles and sieges, so absorbing to men.[22] In the letter 'On the Uses of History', she observed, 'The more History approaches to Biography the more interest it excites'.[23] Whenever a historical context is evoked in a Brontë novel, individual actions, experiences and emotions are at its centre. Helen Burns's discourse on Charles I provides a characteristic instance:

'This afternoon . . . I was wondering how a man who wished to do right could act so unjustly and unwisely as Charles the First sometimes did; and I thought what a pity it was that, with his integrity and conscientiousness, he could see no farther than the prerogatives of the crown. If he had but been able to look to a distance, and see how what they call the spirit of the age was tending! Still, I like Charles – I respect him – I pity him, poor murdered king! Yes, his enemies were the worst: they shed blood they had no right to shed. How dared they kill him!' (I.vi.57)[24]

Charlotte Brontë's letters also testify to a tendency to view dramatic events in terms of their causes in the conduct of individuals and their effects on those individuals' lives.[25] In addition, the warp of 'the Brontës' web of childhood' was of course made up of the histories of imagined personages.[26] Neither as juvenile chroniclers of imaginary realms nor as adult commentators on past history and current affairs did the Brontës display much interest in collectively composed undertows of sociopolitical change: however vital it might have been for statesmen to consult the 'spirit of the age',[27] what mattered to them was what influential people actually did.

No two people were more influential in early-nineteenth-century Europe than the men after whom young Charlotte and Branwell Brontë named their toy soldiers. From an English perspective, Napoleon and Wellington still towered over all other protagonists on the world stage for decades after their military encounters. The latter never achieved the lasting international stardom Charlotte Brontë predicted for him; but even in his old age and irrespective of the policies he espoused, he was her hero.[28] Branwell's predilection for all things French, often commented on by students of the Brontë juvenilia, repeatedly manifested itself in allusions to Napoleon.[29] The favourable character of those allusions is no surprise; but the expressions of Charlotte's attitude to Napoleon display a remarkable range.

The omniscient narrator of *Shirley* heaps abuse on 'the Corsican bandit' (I.x.167), but even this novel contains a variety of views on Napoleon. It is interesting that Robert Moore, the character with the best claim to being the book's hero, expresses an opinion common among British intellectuals in the early nineteenth century (Byron among them):[30] Napoleon was a Moses figure, leader of gallant Israel/France in her struggle against the 'old over-gorged empires and rotten dynasties' of corrupt Europe; and the only sad thing is that 'the conqueror of Lodi', who was 'fit to head and organize measures for the regeneration of nations', had betrayed the Revolutionary ideals in '[condescending] to become an emperor' (I.iii.39–40). In the last chapter of *Shirley*, even the narrator invests the 'robber' of chapter I.x with epic grandeur, presenting the collapse of the Grande Armée in cosmic-cataclysmic terms (III.xiv.635–6).

Complexity also characterises Lucy Snowe's comparisons of M. Paul Emanuel to 'the great Emperor' at the point when the reader realises that the heroine of the story is falling in love with the choleric professor. The similarities between the two men hardly constitute compliments to either of them: it is Napoleon's hot temper, love of power and 'eager grasp after supremacy' (XXX.348–50) that Lucy sees in M. Paul. At the same time, these characteristics are part and parcel of the man's passionate nature, and it is that nature which conquers the equally passionate – though outwardly demure – Lucy.

This pattern of ambivalence can be traced back to the 1843 essay on the death of Napoleon which Charlotte Brontë submitted to Constantin Heger for his perusal and corrections. As perceptive scholars have observed, there is a peculiar inconsistency in the essay: it sets up Wellington as Napoleon's peer and then argues that Wellington was the greater man because he displayed precisely those virtues which the essay-writer had just relegated to the realm of mediocrity: coolness and balance.[31]

The contradictoriness that characterises Charlotte Brontë's writings about Napoleon, with or without adjacent references to Wellington, arises from the cohabitation of 'two souls': she was a staunch British patriot with a streak of Francophilia. As any praise of Wellington in Charlotte's fiction can be read as a direct expression of the author's own opinion, Mr Helstone's tribute to 'the fit representative of a powerful, a resolute, a sensible, and an honest nation' (*Shirley* I.iii.38) may serve as an example of her fused patriotism and hero-worship. On the other hand, Charlotte's appreciation of relentless French cerebralism comes out in her characterisation of Louis-Adolphe Thiers (in a letter to W. S. Williams): 'Can [the rulers of France] set aside entirely anything so clever, so subtle, so accomplished, so aspiring, in a word, so thoroughly French as he is?' Her praise for Thiers's administrative ability is followed by an invocation of Napoleon: 'I always think he writes as if the Shade of Bonaparte were walking to and fro in the room behind him . . . Thiers seems to have contemplated Napoleon's character till he has imbibed some of its nature' – including, of course, ambitiousness.[32]

British nationalism combined with an admiration for French capabilities, with or without a bow to Napoleon, was not a Brontëan peculiarity. Indeed, the Brontë children could have absorbed it from some of their schoolbooks. Published in 1795, the English version of Nicolas Lenglet du Fresnoy's geography book certainly accorded special treatment to the British Isles; but it still described France as 'the most powerful nation of Europe'. Her people, the reader is informed, 'are blessed with a ready conception, and have of late greatly advanced the republic of letters; and even some of the female sex are now famous through the learned world for their singular talents'. Any young girl engaged in the writing of imaginative literature on a massive scale would find such a statement inspirational. However, these great intellectual powers are not matched by moral rectitude: for all their charming ways, the French are 'complete masters of the art of dissimulation'.[33] No ethical indictment could have been more damning in Charlotte Brontë's eyes.

Even Charlotte's copy of Richmal Mangnall's *Historical and Miscellaneous Questions* combines British patriotism with acknowledgements of Continental achievements. The question 'What great events mark the opening of the nineteenth century?' is provided with the answer, 'The union with Great Britain and Ireland: Bonaparte (unquestioningly a man of great abilities) was chosen chief consul of the French republic for life: this title was afterwards exchanged for that of Emperor'.[34] The idea of British children learning these phrases by heart and reproducing them on cue, parenthesis and all, is a beguiling one, especially in view of the fact that Britain and France were at war when this edition of Mangnall's *Questions* was published. The perils of the time are evident in the section on the English constitution, which ends with an impassioned plea to defend the laws of England ('the admiration of other nations, the pride of our own'). These patriotic sentiments seem to have found an echo in the schoolgirl Charlotte Brontë: next to Mangnall's passionate desire that British homes 'may . . . ever be preserved inviolate!' on p. 141, three small flowers are drawn, and the word 'inviolate' is twice underlined in pencil.

Charlotte's copy of Mangnall's *Questions* contains 'abstracts' of a large number of topics, including a sixty-page 'Abstract of British Biography'. Grouped under individual letters but then arranged according to the death year of the listed persons, the entries in this mini-*DNB* are remarkable for their fairness, even generosity, to people with whose opinions and policies Mangnall manifestly disagreed. In the context of history, it is also worth observing that Mangnall speaks warmly of Edward Gibbon (p. 233). Unreserved praise for Gibbon in a schoolbook read by large segments of Britain's literate female youth is remarkable in view of Gibbon's patent scepticism against Christianity. Not all writers on female education in the early 1800s were prepared to allow girls free access to Gibbon. For example, M. A. Stodart's *Hints on Reading* of 1839 insisted that female readers restrict themselves to Bowdler's revised version, as Gibbon's anti-Christian innuendoes were more harmful than out-and-out attacks would have been.[35]

Apparently nobody harboured such qualms with regard to the Brontës. As Christine Alexander has shown, the character Lady Zenobia Ellrington in Charlotte Brontë's juvenile fiction has points in common with Zenobia, Queen of Palmyra, as portrayed in Gibbon's *Decline and Fall*. Alexander mentions the Keighley Mechanics' Institute library as one possible provider of Gibbon to Charlotte, but there would have been other complete sets on shelves close to her before 1841.[36]

However, Gibbon was not among the historians that Charlotte recommended Ellen Nussey to read in the letter of 4 July 1834. Aged 18, Charlotte only found David Hume and Charles Rollin worth her friend's attention – her airy admission that she had never read 'the Universal History' herself made it most unlikely that Ellen would attempt it.[37]

Charlotte's choices were unexceptionable by any standards, including Roe Head's where they were studied, in accordance with Hester Chapone's *Letters on the Improvement of the Mind*.[38] Rollin's works on ancient history featured in compilations of suggested reading matter from the late eighteenth to the mid-nineteenth century. The fact that they had to be studied in French was no bar to Catharine Macaulay's proposing that Rollin's *Histoire ancienne* introduce a serious course of historical reading for 14-year-olds.[39] That is not surprising, however, as Rollin's early-eighteenth-century French is lucid and readable. Decades later, Rollin's alleged failure to give sufficient attention to probability did not prevent the authors of *Systematic Education* from wanting young students to benefit from his 'genuine and entertaining abstracts' of the ancient historians.[40] The Scot Hume's name tended to be accompanied by reservations, partly owing to discrepancies between his strongly stated opinions and the carefully articulated views of English writers on education.[41] It was too powerful a name to be omitted, though, whatever qualms might be voiced about his values, religious as well as scholarly – Hume was no more an orthodox Christian than Gibbon. Elizabeth Appleton advised governesses to select from the 'celebrated works' of both men 'according as [they] may think proper', and her attitude seems to have been representative.[42]

One reason why writers on education felt obliged to warn their readers against Gibbon was his treatment of the English language. Time and again, the great historian's 'luxuriancy of diction' was held up as a dangerous example on grounds best examined under another heading.

THE ENGLISH LANGUAGE

Another book recommended at the back of Goldsmith's geography book articulates an objection frequently made against Gibbon's prose style. On the over-use of adjectives, David Irving's popular *The Elements of English Composition* dispenses good advice at Gibbon's expense:

> When used sparingly and with judgment, [adjectives] have a powerful influence in enlivening the expression; but nothing has more of an opposite effect than a profusion of them. When scattered with too liberal a hand, they lengthen the sentence, without adding proportionate vigour; they betray a violent effort to say something great or uncommon. A profusion of this kind is one of the principal faults in the rich and elegant style of Gibbon.[43]

The author of the manual *Advice to Governesses* suggests that an early fondness for Gibbon encourages a taste for orotundity, likely to result in a preference for Young's poetry over that of Milton and Pope.[44] That such a taste is unfortunate is never said outright, but the implications are unmistakable.

The staples of the study of English in the first half of the nineteenth century were reading, spelling, composition writing and grammar. Generations learnt to spell on the basis of William Mavor's *English Spelling Book*, which retained its popularity despite complaints that it contained words that young learners found strange.[45] The American grammarian Lindley Murray's *English Grammar, adapted to the Different Classes of Learners* was another classic that stayed around for the best part of a century after its first appearance in 1795. Besides orthography, morphology (called 'etymology'), syntax, punctuation, versification, and a potted history of the English language, Murray's book offered its students an appendix containing 'Rules and Observations for Promoting Perspicuity and Accuracy in Writing'. While it is easy to sympathise with the countless pupils who suffered from having to memorise Murray's grammatical rules and submit to endless parsing exercises, it must be said that the appendix provides excellent advice on how to develop an effective prose style.[46] Similar values ('purity, propriety, and precision') were upheld by another popular grammar, W. Pinnock's *A Comprehensive Grammar of the English Language*.[47]

As apprentice writers all the Brontës experimented with a wide range of styles, both in their imaginative writings and in their letters. Charlotte's mature correspondence displays great stylistic variety, too, from warm intimacy to hard-hitting professionalism. Years of practice preceded the development of the three sisters' distinctive fictional styles.[48] They had tried their hands at all the main *belles lettres* genres as well as at journalism and essay-writing, and the seeming effortlessness that characterises the handling of idiom in their published work rested on immense labours. Their ears for style and idiom had been trained in a literal sense through their early dramatic writings and through much reading aloud, a factor easily overlooked in a later age where such skills are poorly developed. For Emily and Charlotte Brontë, the latter particularly, their period of professionally supervised creative-writing practice in French entailed a good deal of reading aloud by a master of the art, Constantin Heger.[49]

Biographers have dwelt on Charlotte Brontë's mortification on finding that her knowledge was deemed insufficient for a place in the senior class at Roe Head, notably in respect of geography and grammar, when she arrived there in 1831, aged 14.[50] She swiftly remedied the deficiencies, however, and one of the ways in which she did so will have involved rote-learning from Murray.[51]

The humiliation at Roe Head in 1831 was not the first time Charlotte had been found wanting where systematically acquired knowledge was concerned. On admission to Cowan Bridge, she had been found to be completely ignorant of 'Grammar, Geography, History or Accomplishments', though she was perceived to be '[a]ltogether clever of her age'.[52] As that age was eight, these shortcomings were not to be wondered at. Even so, the repeated observation by school staff that the Brontë girls had not been systematically taught is a reminder of the extent to which they were autodidacts, and the chief means of their self-education was always free reading.

From their early years, that free reading coexisted with free writing, without the benefit of regular instruction in grammar, spelling and composition. Pernicketiness over formal matters did not trouble the youthful members of their writers' workshops, and no censorious adult interfered. It has often been observed that the Brontës were poor spellers in their early years.[53] Emily's progress with regard to orthography is difficult to chart, but the effect of formal schooling on Charlotte is obvious. Even the poorest schoolteacher was expected to be able to spot and correct inaccurate spelling.[54] Charlotte was being trained for a professional teaching career and could not afford to slip up in this respect – although her punctuation remained erratic all her life.

There are no records suggesting that Charlotte Brontë chafed at studying Murray and Pinnock, and she seems to have been successful in imparting her new-found skills to her sisters. Nor do her novels contain any hint that she found it unduly irksome, still less superfluous. For instance, it is thanks to 'six long years of drilling in the simple grammar of the English language' that Eulalie, beautiful but dim-witted, can manage to win third place in English in Mlle Reuter's school (*The Professor*, XIV.111). Systematic knowledge of grammar was a prerequisite of learning French and other foreign languages without which no prospective governess stood a chance of securing a reasonably decent position. A 'dry study' it might be, but no girl undergoing a 'sound English education' could be allowed to neglect it.[55] Where another dry subject was concerned, ambitions were lower: advanced mathematics rarely featured in the education of girls in the early nineteenth century, and this was a field in which the Brontës showed little interest, either as teachers or as writers of fiction.

MATHEMATICS

'Arithmetic' was a component of the 'sound English education', but few young women moved far beyond its four fundamental rules in the first half of the nineteenth century. Boys of all classes might wrestle with Euclid, Bonnycastle's *Algebra* and trigonometry; but a girl's mathematic ability was commonly deemed sufficient if she mastered fractions and decimals.

Writers on education for girls struggled with a problem complex in which contradictory notions and experiences made practical advice hard to deliver. On the one hand, they opposed and resented the idea that the female brain could not cope with mathematics; on the other, they were obliged to recognise that it was an unpopular subject among the girls themselves. Well might a Margaret Thornley extol the enhancement of mental power and acumen gained by a young woman who reasons her way through to the correct solution of a mathematical problem;[56] classroom reality usually presented a more sombre picture. In 1849 Mary Maurice articulated the core of the difficulty with arithmetic:

[T]here is no science more valuable when well taught, because of the precision and correctness of mind which it produces, from the certainty of arriving at truth, and the exercise of comparison it calls forth in considering the relative value of numbers. When taught in the ordinary way, nothing is more perplexing and distasteful than arithmetic – the why, and wherefore, of the abstract rules are so mysterious, and puzzling questions disturb a child's mind as to how it can be honest to borrow a sum of one and then return it to another.[57]

No wonder early-nineteenth-century governesses and schoolmistresses had to make the best of a bad job by encouraging girls and their parents at least to appreciate the practical usefulness of arithmetic. A woman who can do sums in her head will not be cheated by tradesmen; and if she is forced to earn her own living by adopting a trade herself, arithmetic and a knowledge of book-keeping will be vital to her success in business.[58] Even if she is not compelled to earn money, basic mathematical skills will enable her to keep the household accounts in good order.[59] Elizabeth Appleton's sigh of resignation is still audible across nearly two centuries: having mastered the four rules of arithmetic around the age of 12, a girl might

be conducted as far as vulgar fractions, if it be considered *necessary* to the future convenience or pleasure of a female; but I would recommend that the taste and disposition of the learner be consulted, and would, especially, plead for moderation in the cyphering tasks.[60]

None of the Brontë sisters is on record as having relished the mind-sharpening and inexorably truth-orientated character of arithmetic. If they studied their father's Irish mathematics book, Elias Voster's *Arithmetic in Whole and Broken Numbers*, they will not have been encouraged to dwell in the realm of figures; among the exercises of dubious 'relevance' that it sets before its readers are 'How many Minutes are in 1709 years?' and 'How many Sparrows, 10 for 1 Penny, would pay for an Horse worth 20 *l.*?'[61]

Nor does any Brontë heroine shine in the subject. In fact, young Jane Eyre at ten doing 'a sum in long division' is the closest thing to a mathematical prodigy among them (I.vii.61) – and even she struggles with it. To make matters worse, young women's ignorance of mathematics supplies ammunition for men bent on worsting them in arguments. Robert Gérard Moore's assistant Joe Scott scores a point against Shirley and Caroline in their debate on women in religion and politics when he tells the 'young Misses' that their 'learning' consists of a 'superficial sort o' vanities':

'I can tell – happen a year sin' – one day Miss Caroline coming into our counting-house when I war packing up summat behind t' great desk, and she didn't see me, and she brought a slate wi' a sum on it to t' maister: it war only a bit of a sum in practice, that our Harry would have settled i' two minutes. She couldn't do it; Mr. Moore had to show her how; and when he did show her, she couldn't understand him.' (II.vii.330)

The girls' ensuing expostulations are feeble; Joe has obviously hit home. Similarly, Lucy Snowe must submit to having her faulty grasp of arithmetic characterised as a thing 'which would have disgraced a charity-schoolboy' (*Villette* XXX.350–1). What makes this unanswerable put-down from

M. Paul particularly galling for Lucy is that he does not like mathematics himself and is an abject failure as a maths teacher:

[H]is humour was visibly bad – almost at its worst; he had been giving a lesson in arithmetic – for he gave lessons on any and every subject that struck his fancy – and arithmetic being a dry subject, invariably disagreed with him: not a pupil but trembled when he spoke of figures. (XXVIII.324)

M. Paul's fancy does not seem to have been very vigorously struck by mathematics; he is obviously an arts person. So are all the main protagonists in the Brontë novels, insofar as they evince any academic bent at all. Even William Crimsworth, who tells his brother that he 'studied Mathematics' at Eton (II.15), is never seen to capitalise on his proficiency in that subject. Nor does his brother, the hard-nosed businessman, care about it – 'Stuff!' is his reaction, and when William is hired as a clerk it is because of his knowledge of French and German. Two other languages (English and Latin) win him his teaching post at M. Pelet's. Frances Henri has taken a course each in 'grammar, history, geography and arithmetic' (XVII.130–1), but she is only ever required to teach the first three (XXI.177). The prospectus of the 'Misses Brontë's establishment' listed the subjects covered by the basic charge of £35 per annum as 'Writing, Arithmetic, History, Grammar, Geography, and Needle Work'.[62] It is not too bold a guess that such tuition in mathematics as might have been provided would have fallen short of Mary Maurice's ideal.

NATURAL SCIENCE

With regard to the natural sciences in contemporary female education, the pattern is similar to the one that prevailed in respect of mathematics: there was some disagreement as to whether they were a proper subject of study for girls; references to them in the Brontë novels are not numerous; and the sisters themselves do not seem to have taken a very great interest in them. It is hard to escape the suspicion that Lucy Snowe's and Paulina de Bassompierre's shared inclination towards the arts rather than the sciences is germane to a general Brontë preference.[63] If so, it was one they have shared with many generations of women up to the present time.[64]

Not that there would not have been any women role models to emulate, or instruction material to be had. Mary Somerville's success with *The Mechanism of the Heavens* (1831) was as triumphant as Harriet Martineau's with *Political Economy* a year later, and in 1842 Janet Taylor published her *Epitome of Navigation and Nautical Astronomy, with the Improved Lunar*

Tables.[65] The libraries of Mechanics' Institutes, including the one at Keighley, contained large numbers of books about science – naturally enough, as the promotion of general scientific knowledge among the lower classes was one of the Institutes' main objects. The admirable Mrs Marcet had written a two-volume work called *Conversations on Chemistry* which was 'especially addressed to the female sex'; it ran into a number of editions.[66] The consistently ambitious Anna Laetitia Barbauld had recommended girls to study astronomy, chemistry and physics as well as natural history and botany.[67] If the Brontës did not make chemistry or physics favoured objects of study, it is hence a fair assumption that this was not because they did not know of any precedent for such studies among women, but because they found these sciences less absorbing than other subjects.[68]

One of those other subjects was natural history, whose modern counterparts, zoology, botany, geology and biology, belong under the umbrella of the natural sciences.[69] From the painstaking copying of animal pictures performed by the Brontë sisters to the child Jane Eyre's hours closeted with Bewick's *History of British Birds*, the lives and works of the Brontës constantly testify to their interest in fauna.[70] References to botany in *Agnes Grey* (XIII.106–107) and *Shirley* (II.x.373) indicate an interest in plants as well. In the latter novel, an authorial-narratorial interpolation ('a digression', says the omniscient narrator) of more than half a page explains why Caroline Helstone preferred William Farren as wheeler of her garden-chair during her convalescence: they 'took a similar interest in animals, birds, insects, and plants: they held similar doctrines about humanity to the lower creation; and had a similar turn for minute observation on points of natural history' (III.ii.445). The natural world plays a major role in all the Brontë novels, its manifestations ranging from mystical forces acting powerfully on leading characters to detailed and informed observations on flowers and birds. *Wuthering Heights* supplies a memorable instance of the scope of this element in the scene where more-than-half-mad Catherine raves about the moors, Penistone Crags and her old home at the Heights, identifying the birds that supplied the feathers in her pillow, species by species (I.xii.108).[71]

One of the books recommended by Charlotte Brontë in her suggestions-for-reading letter of 4 July 1834 to Ellen Nussey was Gilbert White's *The Natural History and Antiquities of Selborne*, first published in 1789.[72] The emphasis on 'minute observation' in the Brontë references to the study of natural phenomena is a characteristic that recalls White's exactly recorded evidence of his own senses. The appearance of the 1827 edition of White's work ensured that no English student of the endemic flora or fauna was ignorant of this classic of natural history, irrespective of age, status or sex.

While several contemporary works on female education did mention chemistry, physics and astronomy, natural history is much more to the fore in them. There were many books on the phenomena of the natural world besides White on Selborne. Feeding an enduring craze, some of them sold huge numbers of copies.[73] Quite a few were written by women with women readers in mind.[74] In fact, there seems to have been a presumption that natural history was somehow 'science lite', an effeminate kind of part study, part amusement.[75] Most books on natural history would combine contemplation and detailed observation with references to scientific categorisation (Linnaeus looming large in any popular discussion on botany), to end in some sort of tribute to the Creator. These were the last few decades in the modern history of natural science and Christian orthodoxy in which the two could coexist in harmony, even enhance each other – Darwin published *The Origin of Species* in 1859.[76]

CHAPTER 8

Religion and education

A present-day reader might find the sound-English-education curriculum presented above curiously wanting in religious instruction and wonder about the early-nineteenth-century equivalent of the 'RE' subject. The answer is that religion was supposed to be everywhere. Not only did Scripture reading, prayers, hymn singing and Biblical history account for a substantial share of the daily curricular activities; religion was to provide the impetus and the foundations of any endeavour to educate the people, and the Bible was to permeate instruction on every subject. For instance, arithmetic might be practised by subtracting the number of chapters in one book of the Bible from that of another. Natural history should not only constantly remind pupils of the wonders of the Creation; wherever possible, discussions of species of plants and animals would proceed from Biblical loci.[1]

As Britain had not had a Frederick II nor experienced Revolutionary/Napoleonic rule, secularism did not manage to assert itself in popular education until most of the nineteenth century had passed. As Chapter 1 indicated, the history of elementary education in Britain up to the implementation of the Education Act in 1870 is to a large extent made up of a bewildering series of conflicts between different religious and political-ideological factions.[2] It is impossible to point to heroes and villains in those decades of angry confusion. In 1839, for instance, a man whom one might expect to find on the side of the angels, Frederick Denison Maurice, was a passionate opponent of state authority over education. Asserting the supremacy of the Church of England in the strongest terms, Maurice said that the function of the Church was 'the function of proclaiming truth to men' – and there was no arguing with that position.[3] His conviction that there can be no distinction between the religious and the secular made it impossible for him to accept any dimension of secularism in the context of education, and his feelings were shared by many combatants in different camps.[4]

In 1846, however, a leading Yorkshire cleric presented a scheme that implicitly tolerated such a division in a bid for national unity. Dr Hook's proposals on popular education accepted that 'in any measure of education the State must admit the co-operation of Dissenters as well as that of the Church'.[5] His pamphlet went through eight editions in three months, and as was pointed out in Chapter 1 above, it was well known in the parsonage of Haworth. Hook did not regard his proposals as weakening the religious element in education: on the contrary, entrusting it to professionals (clergymen and Dissenter ministers) would assert its dignity. No longer would the Bible be a mere schoolbook, a quarry for arithmetic and spelling exercises; passing from the hands of ignorant monitors to those of men of God, it would regain its status as Holy Writ.[6]

Irrespective of the extent to which it was made to serve as a schoolbook, the chief source of religious knowledge in schools and homes was, of course, the Bible. Familiarity with the Scriptures was tirelessly promoted by two important bodies founded for that purpose, the Society for Promoting Christian Knowledge – the SPCK – and the British and Foreign Bible Society. In his prose tale *The Maid of Killarney; or, Albion and Flora*, the young family man Patrick Brontë compared these societies to two great rivers: the SPCK was like 'the stately Thames', staying in and enriching England, whereas the latter was 'the mighty Nile, into which countless rivers pour their tributary waters'.[7] From six to eight a.m., Flora, the heroine of this story, studied 'the Scriptures, and other books of a divine nature and tendency'. She would end the day as she began it, 'with lively and spiritual exercises, full of heavenly enjoyment' (pp. 86–7). Praising a poor woman whose family are starving but whose religion remains firm, Flora says, 'Through infinite mercy, your good education is not lost. You feel, and you speak like a Christian, and a woman of sense' (p. 146).

Observations of this nature, in which the value of a person's education is assessed in terms of his or her religious soundness and moral stamina, were entirely in accord with early-nineteenth-century views on education, regardless of which camp they emanated from. Writers on female education never wearied of reminding their readers that the cultivation of the understanding is a religious duty, and that a good instructress must make Christian principle her ruling object in everything.[8] *Blackwood's* constantly insisted that unless reading and writing skills were shored up by 'the one sole panacea for every variety of evil in every order of men', namely religion, they would do nothing but harm.[9]

Agnes Grey thus conforms to contemporary ideals when she dreams of '[making] Virtue practicable, Instruction desirable, and Religion lovely and comprehensible' (I.9). However badly she fails in all these respects, she holds on to that 'reverence for matters connected with Religion' noted, she says, by the Murray pupils as one of her peculiarities (VII.70). Like the successful maternal teacher in Mary Maurice's *Aids to Developement* [sic], Agnes never loses her conviction that divine wisdom is the highest form of knowledge. Her advice to Rosalie, Lady Ashby, to let religion teach her how to live is not delivered with great optimism, however. In fact, the failure of teachers to inspire Christian devoutness in their charges is a striking feature of the Brontë fiction.

Not only are the young Bloomfields and Murrays impervious to Agnes' attempts to make religion 'lovely and comprehensible', other children in the Brontë novels are no more amenable to religious instruction than they. Heathcliff's resentment at being punished by being made to learn Scripture names by heart and read sermons would be understandable even in a less rebellious child (*Wuthering Heights* I.vi.41). A graphic scene from *Jane Eyre* speaks of religious instruction falling on stony ground:

The Sunday evening was spent in repeating, by heart, the Church Catechism, and the fifth, sixth, and seventh chapters of St. Matthew; and in listening to a long sermon, read by Miss Miller, whose irrepressible yawns attested her weariness. A frequent interlude of these performances was the enactment of the part of Eutychus by some half dozen of little girls; who, overpowered with sleep, would fall down, if not out of the third loft, yet off the fourth form, and be taken up half dead. The remedy was to thrust them forward into the centre of the school-room, and oblige them to stand there till the sermon was finished. Sometimes their feet failed them, and they sank together in a heap; they were then propped up with the monitors' high stools. (I.vii.60–61)

No measures undertaken to punish the bodies of such hapless mites would be likely to increase their spiritual welfare, *pace* Mr Brocklehurst. The *lecture pieuse* at Madame Beck's school is so soporific that whatever interruption M. Paul might devise is welcomed by the bored girls, including the 'sleepy pupil' whose lot it was to trot out the 'besotted' religious literature deemed suitable for the schoolgirls.

It is interesting that successful tuition in the Brontë novels is hardly ever associated with religion. True, William Crimsworth approves of the way in which Frances concludes an essay by means of invoking eloquent 'religious Faith' (*The Professor* XVIII.138), and Lucy Snowe has no difficulty teaching the Beck children prayers and a hymn in English (*Villette* VIII.73) – but these two glimpses of untroubled piety do little to counteract the impression that pupils in the Brontë novels fail to benefit from such religious instruction as they receive. It would of course be fair to say that the fault was in the methods, not in the matter itself; but in that case one may well wonder at the absence of successful pedagogy invested in the teaching of religion to children. Even the pious Helen Huntingdon is never seen to educate her little boy 'for Heaven' (*The Tenant of Wildfell Hall*, XXVIII.228) by means of 'target-orientated' religious lessons.

Part of the answer might be found in Patrick Brontë's benefactor Henry Venn's frank admission that he himself avoided 'surfeiting a child with religious doctrines', having concluded that 'too frequent talking [to children on religious matters] is a weariness to them'.[10] The Brontë novels were written by experienced teachers – Sunday-school teachers, too – who had had ample opportunity to discover the wisdom of Venn's tactful restraint.[11]

When Mr Hall in *Shirley* catechises the Farren children, he does so to distract them until their mother can satisfy their hunger (I.viii.141), turning what might have been a tiresome exercise into a game ('You begin, Ben. What is your name?') The perfect clergyman would not make the mistake of trying to press religious morality on children with empty stomachs.[12]

The absence in the Brontë novels of laudable religious instruction is not due to irreligiousness on the authors' part but to the recognition, so frequently and insistently demonstrated, that spiritual progress comes from within the individual. An able instructor can help another adult along on that progress, but only if he or she manages to tap into the other person's inmost feelings (as happens, for instance, with Mr Weston and old Nancy Brown in *Agnes Grey*, ch. XI; Jane Eyre's lesson in religion from Helen Burns is transmitted by way of the child's love of her friend and only comes to fruition in adulthood). Where young minds are concerned, discreet moral guidance and good examples manifested in unimpeachable everyday conduct are seen to be far more effective in fostering real virtue than preaching of any kind.

The Brontë distaste for religious ranting was clearly a family characteristic, and their tendency to discretion in respect of religious profession could only have been encouraged by Hannah More's *Moral Sketches*, of which Patrick Brontë owned a copy. Having encouraged study of the Bible as a means of obtaining self-knowledge, More continued, 'Be not impatient . . . to make a public disclosure of your sentiments. Religion is an interior concern'.[13] This sentence is underlined in the Haworth copy.

If there is a dearth of religious instruction proper in the novels of the Brontës, they – especially Charlotte's – overflow with Scriptural allusions. Scripture was one field where the Brontës themselves needed no tuition outside the home.[14] Charlotte's schoolmates at Roe Head were awed by her command of the Bible. Her knowledge of Holy Writ was as impressive as her easy familiarity with poems to which her schoolmates had to devote hours of laborious study, and not unrelated to it in that it was built on interest and pleasure. '[N]o girl in the school was equal to Charlotte in Sunday lessons', according to Ellen Nussey who added, 'she was very familiar with all the sublimest passages [in the Bible], especially those in Isaiah in which she took great delight'.[15] Charlotte Brontë's knowledge of the Bible thus seems to have been the result not of mechanical memorising, but of voluntary immersion in texts that excited her. Developing one's mental powers may have been regarded as a religious duty in the nineteenth century; but then as now, no pedagogical system could rival the power of individual inclination even in – maybe especially in – the study of religion.

CHAPTER 9

The accomplishments

If religion was to be 'the groundwork of [all] education',[1] and 'the usual accomplishments' were regarded as the second pillar of girls' education from the middle class upwards, a religious dimension should have been present in that part of the female curriculum as well. Some commentators on education certainly attempted to remind their readers that any human effort ought to harmonise with, even uphold, Christian values and principles. Priscilla Wakefield's observations on the merits of artistic pursuits supply a typical example:

Drawing, not merely for the purpose of making pleasing pictures, and obtaining applause, but for that capacity it gives to a proficient, of representing any object with ease and accuracy, is both a useful and an amusing qualification: nor are its good effects confined to the exercise of the art alone; it strengthens the habit of observation, and facilitates the acquisition of natural history, which is a study at once delightful and valuable; and it promotes a reverential admiration of the wisdom and goodness of the Great First Cause.[2]

Even so, the continuous maintenance of a religious element in the accomplishments curriculum was an uncongenial, not to say hopeless, task. To begin with, the Bible could not serve as a universal teaching aid in a skills-orientated context. Of course, musical practice could comprise hymns as well as secular songs; drawings could feature ecclesiastical buildings and Biblical images; and works in foreign languages might be chosen partly for their devotional content. Still, the whole female-accomplishments sphere was inherently secular, and this is one of the reasons why it engendered such mixed feelings among commentators on female improvement.

A present-day reader cannot help being confused by the contradictory picture presented by the late-eighteenth- and early-nineteenth-century debate on the accomplishments. On the one hand, they were obviously desirable: every respectable middle- and upper-class girl required the attribute 'accomplished' to have any sort of social standing, and instruction in the accomplishments was a comparatively prestigious teaching job in schools; no contemporary reader of *Jane Eyre* would have been surprised to find that it is Miss Temple who teaches music and drawing at Lowood. The best teachers rarely come cheap, and parents who wanted their daughters to receive such instruction would usually have to pay extra. In other words, it was a luxury, and as such both coveted and a reason for self-satisfaction on the part of those involved in it. On the other hand, no discussion of the accomplishments in a work written for audiences interested in the education of girls omitted to sound a warning note. No adjectives were so often associated with 'the accomplishments' in such works as 'showy' and 'superficial'. The writers of manuals on female education were tireless in their exhortations not to invest too much time and labour in schooling 'the fingers, the ears, the tongue, and the feet' of young females 'in all those little arts and elegancies that are calculated for momentary and external effect'.[3] Elizabeth Sandford spoke for many when she depicted those skills as a non-essential bonus:

Accomplishment, unless it is the ornament of a cultivated mind, is like a fine dress upon a vulgar person . . . Accomplishment is a graceful addition when the groundwork is complete; but it is no substitute for the essential branches of education, no apology or cloak for imperfect knowledge.[4]

The Brontë children will have read similar strictures on female education from the Ettrick Shepherd, who complained that young girls and women had no time to reflect over anything, 'sae that their acquirements, or accomplishments, as they ca' them, are ower mechanical, and dinna melt into, and set aff ane anither'.[5]

In other words, accomplished women enjoyed respect and admiration – but the acquisition and exercise of their skills were hedged with reservations and misgivings. This duality is very much a feature in the fiction of the Brontës, where profoundly gifted women artists are contrasted with slick performers whose sole aim is to impress. Indeed, the Brontë novels may be seen as part of the nineteenth-century debate on how this seeming inconsistency in female education might be resolved.

Even the servant Bessie from Gateshead knows what an educated young lady should be capable of. Her questions to 18-year-old Jane Eyre form a concise recapitulation of the accomplishments curriculum: 'What can you do? Can you play the piano? . . . and can you draw? . . . and have you learnt French?' (I.x.91–2).[6] Satisfied on all these points, and reassured that Jane can also 'work on muslin and canvass', Bessie exclaims, 'Oh, you are quite a lady, Miss Jane!'

Bessie's visit brings the first intimation of Jane's paternal uncle, Mr Eyre of Madeira, whose wealth and connections play such important roles in the plot of *Jane Eyre*. While in no position to know anything about his money, Bessie recognised his social standing when he visited Gateshead to see his young niece: 'He looked quite a gentleman' (I.x.92). The collocation of class and accomplishments is not fortuitous. Thanks to her own efforts, Jane Eyre has secured her social position as a gentleman's daughter, albeit orphaned and impoverished. Bessie is delighted with Jane's success in asserting her caste by means of obtaining the capabilities associated with the upper strata in society: 'I know . . . you will get on whether your relations notice you or not'.[7]

Why were the accomplishments so highly prized? Maria Edgeworth supplies part of the answer:

Accomplishments, it seems, are valuable, as being the objects of universal admiration. Some accomplishments have another species of value, as they are tickets of admission to fashionable company. Accomplishments have another, and a higher species of value, as they are supposed to increase a young lady's chance of a prize in the matrimonial lottery. Accomplishments have also a value as resources against *ennui*, as they afford continual amusement and innocent occupation. This is ostensibly their chief praise; it deserves to be considered with respect. False and odious must be that philosophy which would destroy any one of the innocent pleasures of our existence.[8]

The aspect of entertainment is easily underestimated in an age where first-class music, theatre, opera and so on are available at the pressing of a button. Part of the marriage-market value of the accomplishments was connected with their anti-*ennui* potential. Not only would an accomplished wife be able to cheer her husband with live music during dull evenings; she would also render his home more attractive to his connections and associates.[9]

In such circumstances, hymns and oratorios would not be appropriate: their entertainment value was far below that of popular songs, foreign and domestic, and of light instrumental music by the favourite composers of the day. Similarly, pretty drawings of birds, flowers and handsome persons were much more likely to delight fashionable people than representations of religious motifs. This is another major reason for the essential secularity of the accomplishments. The most worldly of them all, dancing, relied on the availability of domestic musicians: without their skills, the prime marriage-market 'shows' could not have taken place (Jane Austen springs to mind).

MUSIC AND DRAWING

No wonder, then, that the accomplishments – music and drawing especially – were attended with such unsettling connotations to commentators on female education. Tainted by their association with the non-spiritual aspects of human relationships, accomplishments encouraged all sorts of vanity. To make matters worse, they could be acquired without intellectual or moral endeavour and hence did little to improve the mind, the avowed aim of all educationists and conduct-book writers. While assiduous practice on piano or harp entailed an element of disciplined effort and was laudable to that extent, it was still a matter of exercising fingers rather than thoughts and feelings.

It is intriguing that music executed by talented women for purposes of social entertainment is so unfavourably represented in the novels of the Brontë sisters. After all, the Brontës took their own music seriously, benefiting from such instruction as their father could afford and taking considerable time and trouble to obtain sheet music. Emily was skilful enough to be paid for giving piano lessons to pupils at the Heger pensionnat.[10] Charlotte may have been discouraged from playing owing to her poor eyesight, but Anne and Emily were obviously both able musicians and fond of music. The sheet music and music books, including three *Musical Library* volumes of 1844, that the Brontës owned tell of their familiarity with Mozart, Handel, Haydn, Beethoven and Purcell as well as with the 'newest foreign composers, especially of the German school . . . with English words'.[11] Exercises familiar to piano learners of later ages were known to the Brontës, too, including Czerny's *études*, complete with fingering. The Haworth music collection also contained settings of Scots airs, including 'Scots Wha Hae', and traditional English drawing-room songs. In other words, music was both prized and practised in the Parsonage. It is the more surprising that nobody plays the piano in *Wuthering Heights* and that those who do, and sing to their own and others' accompaniment, in *The Tenant of Wildfell Hall* are corrupt and corrupting characters.

The only accomplishment that Arthur Huntingdon truly appreciates is musical ability, and both his mistresses possess it. Miss Myers, whom Arthur brings to his home under the pretext of her being a governess to his son, has a fine voice; she 'could sing like a nightingale, and accompany herself sufficiently well on the piano; but these were her only accomplishments' (XLIII.367). Before Helen has received proof of her relationship with Arthur, Miss Myers spends evenings with the spouses in the drawing-room where she entertains the master of the house, pretending to sing and play to both husband and wife. Helen has experienced similar scenes before, during her husband's affair with the similarly gifted Annabella Lowborough. Her jealousy of Annabella was increased when the latter sang and played, and played up, to Helen's husband. Forced to recognise Annabella's superiority as a musician, she stated, sadly and baldly, 'I can amuse and please him with my simple songs, but not delight him thus' (XXVI.218; see also XIX.155–6).

Blanche Ingram in *Jane Eyre* is another siren who uses her musical skills in an attempt to capture the man of her choice. Miss Ingram and Mr Rochester spend much time together by the piano, and Jane Eyre has to suffer the mortification of discovering that Mrs Fairfax's advance praise of Blanche's musical ability was amply warranted. The fact that Rochester had summarily dismissed Jane's own musical attainments does not help (I.xiii.124).

By contrast, artless songs sung to entertain, soothe or comfort someone whom the singer cares for, or the singer herself, are shown in a favourable light throughout the Brontë novels. Bessie's singing used to fill the child Jane with 'lively delight', though the sad ballad of the poor orphan child makes her cry (*Jane Eyre* I.iii.21–2); Nelly Dean lulls little Hareton to sleep with a similarly mournful song (*Wuthering Heights* I.ix.67). The six pages devoted to the introductory account of the Yorke family home Briarmains contain another instance: one reason why Mr Yorke does not hear the doorbell is that his little daughter Jessy has been singing a Scots air to him; Mr Yorke 'delights in Scotch and Italian songs, and has taught his musical little daughter some of the best' (*Shirley* I.ix.152). Hortense Moore's skilful guitar-playing and singing are usually marred by her 'formal and self-important character' (I.vi.78); but when her brother suggests that she cheer them both by singing their mother's favourite songs, affection informs her delivery, which then excites Caroline's sincere admiration (I.vi.87–8). It is because of the grotesque artifice with which little Adèle has been taught to sing songs wholly inappropriate for a little girl that Jane Eyre is revolted by her display – a disgust directed against the tastelessness of the child's elders, not against the child herself and not against the song as such (*Jane Eyre* I.xi.102).

It is hence want of sincerity, of genuine warmth and devotion to the pursuit for its own sake, that vitiates accomplished musical performers in the fiction of the Brontës. In the two novels that feature morally inferior singers, the heroines are accomplished in another art: Helen Huntingdon is forced to put her love of drawing and painting to use in earning her living; and Jane Eyre secures, if not captures, Mr Rochester's interest by means of some remarkable sketches the execution of which gave her 'one of the keenest pleasures [she had] ever known' (I.xiii.126).

While two of the Brontë sisters were respectable amateur musicians – and all seem to have enjoyed, and had an ear for, music – all three of them were skilful pictorial artists. As Christine Alexander and Jane Sellars' monumental *The Art of the Brontës* showed, Branwell was not the only Brontë sibling to harbour professional artistic ambitions.[12] All the young Brontës had drawing lessons from well-known local teachers, went to exhibitions and studied such art reproductions as they could lay their hands on.[13] The link between literature and art was present in their writings from the start, as Alexander and Sellars have shown, and the representations of art and artists in the novels are characterised by the assurance of the experienced practitioner.

Natural inclination is probably one factor in the Brontë preference for the pictorial arts, but practical circumstances will have mattered, too. Pen and paper, and even paints, were more mobile and affordable tools than musical instruments, and many books and periodicals available to the young Brontës supplied materials for them to copy and draw inspiration from.[14] Besides, they were studious and intellectually ambitious, and they lived in a period which recognised that drawing was a more 'serious' accomplishment than singing and playing. It was less associated with the courtship-related activities whose ultimate purpose was to captivate, and it did not afford such obvious opportunities to shine in company. *The Complete Governess* admitted that drawing was less popular than music in that it was 'less calculated for temporary show', but defended it as an inherently superior occupation: requiring more general knowledge, it had closer ties with mental education.[15]

Albeit less imbued with seductive properties than music, art is the accomplishment that invests the heroines of *Jane Eyre* and *The Tenant of Wildfell Hall* with particular fascination in the eyes of the men who fall in love with them. Much has been written about the three water-colours which arrest Rochester's jaded eye as he leafs through Jane Eyre's sketches.[16] The subjects are sensational and grim – a shipwreck with a female corpse whose bracelet has been salvaged by a cormorant, and two personifications of the Evening Star and Death, both set in majestic and forbidding scenery (I.xiii.125–6). Hardly congenial to present-day notions of good art, they would surely strike a spectator of any period as 'peculiar' 'for a school girl' (Rochester's words, I.xiii.126). Not the least remarkable quality is their origin in the artist's imagination: art taught as an accomplishment, in schools and homes, was very much a business of copying, from models or from Nature.[17] Similarly, the romantic teenager Helen Lawrence had created heavily symbolic scenes drawing on her own imagination, among them a picture of young love which would strike modern spectators as unbearably sentimental (*The Tenant of Wildfell Hall* XVIII.149–52; Anne Brontë devoted a full page to her narrator's description of the picture).

Arthur Huntingdon has no difficulty in interpreting the painting, in a manner flattering to himself. Gilbert Markham's responses to the older Helen's work are more interesting, not least for what they tell the reader about the man himself. It is a seasoned observer who comments on the development of the professional artist 'Mrs Graham': he perceives that the 'careful minuteness of detail' that characterised the young and artistically insecure artist has disappeared from her mature work, which possesses greater 'freshness of colouring and freedom of handling' (V.44). This development suggests growing assurance on the part of the painter, as well as awareness of the changing attitudes to colour in early-nineteenth-century art.[18] Another noteworthy passage is the following exchange, prompted by Helen and Gilbert's contemplation of 'little clusters of foliage' with the sun behind them:

> 'I almost wish I were not a painter,' observed my companion.
>
> 'Why so? one would think at such a time you would most exult in your privilege of being able to imitate the various brilliant and delightful touches of nature.'
>
> 'No; for instead of delivering myself up to the full enjoyment of them as others do, I am always troubling my head about how I could produce the same effect upon canvass; and as that can never be done, it is mere vanity and vexation of spirit.' (IX.79)

Consciousness of the gulf between idea and expression, agonisingly familiar to artists of all descriptions, stamps Helen and her creator as professionals.

Helen cannot afford to paint for her own pleasure alone, and her pictures duly conform to the prevailing taste for landscapes, picturesque buildings in ditto settings and human figures in predicaments conducive to moral reflection. Her secluded existence at Wildfell Hall is a real occupational disadvantage, as it entails 'a sad dearth of subjects' (V.43);[19] and it is the prospect of a fine sea view that persuades her to take part in an excursion with a party of young people. The fact that Gilbert understands Helen's work is a circumstance in her favour, reminding the reader that the spoilt young gentleman farmer is, after all, a man of taste and feeling, as well as an incarnation of the Classical *beatus ille* ideal and a faithful steward.[20]

The way in which Helen Huntingdon and Jane Eyre turn to their art when beset with strong feelings, finding an outlet, if not always solace, in their work, demonstrates that drawing and painting are part of their very natures. They also devote much labour to their artistic projects. At a late stage in the narrative, Helen recognises that she needs to hone her skills in order for her products to become saleable (XXXIX.337); but she was a painstaking artist even before '[t]he palette and . . . easel, [her] darling playmates once' perforce became her 'sober toil-fellows'. Asked whether she had '[sat] at them long each day', Jane Eyre answers that the pictures were all she had to do during her last two vacations, and that 'the length of the Midsummer days favoured [her] inclination to apply' (I.xiii.126). This is an acknowledgement that she worked long and hard to realise her visions, and Rochester recognises her effort in speaking of her 'ardent labours'.

To such a person, the suggestion that the success of her work was at least partly due to another and more expert hand is an insult, and Jane is understandably stung when Rochester speculates that a drawing-master helped her (I.xiii.124). It was not an unnatural suspicion, though: pictures partly executed by instructors appear in many contemporaneous texts on the accomplishments, fictional and non-fictional. Back in 1788, Mary Wollstonecraft had spoken sardonically about girls who imagined themselves artists just because they had 'a drawing or two (half done by the master) to hang up in their rooms'.[21] Many subsequent writers on girls and education bore witness to youthful weariness with artistic projects, which would then be left to the teacher to finish. One instance occurs in *Agnes Grey*, where Agnes is obliged to carry out 'the principal parts' of Rosalie Murray's drawings. Rosalie only works at such 'showy accomplishments' as will allow her to shine, especially the music which is the most attractive of the accomplishments in the eyes of her matchmaking mother (VII.62–3).[22]

Blanche Ingram is also afflicted by such a parent and similarly bent on colluding with her to capture the biggest prize in the local marriage-market. She is, of course, ignorant of the fact that Rochester has been caught that way before by another black-haired beauty and is unlikely to repeat the experience, quite apart from his being in love with a very different woman.[23] The pair Blanche – Jane actually provides a very good illustration of the opposite poles of the accomplishments issue. Blanche is a proficient musician, but everything about her, including her singing, is corrupted by her essential phoneyness. Jane despises her too much to be jealous of her:

She was very showy, but she was not genuine: she had a fine person, many brilliant attainments; but her mind was poor, her heart barren by nature: nothing bloomed spontaneously on that soil; no unforced natural fruit delighted by its freshness. She was not good; she was not original: she used to repeat sounding phrases from books; she never offered, nor had, an opinion of her own. She advocated a high tone of sentiment; but she did not know the sensations of sympathy and pity: tenderness and truth were not in her. (II.iii.185–6)

Jane, by contrast, is genuine, an 'original' all through.[24] She gives all she has to the work in hand, whether it is connected with study, drawing or 'cleaning down' Moor House. The forces that drive her come from within. True to herself at all times and at all costs, she is constantly on her guard against the greatest danger to her integrity: self-deception induced by treacherous feelings fostered by self-indulgent inclinations. The 'dictates of conscience' (II.iv.201), intermediaries between God and his created beings, guide her; in extreme situations she begs God for direct guidance, and her prayers are answered.[25] Blanche is all veneer; her accomplishments are gleaming patches on the surface of something that has no substance.[26] Conversely, Jane's accomplishments are rooted in that which is her substance, her God-given personality for which she is alone responsible. Her artistic work emanates from the same source as those guiding forces to which she struggles so hard to be faithful, 'the finest feelings of the heart'.

That expression is a quotation from Patrick Brontë's *The Maid of Killarney*, where the 'original' Dr O'Leary – whose views are constantly supported by the narratorial perspective – comments on the modish intrusion of foreign languages in young ladies' music:

'I always like to see more of nature than art in music. Many prefer execution; but I cannot bear to have the eye entertained at the expence [sic] of the finest feelings of the heart. Those performances have the most genuine music in them, which make us feel the most. Nor do I like the modish method of singing. They often entertain our English and Irish ears with Italian words; but, indeed, it matters not in what language they sing, they so fritter it all away into a whisper, that you cannot understand them.' (Page 59)

MODERN LANGUAGES

The extent to which girls should learn foreign languages, the third staple of the accomplishments curriculum after music/dancing and art, was much discussed in the early nineteenth century. These discussions are reviewed below; but another question should be dealt with first. It is a question which immediately occurs to a present-day student of girls' education in the early nineteenth century, but which does not seem to have been a matter of concern to contemporary writers: why did the study of modern languages belong to the 'accomplishments' division of the female curriculum? After all, surviving records of the pursuit testify to its having been an intellectually demanding one. Granted that the acquisition of a foreign language involved listening to and imitating correct pronunciation and was skills-orientated to that extent, 'fagging away' (as Charlotte Brontë put it) at grammar was still a vital component. Nor was this strenuous occupation the only mentally taxing aspect of language study: the student was also expected to master the basics of the foreign language's literary history and its prosody. For instance, the French and German schoolbooks studied by the Brontës contain sections detailing literary categories, metrical units and so on.

One answer might be that whereas nobody doubted that mastering a foreign language involved hard work, it was not essential and it was not English. The 'sound English education' certainly comprised knowledge of other countries' topography and modes of governance, past and present; but such facts were part of studies in which British conditions had pride of place, and much of their relevance was seen in terms of their bearing on those conditions. There is nothing remarkable about such priorities, of course; even today most elementary-school tuition all over the world begins at home. Nevertheless, the fact that young women's learning of modern languages was thought of in terms of desirable outwork gives one pause, especially in conjunction with the core-fabric status of the Classical languages in the education of young men.[27]

A sense of imbalance was clearly felt in the nineteenth century as well, though, and some writers took pains to counteract the view that foreign languages were little more than an ornament designed to enhance the social prestige of an 'accomplished' young girl. Sarah Ellis pointed out that having learnt other languages amounted to having 'gained possession . . . of the *keys* of vast storehouses of knowledge', for the use of which the thus accomplished woman was 'responsible to society'.[28] Similarly, Anna Laetitia Barbauld maintained that learning French was mandatory not in order to impress people but to be able to read its masterpieces of polite literature.[29] A good command of English was everybody's first priority, however, and scathing things were said about the 'lingomania' which produced young women 'so learned in foreign languages, that they scarcely [knew] how to articulate their mother tongue'.[30]

Whatever a writer on education for middle- and upper-class girls thought of the desirability of German and Italian (a topic addressed below), he or she would agree on one thing: French was a necessity. No prospective governess would be taken on without it;[31] and no school for young ladies had a hope of prospering without offering tuition by staff able to teach at least reasonably authentic-seeming French. There were practical reasons for this, in addition to the joys of cultural refinement: in the early nineteenth century, foreign travel had become a reality for non-privileged members of British society;[32] and French was by far the most useful language to a Briton travelling on the Continent.

The Brontës' Brussels scheme, sometimes depicted as a daring and speculative venture, hence made perfect sense. Paris might have been even more desirable; but it would have been more expensive, they had friends in Brussels, and whatever Charlotte Brontë came to think about Belgium and the Belgians, the country was known to possess fine schools.[33] As things turned out, the tuition in French that Charlotte and Emily received from Constantin Heger would have been hard to improve on in any place or time.

It is difficult to ascertain how much French the elder Brontë sisters knew on arrival at the Pensionnat Heger. Charlotte had studied the language at Roe Head and presumably passed some of what she learnt on to her sisters. Her oral proficiency seems to have been relatively undeveloped, but her written work was clearly much better, and she was swiftly promoted from the beginner's tasks she had been set at first.[34] Thanks to Sue Lonoff's edition of Charlotte and Emily's Belgian essays, it is now possible to study their development as writers of French in some detail. Comparisons between the two do not leave all the honours with Charlotte: for instance, even on the basis of Emily's first uncorrected essays one may conclude that she was as well acquainted with French grammar as her sister.[35] By any standards, both young women were admirable writers of French as a foreign language who developed skills commensurate with those of native writers of no mean ability. In other words, the primary objective of their stay in Brussels was handsomely achieved.

Whatever the quality of instruction in French at Roe Head, the Brontë sisters had been in a position to teach themselves the language. Charlotte had acquired Porny's *Grammatical Exercises* in 1831, and she does not appear to have been its sole user; the very elementary French words, with translations, on the inside cover are more likely to be Anne's markings than hers.[36] Whatever the shortcomings of the book (for one thing, one wonders why certain words are translated in the exercises and not other and more difficult ones), it will have been a useful tool for the autodidact. Porny had a clearly articulated pedagogical agenda, and numerous examples and practical exercises accompany the rules. The section on 'Gallicisms' explains 'particular French expressions, which are very difficult to be understood by Learners, as they cannot be rendered into English *verbatim*' (p. 146); one of them is 'il me tarde de' – 'I long to' – which Emily used in her letter *devoir* of 26 July 1842.[37] An intelligent and dedicated pupil who moved on to Porny from

Tocquot's elementary, but very helpful and everyday-orientated, *A New and Easy Guide to the Pronunciation and Spelling of the French Language* will have been able to give herself a reasonably good grounding in French even without formal tuition.[38]

Charlotte Brontë had loved French long before she met and fell in love with her French master in Brussels; but that experience obviously added to her enduring fascination, even obsession, with the language. As Brontë scholars have noted, snippets in French became increasingly frequent in her novels, to the point where her publisher had to restrain her.[39] All her heroines have either native-quality (Frances Henri) or next-to-native-quality French: Jane Eyre acquired it at Lowood, where she spent much time perfecting her pronunciation with a long-suffering Mademoiselle; Shirley's and Lucy's French is good enough to enable them to compose remarkable essays in that language.

Whatever level of proficiency Caroline Helstone had reached when her uncle forbade her to continue her French lessons with Hortense Moore (*Shirley* I.x.168–9), it was high enough for her to be able to talk informally and parse sentences in that language (I.v.68, I.vi.77). More than that, she could recite poetry, displaying a particular fondness for André Chénier's 'La Jeune Captive', whose last two stanzas are reproduced in the book (I.vi.94).

That poem had special significance for Charlotte Brontë, who had studied it in Brussels and alluded to it in one of her essays for Heger.[40] It is natural for works and authors associated with Heger to occupy special places in Charlotte Brontë's mind. The French Romantics feature among them, notably Bernardin de Saint-Pierre, Chateaubriand and Lamartine (but they also include Pascal's *Pensées*, of which Heger gave her an edition). Contrary to an assumption expressed by some Brontë scholars, a taste for these writers was not particularly 'advanced' at the time, at least not in England.[41] Bernardin de Saint-Pierre was recommended by several leading writers on education for girls, along with the ubiquitous Bossuet, Corneille and Racine, who also crop up repeatedly in Charlotte's fiction.[42] Indeed, her predilections, and those of her protagonists, where French literature is concerned are distinctly unadventurous.

It is worth observing that Charlotte Brontë disapproved of Rousseau – not on account of the irreligiousness which made him anathema to many contemporary Christians in Britain and elsewhere, but for his sentimentality. This was a quality she consistently condemned, praising George Sand for her comparative freedom from it.[43] It would have been natural to expect the Brontës, who loved liberty so ardently, to be admirers of Rousseau, but this was not the case. Anne and Charlotte's practical experiences of and with undisciplined children might have checked any inclination towards Rousseauan idealism, at least as regards child development.[44] More importantly, such an inclination would have run counter to their adult conviction that the sweetest fruits in life are earned along the path of self-improvement by dint of labour and endurance. Maybe it is no coincidence that Mr Rochester's French paramour, Céline Varens, bears a surname that conflates those of Rousseau's better-known mistresses, Louise de Warens and Thérèse le Vasseur.[45]

In view of the strong presence of French in Charlotte Brontë's novels, its absence from *Wuthering Heights* is striking. Apart from the odd phrase – 'mauvaise honte' in *Agnes Grey* (VI.53) and 'spirituel' in *The Tenant of Wildfell Hall* (LI.447) – it is also missing from Anne's fiction. So are allusions to French literature and culture. With the possible exception of E. T. A. Hoffmann (see below), Continental writers and their works have left few obvious traces in the work of the younger Brontë sisters.

This difference between the sisters might be interpreted as a sign of a comparative lack of interest in other languages on Emily and Anne's part, but such an assumption would be misguided. True, they did not glory in their linguistic prowess as Charlotte did, quite apart from their not having had her special emotional reasons for immersing herself in French. That does not mean that they were any less dedicated or indeed proficient, however. While the extrovert side of Charlotte's personality made it natural for her to put her knowledge on display, Emily and Anne were far more reserved, both as private persons and as authorial personae.

In fact, Anne once resorted to foreign languages as a way of simultaneously articulating and veiling a very personal response. Opposite stanzas three and four of the anonymous poem 'Sabbath Evening Twilight' in *Sacred Harmony*, an anthology of religious poems that she acquired shortly before leaving Thorp Green in 1845, she pencilled two brief comments: 'et moi aussi' and 'und ich auch'.[46] The two stanzas describe intense memories of past happiness, 'bright scenes of love and youth', rushing in on a grateful soul. It is easy to imagine Anne at Thorp Green identifying with these aching moments of remembered joy, irrespective of whether one associates them with William Weightman, with the days of untroubled Gondal symbiosis or simply with a happy childhood before the tribulations of young adulthood. Anyone who commands other languages than his or her mother tongue is familiar with the temptation to resort to them when expressing something sensitive. Anne's touchingly laconic comments show that French and German were more to her than mere marketable skills.

Nevertheless, the market value of German was a very good reason for an intellectually ambitious early-nineteenth-century governess to study it. German was fashionable in the 1830s and 1840s;[47] and contemporary readers of *Jane Eyre* will have had no difficulty in grasping the starkly articulated rationale with which the Rivers sisters account for their German studies to their materialistic servant, Hannah: 'We mean to teach it some time – or at least the elements, as they say; and then we shall get more money than we do now' (III.ii.333).

The opportunities to study German were an additional reason for Charlotte and Emily Brontë to go to Brussels rather than Paris, as Flemish-speaking Belgium bordered on German-speaking areas. The prospect of being able to add German to the attractions of the 'Misses Brontë's establishment' undoubtedly made business sense. Some commentators on female education wondered at the current craze for what Sandford called 'this most difficult tongue'.[48] Sandford saw little point in it, especially as the literature of Germany, to say nothing of its philosophy and theology, was not thought entirely suitable for young women.[49] Such an attitude was not incomprehensible in view of – to mention three random examples of the turbulence in intellectual Germany in the late eighteenth and early nineteenth century – the furore over Strauss' *Das Leben Jesu* (published in 1835, the year before Sandford's book appeared), the *succès de scandale* of Schiller's *Die Räuber* some decades earlier and the controversy over Fichte's alleged atheism.[50] Characteristically, however, no such qualms interfered with Charlotte and Emily Brontë's plan to master what the former's Diana Rivers calls 'this crabbed but glorious Deutsch' (*Jane Eyre* III.ii.333).

Instruction in German was hence part of the package for the Brontës at the Pensionnat Heger, and Charlotte continued to take German lessons from one Miss Mühl after her return to Brussels without Emily in 1843.[51] A letter in German written by way of exercise, partly corrected by her teacher but still full of faults, shows how far she had come in June 1843. Her grammar leaves much to be desired: she repeatedly offends against German word order, and there are preposition errors (including the classic 'nach Haus' instead of 'zu Haus') as well as erroneous inflections – but by and large the writer is someone who can make herself understood in German and should at least be capable of teaching 'the elements, as they say' (*Jane Eyre* III.ii.333). Shortly before writing the letter, she had been given a New Testament in German by M. Heger and inscribed it 'Herr Heger hat mir dieses Buch gegeben' – valiantly penning some of the words in German longhand, always notoriously difficult for foreigners (and virtually unreadable to most present-day Germans below retirement age).

While Charlotte was struggling with her German in Brussels, Anne began to teach herself what Sandford called 'this most venerable of modern tongues'.[52] It has been suggested that she wished to follow Emily's lead in this respect, which is of course possible;[53] but as we have seen German was a desirable accomplishment for any governess, let alone for a prospective schoolteacher. The *Rabenhorst Pocket Dictionary of the German and English Languages* (5th edn of 1843) which Anne bought in September 1843 was ideal for a beginner in that the German words were not set in black-letter type. Some six months later, she purchased another useful volume, John Rowbotham's *Deutsches Lesebuch* of 1837.[54] As its complete title suggests, it is an ambitious work: not only does it contain three different kinds of translation into English – an interesting pedagogical device in itself –, it also offers generous selections from, among others, Goethe and Schiller. Another peculiarity is translations into German from Shakespeare (*Henry IV*, *Hamlet*) and from Byron's *Manfred*, well known to the Brontës. The interlinear translations are sometimes hilarious, as the German syntax has had to be bent to accommodate the English;[55] but it must have been a treasure-trove to a serious student like Anne.

It is hard to guess how much German Emily Brontë knew.[56] The classic image, passed on by biographers from Gaskell onwards, of Emily kneading the dough of her famous bread in the Parsonage kitchen with a German book propped up in front of her may have encouraged exaggerated estimates of her proficiency. However, her assured handling of French grammar after little formal instruction in that language suggests a mind capable of dealing with a difficult inflected language, as does her skilful parsing of Latin.[57] Whatever her actual competence in German, there was no need for her to have read E. T. A. Hoffmann in the original language;[58] both *Das Majorat* and *Die Elixiere des Teufels* were translated into English in the 1820s, as was well known to any attentive reader of *Blackwood's* and *Fraser's*.[59] The spirit of German Romanticism has often been seen standing next to both *Wuthering Heights* and Emily's later poems, but its position is far from unchallenged. As a *BST* article entitled 'Farewell to Hoffmann?' points out, whether or not Emily Brontë had read the German Romantics she had most definitely read the English ones, and the strands that made up her unique vision resist prising apart.[60]

The place where the spirit of German Romanticism asserts itself most firmly and memorably in the Brontë fiction is Moor House in *Jane Eyre*, on the wild night when Jane knows she must find food and shelter there or die. Peering through a tiny window, she sees and hears two young women reading sentences in a strange-sounding language. Jane-the-narrator knows what the girl Jane did not: the work quoted by Mary and Diana Rivers is Friedrich Schiller's *Die Räuber*. *Sturm und Drang* hence prevail both indoors and outside, in the dark wet night and in the infernal vision of Franz Moor.[61] This hotpot of wicked deeds and dark deceit seasoned with parricide is an unconventional choice of reading matter for two spinsters in deep mourning for a recently deceased father. Their response to it is more unconventional still: the clergyman's sisters are enthusiastic about the fearsome proclamation of one of the apocalyptic judges, with words such as 'Zorn' and 'Grimm'. 'I like it!' exclaims Diana, echoing her normally so gentle sister Mary's 'That's strong . . . I relish it' (III.ii.332). Labouring over an intensely difficult project which is intended to improve their material prospects, they can still exult over the forceful way in which the foreign language was employed by a writer of genius exploring the depths of evil.

Compilers of works suitable for the eyes of young women might have frowned on Schiller,[62] but he was often approvingly cited in *Fraser's* and *Blackwood's* in the 1830s and 1840s. Nor was he praised by male writers only: Elizabeth Barrett's 'A Vision of Poets' exalted him, along with Goethe (and Burns, Byron and Coleridge, other Brontë favourites); Elizabeth Sewell's Margaret Percival is at one point 'lost in the delights of Schiller's Wallenstein'; and a generation earlier Maria Edgeworth had recorded her surprise that people should take offence at Schiller's play:[63]

Richard the Third excites abhorrence; but young Charles de Moor, in 'The Robbers', commands our sympathy; even the enormity of his guilt exempts him from all ordinary modes of trial; we forget the murderer, and see something like a hero. It is curious to observe, that the legislature in Germany, and in England, have found it necessary to interfere as to the representation of Captain Mac Heath and the Robbers[.]

These are interesting reflections from a writer not normally associated with ethical unorthodoxy; but to the creators of the thwarted bigamist Rochester and the almost-manslayer Gilbert Markham, to say nothing of the possible murderer Heathcliff, they would have seemed perfectly valid.[64]

Schiller's poetry was well known to Charlotte Brontë ever since the years in Brussels, where she translated some of his poems into English and French. One of his ballads, 'Des Mädchens Klage', is quoted in *Villette* (XXVI.304), in a context where it is clear that Paulina is becoming a young woman, and a young woman in love. From the first, then, Schiller is associated with powerful feeling in the life and works of Charlotte Brontë.[65]

One question remains to be addressed under the heading 'Modern languages': what about Italian? In the letter of 29 September 1841 where

Charlotte asks her aunt to subsidise the Brussels project, the order of priority is as follows: 'In half a year, I could acquire a thorough familiarity with French. I could improve greatly in Italian, and even get a dash of German'.[66] These sentences are puzzling – it sounds as though Charlotte knew more Italian than she did French, and could take or leave German. What actually happened in Brussels was that she (and Emily too) acquired a 'thorough familiarity' with German and 'improved greatly' in French, whereas there is, as Margaret Smith observes, no evidence of any study of Italian. The occurrence of isolated Italian expressions in Charlotte's novels does little to support the conjecture that she learnt the language from Miss Wooler, who apparently knew Italian.[67]

If Charlotte did have enough Italian to achieve a working knowledge of the language in the consequence of some 'improvement', it would have looked good on the prospectus of the projected school. Elizabeth Appleton's assertion that 'French and Italian are . . . the only languages taught to young ladies besides their own' (2nd ed., 1816) predated the fashion for German; but Stodart's *Hints on Reading* (1839) did not, nor did Sarah Ellis' *The Daughters of England* (1842) – and both works rank Italian as the second foreign language after French.[68] Travel to the sites of Classical and Renaissance Italy will have been one reason for its popularity; another was the many Italian songs executed in British drawing-rooms. As every trained singer knows, there is no better language than Italian to sing in, and many of the parlour-music favourites of the time came with texts in that language. The Brontës' *Musical Library* volumes always offer an English translation of a German song, along with the original, but Italian texts are usually unaccompanied by English versions. Even if the Brontës were no Italian scholars, they will have wanted to know what it was they sang – and they are unlikely to have '[frittered] it all away into a whisper'.[69]

NEEDLEWORK

The Brontë novels repeatedly convey disapproval of another kind of frittering: the waste of women's time, energy and intellectual as well as physical faculties in useless needlework. Neither Charlotte nor Anne has anything good to say about the finer crafts covered by the term 'fancywork', a pursuit to which middle- and upper-class Victorian Englishwomen devoted countless hours. The kinds of needlework performed by praiseworthy women in the novels tend to be knitting and sewing, whether for charitable purposes or for their own modest chests and drawers. *Shirley* offers particularly numerous and notable examples of irritation with pointless needlework. As an instructor of the well-intentioned but ignorant

Caroline Helstone, Hortense Moore is emphatically and extensively ridiculed. Her taste and judgement in all things – education, dress, house-keeping – are more than a little peculiar, and her priorities when it comes to plying needles are consistent with her general perverseness:

> Mademoiselle, like most Belgian ladies, was specially skilful with her needle. She by no means thought it waste of time to devote unnumbered hours to fine embroidery, sight-destroying lace-work, marvellous netting and knitting, and, above all, to most elaborate stocking-mending. She would give a day to the mending of two holes in a stocking any time, and think her 'mission' nobly fulfilled when she had accomplished it. (I.vi.81)

An often-quoted exchange on needlework in the Brontë fiction takes place between young Rose Yorke and her mother in the chapter called 'An Evening Out' (II.xii, or XXIII) in *Shirley*. The twelve-year-old girl does not deny that she should be made to learn household sewing and does not object even to mending her brothers' stockings and making sheets, but she offends and confuses her mother by stating that she wishes to do more with her life than that (II.xii.400–401).[70] In other words, womanly pursuits are not questioned in themselves; it is their function as tools of subjection and confinement that is rejected.

Embroidery was a pursuit with varied connotations in the nineteenth century. Traditionally an occupation for women of the leisured classes, it had an aura of gentility while counteracting an impression of idleness – the term 'work' for needlework of any kind comprised this activity as well, no matter how far away from the domain of utility the outcome might be. On one occasion the otherwise active Shirley, who is expressly said not to be a great needlewoman ('just about as tenacious of her book as she is lax of her needle', II.xi.386), uses a piece of embroidery as an instrument in her complex dealings with Louis Moore.[71] Taking refuge behind her 'work' (at which she is adept enough to be able to 'ply her needle' standing up; III.v.506), she manages her defensive position partly by recourse to an occupation recognised as peculiarly feminine. Charlotte Brontë may have been 'critical of embroidery and its role in the creation of femininity'; but if so her disapproval will not only have been due to the absence of practical usefulness in a pursuit that entailed both 'confinement and comfort' to women.[72] Two dimensions beyond the gender and utility aspects should be added to the considerations examined by previous scholars.

The first has to do with aesthetics. Where the pictorial arts were con-cerned (see above), tastes have changed enormously over the past century and a half, so that a present-day observer of Jane Eyre's and Helen Lawrence's imaginative artworks would be likely to shudder. Even around the middle of the nineteenth century, however, discerning women were disgusted with much 'fancy-work' not merely because it was of little use, but because it was offensive to good taste. For instance, the fashionable spaniel's head in cross-stitch enriched with beads did not gladden the eye of a mid-nineteenth-century beholder with aesthetic sensibilities.[73] Commenting on such motifs and techniques, the refined Margaret Thornley resorted to strong language: 'in this department of the needle's operations, I see very little that does not torture rather than gratify my taste'.[74] The impatience with fancy-work that is so patent in the fiction of the Brontës would probably have been less marked if the products of such labours had at least been attractive to look at. To cite one instance not mentioned by Hesketh and Parker, the cold, censorious Jane Wilson's days are spent 'in fancy-work and scandal' (*The Tenant of Wildfell Hall*, XLVIII.421) – a collocation which carries a sense of ugliness as well as uselessness. On the rare occasions when a Brontë heroine voluntarily undertakes to manufacture a piece of ornamental handicraft, she takes care that the result should be pretty ('glossy with silk and sparkling with beads', Lucy's watchguard gift to M. Paul, *Villette* XXIX.346).

The second aspect that needs to be considered in the context of the Brontës and ornamental needlework is the creative dimension. In their time, no kind of sewing left any scope for originality. As Sarah Ellis regretfully pointed out, 'the hand [was] more exercised than the head. To imitate [was] more the object than to invent' in female education generally, and nowhere was the absence of ingenuity more glaring than in the realm of needlework. Designs were made by others; neatness in execution was all.[75] The achievement of that ideal failed to engage with any of those faculties that the ambitious young women of Haworth Parsonage aimed to develop: mental, spiritual and emotional strength and integrity, achieved through constant intellectual and moral effort.

CHAPTER 10

Male and female education

Sustained academic endeavour was always a prerequisite for the acquisition of the knowledge and skills which took up most of the middle- and upper-class male curriculum: advanced mathematics and, above all, the Classical languages. The extent to which the Brontë sisters were acquainted with Latin and Greek is discussed below. By way of introduction, some space is given to general remarks about those staples of boys' education, and about the nineteenth-century debate on the extension of Classical learning to girls and women.

THE CLASSICS

If the nineteenth-century female curriculum reviewed above contains apparent contradictions, so does the schooling of boys and young men. As the fundamental difference, openly acknowledged,[1] between male and female education was that boys were destined for the labour market and girls for the home, the prevalence of the Classics in the male curriculum seems an oddity. It is difficult to think of a single profession where, say, natural science, geography, foreign languages and modern philosophy would not have offered far more useful preparation than Latin and Greek – except that of the Church, and here we encounter another anomaly in that most of the texts and authors studied belonged outside the realm of Christianity. It seems obvious to a present-day observer that even future lawyers would have derived greater benefit from studying Kant and Voltaire in their original languages than poring over Homer and Horace; the mastery of legal (to say nothing of medical) Latin never called for the parsing of Cicero or the commission to memory of hundreds of lines from the *Aeneid*. The best tangible use to which one could hope to put the Classics would be teaching them to others; and for most of the nineteenth century, as Section II above showed, that was not an attractive occupation for ambitious young men.

It has been suggested that the very uselessness of the Classics constituted much of their *raison d'être*: entering adulthood with the reputation of being an able Greek and Latin scholar amounted to telling the world that one did *not* have to work for a living.[2] Contemporaneous works, fictional and non-fictional, rarely stress the class-marking/socially-excluding properties of a Classical education; but that does not of course mean that this was not an important consideration, whether people admitted to it or not. It was certainly as impossible for a young man to attain the status of a gentleman without at least appearing to know some Latin and Greek as it was for a young lady to gain access to the middle- and upper-class marriage market without being thought 'accomplished'. Even so, there was a radical difference between those two sets of attainments: unlike the accomplishments, a Classical education was generally acknowledged to train the mind.

To the educational writers and commentators who wanted the Classics to be available to both sexes, the implication that female minds were congenitally inferior to male ones was the most offensive aspect of their opponents' attitude.[3] Harriet Martineau tore the latter's arguments to shreds in *Household Education*:

In works otherwise really good, we find it taken for granted that girls are not to learn the dead languages and mathematics, because they are not to exercise professions where these attainments are wanted; and a little further on we find it said that the chief reason for boys and young men studying these things is to improve the quality of their minds. I suppose none of us will doubt that everything possible should be done to improve the quality of the mind of every human being. – If it is said that the female brain is incapable of studies of an abstract nature, – that is not true: for there are many instances of women who have been good mathematicians, and good classical scholars. The plea is indeed nonsense on the face of it; for the brain which will learn French will learn Greek . . . – If it is said that women are light-minded and superficial, the obvious answer is that their minds should be the more carefully sobered by grave studies, and the acquisition of exact knowledge. – If it is said that their vocation in life does not require these kinds of knowledge, – that is giving up the main plea for the pursuit of them by boys; – that it improves the quality of their minds. – If it is said that such studies unfit women for their proper occupations, – that again is untrue. Men do not attend the less to their professional business . . . for having their minds enlarged and enriched, and their faculties strengthened by sound and various knowledge; nor do women on that account neglect the work-basket, the market, the dairy and the kitchen. . . . For my part, I have no hesitation whatever in saying that the most ignorant women I have known have been the worst housekeepers; and that the most learned women I know have been among the best[.][4]

Similar points had been made before, and not only by women writers. The third edition (1822) of *Systematic Education*, written by three Dissenter ministers, reminded its readers of the fine Classical education acquired by ladies of rank in Queen Elizabeth's day. These male authors' disapproval of the kind of prejudice that drew Martineau's polemics is no less radical and incisive than hers:

> This branch of education . . . as applied to females, has been made the subject of much paltry and unmerited ridicule. The capacity of the female sex for the learning of languages, is at least equal to that of the male; and if classical studies tend to the exercise of the understanding, and to the refinement of taste, why are not these objects as desirable for one sex as for the other? . . . But learned females are said not to acquire the good graces of the other sex. It is asserted that they are regarded with a species of dread and jealousy. – If a reputation for literature keeps fools and coxcombs at a distance from a youthful female, is this circumstance a proper subject of lamentation? and is it expedient, for the sake of such characters, to keep down the female mind, in order to reduce it to the ordinary level of intellectual society? In the estimation of reason, a lovely woman cannot be rendered less lovely, by the high cultivation of her talents; and many examples may be quoted to prove, that intellectual attainments are so far from being inconsistent with feminine graces, that they confer upon them additional attraction. (20–21)

What present-day readers may overlook in such passages is the link between mental development and ethics in the nineteenth century (and before). When Martineau suggested that engagement with the Classics would lend greater seriousness to a young woman's personality, she was saying, in effect, that an improved mind meant an improved character. Similarly, the authors of *Systematic Education* maintained that if shallow young men were frightened off when encountering a trained mind in a young woman, she was well rid of them. Studying the Classics meant acquiring true learning and with it virtue. If the result was spinsterhood, the virtuous woman would be better off than she would have been if married to an uncongenial partner – and 'an opportunity for intellectual pursuits' was one of the prime advantages of the unmarried state.[5]

Granted that the idea of girls studying the Classics, however repugnant to some people,[6] was acceptable to quite a few writers on education, how would female pupils go about learning Latin and Greek? Not many schools for girls offered tuition in Latin and still fewer in Greek, and few governesses were Classical scholars. The obvious potential source of instruction in the Classics was a well-educated father willing and able to teach his offspring.

Patrick Brontë was such a father, but the extent to which he may have taught his daughters Latin is uncertain. Conversely, it is clear that he took care to ensure that his only son obtained as good a Classical education as the paternal tutor's limited time permitted.[7] In addition, the blank pages in his copy of *A Concordance to the Holy Scriptures* testify to Mr Brontë's desire that Branwell's knowledge of Greek and Latin should be of practical use to the young man. Under the heading 'In June 1839 – I agreed with Branwell, that, under Providence, we should thoroughly read together, the following classics, in the following order only –', Patrick Brontë listed the first six books of the *Aeneid*, the four Gospels in Greek, the first three books of the *Iliad*, 'some of the first Odes of Horace' and *Ars Poetica*, adding that he and Branwell would also '[translate] some English into Latin', in the time-honoured English manner. It is an unexceptionable bibliography of texts for an elementary course of reading in the Classics. The Branwell who was to study it with his father was no beginner – he had, among other things, produced respectable translations of Horace – but a young man (at 22) whose career options included tutoring. If he were to take up such a post, these were precisely the works he would be teaching.[8] The scheme outlined by Patrick Brontë thus amounted to two Classics coaches getting together over core texts, the elder and more experienced instructor preparing the younger for entering the profession which had been the means of his own social advancement. Another incentive may have been a wish on the father's part to 'steady' the son by recourse to what was generally thought to be a particularly character-building kind of study.[9]

Where the Classical learning of Patrick Brontë's daughters is concerned, the hard evidence consists in translations of Latin texts in Emily Brontë's handwriting and a copy of Valpy's *Delectus* inscribed and marked by Anne Brontë. Edward Chitham has made out a convincing case for Emily's command of Latin: around the age of 20, she was clearly sufficiently able not only to translate but to comment on her work in an informed manner.[10] Anne is unlikely to have matched Emily's competence. However, her characteristic markings in the first few pages of *Delectus* suggest that she was at least preparing to study this primer of primers in the same systematic manner that she adopted in her ambitious self-educating projects involving the Bible and the *Sacred Harmony* anthology.[11]

Emily Brontë had far better opportunities to advance in her study of Latin around 1838–40 than Anne had in 1843, when she acquired her *Delectus* – probably, as Juliet Barker suggests, to teach the basics to the Robinson girls at Thorp Green.[12] First of all, Emily was at home, apart from her six months at Law Hill, and despite her housework she was in control of her life in a way

Anne could only have dreamt of. Second, she had access to a Classics scholar in her father. It is hard to imagine Patrick Brontë frowning on Classical ambitions in his talented daughters. If he did not invest much time in actually teaching them – and we do not know for certain that he did not – that can only have been due to one thing: chronic lack of it. Patrick Brontë was an immensely active and busy man with constant and partly unforeseeable calls on his time. If he put Branwell's interests in that regard before Emily's, he had urgent reasons for doing so: what was a necessity to the son was a bonus to the stay-at-home daughter. In fact, the joint study programme of the two Brontë men does not seem to have been fully realised, and the cause may just as easily have been the elder's lack of time as the younger's lack of persistent application (a combination of the two seems likely).

If Emily's and Anne's knowledge of the Classics is at best a subject for educated guesses, Charlotte's is a matter of pure speculation. Scholars and critics who have indulged in it have usually quoted Thackeray's comment to the effect that if the writer of *Jane Eyre* was female, she must have had a Classical education.[13] It is also sometimes intimated that Charlotte regretted not having learnt Latin and Greek, and there have been hints of a grievance on her part in that direction.[14]

With all due reservation for the speculative character of the following remarks, the idea of a resentful Charlotte Brontë feeling hard done by because she never learnt Latin or Greek does not seem convincing. If she did harbour such a grievance, one would have expected to find it expressed, however indirectly, somewhere in her writings or in the records of her life. Unlike her sisters (Emily was characteristically disinclined to allow any other person's feelings or opinions about anything to stand in her way, and Anne soon learnt to keep her difficulties and disappointments to herself), Charlotte Brontë was usually able to give vent to her frustrations somehow. Resign herself she might; but suffering in silence was not her way.

The passage in *Villette* where Lucy Snowe speaks about M. Paul's suspicion that she had received a Classical education may be considered in relation to Charlotte Brontë's own feelings on the matter:

> At moments I *did* wish that his suspicions had been better founded. There were times when I would have given my right hand to possess the treasures he ascribed to me. He deserved condign punishment for his testy crochets. I could have gloried in bringing home to him his worst apprehensions astoundingly realized. . . . Oh! why did nobody undertake to make me clever while I was young enough to learn, that I might, by one grand, sudden, inhuman revelation – one cold, cruel, overwhelming triumph – have for ever crushed the mocking spirit out of Paul Carl David Emanuel! (XXX.354)

First of all, of course, we must bear in mind that the speaker here is Lucy Snowe, not Charlotte Brontë. These passages may have a basis in the latter's relationship with M. Constantin Heger, or they may not; that point is not of primary interest in this context. Second, and more important, what rises from these pages of *Villette* is not the acrid smell of a grievance: it is the scent of humour. These comic passages belong to the funniest parts of a fairly grim book. Charlotte's irony is not exclusively reserved for the obviously prejudiced M. Paul, whose notions on intellectual women are exposed to exuberant ridicule. Lucy suffers a touch of it, too, when she hotly wishes his suspicions had been well-founded – not so that she could have 'revelled on flowers of Hymettus', but so that she could have brought discomfiture on the man she is more than half in love with. This glance at a vexed educational issue hence takes the form of an amusing contretemps between hero and heroine rather than that of rancorous satire.

Such good humour allows for the suspicion that her siblings' knowledge of Latin, and in Branwell's case Greek, was not a sore spot with Charlotte Brontë. On the contrary, Emily and Anne's ability was a potential asset to the 'Misses Brontë's Establishment', which offered tuition in French, German and Latin at an extra cost of a guinea per quarter for each. The younger Brontë sisters' attainments in this field must have been more than rudimentary for Latin tuition to be offered by the conscientious Brontës, who went to such trouble and expense to fit themselves for running a school (that their busy father should have been expected to supply such instruction on a regular basis seems unlikely).

It was not surprising that Thackeray spoke of a Classical education in connection with *Jane Eyre*: the book, and Charlotte Brontë's fiction generally from an early age, is dotted with allusions to Classical personages and conceptions. However, such easy familiarity with, for instance, Classical mythology did not require protracted struggles with *Delectus* or the Eton Grammar. Quite apart from all the pertinent references Charlotte will have picked up during family conversations, there were dictionaries which enabled any person with her keen intellect and retentive memory to handle Classical allusions with assurance. One of them was J. Lempriere's *Bibliotheca Classica*, of which there was a copy in the Parsonage.[15] It must have been an immensely useful volume: not only are all sorts of names (including names of countries, rivers, towns and so on) explained; references to Classical works where they occur are provided, too.

In addition, there were compilations intended to supply students with the kind of wider cultural and historical context that Tom Tulliver lacked at Mr Stelling's.[16] Benjamin Johnson's *A Grammar of Classical Literature*, one of the books recommended at the back of Goldsmith's *Geography*, is an especially interesting example.[17] Its paragraphs were equipped with numbers and clearly intended for memorising, the small-type 'Observations' supplying extra information in between.

What makes Johnson's handbook particularly intriguing to a reader of *Jane Eyre* are its descriptions of Vulcan and Apollo:

Vulcan, kicked out by Jupiter, was one whole day . . . in the fall, and lighted on the island of Lemnos, but was crippled ever after. . . . His breast is hairy, his arms nervous and brawny, and he appears all sooty, squalid, and discoloured. (80–81, paragraphs 307 and 311)

[Apollo] is represented as a tall beardless young man, with long hair and a handsome shape . . . his head crowned with laurel, and surrounded with rays of light. (76, paragraph 284)

The accompanying illustrations show the former much sturdier and more muscular than the boyish and beautiful Apollo. Such representations lend added poignancy to the little dialogue towards the end of *Jane Eyre*, where Jane teases Rochester about St John Rivers:

'Your words have delineated very prettily a graceful Apollo: he is present to your imagination, – "tall, fair, blue-eyed, and with a Grecian profile". Your eyes dwell on a Vulcan, – a real blacksmith, brown, broad-shouldered; and blind and lame into the bargain.'

'I never thought of it before; but you certainly are rather like Vulcan, sir.' (III.xi.441)

The contrast envisaged by Rochester between himself, crippled ever after like Vulcan, and his angelically radiant rival engenders a jealousy sharp enough to supplant 'the gnawing fang of melancholy', as Jane intended. With books like Johnson's around, the full impact of the scene could be felt without any Classical erudition on the reader's part.

Jane-the-protagonist is no Classical scholar. There are no references to her having tried to emulate Helen Burns, who impressed the child Jane with her ability to 'read and construe' Virgil (I.viii.73). Hearing the Rivers sisters quote Schiller, she does not know whether the 'unknown tongue' is Greek or German (III.ii.332). Although Lowood's superintendent knows Latin, there is no room for it in the school's curriculum. It would have been odd indeed if an early-nineteenth-century educational institution for girls from impecunious families had offered tuition in the Classics, as its creator knew.

Helen Burns is said to have learnt Latin by the same means as the other young girls in the Brontë novels who have more than a smattering of

Classical learning: through a father's instruction. Agnes Grey and her sister Mary study all other subjects with their mother, but Latin tuition is the clergyman father's province (*Agnes Grey* I.2). Cathy Linton has no tutor but her studious father, who inspires her with a love of books that does not, apparently, stop at volumes in Latin and Greek (*Wuthering Heights* II.xvii.266–7).[18] The presence of books in the Classical languages in Hareton's room is not surprising: he is, for all his ignorance and semi-illiteracy, the son of a college-educated man. Even so, his small store cannot compare with the library at Thrushcross Grange, Edgar Linton's refuge during times of domestic trouble. That the library contains volumes in French and in the Classical languages is clear from Nelly Dean's statement to Mr Lockwood, to the effect that she has looked into all the library books apart from them – and even 'those [she knows] from one another' (I.vii.55).

Matthewson Helstone's Greek and Latin books are no more use to his niece than Edgar Linton's were to Nelly (*Shirley* II.xi.389). The narrator of *Shirley* leaves the reader in no doubt that Helstone's neglect of Caroline's education is a grave dereliction of duty; but one may well wonder what to make of the following exchange between Caroline and Shirley. Having argued that women are much better at portraying men than the other way around, Shirley says that she will prove that in a magazine contribution written 'some day when [she has] time, only it will never be inserted: it will be "declined with thanks," and left for [her] at the publisher's'. Caroline's response lays the blame for this imagined failure not on sexist publishers (Shirley's masculine first name would protect her from such prejudice in any case) but on Shirley's deficient education:[19]

'[Y]ou could not write cleverly enough; you don't know enough; you are not learned, Shirley.'
'God knows, I can't contradict you, Cary: I'm as ignorant as a stone. There's one comfort, however, you are not much better.' (II.ix.352–3)

The puzzle here is that Shirley Keeldar's education had been entrusted to a superior governess, Mrs Pryor (in reality Mrs James Helstone), who refused to bring up her own daughter – and the result, both girls acknowledge, is much the same. If one does not want to dismiss this seeming inconsistency as a case of authorial inattentiveness, it can be accounted for in two mutually complementary ways: Mrs Pryor's priorities, like those of any respectable nineteenth-century governess, would have been ethical, not intellectual – and if we take 'learned' to refer to the orthodox education for males, 'ignorant' standing for the absence of systematic/scholastic 'learning', the problem disappears. There are good reasons for this reading: for centuries, a 'learned' woman was commonly thought of as someone who had mastered at least part of the standard Classical curriculum.[20] It is no surprise to find the energetic Shirley disinclined to undertake this kind of study, even if one assumes that Mrs Pryor had been capable of teaching her the 'Latin grammar' that Shirley says she would only study to purchase a respite from Louis Moore's questions (III.v.506).

To be sure, such an assumption would ascribe unusual attainments to Mrs Pryor. Latin and Greek were rare among the early-nineteenth-century governess's qualifications. As contemporary readers of *Agnes Grey* will have known, the heroine would never have been hired by a family like the Murrays if she had not been able to offer Latin as one of hers: her relative inexperience, her extreme youth and her demand for as high a salary as fifty pounds could only have been offset by an ability to give the young sons a good grounding in Latin. In the event, she is, of course, seen to fail dismally as a Classics instructor, not because she lacks the necessary knowledge but because she is unable to compel her boy pupils to apply themselves to their studies:

Master Murray . . . was about eleven when I came, a fine, stout, healthy boy, frank, and good-natured in the main, and might have been a decent lad, had he been properly educated, but now he was as rough as a young bear, boisterous, unruly, unprincipled, untaught, unteachable – at least, for a governess under his mother's eye; his masters at school might be able to manage him better – for to school he was sent, greatly to my relief, in the course of a year; in a state, it is true, of scandalous ignorance as to Latin, as well as the more useful, though more neglected things; and this, doubtless, would all be laid to the account of his education having been intrusted to an ignorant female teacher, who had presumed to take in hand what she was wholly incompetent to perform. I was not delivered from his brother till full twelve months after, when he also was despatched in the same state of disgraceful ignorance as the former. (VII.65)[21]

Agnes' expectation that the boys' shortcomings in respect to Latin will be ascribed to her incompetence may be noted as a highly realistic touch – but seven words in the long sentence that articulates it are even more worth observing. Studious and self-disciplined Anne Brontë, who had grown up in a home where the Classics were venerated and who had tried to master the basics of Latin herself, made her narrator, a Latin scholar, express the opinion that the Murray boys' 'scandalous ignorance as to Latin' was not the worst of it: they were also unacquainted with 'the more useful, though more neglected things'. As Agnes' job where the boys were concerned consisted in preparing them for school, it was clearly her duty to concentrate on Latin, grammar and mathematics – to the exclusion of 'more useful' subjects, such as, presumably, the history and geography which featured so largely in the female curriculum. It is a telling phrase.

Taken altogether, the references to Classical learning in the Brontë novels do not convey a sense of frustration on the part of girls and women at being wholly or partly excluded from the study of Latin and Greek that dominated the school years of their male counterparts. The child Jane Eyre's awe of Helen Burns's ability to read Virgil is the only instance where Classical attainments in a female are represented as something overwhelmingly admirable – and not even Jane is shown to develop a desire to master the same skills.

With reservations against drawing on fiction to speculate on biography, it does seem unlikely that the Brontë sisters resented or even regretted the relative absence of Latin and Greek in their lives, studies and employments. If they had wanted more in the way of Classical learning, they could and surely would have taken steps to obtain it. The presence of Latin in the prospectus of their intended school was a good (though, as it turned out, insufficient) sales argument; but its placing is significant. Under French and German, as an 'extra', it was, in effect, presented as an accomplishment: a valuable additional attainment, but not necessary and not part of that 'sound English education' that was the sure foundation of character development.

If the Brontë sisters did not in fact feel that the lack of Classical erudition in a woman entailed an element of injury or inferiority, they were far from unique in their day. However much Harriet Martineau and other so-called blue-stockings may have averred that 'every woman who pretends to a commonly good education now reads latin [sic]', there were quite a few people, of both sexes, who regarded the Classics as a bonus rather than a necessity – for anybody.[22]

Such opposition to the Classics-dominated male curriculum was nothing new. John Locke had been one of its most notable critics in the seventeenth and eighteenth centuries, throughout the latter of which a utilitarian groundswell could be felt, not least in the writings of Addison, Steele and Defoe. Their views were conveyed in fiction as well as in essays and other kinds of non-fictional prose. For instance, *Robinson Crusoe* was a powerful carrier of the useful-knowledge message to wide audiences decades before the Society for the Diffusion of Useful Knowledge was created.[23] A component in the protracted ancients-versus-moderns battles, the role of the Classics in education was a disputed subject for generations.

Although the pro-Classics persuasion was strong during the first half of the nineteenth century, with fresh enthusiasm for Greek,[24] it was not unchallenged.[25] For instance, the phrenologist George Combe, well known to the Brontës, rejected the Classics utterly, arguing that whereas Latin and Greek were worthy of study when 'rediscovered' in the Renaissance, there was 'no *knowledge* relating to the physical and moral worlds contained in these languages, which [did] not [now] exist clearly expressed in English'. Forcing children to labour with 'difficult, copious, and obsolete languages' was 'an outrage upon Nature, – tedium, disgust, and suffering invade the youthful mind'. To anyone who intended to go in for commerce or manufacture, Latin and Greek were worse than useless, in Combe's opinion.[26] Combe also reminded his audience and readers that some of the most 'eminent' authors in the English language, for example Shakespeare, Cobbett, Burns and 'a whole host of female writers', knew little of the 'dead languages' and were none the worse for that.[27]

The existence of views like Combe's accounts for the anxiety expressed by *Blackwood's Edinburgh Magazine* in 1836. The author of a piece called 'The Future' was pessimistic about developments in education, which was just undergoing 'a vast and degrading change'. The Classics, he lamented, were threatened by all the new talk about money, mechanics and manufacture; indeed, they were in the process of being 'scouted and abandoned'.[28] This is not how matters will have seemed to an observer in the English shires; but the Brontës had, as has often been pointed out, something of a Scots bias as intellectuals. They may well have been exposed to north-of-the-border ideas about the desirability of an education whose main function was to prepare pupils for work, not for statecraft, diplomacy or refined leisure.

That is all the more likely in view of the Scots influence on the northern counties of England:

Lancashire and Yorkshire were industrially in advance of the northern kingdom, but it was only after they had been stirred from Scotland that educational need created an educational demand. In elementary education Bell and Lancaster were English, for Scotland already had a school in every parish, but its great reformers, Robert Owen, Wilderspin, and Stow, all worked in Scotland. The *Edinburgh Review* was the main critic of the English universities and public schools. The early advocates of science – George Combe, Birkbeck, Hodgson, and William Ellis – were all either Scots or educated in Scotland. Adult working-class education started there. The new subjects were welcomed in the Scottish universities.[29]

The idea of useful knowledge, conducive to gainful employment, forms a suitable context in which to view the vehement attack on the patriarchal oppression of women in *Shirley* II.xi (ch. 22 in some editions). That head-on assault on male complacency, condescension and uncomprehending cruelty is made even more remarkable by being assigned to the outwardly meek

Caroline Helstone. The burden of her accusations is that men destroy
women by denying them fruitful employment, confining them to
monotonous and even pointless domestic pursuits. The outcome, says
Caroline, is listless, narrow-minded females in poor physical and mental health. Even this indignant plea is not devoid of humour: it is pointed
out that such feminine models as 'Lucretia, spinning at midnight in the
midst of her maidens' and Solomon's virtuous woman were inconsiderate
to their staff.[30] Caroline has her reservations about the former; but she
recognises the latter as a 'worthy model' because the Biblical paragon was a
manufacturer, a businesswoman and a clever manager.[31] In other words, the
'royal standard' she sets is one of successful commercial entrepreneurship.
This, then, is the sphere of activity in which one of *Shirley's* two heroines
wants to see women employed, not in the Classical scholar's study.

HEALTH AND EXERCISE

It is universally acknowledged that too much time spent in studies is delete-
rious to the health, and the desirability of physical activity for the young has
been recognised for centuries (again, Locke was a strong proponent). The
idea that it was good for young people to move about briskly according to
some sort of general pattern gradually gained ground in the early 1800s. One
of its eighteenth-century pioneers was one Mr Elphinston, who ran a private school in Kensington and argued that 'bodily exercise invigorates also
the mind'.[32] About half a century later, the Hills at Hazelwood (a famous
experimental school which educated boys only) were among the first in
their century to attach importance to gymnastics and games.[33] The ben-
eficiaries of physical education in the early stages were almost exclusively
male: the value of exercise took longer to spread to the realm of female
education, where dreary 'crocodile' walking was all the physical movement
pupils experienced long after boys began to receive regular physical training.
It should be noted, though, that girls as well as boys devoted much time to
vigorous folk dancing and singing at Robert Owen's New Lanark schools
for working-class children in the early nineteenth century. Like Elphinston
before him, Owen believed in the character-building properties of 'bodily
exercise'.[34]

By the mid-1830s, fashionable mothers were urging their daughters to
do calisthenic exercises in order to be able to move more gracefully;[35] but
schools still remained slow to take to the idea of physical education for
girls. As late as 1864, one Archibald Maclaren, writing about girls' schools,
complained that 'the two-and-two walk is the sole . . . form of exercise that

appears ever to have presented itself as being necessary or even desirable'. He strongly advocated outdoor sports – such as ball-and-racket games – for girls as a major health-promoting measure.[36]

As their writings show, the Brontës were well aware of the necessity for girls to build up and conserve their strength by means of plentiful outdoor exercise. Charlotte's description of Madame Beck's first-rate health-promoting régime includes 'a provision for exercise which kept the girls healthy' (*Villette* VIII.73). Similarly, the medical assistant charged with the ungrateful task of preventing further typhus deaths at Lowood insists that the few girls who have not yet caught the disease take 'frequent exercise to keep them in health' (*Jane Eyre* I.ix.76).[37] Agnes Grey regrets the inconsiderateness of the Murray children in choosing to do their lessons outdoors; she sometimes catches cold as a result, whereas the youngsters suffer no ill effects from sitting on damp grass or being exposed to the evening dew. Even so, she admits that '[i]t was quite right that they should be hardy' (*Agnes Grey* VII.68).

Agnes' word 'hardy' recalls *Wuthering Heights*, where Catherine Earnshaw Linton mourns her lost strength in memorable terms: 'I wish I were out of doors – I wish I were a girl again, half savage and hardy, and free' (I.xii.111). Before her first and last serious illness, Emily Brontë was as robust as any male contemporary, and it is natural to relate her prowess to that of the elder Catherine: when Heathcliff and Catherine were adolescents, running wild for hours on end as soon as they could escape Hindley's rule, she was as strong and swift as he. In their race from the Heights to the park of the Grange, 'without stopping' – no mean feat, as the distance is nearly four miles (admittedly downhill) – the reason for Catherine's defeat, artlessly articulated by her mate, was 'because she was barefoot' (I.vi.41). At that time of her life, she was obviously the 'stout, hearty lass' Mr Kenneth remembers when summoned to her sick bed at the Grange (I.xii.114).

The Brontë fiction was part of a current of exhortations and pleas for more vigorous fresh-air activity for girls. For instance, Sarah Ellis felt strongly about the need for female youth to lead physically active lives:

I would ask for [woman] a fresh, pure, and invigorating atmosphere, in which she may breathe with freedom, free exercise for her limbs, and occasionally the indulgence of that wild excitement, that thrilling ecstasy, and that unbounded exhilaration of mind and body, which a free and joyous life in the country can best afford. . . . I would earnestly recommend that girls should often be associated with their brothers in their sports, that they should climb with them the craggy rock, penetrate the forest, and ramble over hill and dale[.][38]

Slowly, progress was made in the late 1840s and early 1850s. In 1854, Bessie Rayner Belloc stated that '[t]he physical education of females is much better than it was'; she attributed this development to the successive dissemination of the views of George Combe and his brother Andrew.[39]

The preceding review of the differences between the nineteenth-century male and female curricula with reference to the lives and writings of the Brontë sisters suggested that neither they nor the female protagonists they created regarded these differences as a cause for female discontent. That does not amount to viewing Charlotte, Emily and Anne Brontë as passively resigned to patriarchal values and policies. On the contrary, they come across as sturdy intellectuals in harmony with the utilitarian forces that would ultimately be victorious in education. However much Charlotte Brontë revered Thomas Arnold as a Christian reformer, where education is concerned the views articulated in her novels are more in tune with the ideas of such mid-century promoters of useful knowledge and physical exercise as F. D. Maurice and Charles Kingsley. They belong in the tradition that extends from the Enlightenment challengers against the traditional Classics-dominated male curriculum to late-nineteenth-century reformers such as Herbert Spencer. However nonsensical his espousal of phrenology may seem to a later age, the presence of George Combe in the intellectual milieu of the Brontës is indicative of an orientation towards those ideological currents that may, with hindsight, be termed 'progressive'.

Another indication that Charlotte Brontë belongs in this ideological context is supplied by the most 'sociopolitical' of her novels, *Shirley*. Robert Moore, who had been educated in Belgium, is a businessman who overcomes difficulties to become rich and powerful. His younger brother Louis was sent to England to acquire gentility in the course of a typical public-school education and is afterwards fit for nothing but tutoring (I.v.64). William Crimsworth in *The Professor*, in whose career the goodwill and financial advice of two businessmen are instrumental, only prospers when he is able to stop teaching as a hired master and join his wife in starting a school;[40] and *modern* languages, not the Classics, form his passport into the labour market.[41] Forced to give up his first plan to become a tradesman (I.6), he succeeds – brilliantly – when he converts the Crimsworths' educational attainments and experience into a commercial product and invests their profits wisely. In other words, the market-player trumps the retiring scholar – in the short run.

In the end, however, entrepreneurial triumph paves the way for a life of contemplation: Charlotte Brontë makes William and Frances Crimsworth retire as soon as they can afford it, leading a life of domestic bliss in their rural retreat. In so doing they fuse the notions of commercial and professional success that were so characteristic of their time with that more ancient conception of the good life, the *beatus ille* ideal familiar to every English secondary-schoolboy in the nineteenth century.

CHAPTER II

Beyond the schoolroom: reading and the Brontës

The quiet life of country gentlefolk is the situation in which the Brontë fiction leaves not only the Crimsworths but the Rochesters, the Moores at Fieldhead, the Markhams and the Earnshaws (the last three couples, it might be noted, on estates brought into the marriage by the female partner). Where there is no need to labour for gain, Brontë protagonists do not, preferring to cultivate their minds and relish the beauties of the countryside at leisure. Their best companions are their loved ones and books enjoyed in comfortable libraries.[1]

It was a kind of existence known to many aspiring late-eighteenth- and early-nineteenth-century middle-class people through the works of that latter-day Horace, William Cowper, one of the most popular writers in the lifetime of the Brontës.[2] He was a favourite with the whole family, as is clear not only from biographies from Mrs Gaskell onwards but also from the sisters' works.[3] To them, Cowper was above all the poet of 'The Castaway'; but though they were especially drawn to his renditions of human suffering, they were familiar with all of Cowper, including the eulogies to contented retirement in *The Task*.

The Brontë partiality to Cowper makes a convenient starting-point for a survey of their relationship with the world of books outside the set texts of the schoolroom. While something will be said about what, how and why the Brontës read, the full extent of their reading and its implications for their writing calls for a book of its own; as Michael Wheeler pointed out decades ago, '[s]tudents of the Brontës have long recognised that the sisters' reading provides as many clues to the source of their inspiration as do their biographies'.[4] What the following pages offer is a look at what reading meant in the time of the Brontës, especially in the context of self-improvement and woman's role in society, and some observations on the functions of literature and reading in the Brontë fiction.

Apart from Cowper's serving to remind us that a good deal of the Brontës' core reading stemmed from the eighteenth century, he makes a useful point of departure for two reasons: he articulated the Brontës' vision of earthly happiness as well as the sources of some of their most acute distress; and he provided Charlotte with food for thought about the functions of creative writing, from both the writer's and the reader's point of view (in *Shirley*; see below). That the Brontës were writers for nearly as long as they were readers needs to be borne in mind by anyone who examines what reading meant to them. So, however, does another circumstance that is more central to this book: much of their reading was undertaken with a view to making them better equipped for imparting instruction. Like all great readers, they read for a variety of reasons and in different ways that are not always easy to keep distinct from one another. One distinction may be made, though, and that is the one between reading and study. The ensuing subsection looks at these two occupations and the sphere where they were pursued: the home, with its own particular demands on a woman's time and energy.

READING, STUDY AND DOMESTICITY

The home of a middle-class English family of independent means and intellectual tastes was no castle of indolence in the early nineteenth century. Running a household was not a sinecure even for people who could afford to keep servants, and during such leisure as they commanded they would be expected to cultivate their minds and pursue other character-improving activities. The foremost of these was study: a pursuit that entailed the active understanding and committing to memory of large portions of knowledge. This knowledge should be so coherent and so well digested that it formed personality-enhancing insights. Acquiring it called for contemplation and reflection, rather than the storing-away of sundry items of information for semi-automatic reproduction that featured in even the best schools. There could be no better place for such ambitious endeavours than a comfortable home where household members studied together. Haworth Parsonage was such a home, however modest its comforts, and the attractions of a community of like-minded family members formed part of the devotion that bound the intensely intellectual Brontë sisters to it from first to last.

One of the most memorable collocations of the concepts 'reading' and 'study' in Brontë-related materials occurs in a letter written by Charlotte Brontë to W. S. Williams, her publisher's reader, in January 1849; Emily had died a couple of weeks earlier. Williams had apparently envisaged the two surviving sisters engaged in mental labours, but Charlotte replies that they 'do not study; Anne cannot study now, she can scarcely read'.[5] A subsequent letter to the same recipient speaks of books sent by Smith,

Elder as 'our welcome and congenial resource when Anne is well enough to enjoy reading', as the following lines imply that she sometimes was.[6] These passages draw a line between cerebral effort and pleasurable perusal, two activities based on the same medium – the printed word – but engaging different faculties.

This distinction was observed by authorities on character-building endeavours who had accompanied the Brontë sisters since girlhood. A particularly interesting example is Isaac Watts, whose *The Improvement of the Mind* was given to Anne as a prize for good conduct at Roe Head.[7] Having stated that knowledge is acquired by five complementary methods – observation, reading, instruction by lectures, conversation and 'meditation . . . which . . . is called study' – Watts said:

Meditation or study includes all those exercises of the mind, whereby we render all the former methods useful for our increase in true knowledge and wisdom. It is by meditation that we come to confirm our memory of things that pass through our thoughts in the occurrences of life in our own experiences, and in the observations we make. It is by meditation that we draw various inferences, and establish in our minds general principles of knowledge. It is by meditation that we compare the various ideas which we derive from our senses, or from the operations of our souls, and join them in propositions. It is by meditation that we fix in our memory whatsoever we learn, and form our own judgment of the truth or falsehood, the strength or weakness, of what others speak or write. It is meditation or study, that draws out long chains of argument, and searches and finds deep and difficult truths which before lay concealed in darkness.[8]

Watts asserted that reading comprises many virtues, but that it is study that 'conveys the notions and sentiments of others to ourselves, so as to make them properly our own . . . [Our own judgment concocts] our intellectual food, and turns it into a part of ourselves'.[9]

A century later, Elizabeth Sandford made similarly exalted claims for study, reminding her readers that it is more than '[t]he mere act of receiving instruction': study 'furnishes the mind with matter to reflect on, and habituates it to think', involving 'the *entire* application of the mind'.[10]

Both Watts and Sandford emphasised that mental improvement was desirable in women as well as in men. Watts invited any female reader of his book to apply its contents to herself by the simple means of changing the gender of any masculine words in it;[11] Sandford pleaded for women to be granted access to the kind of training that would enable them to progress along 'the path of true wisdom'.[12] The contrast is an interesting one: what the eighteenth-century divine regarded as a natural option for a woman was a cause whose female champion comes across as distinctly defensive a hundred years later. The fact that Watts was a man and Sandford a woman is a relevant circumstance here, but hardly enough on its own to account for the difference: Sandford's embattled position must also be seen in the context of the debate on the middle-class woman's role in society which was taking a new turn in the 1830s.

Several factors contributed to the anxiety about the proper place and functions of the female sex in the 1830s and 1840s.[13] First of all, this was a time of general sociopolitical upheaval, with Parliamentary reform, Chartism, sectarian schism and so forth, revolutionary movements on the Continent supplying a rumbling *obbligato*. Educational developments during this period of unrest were complex, as preceding sections/chapters have indicated. For instance, the spread of literacy was not regarded as a favourable development by those who felt that – as a *Blackwood's* contributor put it – 'the extension of the power of reading to almost all the youth of the lower orders . . . has . . . produced the restless and feverish temper of the present times'.[14] Working-class men thus read seditious and otherwise allegedly harmful matter, of which there was a great deal. Indeed, there were unprecedented masses of publications of all kinds; as John Stores Smith put it in 1850, 'the ceaseless flux of printed matter that floods upon us' was a new – and, in Smith's opinion, not entirely welcome – development.[15] Many noted that the traditional predominance of religious matter in the production of books had vanished and were concerned about the concomitant secularisation of society. Commentators on condition-of-England issues were aghast at the irreligiousness of the so-called lower orders, where few children had any Biblical knowledge to speak of, let alone a sense of Christian morality rooted in religious instruction from responsible elders.

A soothing, steadying influence was needed in these troubled times; and regardless of the party-political domicile of a participant in the contemporary debate, he or she knew where it would have to come from: a religiously devout womanhood trained for and dedicated to housewifely duties. Looking around them, however, debaters saw far too few self-disciplined and self-sacrificing rulers of the domestic sphere. Instead, women competed for top prizes in the marriage-market – a market where accomplishments netted greater gains than the 'solid acquirements of mind' extolled by writers eager to 'raise the female character'.[16] Such writers were not only worried by the prevalence of the accomplishments. 'Blue-stocking' activity posed another threat to young women's acquiring the practical competence and submissive temper that would enable them to create the secure domesticity in which an improved British population should be formed.

Not even the most enthusiastic advocate of advanced studies for women could afford to leave his or her readers in any doubt that the chief object of a studious female was to be a virtuous and capable home-maker. Even Harriet Martineau took pains to point out that the most learned women also made the best housekeepers.[17] Charlotte Brontë's much-quoted correspondence with Robert Southey may be contemplated in this context: Southey reminded her that she had 'not yet been called' to a woman's 'proper duties', and that when (not if) she was, she would have little time for writing. In her answer, Charlotte resisted the implication that her home-making skills were unpractised: '[f]ollowing my Father's advice . . . I have endeavoured not only attentively to observe all the duties a woman ought to fulfil, but to feel deeply interested in them'.[18] This mutual genuflection before the ideal of the domestic female has grated on readers for generations;[19] but it must not be forgotten that both correspondents also acknowledged the power of literature, and that Southey regarded it as a force for good when sensibly handled – even in the life of a woman.

It is tempting to dismiss Charlotte's obeisance to womanly duties in her letter to Southey as a piece of defensive lip-service to the prevailing notions of the day, but such a gesture raises the danger of anachronistic reasoning. The curriculum at Morton School, for example, is worth contemplating in this context: among the marks of improvement in her 'scholars' that give Jane Eyre the greatest satisfaction are personal cleanliness, pleasant manners and neat (needle)work. When *Shirley* speaks out against the mistreatment of England's young women, confined to homes where they are denied the stimulus of meaningful occupation, the narrator's chief target is the waste of at-home daughters' time and faculties in useless pursuits about the house. Neither the Brontë fiction nor records of the sisters' lives suggest that they found traditional female employments repulsive or unworthy in themselves.[20] In fact, all three sisters took pride in executing them well.

READING AND STUDY IN THE FICTION OF THE BRONTËS

While there is no overt rebellion against domestic duties in the lives and works of the Brontës, reading and study certainly occupy much more space than housework of any description in the lives of those of their female characters who are able to choose their occupations. For instance, Diana and Mary Rivers took after their mother, 'a great reader', having 'liked learning . . . almost from the time they could speak' (*Jane Eyre* III.iii.343; these are Hannah's comments and they also apply to St John). When released from drudgery thanks to Uncle Eyre's inheritance, Diana, Mary and Jane Eyre herself spend much of their time in 'regular studies' (III.viii.396) whose laboriousness the narrator does not disguise. Lucy Snowe seeks a remedy for heartbreak in 'hard' study and 'a course of regular reading of the driest and thickest books in the library' (*Villette* XXIV.267). The forbiddingness of that occupation recalls Diana Rivers' 'Encyclopaedic reading' (*Jane Eyre* III.viii.396), another 'systematic' – as opposed to 'desultory' – self-educating pursuit (and one that Jane has not the slightest desire to emulate). Relieved from some of her teaching duties at Horton Lodge, Agnes Grey devotes more of her time to 'reading, study, and the practice of music' (*Agnes Grey* XI.85). The books in the library that is Edgar Linton's haven are also handled by his housekeeper and in due course studied by his daughter. Frances Henri worries that her efforts to support herself will leave her too little time and strength 'for reading or study' (*The Professor* XXI.177). Helen Huntingdon's husband, who never looks at any other printed matter than 'newspapers and sporting magazines', 'will not let [her] rest' till he has forced her to close any book she is reading (*The Tenant of Wildfell Hall* XXIV.197).

No villainous character, male or female, in the Brontë novels is studious; for instance, Heathcliff 'never reads' (*Wuthering Heights* II.xvii.266). Similarly, no virtuous man or woman is without intellectual aspirations; even William Farren in *Shirley* is lent books by the two heroines (II.vii.323). Not only are study and reading praiseworthy in members of both sexes, they are instrumental in breeding intimacy between men and women, too. Such intimacy can be invasive in an unfavourable sense, as Jane Eyre's and St John's becomes to her; but more often it assists the development of true love, as numerous instances from the novels testify.

The quoted examples from the Brontë fiction show that the writers repeatedly distinguished between 'reading' and 'study', just as Watts and Sandford did. The respective orientations of the two pursuits are seen to be different in that study is geared towards stocking and exercising the intellect, whereas reading develops the emotions, the aesthetic sensibility and the moral sense.[21] Naturally, there is confluence in that both occupations improve the whole, balanced personality in which a clear brain guides sympathetic feelings.[22] Besides, as the Riverses' reading of Schiller suggests, a text studied for the purpose of broadening a person's intellectual attainments may well excite the emotions, too.[23] Nevertheless, the Brontë novels frequently illustrate how different kinds of engagement with written works involve the affective and the cerebral faculties respectively.

As a scene from *Shirley* shows, reading is not a less profound activity than study in the fiction of the Brontës. The schooling of the feelings through literature is certainly no mere pastime in the chapter that Charlotte Brontë called 'Coriolanus' (I.vi).[24] Caroline Helstone, masterful for once, gives her millowner cousin Shakespeare's *Coriolanus* to read aloud, her stated purpose being 'to stir you; to give you new sensations . . . to make you feel your life strongly, not only your virtues, but your vicious, perverse points' (I.vi.89). By having Robert Moore 'take some of [Shakespeare's] soul into [his]', the otherwise so diffident girl assumes the authority and role of the instructor. As Robert reads on, his personal identification with Coriolanus moves from haughty relish to sombre recognition, not of a 'fault' – that is Caroline's word, and the proud man does not acknowledge it – but of an aspect of his personality which gives him pause.

The scene is quite extensive, covering about four pages which immediately lead over to another literary experience. Having read the comic scenes from *Coriolanus* with spirit and humour, Caroline – at Robert's request – repeats André Chénier's wistful poem 'La Jeune Captive', for which she had expressed a preference.[25] Watching her, Robert comes as close to falling in love with her as his rigid self-control will permit him. He swiftly pulls back before this new 'weakness' and 'phrenzy', fearing its ruinous effect on the ambitions that rule his life. The outcome of the double reading lesson is hence inconclusive; but it marks a station in Robert Gérard Moore's *éducation sentimentale*, and it is worth observing that his mentor is the girl whose superior moral worth he bows to at the end of the novel (III.xiv.640–1): ignorant and inexperienced she may be, but she possesses greater human wisdom than he, and that wisdom has been fostered by her reading.

It is Caroline Helstone, too, who repeats Cowper's 'The Castaway' on another occasion. This time Shirley is her listener, and again the execution is congenial. Like Anne Brontë in her poem 'To Cowper', and like many other Cowper admirers before and since, Charlotte Brontë's heroine utters the hope that Cowper's death translated him from earthly anguish to celestial bliss (II.i.226).[26] The recital sets off one of the most interesting conversations about literature in the fiction of the Brontës. Shirley and Caroline discuss Cowper's personality, Caroline bringing in Rousseau for comparison, and again the outwardly submissive Miss Helstone speaks with an authority that is almost stern. Like Robert before her Shirley recognises that authority, and she changes the subject – to Robert Moore (II.i.228).

One reason why Caroline can assert herself so forcefully through poetry is that she has learnt it by heart and thus appropriated it, being in the habit of doing so when she encounters '*real* poetry' (I.vi.95). Although 'The Castaway' is partly her own in more ways than one, she is not moved to tears by it: when Shirley expresses her surprise that her friend's voice remained steady throughout the recital, Caroline makes a memorable reply:

'Cowper's hand did not tremble in writing the lines: why should my voice falter in repeating them? Depend on it, Shirley, no tear blistered the manuscript of "The Castaway." I hear in it no sob of sorrow, only the cry of despair; but, that cry uttered, I believe the deadly spasm passed from his heart; that he wept abundantly, and was comforted.' (II.i.227)

It is hard to envisage anyone but a professional author of *belles lettres* behind these lines where the traditional notion of giving vent to emotion in writing is invested with a peculiar seriousness. Somewhat earlier, Caroline expressed her belief that the 'gift of poetry – the most divine bestowed on man – was . . . granted to allay emotions when their strength threatens harm' (II.i.227). Her belief coexists with contempt for those who write poetry to flaunt their learning and skill. Feeling, in her view, is the raw material of genuine poetry; but its overflow on to the page is a process whose terms the poet cannot dictate. A timely utterance gives the feeling relief, to misquote Wordsworth; but the timing of that utterance is beyond human control. While the views that Charlotte Brontë placed in Caroline's mouth are entirely in agreement with the most exalted Romantic conceptions of poetry, their severity anticipates the lofty austerity with which T. S. Eliot was to reject the giving-vent idea 70 years later.[27]

The passage becomes even more remarkable when considered in relation to the conflicting attitudes to women and poetry in the early nineteenth century. While Sarah Ellis asserted that poetry elevates a woman's mind and that '[a] woman without poetry, is like a landscape without sunshine', M. A. Stodart regarded it as a dangerous force: it was, she said, her own passion and her 'bane even in childhood . . . I know [poetry] to be deceitful and treacherous, and a very Circe'.[28] Antithetical as these views are, they have one thing in common: recognition of the power of poetry.

It is in that context that Jane Eyre's passionate tribute to Sir Walter Scott, and to poetic genius *per se*, belongs. The person who brings her a copy of Scott's *Marmion*, 'a new publication', is St John Rivers, whose rigorous nature is not incompatible with giving a young woman a verse romance to read.[29] The work sets off a dozen passionate lines in which the narrator acknowledges that 'the golden age of modern literature' has passed, but that poetry and genius still exist, indeed still rule, despite the envious efforts of small minds to destroy them (*Jane Eyre* III.vi.370).[30] The proper domicile of these '[p]owerful angels' is Heaven, from which they spread their 'divine influence'. A more decided counterblast to warnings such as Stodart's is scarcely imaginable.

Opinions as to whether women – young women particularly – should be allowed to read fiction were less polarised, but the question was still a live issue in the early nineteenth century. The trouble with fiction had been articulated by Hester Chapone:

> I would by no means exclude the kind of reading which young people are naturally most fond of; though I think the greatest care should be taken in the choice of those *fictitious stories* that so enchant the mind; – most of which tend to inflame the passions of youth, whilst the chief purpose of education should be to moderate and restrain them.[31]

M. A. Stodart was as concerned about the perils of fiction as Chapone, but she grudgingly admitted that 'a really well-written novel may occasionally be useful, as a species of relaxation to the mind after severe and long-continued labour'.[32] Even the heroine of Patrick Brontë's *The Maid of Killarney* was allowed 'a few Novels . . . which are not only harmless, but very entertaining and instructive'.[33]

Ironically, the only intimation in the Brontë fiction that novel-reading may indeed 'enchant the mind' with disastrous consequences occurs in *Wuthering Heights*, where Heathcliff explains Isabella's 'delusion' about his character as the outcome of her having imagined him 'a hero of romance' (I.xiv.133).[34] It seems plausible enough on the face of it, and Heathcliff's management of the early relationship – secret trysts, an elopement – would feed into the preconceptions of a wilful teenage girl with no experience of the world and a taste for fictional love stories. Even so, the few phrases that the as-yet-deluded Isabella uses about Heathcliff smack more of conduct literature than of romantic fiction ('he has an honourable soul, and a true one, or how could he remember [Catherine]?', I.x.91), and Heathcliff is hardly a reliable informant.

Those who would forbid or at least restrain women's reading of fiction must have realised, at least intermittently, that they were fighting a losing battle. For one thing, circulating subscription libraries were everywhere, helping to indemnify readers with modest means against the steeply rising prices of new books on the coat-tails of Scott's phenomenal success.[35] Glumly recalling bygone days when the 'dear box' from Hookham's subscription library arrived, a character in Frances Trollope's *The Vicar of*

Wrexhill (1837) speaks of the 'eager rejoicings of the whole family' at the sight of new 'lively novels and fancy-stirring romances' (fortunately the reign of the 'Evangelical Magazines, Christian Observers, Missionary Reports, and Religious Tracts' that replaced them was short-lived).[36] Mrs Ellis was no more wary of fiction for young female readers than of poetry, freely allowing that girls should have access to 'lighter works' such as novels, in addition to books on 'history, science, and even weightier themes'.[37]

However, an element of anxiety about proper reading matter for women is palpable in works on female education throughout the lives of the Brontës, father and children. The sisters were well aware of it, and surely grateful that no censorship was exercised over their own reading. This anxiety supported a whole courtesy-literature sub-genre, that of recommendations for reading. The conclusion of the often quoted letter written by the 18-year-old Charlotte Brontë to Ellen Nussey on 4 July 1834 looks like a deliberate attempt in this sub-genre.[38] The books Charlotte recommended to her less well-read friend – at the latter's request, she says – are much the same as the ones found in numerous published compilations of works thought suitable for young female readers. Charlotte's somewhat pompous assertions about the moral properties of works and readers are also paralleled in published 'letters' from *femmes savantes* to women friends, daughters and nieces.[39]

Many contemporaneous books on the education of girls contain lists of permissible authors, British and foreign. Among writers who were demonstrably known to the Brontës and who constantly feature in such lists are – besides the ubiquitous Shakespeare, Milton and Cowper – Bunyan, Addison and Steele, Pope, Johnson, Defoe, Thomson, Young, Burns, Wordsworth, Coleridge and Southey, and, of course, Scott. Many compilers would make a point of recommending women writers and praise them warmly as leading authors in their own right, worthy of being read by both sexes. Hannah More, Felicia Hemans and Anna Laetitia Barbauld are examples well known in Haworth Parsonage; exalted claims were also made for Joanna Baillie.[40] Occasional writers would mention Mary Wollstonecraft with respect – not an unproblematic stance in view of her notoriety, even several decades after her death.[41] A writer who occurs more frequently in these compilations than one might have expected is another infamous celebrity, Lord Byron: in 1835, for instance, the Sarah Stickney who later became Mrs Ellis boldly praised *Cain* for its skilfully portrayed female characters.[42]

Where both *belles lettres* and other kinds of writing are concerned, the preeminence of eighteenth-century writers in recommendations for reading and study is striking. In the *belles lettres* category, eighteenth-century poets are usually out in full force, including, in addition to those mentioned above, Gray, Collins, Shenstone and Akenside. Non-literary writers typically include Isaac Watts, a household name in Haworth Parsonage, and the Edgeworths. The persistence of reputations forged in earlier times is also noteworthy. Examples include John Locke's works from the turn of the century 1600–1700, including *Some Thoughts Concerning Education* of 1693, Bishop Joseph Butler's *Analogy* of 1736 and William Paley's *Horae Paulinae* of 1790 (Patrick Brontë owned a copy of the latter). The authority of Paley's *Evidences of Christianity* (1794) was still respectfully invoked in the 1830s, although signs that Paley's glory was beginning to fade are discernible.[43]

In view of what has been said above, Juliet Barker's statement that the eighteenth century 'was the period with which the Brontës were least familiar and with which they had least affinity' seems odd.[44] At the very least, they were certainly thoroughly acquainted with the Pre-Romantic poets and had read parts of Johnson, Swift and Defoe. The gulf between the eighteenth century and the second quarter of the nineteenth probably seems wider to today's literary scholars than it did to keen readers at the time of the Brontës. Present-day researchers are also too apt to assume that values and opinions which were first articulated a couple of decades into the 1800s are somehow more 'progressive' than those formulated 50 or 150 years earlier. This is a mistake, as – for instance – the perusal of works on education by Locke, the Edgeworths and Erasmus Darwin soon persuades the reader.[45] Indeed, it is tempting to speculate that an 1820s and 1830s household where eighteenth-century notions still prevailed might have been less restrictive to imaginative and intellectually precocious youngsters than one where the elders were eager to keep up with the latest fashions in child-rearing.

GLUTTONS OF BOOKS – THE BRONTËS' APPETITE FOR READING

The spread of literacy in the early nineteenth century did not always entail the infusion of text-borne excitement into young minds. Richard Altick has painted a dreadful picture of children taught to read by being force-fed at best dull and at (a frequent) worst incomprehensible chunks of texts. Not only was the content of such texts devoid of interest for the young reader; any glimmer of pleasure in the new skill would often be extinguished by the mode by which it was instilled, with relentless parsing, accounting for derivations and memorising.[46] Silent reading was unknown in schoolrooms, and insofar as books were seen there at all – rather than the flash-cards popularised by the monitorial system – they would be of a religious orientation and hence (as enlightened clergymen with educational experience, such as Patrick Brontë, knew) unappealing to youngsters. The result, in Altick's words, was 'a deep distaste for the printed word in countless pupils'.[47]

A more complete contrast to Haworth Parsonage in the 1820s and 1830s can hardly be imagined. A factor mentioned by Altick (pp. 152–3) may serve as a vehicle of transition from the schoolroom horrors sketched above to the home of the Brontë children: the availability of narratives. The small lending-libraries attached to some schools saw children hungry for stories making do even with accounts by missionaries, as long as there was a tale in there.

The young Brontës were lucky to grow up with *The Pilgrim's Progress*, *Gulliver's Travels*, *Robinson Crusoe*, the *Arabian Nights*, Aesop's *Fables* and James Ridley's *Tales of the Genii*. They will not have been told that the Bible should not be read as a story-book, a stricture levelled at many nineteenth-century children found to enjoy the Scriptures for the wrong reasons.[48] The story element in other works not usually thought of as primarily narrative in character – the *Aeneid* translated, *Paradise Lost*, Johnson's *Rasselas* – will have helped the young Brontës make their way through increasingly demanding literary works, the story-lines in Shakespeare's plays having a similar function.

The Brontë children's enthusiasm for literature is all over their juvenilia. Their home-made magazines remind us that much of their early acquaintance with the literary giants of the time, and of past times – in Britain and elsewhere – was mediated through periodicals, first of all *Blackwood's* and *Fraser's*. As recent scholarship, above all the magnificent work by Christine Alexander, has shown, such periodicals encouraged a heroisation of men of letters in the children. They gleefully adopted the disputatious tempers and self-assertive styles employed by magazine contributors in their own writings, including letters, teaching themselves to evolve different narratorial *personae* and attitudes.[49] Periodicals were full of stories that were more easily digested, especially by juvenile readers, than worthy tomes;[50] in a sense *Blackwood's* and *Fraser's* bridged the gap between the lightest reading and serious engagement with texts, rather as the *Classics Illustrated* and the *Reader's Digest* did in the twentieth century. As Heather Glen has pointed out, 'annuals' with such titles as *Forget Me Not*, *The Literary Souvenir* and *Friendship's Offering* will have made considerable impressions on the growing girls.[51] The *Leeds Mercury* and *Leeds Intelligencer* also contained some light reading, under headings such as 'Literary Selections', 'Extracts from

New Books' and 'Miscellaneous', offering titbits from newly published works.

For these youngsters, reading was, in other words, fun, giving them some of the greatest pleasures they knew and opening wide ranges of exciting experience to them, including creative activity. Branwell's letter to Wordsworth speaks of reading being a kind of craving, like eating and drinking.[52] Juvenile readers in the Brontë fiction are similarly motivated by pleasurable passion: young Victor in *The Professor* is 'a glutton of books' (XXV.242), and little Arthur reads to his mother 'with wonderful fluency', which suggests both aptitude and interest (*The Tenant of Wildfell Hall* VII.56). The child Jane Eyre 'liked reading, though of a frivolous and childish kind', as the mature narrator says (I.v.49). It is this favourable view of books and reading that emboldens her to speak to Helen Burns, engrossed in *Rasselas*.[53]

Helen's engagement with *Rasselas* is something much more serious and profound than Jane's fondness for thrilling tales and pictures. Completely absorbed in its last pages, the older girl kneels by the fire whose last glow sheds a feeble light on them, 'silent, abstracted from all round her by the companionship of a book' (I.vi.55).[54] The combination of 'silent' and 'companionship' is significant: the early nineteenth century was a time when seeking congenial society between the covers of a book perused in silence was becoming a common and accepted pastime in a way it had not been before, especially not for a woman.[55] Priscilla Wakefield might acknowledge, in 1817, that '[b]ooks are the best substitutes for the charms of society: they amuse the imagination, and enrich the mind with knowledge, when company cannot be collected';[56] but her description allowed for the idea of reading aloud in a small family circle, a pursuit regularly recommended by conduct-book writers.[57] Retiring into quiet reading could be regarded as a rejection of such society as there was. Some Brontë protagonists take exception to their spouses' withdrawing from them into libraries and books; such objections prove the unworthiness (in the case of Arthur Huntingdon) or at least incompatibility (Catherine Linton) of the resentful characters.[58] Shared reading and discussion of books is still very much a feature of rewarding human interaction in the fiction of the Brontës.[59] So, of course, was shared writing in their lives.

However, *Villette* affords us a fascinating glimpse of a kind of solitary engagement with books that seems thoroughly modern. Lucy Snowe describes the process of writing an essay in a manner known to most people who ever had to present a piece of research in a manner accessible to a demanding, though not necessarily specialist, audience:

. . . I got books, read up the facts, laboriously constructed a skeleton out of the dry bones of the real, and then clothed them, and tried to breathe into them life, and in this last aim I had pleasure. With me it was a difficult and anxious time till my facts were found, selected, and properly jointed; nor could I rest from research and effort till I was satisfied of correct anatomy[.] (XXXV.401)

It is hard to do more than speculate about the extent to which the toilsome studies on which all three Brontë sisters spent so much time brought intrinsic personal enjoyment, beyond the gratifying awareness of self-improving endeavours diligently performed. It has recently been suggested that Emily Brontë was not seriously interested in education, at least not after her teaching experiences at Law Hill and in Brussels.[60] Anne's years of patient systematic study may have been dictated by duty and little else. In the quoted passage from *Villette*, however, Charlotte Brontë describes a process where the mastering of fresh knowledge joins advanced reflection and structuring work – all jobs whose sustained arduousness has defeated the most brilliant minds – in a way that also brings a creative impulse into play. '[I]n this . . . I had pleasure' – and as the writings of the Brontës have afforded such variegated pleasure to so many, from the avid juvenile reader to the staid academic, it seems fitting to end this review of the Brontës' engagement with books on that note.

IV

Strategies and methods

Introductory Remarks to Section IV

The range of educational milieux in the Brontë novels is immense. Pupils of both sexes, all ages and very different social origins are instructed in all sorts of places – from the day nurseries of rich homes to the halls of large institutions of learning – by teachers of the most varied kinds. What these pupils and their real-life counterparts learnt was the topic of the preceding section; it remains to examine how they were taught. Looking at the Brontë works in the context of education in the early nineteenth century, how might successful educational activity be defined, what makes a teacher successful (or not) and in what ways can the fiction of the Brontës be seen to interact with the late-eighteenth-century and early-nineteenth-century pedagogical debate?

Before these questions can be answered, the 'range' concept should be contemplated from another perspective as well: that of quality. The difference between the best and the worst school in any system at any time is considerable. In the lifetime of the Brontës (as in our own), it was vast. The best-known novelists of the day left us a long list of appalling educational establishments, Dotheboys Hall and pre-reform Lowood Institute featuring at the top (or bottom, depending on how one looks at it). It has been suggested that the prevalence of horror schools in nineteenth-century fiction might be at least partly due to writers' knowing that it was 'the done thing' to be indignant about unsatisfactory education, even if one did not know a great deal about it.[1]

That idea begs the question of how much in the way of real insight we present-day scholars possess. As Harold Silver has reminded us, we do not know as much as we think we do about what actually went on in nineteenth-century schoolrooms.[2] There was probably a good deal of first-class pedagogical achievement of which we know little or nothing. Studying the Brontë novels and what we know of the sisters' lives is one way of filling in some of the blank spaces of our ignorance. Of course, the documentary value of works of fiction is notoriously uncertain; but after all the seven books were written by professional teachers, with experience of both domestic and school tuition at all levels and in two countries, and education is a persistent concern in them. Although the best-known school in the Brontë fiction is Lowood in the bad old days, that is in fact the only school in the Brontës' books to make it to the horror list. The others are good-enough institutions; indeed, the fictional narrators suggest that three of them are models of their kind: Mrs Crimsworth's school in Brussels, Mrs Grey's establishment in A– and the Externat de demoiselles in the Faubourg Clotilde, run by Lucy Snowe.[3]

This fourth section of *The Brontës and Education* is concerned with how teachers are seen to help pupils learn and grow into worthy and well-educated adults. The section is divided into two chapters. The first places the Brontë novels in the context of the pedagogical developments that took place in the lifetime of Patrick Brontë and his children. As those developments were to a considerable extent driven by ideas that evolved in the eighteenth century, at home and abroad, the historical and geographical scope is wide, extending from Jean Jacques Rousseau in 1760s France to James Kay-Shuttleworth in mid-nineteenth-century Britain.

The second chapter moves from the level of ideas to that of everyday practice in the schoolroom. The focus is on the nuts and bolts of instruction, such as ensuring silence and order, promoting progress and disciplining young transgressors.

The issue of rote learning was a matter of both policy and practice. The second chapter hence ends with a consideration of this vital question, a consideration which leads up to a brief sketch of the ideal pedagogue in the fiction of the Brontës.

CHAPTER 12

Pedagogical purposes and principles

As previous chapters have pointed out, character development was regarded as the most important function of any educational undertaking in the nineteenth century. In the words of the great Continental educational philosopher Johann Friedrich Herbart (1776–1841), 'The one and whole work of education may be summed up in the concept of morality'.[1] However desirable academic ability and well-practised accomplishments might be, educationists at home and abroad were forever asserting that good manners and virtuous habits, exercised within the social framework to which the pupil belonged, were the true marks of a good education, whether it was provided by Eton, a governess or the village school.

The Brontë fiction as a body supports that view. The academic attainments of William Crimsworth, Louis Moore and M. Paul would not have invested them with hero status in Charlotte Brontë's novels without their personal virtues. The chief of those virtues are truthfulness, uprightness and good feeling, qualities signally lacking in other learned gentlemen, such as Messieurs Pelet and Rochemorte.[2] Similarly, as a preceding chapter showed, all the accomplishments of Annabella Lowborough and Blanche Ingram are powerless to win them happiness: without personal worth they cannot even secure their worldly aims in the long term.

It should be borne in mind that the predominance of character formation was not a 'conservative' attitude in education: every theorist, whatever his or her nationality, religious faith and political allegiance, was fundamentally concerned with the making of good human beings. Ideas about what a good human being was varied, of course; but the conviction that it was the business of education to improve the human race was common to all. The seriousness and urgency of that conviction inform the many schemes in which ardent educationists invested their time, energy and such funds as they could lay their hands on. Experimental schools operated for a limited period of time – sometimes, as in the case of Hazelwood and Cheam under Mayo, for less than a decade – but part of their legacy is still with us today.[3]

The late eighteenth and early nineteenth centuries in Britain witnessed radical developments in the way people thought about how children and young people should be taught, and why they should want to learn any-thing in the first place. There was a strong native tradition to build on, including, among others, John Locke and later Henry Home, Lord Kames. Even so, and despite the superiority of freeborn Britons so persistently maintained by patriots like Charlotte Brontë, much of the inspiration for the men and women who transformed British teaching in the lifetime of the Brontës (father and children) came from the Continent. Nobody who took the slightest interest in education in the early nineteenth century could avoid the powerful currents that emanated from France, Switzerland and Germany; and Continental concepts such as *Didaktik* were well known among, and used by, British educationists.[4]

Jean Jacques Rousseau's *Émile, ou Traité de l'éducation*, first published in 1762, was snatched up by British intellectuals, notably David Hume. However, something of the ambivalence that characterised Rousseau's own experiences in Britain adheres to his name whenever it crops up in the works of British educationists in the late eighteenth and early nineteenth centuries: his importance is acknowledged, sometimes handsomely; but there are eddies of disagreement, embarrassment and – occasionally – hostility.[5]

Rousseau's idea that the young child's natural instincts are sound and that subsequent corruption comes from the world in which he or she grows to adulthood was of course highly controversial from a theological point of view. Not only did Rousseau have to flee from Roman-Catholic France as a result of professing such opinions; they roused much consternation among British Protestants as well. The anxiety about original sin that caused loving Evangelical parents to adopt oppressive surveillance policies and harsh corrective measures towards their offspring obviously ran counter to Rousseau's views.[6] The vehemence of the clash between these irreconcilable conceptions contributes to the sense of unease which is so often felt in works by British writers on education between 1770 and 1830 as soon as Rousseau is mentioned.

Transposed to the realities of the schoolroom, this clash manifested itself in the distinction between teacher-driven and pupil-driven teaching. In the latter, Rousseau's influence was mediated by the Continental educationists he inspired, above all Johann Heinrich Pestalozzi and Philipp Emanuel von Fellenberg (and, somewhat later, Friedrich Wilhelm August Fröbel). These men evolved school policies which were in fact far removed from the *Émile* model, whose inadequacy as a practical educational programme many an early Rousseau devotee had been forced to acknowledge.[7] However, they proceeded from a Rousseauan conviction that the child's natural desire to learn about the world is the mainspring of successful education. Pestalozzi encouraged spontaneity and self-activity among his pupils while adhering to a systematic principle: a grasp of simple facts and circumstances would gradually lead to an understanding of complex phenomena and processes. This kind of learning engaged the individual pupil's complete attention, fostering a kind of intuition or mental energy which Pestalozzi called *Anschauung*.[8]

Pestalozzi's model establishment in Yverdon in French-speaking Switzerland attracted a number of British visitors over the years; there was even talk of a 'colonie britannique'. Among the distinguished British visitors who came to see Pestalozzianism in action was Dr Charles Mayo, who applied Pestalozzian ideas and practices in his own experimental school.[9] In the early decades of the nineteenth century, Pestalozzi's and Fellenberg's pedagogical theories became generally known throughout the British Isles. From the 1830s onwards, they had a particularly influential advocate in James Kay-Shuttleworth. While Kay-Shuttleworth's powerful hands-on reform work started out from the situation in Britain, part of his ideological groundwork was hence imported from the Continent.[10]

One British visitor to Yverdon came away convinced that his own educational system was superior to Pestalozzi's. Nobody who knows anything about Dr Andrew Bell's personality will be surprised to hear that he was unimpressed with Pestalozzi's life's work in comparison with his own.[11] To be fair to Bell, his monitorial system was practised on an entirely different scale from Pestalozzi's pedagogy.[12] Bell's project was the massive extension of literacy among the poorer classes, and this, with all its shortcomings, his and Lancaster's method accomplished. Old pictures of monitorial schools show hundreds of children's faces turned towards a few teenage boys, the 'monitors', who are themselves monitored by a single schoolmaster.[13] It is hard to imagine a more extreme representation of a teacher-driven system, implemented with a minimum of teachers and without even the faintest element of individually motivated exploration on the pupils' part.[14]

At the time when the Brontë sisters took up education as a profession, the names Bell and Pestalozzi were sufficiently established to be referred to in passing by anyone who spoke about teaching. In 1831, for instance, Elizabeth Sandford ruefully admitted, starting out from the Thomson quotation about the 'Delightful Task!' that had long been a cliché in works on education:

Instruction is not without its trials. We have heard, in poetry, how delightful it is to 'rear the tender thought;' but we doubt whether any of us can altogether sympathise with the beau idéal of the bard. In spite of Bell and Pestalozzi, it must ever be a work of patience to teach grammar and orthography.[15]

LEARNING AS LABOUR IN THE BRONTË NOVELS

The dimension of hard slog in education, for teacher and pupil alike, is present throughout Charlotte and Anne Brontë's novels. Some of the sharpest irony expressed by the narrator of *Agnes Grey* is reserved for parents who fail to realise that 'nothing can be taught to any purpose without some little exertion on the part of the learner' (VII.64). Mrs Murray's sole concern is that her children should be comfortable and a credit to her, 'with the least possible exertion on their part, and no exercise of authority on mine' (VII.60).

Irrespective of whether its author intended it, *Agnes Grey* may be regarded as an anti-Rousseau voice in the contemporary debate on education. In this book, extreme youth in a child does not bespeak healthy innocence, far from it. When, aged four, little Fanny Bloomfield entered the schoolroom, she was 'a mischievous, intractable little creature, given up to falsehood and deception, young as she was' (III.30), says Agnes-the-narrator. As Agnes gives the reader to understand that the child's parents had little to do with their second daughter, Fanny's viciousness cannot very well be imputed to their bad influence. As for the nurse Betty, the fostering of such flaws as false-ness does not seem to have been on her – essentially survival-orientated – agenda ('she had not the task of teaching, nor was she so responsible for the conduct of her charge'; IV.41). In other words, it is impossible to see even this child, the youngest pupil in the book, as trailing any clouds of Rousseauan glory. In fact, the much older hoyden Matilda Murray seems downright sound in comparison.

In Charlotte Brontë's novels, falseness in a pupil is characteristically associated with foreignness and especially apt to be activated in situations involving work. Given the opportunity, work-shy Continental-European pupils will resort to cheating as a means of escaping the demands made by their teachers. Hence Madame Beck's constant surveillance: according to Lucy Snowe, the directress herself admits that her régime would not have been necessary with young Englishwomen, on account of their 'more real and reliable probity'; but with Continental children, who have never enjoyed freedom under responsibility, it is the only option (*Villette* VIII.73). In the same context, Madame Beck also acknowledges that English girls are intellectually superior. The narrator of *Villette* delivers another kick at foreigners in her description of Fräulein Anna Braun's surprise at Lucy and Paulina's progress in German; Fräulein Braun, after all, was '[a]ccustomed to instruct foreign girls, who hardly ever will think and study for themselves – who have no idea of grappling with a difficulty, and overcoming it by dint of reflection or application' (XXVI.303). Lucy Snowe is not, of course, Charlotte Brontë; but in view of the work ethos that pervades Charlotte's writings, it is hard to read this as anything but a resounding condemnation of Continental-European policies and practices in education from someone who claims to have experienced them at first hand.

Only one of the Brontë novels marks a departure from the idea that valuable knowledge cannot be gained except through hard work. It is interesting that Emily Brontë, who was obviously capable of massive intellectual endeavour, allows several characters in *Wuthering Heights* to speak like highly educated people without implying that their attainments were bought at the price of effort. Heathcliff's reappearance after three years with the address and bearing of a gentleman is the most striking example.[16] It is not the only one, though. Nelly acquires the polish that Lockwood comments on by looking into Edgar Linton's library books, which does not sound especially strenuous; the curate's services as a tutor are presented as an option rather than a necessity for Linton Heathcliff, and his attentions to the first generation of children at the Heights and the Grange are only mentioned in passing (I.v.35, in a parenthesis, and I.vi.40); and despite Nelly's statement that Hareton 'was not to be civilized with a wish' (II.xviii.280), the process seems remarkably smooth (II.xix.286). Young Cathy's education is administered by one teacher only, the paternal tutor who knows how to make it 'an amusement' (II.iv.167). Nelly adds, 'fortunately, curiosity and a quick intellect urged her into an apt scholar; she learnt rapidly and eagerly, and did honour to his teaching'. The odd reference to stumbling and tottering (II.xvii.267) does not detract from the impression that book-learning comes with a minimum of trouble in *Wuthering Heights*.

One possible reason for this discrepancy between *Wuthering Heights* and the other Brontë novels is mentioned elsewhere.[17] Another is that Emily Brontë did not regard intellectual pursuits as inherently laborious, either because they constituted 'an amusement' to her or because her intellectual abilities were so extraordinary as to allow her to acquire a good deal of knowledge without great sustained effort, or both these factors combined. After all, she had considerable freedom in her self-education and hence ample opportunity to learn what interested her. Apart from the short spells at Cowan Bridge and Roe Head she was never subjected to an institutional curriculum, and her reluctance to perform the tasks M. Heger set her and Charlotte (see below) suggests someone who was not accustomed to allowing others to dictate what or how she should study.

According to one scholar, Emily may have found the teaching at Roe Head 'childish and unstimulating', entirely inadequate to satisfy her 'thirst for education'.[18] If one accepts that she did experience such a thirst and satisfied it in ways that entailed hard work on her part, the absence of a hard-slog dimension in her novel may be accounted for by other means than an assumption that she did not care about education. To indulge in some brief biographical speculation, perhaps all the talk of 'fagging' and 'exertion' that Emily Brontë heard from other family members provoked her into allowing her fiction to display a more insouciant attitude.[19]

The point matters because the suggestions in *Wuthering Heights* that education is somehow optional and may be acquired without labour coexist with repeated indications that it is essential to the development of characters and plot.[20] While it would be wrong to say that education is unimportant in *Wuthering Heights*, the focus is not on the process of acquiring the status and habits of an educated person, but on the possession or lack of that status and those habits. The swift civilising of adult Hareton could be interpreted as implying support for the idea that a successful education does not necessarily have to be acquired by toiling children, and seen as conveying a measure of support for Rousseau to that extent.[21] Another circumstance that brings Emily Brontë closer to Rousseau than her sisters is the strength of the as yet unwarped love between Heathcliff and Catherine as children.[22]

MOTIVATION IN LEARNING AND TEACHING

Hareton Earnshaw certainly has a powerful motivation for study, and while late-eighteenth- and early-nineteenth-century educationists may not have used that particular word, they were very much aware of the phenomenon. All agreed, in one way or another, that the acquisition of an education entails both pleasure and pain. Having accepted that, their next question was how the pleasure could be cultivated and the pain made bearable.

Realising that there is no pleasure in being made to do something one has no mind to, the teachers of two centuries ago exercised great ingenuity in stimulating their pupils' thirst for knowledge. Appealing to the young person's natural curiosity was an obvious method for which no foreign authorities had to be invoked. Indeed, the much-maligned Richmal

Mangnall stated that her questions on history were 'intended to awaken a spirit of laudable curiosity in young minds'.[23]

A sure way of extinguishing such curiosity is to confront the learner with unintelligible material. Another pedagogue whose work was studied by the Brontë children, 'Mr Porny' (Antoine Pyron du Martre), prided himself on explaining every rule as he went along. Step by step, everything is made clear to the *'young Tyro'*, who is 'led gradually, as it were by the hand, from *known Parts to those that are unknown'*.[24] The picture evoked by such images is that of an enquiring mind moving forward of its own volition and on the strength of conquered knowledge, in accordance with the best European pedagogical traditions. In the words of a seventeenth-century educationist, approvingly quoted in the House of Commons on 20 June 1839: 'aidez seulement leur esprit, et mettez les en chemin de trouver ces vérités dans leur propre fonds'.[25]

The hands that lead 'young Tyros' need to be attached to kindly and good-natured preceptors, and the educationists of two hundred years ago were perfectly conscious of the fact. Time and again, writers of recommendations for teachers of all sorts emphasised the importance of, as Mary Maurice put it, '[cultivating] in themselves a cheerful spirit'.[26] One of the better-known teachers' manuals, Jacob Abbott's *The Teacher*, stressed the usefulness of humour in the classroom.[27] Kindness was the watchword in Robert Owen's New Lanark school, where the pupils' 'happiness' was as essential as – indeed, a vital part of – the formation of their characters.[28] In the words of a scholarly tribute to the British forerunner of Fröbel, Samuel Wilderspin, this father of modern infant schooling in England 'knew that cheerfulness is the sky beneath which everything flourishes'.[29]

Similarly, educationists in the time of the Brontës were well aware that the best teaching presupposed the pupils' acceptance of and interest in their masters' plans for their instruction. Pupils should be encouraged to regard the success or failure of their school as a matter of personal concern.[30] In Abbott's words, 'the co-operation of the majority . . . is absolutely essential to success'.[31]

Delight in learning for its own sake was another recognised motivating factor long before Fröbel, in whose writing and practice it was especially prominent.[32] In order for the acquisition of knowledge to be enjoyable, two conditions must be met: the subject-matter must be of some interest to the pupil, and his or her capabilities must be adequate.[33] Reading and writing, for instance, should not be forced. (A particularly appealing and characteristically concrete example from the Edgeworths' *Practical Education* is the warning against putting too young children under pressure to write '*a pretty letter*'.[34]) A reader published around 1840 was intended for children who had just 'overcome . . . the mechanical difficulty of reading' and were '*beginning to enjoy* the perusal of a book'. The aspect of enjoyment is clearly crucial, pieces of poetry being included to 'improve the taste and excite the affections'.[35]

Richard Altick's gloomy picture of the reading matter available to children in elementary schools should not obscure the fact that luckier beginners might take their first steps aided by the works of first-class writers for juvenile readers. As M. A. Stodart put it in 1842, 'It is observable that none but women of the highest talent, have really succeeded in writing for children', mentioning Anna Laetitia Barbauld and Maria Edgeworth as examples.[36] These writers' stories for children were great favourites in homes able to buy or borrow them. It is significant that Lucy Snowe makes Désirée Beck work with 'some little essay of Mrs. Barbauld's' (*Villette* VIII.76). While Edgeworth's many stories for juvenile readers, including the book-length *Harry and Lucy*, contained a patent moral dimension, they were lively and entertaining, and children enjoyed them. At the same time they were less sensational than Mary Martha Sherwood's *The History of the Fairchild Family* (1818), which was frowned on by a number of writers on education for girls.[37] Barbauld and Edgeworth might be criticised on religious grounds;[38] but the general esteem in which they were held as women of letters ensured that their works for young children conquered nurseries even in households where light entertainment was regarded with suspicion, imparting at least some degree of pleasure to reading lessons.

While Barbauld and Edgeworth were consistently praised for their works for children, early-nineteenth-century British writers on education often complained about the lack of good schoolbooks. To some extent this dissatisfaction was associated with disapproval of rote-learning.[39] Mrs Marcet's volumes were usually exempt from criticism, though, and it is not difficult for a present-day reader to see why: Marcet's pedagogical skill shows in the way she guides children into her subject-matter, involving them and encouraging them to feel pleased with their progress.[40] Harriet Martineau testified to the esteem in which she was held: 'Mrs. Barbauld's "Early Lessons" were good; Miss Edgeworth's were better, but Mrs. Marcet's are transcendent, as far as they go'.[41]

Sunny scenes of joyous learning are comparatively rare in the fiction of the Brontës, but all the motivating factors reviewed above appear in the novels, too. For instance, Helen Burns knows so much about Charles I because she takes a keen personal interest in the martyred king and the processes that led to his downfall. The reason why the daydreamer manages to stay alert during Miss Temple's lessons is that the superintendent supplies fresh food for Helen's capacious intellect and knows how to make it tasty: she 'has . . . something to say which is newer than my own reflections: her language is singularly agreeable to me, and the information she communicates is often just what I wished to gain' (*Jane Eyre* I.vi.57; see also p. 53).[42]

If references to the positive delights of receiving instruction are not numerous in the Brontë fiction, nor are instances of keen pleasure in teaching. To be sure, Frances Crimsworth '[seems] to feel a certain enjoyment in the occupation' of teaching, according to her husband (*The Professor* XXV.231) – although that is surely a remarkably guarded phrase from a narrator who is himself a professional in the field of education, in a work of fiction by an experienced teacher (one even senses a degree of surprise that anybody should take real pleasure in imparting instruction). Like Miss Temple, Frances is eloquent in communicating her favourite subjects. M. Paul in *Villette* is sometimes an exhilarating teacher and sometimes an atrocious one, depending on whether the subject agrees with him. Madame Beck, ever self-possessed, does not need to be personally inspired to teach well: what makes her a successful pedagogue is her ability to present the subject-matter effectively. Even Lucy, who detests her, is 'pleased and edified with her clear exposition of the subject in hand' – a handsome tribute from one fictional professional to another, formulated by someone who was herself a professional in real life (*Villette* XXXV.398).

It has come to be seen as an accepted fact that the Brontë sisters themselves were not good teachers, and the available evidence does favour such a view. Certainly the eruption of anger at pupils disturbing young Charlotte Brontë's thoughts does not suggest a natural aptitude for teaching.[43] If it is true that Emily as a teacher at Law Hill said she preferred the school dog to the pupils, a similar aversion may be suspected in her case.[44] The fact that the Robinson girls were so warmly attached to Anne appears to have had more to do with her personality than with inspirational teaching.

However, it seems somewhat uncharitable to say, as many have done, that the Brontë sisters disliked children.[45] They may not have had the knack of getting on with *all* children that some enviable people possess, but the absence of that particular skill does not justify talk of a general dislike. All three of them were more or less ill at ease among strangers of all ages. Besides, Charlotte and Anne's governessing experiences were hardly conducive to the development of a general affection for children. Occasional passages in Charlotte's letters speak of a certain fondness for a particular child;[46] and as Edward Chitham has pointed out, Anne Brontë clearly had a maternal streak.[47]

In other words, the Brontë sisters probably liked some children and disliked others, as most people do – but two circumstances support the notion that their pedagogical abilities and ambitions were indeed limited. One is the disgust Charlotte articulated with reference to teaching, in letters and other documents such as her Roe Head Journal. Emily's and Anne's obvious unhappiness in their teaching positions belongs in this context, too. All teachers know that complaining about their jobs and their pupils will somehow, in some degree, reflect badly on themselves as professionals – however dreadful the circumstances, a failure is still a failure. It is surely significant that this aspect did not bother the Brontës. True, the recipients of their complaints were close friends, family members and diaries – but the intensity of the combined hostility and misery is telling.

The other circumstance which indicates that 'the old business teach – teach – teach' was nothing so much as a wearisome duty, at least for Charlotte Brontë, is a literally negative one.[48] It is the complete absence, in all the Brontë writings, of the experience which (the salary excepted) does more than anything else to keep good pedagogues in their jobs: the experience of 'getting through', of seeing and feeling the spark fly across. Charlotte Brontë described it from the point of view of the pupil-recipient or the spectator, never from that of the teacher. None of her protagonists continues to teach after it ceases to be an economic necessity, and renouncing it brings no regrets, either in the short or the long term. It is hard to escape the conclusion that instructing the young is a chore which, if anything, impedes the life-long self-instruction project – the 'reading and study' – that the Brontë fiction represents as the mandatory pursuit of every morally responsible and thinking individual.[49]

A MASTER AND HIS ANCESTRY: THE PEDAGOGY OF CONSTANTIN HEGER

In Brussels in 1842, Charlotte and Emily Brontë were taught by a peculiarly spark-emitting pedagogue. 'They wanted learning. They came for learning. They would learn', as Gaskell's *Life* of Charlotte Brontë so memorably declared;[50] and the outcome of their quest is evident throughout Charlotte's writings, especially, of course, *The Professor* and *Villette*. The ensuing review of Constantin Heger's pedagogical principles and practices forms a transition between the two chapters of this section.

Thanks to Sue Lonoff's edition of Charlotte and Emily's Brussels essays, we possess meticulously presented first-hand records of Heger's work as an essay supervisor. The other main sources that offer themselves to a student of

Constantin Heger as a teacher are Gaskell's *Life*, where the author draws on conversation with Heger himself in 1856;[51] Frederika Macdonald's *The Secret of Charlotte Brontë* of 1914;[52] Erik Ruijssenaars' two booklets on Charlotte Brontë's Brussels;[53] and a recent article by Sue Lonoff on Charlotte Brontë's education.[54]

Both Gaskell and Macdonald must be treated with caution as sources of information on the Brontës in Brussels. To begin with, their accounts are based on what they were told, and experienced, in the mid- and late 1850s, after Charlotte Brontë's death and a good many years after her and Emily's sojourn in Brussels. Then there is the matter of their personal agendas: Heger and Gaskell had a joint interest in concealing Charlotte's passion for her Brussels master;[55] and Macdonald was reminiscing about her distant teens, writing in affectionate memory of a recently deceased brother who had shared her Brussels past. In addition, Macdonald had read both Charlotte's novels and Gaskell's biography, which disqualifies her book as a Brontë-independent source. Even so, neither writer had any reason to invent details pertaining to Heger's pedagogical ambitions and his modes of instruction, and the compatibility of their accounts in those respects is reassuring. Lonoff, who (rightly) questions the odd detail in Heger's statements to Gaskell, does not doubt their essential good faith.[56] Consequently, a presentation of Constantin Heger's teaching aims and methods on the basis of Gaskell's and Macdonald's books ought to be reasonably reliable.

There is no need to recapitulate the many existing accounts of Heger's work on the Brontës' essays in detail. Suffice it to say that his dedication to his English pupils' development as prose writers is in evidence all over their work, especially Charlotte's. While the medium was French, and grammatical and idiomatic correctness was paramount, Heger's concern with argumentative and metaphorical effectiveness, register and tone must have done much to develop Charlotte's gift for persuasiveness in English, too. Ironically enough, her mature literary style only emerged when she abandoned the high-flown rhetoric which matched Heger's own predilections a little too well.[57] In other words, Heger's pedagogical success as Charlotte Brontë's essay supervisor was of the highest order: his teaching did not impose the instructor's personal preferences on the student, it empowered her to develop her own voice. The tools he gave her were wider knowledge, increased linguistic and analytical proficiency and greater intellectual rigour.

Macdonald's chapter on her first meeting with 'Charlotte Brontë's Professor' starts out from Heger's motto to the effect that teaching may be a matter of sowing rather than of outright bestowal – 'quelquefois, donner, c'est semer'.[58] That principle expresses an attitude recommended by pedagogues since Antiquity: humility before the preceptor's role.[59] However, it should not be interpreted as a strategy of self-effacing support of the 'adviser' or 'facilitator' kind often recommended in present-day pedagogical guidelines: Heger was by all accounts an authoritative teacher, who dominated his classrooms and lecture-halls completely. Charismatic, enthusiastic and eloquent, 'he told people what they ought to think about things', in Macdonald's artless phrase.[60] If he saw himself as a sower, he reserved the right to choose his seeds and where, how and when to sow them.

Fascinated by the man's magnetic personality, Charlotte Brontë was soon happy to submit to his authority; the unaffected Emily, not surprisingly, resisted it. If there is any record of Emily's willing submission to any externally imposed régime, it has not found its way into the core works of Brontë scholarship. Whatever has been said, especially in recent years, about Charlotte's fashioning her sisters' posthumous reputation, one sentence from her 'Biographical Notice of Ellis and Acton Bell' stands out as unchallengeable: 'her nature stood alone'.[61]

The method that Heger proposed for training the sisters' language awareness was one that Emily would be especially disposed to reject: imitation of the styles of eminent authors.[62] In Gaskell's words, '[she] said that . . . by adopting it, they should lose all originality of thought and expression'. Characteristically, it was an instant response. Charlotte's slow, reluctant acceptance was equally characteristic: 'she also doubted the success of the plan; but she would follow out M. Héger's advice, because she was bound to obey him while she was his pupil'.[63]

Charlotte's attitude is significant for a reason ignored by previous Brontë critics: it is that of a professional in education. Since the days when pedagogical principles in the Western world began to be articulated in writing, in Classical Antiquity, the pupil's duty to submit to the master's guidance has been one of the two rules for successful instruction (the other being the master's obligation to teach well).[64] A woman who wanted to run her own school needed to understand the first principles of education, and from that point of view Charlotte's reaction to Heger's proposal was much more mature than Emily's.

Learning by imitation is not a highly esteemed pedagogical method in our own time, and a present-day reader will probably instinctively sympathise with Emily; but for thousands of years it was a mainstay of education. It is easy to imagine the mind-shackling effects of this method in the hands of indifferent instructors. When employed by an able teacher, however, it could be a step towards a level of attainment where an acute intelligence would be able to move with an assurance all the greater for the practice. That Heger was such a teacher is clear from his ambitious essay-marking; and in Charlotte's case at least (as many scholars have pointed out, the effect of his teaching on Emily is much harder to assess) the results justify the means.

It should be borne in mind that imitation as a pedagogical instrument in the hands of a good teacher was meant to be an exercise promoting rhetorical and stylistic awareness, not a drill intended to repress individual style.[65] One of Heger's rules for apprentice writers shows that he was conscious of the dangers involved: 'One must not read, before sitting down to write, a great stylist with a marked manner of his own; unless this manner happens to resemble one's own'.[66] Imitation was hence something more than mere parroting; it called for a deliberate effort first to analyse and then to employ what masters of the craft had used to great effect.

A step upward from imitation (doing the same as an admirable achiever) is emulation (doing as well as an admirable achiever). In her insightful article on Charlotte Brontë's education, Sue Lonoff has emphasised that Heger encouraged emulation in his pupils.[67] Emulating the great French writers they studied was an unrealistic aim, of course. However, if they could not hope to equal the 'models of excellence' (Lonoff's phrase) they imitated, they would at least strive for top places among their own peers. Competition along those lines was already familiar to Charlotte Brontë, whose school medals as top pupil in her class at Roe Head bore the inscription 'Emulation Rewarded' and whose *Professor* narrator is confident that 'emulation, thirst after knowledge – the glory of success' will 'stir and reward' his son at Eton.[68]

Emulation is another pedagogical tool that has been employed by educators for thousands of years. Constantin Heger had probably read what Charles Rollin wrote about it in the classic *Traité des études*:

Le grand avantage des écoles, c'est l'émulation. Un enfant y profite de ce qu'on lui dit à lui-même, et de ce qu'on dit aux autres. Il verra tous les jours son maître approuver une chose, corriger l'autre; blâmer la paresse de celui-ci, louer la diligence de celui-là: il mettra tout à profit; l'amour de la gloire lui servira d'aiguillon pour le travail. Il aura honte de céder à ses égaux; il se piquera même de surpasser les plus avancés. Quels efforts ne fait point un bon écolier pour primer dans sa classe et pour remporter les prix! Voilà ce qui donne de l'ardeur à de jeunes esprits; et une noble émulation bien ménagée, dont on aura soin de bannir la malignité, l'envie, la fierté, est un des meilleurs moyens pour les conduire aux plus grandes vertus et aux plus difficiles entreprises.[69]

Heger has been presented as a forward-looking educator, a representative of a 'progressive', post-Rousseau tendency in teaching.[70] In fact, he seems to have been a fairly orthodox follower of the great masters of Western pedagogy through the centuries. On one point after another, his educational ideals as recorded in existing sources are seen to be in agreement with the principles articulated by Rollin, who in his turn drew primarily on the ancients but also on contemporaries such as Fénelon and 'M. Locke, Anglais'.[71]

For instance, Rollin emphasised that one of the teacher's first duties is to become thoroughly familiar with the individual pupil(s), so as to establish a basis for their work together in the pupils' capacities and existing knowledge; similarly, one of Heger's fundamental precepts was to 'study the pupils, to know each one of them'.[72] Macdonald's account of the mixture of fear and affection that Heger inspired in his pupils parallels Rollin's insistence that the teacher must 'se faire aimer et craindre'.[73] Even Heger's use of contemporary literature for educational purposes has a counterpart in Rollin's *Traité*, which frequently draws on writers from the recent past. Rollin the writer may not be quite so up to date in his selection of authors worth bringing into the schoolroom as Heger the teacher was in 1842, but his view of literature as an object of study is similar: it should be taught and learnt '*par rapport à l'esprit et au cœur*'.[74]

These examples of agreement between a French educational classic and Constantin Heger's pedagogical ambitions and practices are not quoted in order to make Charlotte Brontë's professor seem less remarkable than he was. Nor should they be taken to suggest that he was not alive to pedagogical innovation in the late eighteenth and early nineteenth centuries. For instance, Macdonald's anecdote about his having taught her fractions and integers with the aid of a bag of macaroons and half a *brioche* comes across as a beautiful example of a Pestalozzian object lesson.[75] Rather, they confirm what educationists of all ages have known: that first-class teaching was always a matter of opening the minds, senses and feelings of pupils to what the instructor wished to communicate, and that the ways in which that objective may be achieved do not after all differ so very drastically from one century to the next. Whatever methods a pedagogue uses, natural inclination and aptitude have much to do with his or her success.

What made Frederika Macdonald remember Constantin Heger with gratitude all her life, despite his occasional moods, was his love of teaching. This is her account of the moment that led up to the macaroon-and-*brioche* lesson:

The funny and pleasant thing about M. Heger was that he was so fond of teaching, and so truly in his element when he began it, that his temper became sweet at once; and I loved his face when it got the look upon it that came in lesson-hours: so that, whereas we were hating each other when we crossed the threshold of the door, we liked each other very much when we sat down to the table; and I had an excited feeling that he was going to make me understand.[76]

It is a description which Charlotte Brontë would surely have recognised.

CHAPTER 13

Schoolroom practices

While the man whose tutoring left such a profound mark on Charlotte Brontë's life and work taught in a foreign setting, her fiction gives her reader to understand that the best hope of succeeding as a teacher is to be allowed to teach in Britain. The reason is, of course, as the preceding chapter suggested, that the children of freeborn Britons are uncorrupted by the duplicity on which discipline in a Continental-European educational establishment necessarily rests. Falseness being the only way in which foreign young people can cope with the perpetual restraints and surveillance they are subjected to, whatever innate soundness and truthfulness they may have been born with is trained out of them. By contrast, English pupils possess finer feelings which it is the teacher's job to encourage and develop. A shy instructor like Caroline Helstone benefits personally from these feelings; fortunately for her, her Sunday-school girls like and respect her despite her low degree of self-assertiveness:

> By some instinct they knew her weakness, and with natural politeness they respected it. Her knowledge commanded their esteem when she taught them; her gentleness attracted their regard; and because she was what they considered wise and good when *on* duty, they kindly overlooked her evident timidity when *off*: they did not take advantage of it. Peasant girls as they were, they had too much of her own English sensibility to be guilty of the coarse error [of exploiting her shyness]. (*Shirley* II.vi.312)

Irrespective of how this is read – as a piece of fictional wish-fulfilment, for instance, or as a reminiscence of how the author liked to remember Sunday-school girls responding to her sister Anne – it is hard to escape the feeling that Caroline is lucky. That is not the whole story, however: she is a personality, too, and her pupils feel it.

No instructor in the Brontë books is granted unqualified success, in professional and personal terms, unless he or she has a character in which the favourable qualities outweigh the flaws. It is no coincidence that the best teacher at Lowood is likewise the best person within its walls. Agnes Grey attributes the swiftly growing popularity of her mother's school to Mrs Grey's personality: 'she manages things so well, and is so active, and clever, and kind' (*Agnes Grey* XXIV.190). Even Agnes herself, however miserably she may be thought to have failed in both her governess positions, makes some difference for good to her charges. Rosalie Murray wants her to take care of her own child, so that Agnes may make the little girl 'a better woman than [her] mama' (XXI.174); and even the obstreperous Bloomfield brood make some little progress thanks to Agnes' 'unwearied perseverance' before her dismissal.

Nevertheless, it will not have been hard for a nineteenth-century reader of *Agnes Grey* to imagine that a more experienced person would have achieved more with both Bloomfields and Murrays. The Brontë fiction suggests some ways in which an instructor may win his or her charges' respect, thereby establishing a space within which tuition can be imparted and received. The following chapter begins with a look at how that all-important advantage may be secured, scenes from the Brontë fiction interacting with views articulated by eighteenth- and nineteenth-century writers on education. The discussion adheres to a roughly chronological outline, those vital first beginnings being followed by everyday activities and the factors that make for success or failure in the schoolroom.

ASSERTING AUTHORITY

While any reader of *Agnes Grey*, at any time, must sympathise with the wretched narrator, whose task does come across as literally impossible, a trained teacher cannot help noticing that she misses opportunities.[1] Although she tries to endear herself to the self-appointed 'keeper of order' (II.17) in the Bloomfield nursery, young Tom, by admiring his possessions as far as she is able, it is not a good idea to threaten your charge with hell-fire on first acquaintance, however provoked you might be (II.18). She also fails to take full advantage of Mary Ann's impulse to seek Agnes' protection from her brother: by her conduct Agnes shows that she, too, gives in to Tom's bullying ('now go and put on your bonnet', 'you *must* come: I shall allow of no excuses'; II.17). However understandable Agnes' reactions are, they are just that: she is (in current management-speak) reactive, not proactive, and every teacher knows that in order to secure respect from one's pupils one must assert oneself from the very beginning.[2] The cosseted younger daughter of the Grey family is of course totally unable to do so – her whole narrative, as Frawley and others have pointed out, is a pursuit of mature selfhood and autonomy.[3] Agnes herself acknowledges that 'many a girl of fifteen, or under, was gifted with a more womanly address, and greater ease and self-possession, than I was' (II.13).

When William Crimsworth convinces his new employer M. Pelet that he will be an adequate English master, he does so by demolishing the schoolboys' conceitedness and raising himself in their estimation by doing the one thing he can be sure of being better at than they (reading aloud in English; *The Professor* VII.57–8). Pelet acknowledges his success in a significant sentence: 'Je vois que Monsieur a de l'adresse, cela me plaît, car, dans l'instruction, l'adresse fait tout autant que le savoir' (II.58). While most modern dictionaries translate 'adresse' as 'shrewdness', the meaning of the word as used by Charlotte Brontë in this context is not far from that of 'address' in *Agnes Grey*: the manner of speaking to others, of assuming and maintaining control of a communicative context.[4]

No present-day educator will be surprised to hear a school director say that a teacher's ability to secure his or her pupils' attention is as important as the subject-orientated knowledge that he or she possesses. Indeed, this view is now so prevalent as to cause concern in institutions charged with the job of imparting that knowledge, such as universities. In the mid-nineteenth century, when efforts were being made to raise the status of schoolteachers by extending their academic qualifications, such an attitude was more controversial among professionals. After all, greater learning was expected to engender greater respect, to say nothing of better salaries.

Nevertheless, Charlotte Brontë's correspondence shows that the views she made M. Pelet express were not too far removed from her own thoughts on the subject.[5] True, her letters have more to say about the personal qualities of a successful teacher than about classroom conduct, as is natural under the circumstances; but she is adamant that exalted academic ambitions are misplaced, although a good education is always a great boon in itself.

Both *The Professor* and *Villette* contain dramatic examples of ways in which newcomers to classroom teaching ensure obedience. William Crimsworth insults his new boy pupils, calling their English pronunciation 'affreux' (VII.57) and destroying a girl's inept *dictée* after informing her that it is 'honteux' (X.78). Lucy Snowe quells a threatening classroom mutiny by similar means (she reads a 'stupid' piece of work out loud and then tears it up, 'in the face of the whole school'; *Villette* VIII.80). Realising that one rebel still remains to be dealt with, she resorts to the expedient of locking her in a closet – a classic one in the nurseries of bygone times, but unusual in a class of teenagers at any time. Lucy is fortunate in that this particular girl is unpopular, so her subsequent call for silence is not sabotaged by indignant associates (VIII.80–1).

Both William and Lucy are the successors of colleagues who had not been able to curb the rebellious spirits of the large classes they were made to teach. Lucy is aware of the fact from the start; it only gradually dawns on William, but it is natural to imagine that an old Etonian would have memories guaranteed to galvanise his determination to establish order at the very outset. Neither of these two inexperienced pedagogues is given time to think or prepare. M. Pelet, whose authority is such that 'one glance from [his] pensive eye' creates instantaneous silence (*The Professor* VII.56), performs his new master's baptism of fire straight away. Perspicacious and resolute Madame Beck adopts the only means by which 'inadventurous' Lucy could have been induced to come out of her shell: swift and steely determination supplemented by a challenge to Lucy's pride (*Villette* VIII.77–81). Well may Lucy glory in her ability to exercise control – but the greater victory is that of the directress, who controls everything and everyone.

The authority exuded by M. Pelet and Madame Beck is maintained by far subtler means than those adopted by the new teachers in their sink-or-swim situations. Such drastic measures are lacking in contemporaneous teachers' manuals, which is hardly surprising: brutal classroom reality is naturally rather far removed from didactic works intended to encourage and fortify those setting out on a career as pedagogues. Manual writers had to say something about maintaining discipline and motivation by means of punishments and rewards (see below), but most of their space was given to the purposes and ideals of instruction. The pedagogical guides of the nineteenth century were not more explicit than those published today about the fact that no 'method' or 'system' of teaching can even begin to operate unless the master or mistress has managed to establish order, silence and obedience – and that there were always those who fell down on that first hurdle.

ESTABLISHING A BASIS FOR SUCCESSFUL INSTRUCTION

Having ensured that pupils will submit to being instructed, or at least not rebel openly against the instructor's authority, the teacher's next task is to obtain an idea of what the pupils are capable of and pitch his or her efforts accordingly. Writers on education of all periods have emphasised the importance of this step.

In the lifetime of the Brontës, most educational establishments with any academic pretences tested pupils on admission. Charlotte Brontë submitted to such testing three times, at Cowan Bridge aged eight, at Roe Head aged fourteen and at the Pensionnat Heger aged twenty-five. On all three occasions, her abilities were underestimated. Cowan Bridge may, as Juliet Barker suggests, have had a policy of minimising the advance knowledge of pupils in order to inflate the school's subsequent achievement.[6] At Roe Head, it seems to have been Charlotte's inability to recite paragraphs from Lindley Murray's grammar and produce ready-made answers to set geography questions that caused Miss Wooler to consider her unqualified for the senior class. (Her tearful misery on hearing this made Miss Wooler reconsider.)[7] Finally, M. Heger does not appear to have realised that the tongue-tied young Englishwoman had studied French for over a decade and was perfectly able to read contemporary works of fiction in that language; according to Mrs Gaskell, Heger told her that the two Brontë sisters 'knew nothing of French' when they arrived in Brussels.[8]

The woman who was unable to show off her very real attainments created her fictional opposite in little Adèle in *Jane Eyre*, who happily parades her grossly inappropriate accomplishments (I.ix.102–3). Realising that her young pupil is not used to concentrated study, Jane Eyre is careful not to make lessons too long and arduous at first.[9] 'I . . . talked to her a great deal, and got her to learn a little' sounds like an admirable morning's programme with a child who had not spoken her own language with anyone but her nurse for months, but had to be made to understand that schoolroom sessions required some effort on her part.

'Talking' need not be interpreted as insubstantial chitchat; for many eighteenth- and nineteenth-century writers on education, conversation was a better pedagogical instrument than schoolbooks and slates, especially with young children. Jane's method with Adèle parallels that of the model governess Miss Porson in Catherine Sinclair's *Modern Accomplishments*:

> With a judicious mind, and an active, but kind-hearted disposition, she suits her plan to the varying circumstances and tendencies of those she instructs. Christian principle is her ruling object in every thing . . . Miss Porson . . . considers one of the most important means of instructing girls to be by conversation.[10]

It is of course very much easier to devise adequate instruction for one or two children than for a classroom full of restive youngsters. That is the situation faced by William Crimsworth. Having concluded that his boy pupils are unfit for ambitious and protracted work of any description, he places the bar at a height which even the most stupid of them must be able to jump. Once he has done that, though, he is inexorable: no disobedience or impertinence is tolerated for a moment (VII.60–1). One wonders how an intelligent boy would fare in such a classroom, but the reader of *The Professor* is given to understand that a class of Belgian youths is most unlikely to contain such a person. Consequently, William's 'system' serves him well.

Conversely, Hortense Moore's initial assessment of Caroline Helstone's advance knowledge is warped by the teacher's vanity and the pupil's (excessive) modesty. Taking Caroline at her own valuation 'as an irregularly-taught, even ignorant girl', Hortense takes all the credit not only for the bright and hard-working young woman's rapid progress, but even for her command of knowledge she could not possibly have obtained from her instructor (*Shirley* I.vi.76–7). If it had not been for the compassion the reader must feel for Caroline in the hands of a woman who is, in her pseudo-ladylike way, the teacher from hell, the relevant pages in *Shirley* would be one of the most amusing passages in the book.

Charlotte Brontë's description of Caroline's attainments before Hortense began to teach her is suggestive of a biographical parallel. Caroline had tried to educate herself as best she could, says the narrator, and the outcome, though quite inadequate in her own eyes, is at least not despicable: the girl, 'unskilled in routine, had a knowledge of her own – desultory but varied' (I.vi.76). This reads like a characterisation of the adolescent Brontë sisters, pre-Roe Head, from the point of view of a mature professional who had spent years training herself to run her own school.[11]

Ten-year-old Jane Eyre is seen to correspond to that description, too, in that she had never had any systematic tuition before Lowood but had gleaned a certain store of 'desultory knowledge' by her own efforts. Assigned a place in the fourth class at Lowood, she soon masters the unfamiliar routines, above all that of rote-learning, and makes quick progress. Jane has a spur that Caroline lacks: ambition fired by the opportunity to excel, winning promotion and general recognition. The ability of Lowood to place a new pupil where she is able to thrive mentally from the start is an implicit tribute to the academic competence with which even pre-reform Lowood is run.

Domestic tuition of the kind that Agnes Grey strives to impart does not offer the fillips of competition and formal promotion (quite apart from the seeming imperviousness of all her pupils to any attempt to foster academic ambitions). The fruits of experience in education that appear in *Agnes Grey* are seen from the instructor's perspective, not the pupil's. After her first disastrous experiences with the Bloomfields, Agnes Grey avoids making similar mistakes at Horton Lodge. For one thing, she withdraws to her room on arrival to gather strength for the morrow, rather than trying to keep her end up with the young Murrays when exhausted from the journey. In addition, she decides to adopt a formal mode of address towards her pupils, calling them 'Master' and 'Miss' from the start.[12] The resulting absence of cordiality is no disadvantage for the young governess – a youthful instructor is especially likely to benefit from the protection that distance entails – and she need not fear being taken to task for over-familiarity (VII.56–8). Her decision implies an awareness that it is easier for a teacher to relax formality on closer acquaintance than to introduce it at a later stage – another insight born of teaching experience.

SETTING THE COURSE FOR SUCCESS OR FAILURE

Agnes Grey's adoption of the principle of setting modest but inflexible targets is less successful than William Crimsworth's:

> . . . I resolved to give my pupils a certain task, which, with moderate attention, they could perform in a short time; and till this was done, however weary I was, or however perverse they might be, nothing short of parental interference should induce me to suffer them to leave the school-room; even if I should sit with my chair against the door to keep them in. (III.25)

The extent to which Agnes has to resort to force in her first position is one of the most striking aspects of her sufferings as a governess. She runs after her Bloomfield charges, holds them to the floor to prevent them from hurting her and others, lifts, carries and drags them. When young Tom refuses to write, she 'forcibly [draws] his hand up and down' (III.27). With one exception – her shaking Mary Ann and pulling the child's hair when 'exasperated to the utmost pitch' (III.28) – Agnes' use of force is defensive and/or reactive, not offensive; but it is nonetheless exhausting even to read about.[13]

By dint of superior size and strength, Agnes is able to control the physical whereabouts of the nightmarish Bloomfield children, at least most of the time. What she cannot make them do is work, even to the extent of repeating the simplest phrase. Agnes-the-narrator, an experienced teacher and a mother of three, recognises that it was a mistake to let a battle of wills arise which she could not be sure of winning – even the smallest child can defy by silence (III.27). Present-day readers of *Agnes Grey* may wonder what pedagogical purpose might have been answered by a child's being made to enounce a particular set of syllables. However, the meaning and derivation of individual words was a significant part of instruction in the English language, especially for children too young to learn grammar;[14] and it is not difficult to imagine a situation where such instruction would necessitate the pupil's coming out with a certain word.

Despite her good intentions, respectable qualifications and 'Patience, Firmness, and Perseverance' (III.25), Agnes Grey fails even to establish the basic conditions for meaningful teaching and learning in her first situation. Her lack of experience is a factor, but it is hard to imagine even the most seasoned governess succeeding in the circumstances. In both her situations, as she repeatedly laments, her pupils' parents undermine her efforts by withholding the means of asserting and maintaining authority from her. Just as she cannot but fail in the context in which she is placed, Hortense Moore in *Shirley* cannot but succeed in the context that Caroline's grateful obedience creates for her. In every respect enumerated by authors of manuals for governesses and other instructors, Agnes is superior to Hortense: she is better educated, her qualifications including finer tastes and more exalted principles; she has a keener sense of the 'awfulness of the work' involved (Mary Maurice's phrase); and she is a more honest dealer than the self-deluding and self-important Hortense. It takes a professional teacher to depict the power of circumstance – for good and bad – in education with the graphic vigour achieved by the authors of *Agnes Grey* and *Shirley*.

To the reader's relief, Agnes Grey is granted success under more congenial circumstances, as a teacher in her mother's school and in due course of her own children. Another Brontë teacher moves from early failure to subsequent success, and here again the professional author's experience lends credibility to the fictional character's development. Initially, Frances Henri in *The Professor* fails as a teacher of lace-mending in Mlle Reuter's school. The nature of her subject is stated as one reason – lace-mending is not a prestigious occupation, though in great demand in Brussels – and her Protestant religion as another. Despite the narrator's opinion that 'her success as a teacher rested partly, perhaps chiefly, upon the will of others' (*The Professor* XVI.120), Frances gradually improves, albeit still a Protestant teaching the same unglamorous skills without her employer's explicit support. Her transformation is due to changes in her personal life: under the influence of a benign male colleague who encourages her intellectual development and with whom the nineteen-year-old falls passionately in love, she becomes a different person from the pale little 'drudge' who 'liked to learn, but hated to teach' (XVI.120).[15] Her new-found happiness and increased academic prestige make her more cheerful and self-assured, and as her vulnerability decreases her previous tormentors '[lose] their power over her' (XVIII.137).

Frances' development into a successful teacher is hence presented as a matter of personal transformation caused by altered circumstances rather than of acquiring new skills and competence. It is, however, significant that it happens in a school where the young woman is a visiting staff member. The role of a live-in governess would not easily accommodate such a change. In letters to her publisher's reader W. S. Williams, the father of daughters who would need to support themselves, Charlotte Brontë repeatedly dispensed advice about the qualities on which a governess' success depended. As was pointed out above, she stressed the importance of good health and spirits in conjunction with a genuine fondness for children, rating firm, confident cheerfulness far above formal teaching qualifications.[16] Among other things, Charlotte speaks of an 'ignorant nursery-maid' whose possession of these qualities enabled her to manage 'a large family of spoilt children', who nearly drove their governess to distraction, 'with comparative ease'.[17] Margaret Smith is surely right in suggesting that this is an account of Charlotte Brontë's own experience at Stonegappe, the writer herself being the governess who 'went away quite broken in spirit and reduced to the verge of decline in health'. If this is indeed an autobiographical description, Charlotte Brontë's ability to acknowledge her own failure while paying tribute to the maid's success is another mark of professionalism on her part.

The aspect of professionalism is important in this context because the Brontës, Charlotte especially, might be felt to show a deficiency in that regard when attributing success to individual characteristics and circumstances rather than to professional skills. At a time when efforts were being made to professionalise the governess' occupation, Charlotte could be thought to let the sisterhood down by insisting on personal robustness rather than on documented competence. However, she was careful to distinguish between giving *instruction* as a schoolteacher or visiting governess and *educating* a child or children as a resident.[18] It was in the latter capacity, that of a round-the-clock member of the household, that the educator would need stamina, an even temper and an instinctive love of children. Her non-resident fellow teachers would do their work on designated premises at set times and then leave, whereas the governess would be in charge of her pupils outside the schoolroom as well as in it. No amount of occupational training would equip such an educator with the ability to turn a fractious child with whose hair or clothes she had been struggling before breakfast into a model schoolroom occupant an hour or two afterwards, and nobody would know that as well as an experienced governess.

Consequently, it is not surprising that the teachers whose pedagogical ambitions and capabilities are given the most extensive treatment in the Brontë fiction are schoolteachers, not governesses. Jane Eyre and Mrs Pryor in *Shirley* are successful governesses when matched with suitable pupils, in both cases one girl with a friendly disposition (the latter having known misery in less congenial circumstances). Unlike them, Mrs Grey, Mrs Crimsworth, Madame Beck and Miss Snowe run institutions whose success depends on their directresses' professional capability, business acumen and good sense. Personality matters immensely, but the ability to satisfy parents' wishes and pupils' needs is not a matter of personal compatibility on an intimate everyday basis.

ON THE PATH OF LEARNING

When it comes to the mode of conveying knowledge and skills to pupils, first-person Brontë narrators who teach for a living characteristically stress that their employers' chief demand on them is that they should make it easy. It is a matter of '[smoothing] to the utmost the path of learning, [removing] every pebble from the track' (*The Professor* VII.61) and '[smoothing] every difficulty, to reduce it to the level of [Labassecour pupils'] understandings' (*Villette* IX.83). The operative verb occurs in *Agnes Grey*, too: Matilda Murray's mother expects Agnes to 'prepare and smooth the path of learning till she could glide along it without the least exertion to herself' (VII.64).

Such demands are uncongenial to instructors who have been obliged to take on whatever difficulties their lives have thrown at them. Their respect for those who make these demands, and those on whose behalf they are made, suffers in consequence. Disregarding the employers' wishes is not an option, however. William and Lucy make as good a job of 'smoothing the path of learning' as they can, reacting with surprised recognition when encountering a pupil who does not shy away from difficulty (Frances and Paulina – it would of course have to be somebody with English blood in her veins). Contempt for those you teach, and for their elders, is a particularly unfortunate handicap in an instructor (Charlotte's explosive scorn for her Roe Head pupils comes to mind again) – it is questionable whether it is at all possible to teach in a vigorous and interesting fashion when you despise your pupils and yourself for knuckling under to them and their parents.

Agnes Grey's attempts to comply with Mrs Murray's wishes leave Matilda profoundly ignorant. As for the youngest Murray child, Charles, his 'studies' are a parody of home education with a governess:

At ten years old, he could not read, correctly, the easiest line in the simplest book; and as, according to his mother's principle, he was to be told every word, before he had time to hesitate, or examine its orthography, and never even to be informed, as a stimulant to exertion, that other boys were more forward than he, it is not surprising that he made but little progress during the two years I had charge of his education.

His minute portions of Latin grammar, &c., were to be repeated over to him, till he chose to say he knew them; and then, he was to be helped to say them: if he made mistakes in his little easy sums in arithmetic, they were to be shewn him at once, and the sum done for him, instead of his being left to exercise his faculties in finding them out himself; so that, of course, he took no pains to avoid mistakes, but frequently set down his figures at random without any calculation at all. (VII.65–6)[19]

This passage illustrates, again in painfully graphic detail, Agnes' failure to achieve what she was so sure she would accomplish before she went out as a governess: '[making] Instruction desirable' (I.9). In fact, a desire for knowledge for its own sake is something Brontë educators consistently fail to inspire in their charges. Such a desire, where it exists, is seen as innate and/or an aspect of the obligation to pursue self-improvement; it may be stimulated by a congenial teacher for whom the learner cherishes an affection, but the Brontë fiction never portrays a pupil who lacks studiousness and curiosity but who is converted to treading 'the path of learning' willingly thanks to the efforts of a skilful professional pedagogue. True, rural adolescents may learn to better themselves thanks to the efforts of a dedicated schoolteacher, as is the case with Jane Eyre's Morton girls; but the acquisition of formal book-learning plays a subordinate role in this context. Neatness and good manners, and the self-respect they engender, matter a great deal more.

The Brontë novels depict the professional educator's labours as an acceptable form of gainful employment, not as a vocation. Nowhere is this circumstance more starkly articulated than in *Agnes Grey*, whose main protagonist is so brutally disillusioned. Indeed, the unsparingness with which young Agnes' ideals are destroyed is a characteristic that returns in Anne Brontë's second novel. Unjust though Charlotte Brontë was when she maintained that Anne's zeal in describing 'the terrible effects of talents misused and faculties abused' was exaggerated, there is no arguing with one of her statements about her youngest sister and her work: 'She must be honest; she must not varnish, soften, or conceal'.[20] To a reader who is or was also a teacher, the descriptions of protracted everyday torment in the schoolrooms of Wellwood House and Horton Lodge are as harrowing as anything in *Jane Eyre* or *Wuthering Heights*.

The absence of inspirational teaching of the first order – the kind that rouses an eagerness to pursue knowledge for its own sake where there was little or none to start with – in the Brontë fiction is manifest in the lack of pedagogical verve and enthusiasm on the part of instructors. There is no counterpart to M. Heger's little macaroon-and-*brioche* maths tutorial in the novels.[21] Even when the character that Charlotte Brontë partly modelled on Heger himself fires the minds of the young, he is speaking of politics or telling stories, not kindling studious aspirations.[22] The most precious intellectual attainments are not taught; they are learnt, by minds in voluntary pursuit of them.

There is an obvious biographical dimension here, and there is no good reason not to mention it. Sue Lonoff's article on Charlotte Brontë's education argues, persuasively, that teaching encroached fatally on learning in Charlotte's own case. Commenting on her teaching jobs, with the Misses Wooler and as a governess, Lonoff says, drawing on Charlotte's correspondence: 'Teaching robbed her of time and privacy; it drained away her energy for writing. Perhaps less obviously, she had lost the excitement of learning that she had known as a child; routine and repetition had replaced it'.[23] With all due reservations against allowing biography and literary works to comment on each other, the connection seems apparent: in respect of Charlotte Brontë, and maybe Anne Brontë as well, the draining of the 'excitement of learning' was so keenly felt as to impede any infusion of excitement into the novels' depiction of teaching several years later.

An absence of pleasurable excitement in a teacher is one thing; deficient professional conduct is another, and no leading Brontë protagonist who is also a teacher evinces it. In actual teaching situations, fictional Brontë instructors can be seen to act in ways directly relevant to the educational debate of the early nineteenth century in one respect after another. This relevance is clearly seen in their methods of maintaining discipline by encouraging docility and discouraging misbehaviour.

REWARDS AND PUNISHMENTS

Commentators on *Agnes Grey* often point out that the heroine-narrator is peculiarly badly equipped for her governess job.[24] Anne Brontë certainly invested the naïve, overprotected girl's crude awakening with high shock value. Her frustrations and disappointments are attended with varying degrees of anger and sorrow. Among the illusions whose loss causes her the greatest pain and puzzlement is her belief that children can be controlled by means of appeals to their feelings, including their feelings for herself.

However, nobody who was interested in education in the Brontës' time would have dismissed that belief as an impossible ideal. Educationists throughout the centuries had argued that the best way of making children like their studies was to make them like their teachers. Once that first aim was achieved, the young ones would strive to please their masters and mistresses, earning their approval and affection.[25] Seen in that context, Agnes Grey's hope that a cleverly mollified Mary Ann will give in and repeat her one-word lesson, thus earning her governess' good-night kiss, is not unnatural. The child, however, genuinely does not care what her elders feel about her and has no feelings for them. The saddened Agnes, remembering what suffering a withheld kiss from their mother had caused her and her sister in childhood, '[wonders] most of all at this last proof of insensate stubbornness' (III.29).

Rewarding and punishing by bestowing or withholding tokens of affection can of course only work where affection exists and matters. The lovelessness that Agnes Grey encounters in the homes where she teaches thus makes the mildest corrective available to a governess inoperable. As she is not allowed to inflict any regular punishment on the Bloomfield children, the only constructive option open to her is the classic method of positive reinforcement: 'when they behaved tolerably, I would be as kind and obliging as it was in my power to be, in order to make the widest possible distinction between good and bad conduct' (III.25). Sensibly, too, Agnes is careful not to threaten or promise anything she cannot perform. She also tries to entertain the young Bloomfields, explain things clearly and reason with them, in the best Lockean tradition – but it is all to no avail.[26] It is clear that nothing the governess can do to amuse them pleases them nearly so much as their favourite occupations, tormenting animals and rolling about on the floor. In other words, anything-but-noble savagery trumps the only sustained effort at good conduct motivated by good feeling that is made at Wellwood House. It is difficult not to regard this as an implicit condemnation of Rousseau's doctrine of 'natural education'.[27]

No wonder Agnes dreams of 'sound boxes in the ear' and 'a good birch rod' (III.24–5), and it is notable that only fear of Mrs Bloomfield's displeasure prevents her from hitting her pupils. (Their nurse, having proved her inability to 'hold [her] hand off 'em', is dismissed; IV.41.) The issue of corporal punishment was the subject of much discussion in the lifetime of the Brontës (father and children), and here again the gap between principle and practice yawned wide.

Virtually all late-eighteenth-century and early-nineteenth-century writers on education, British and foreign, disapproved of disciplining children by violence and threats of violence. Some allowed that there were cases where nothing else would do, but even then it was not a method that reflected creditably on the chastiser. Catharine Macaulay regretted that so many parents and teachers took Solomon's words about sparing the rod and spoiling the child literally. Having cited 'the humane Fenelon' [sic] in support of her case and reminded her readers that Locke had also argued against corporal punishment, Macaulay continued:

Rousseau, [Madame de] Genlis, and all the later writers of eminence, who have treated on education, have either totally excluded the rod, or kept it for the punishment of hardened obstinacy and disobedience; and such has been the force of truth, supported by argument and eloquence, that severity is in general excluded from every mode of private education.[28]

Regardless of the veracity of the last statement in the late eighteenth century, when Macaulay wrote, and irrespective of how one defines 'private', the situation was different in English schools of all descriptions half a century later. Beatings were common in the British and National schools in the 1830s and 1840s.[29] The great Dr Arnold of Rugby was an inveterate flogger who occasionally went too far even for his admirers.[30] The assumption that teachers hit and walloped errant pupils in most schools is supported by the astonishment of visitors to the Manchester Model Secular School in the mid-1850s to find corporal punishment prohibited there.[31] Also, it was thought noteworthy that William Ellis (Sarah Stickney Ellis' husband) forbade corporal punishment in his Birkbeck schools;[32] and the utopian aspects of the Dutch schools praised by W. E. Hickson were enhanced by his statement that corporal punishment was forbidden in Holland.[33]

Not even the most idealistic educationists deny that all healthy youngsters are occasionally unruly and that unruly youngsters have to be controlled somehow, especially when they come in large numbers. Even the saintly Samuel Wilderspin admitted, 'I have never been able to find out a method to manage two hundred children without [punishment].'[34] Reluctance to administer corporal punishment – not only for charitable reasons; beating children costs staff resources, too – helped create other penalties where skin remained unbroken but hearts bled. Shaming punishments were common, not least in Joseph Lancaster's British and Foreign Society schools (Bell disliked them), and some commentators on education then and now have wondered whether such penalties were not in fact more cruel than flogging.[35] That they were by no means unknown in earlier times is seen from another passage in Catharine Macaulay's *Letters on Education*:

As a succedaneum for corporal punishment some have followed the custom of putting various marks on the little offenders, thus to point them out to their brethren and play fellows, as objects of contempt and ridicule. Such practices are much used in girls [sic] schools; but as they only serve to foster malignity, and blunt the feelings of shame, they ought to be reprobated yet more than the rod; for when the mind has once lost its sensibility, there is no acting upon it with any success.[36]

Every reader of these lines who also knows his or her *Jane Eyre* will think of pre-reform Lowood, in particular the spiteful penalties imposed on uncomplaining Helen Burns by her tormentor Miss Scatcherd. Of course, young Jane's half-hour on the stool where Brocklehurst placed her comes under the heading 'shaming punishment', too. It is significant that the monstrous teacher resorts to *both* those kinds of punishment that educationists frowned on. The verb 'flog' used of Miss Scatcherd's beating Helen on the hands is notable, too, emphasising the brutality of the act and aligning it with the savage beatings that were the order of the day in boys' schools.[37] Ironically, the punishment is seen to be worse than pointless in Helen's case. The untidiness which incurs Miss Scatcherd's wrath – and which Helen freely acknowledges as a fault – is fundamentally due to the girl's living in a world of her own, and she copes with her humiliation by retreating still further into it.

Such fictional stories of cruel disciplinarians may of course invite speculation about what methods the Brontës themselves employed as teachers in extreme situations. One detail repeated across the generations by members of the Ingham/Benson family, with whom Anne Brontë had her first governess post, is that she occasionally tied the children to chairs and table legs. This measure – supposing it was actually implemented – was not in fact such an 'extreme action' as it must seem to an observer of a later age.[38] Nor can it be taken as evidence of 'fury in Anne, comparable to the anger both Patrick and Emily could exhibit'.[39] Joseph Lancaster recommended tethering when no staff hands could be spared to keep a child in check, and though some commentators disapproved of his disciplining methods, he was a well-respected figure in early-nineteenth-century education.[40] Still, having to resort to such means spells defeat in an educator, especially if she had harboured hopes of being able to control her charges by kindness and affection.

The horrors of late-eighteenth-century and early-nineteenth-century schoolrooms depicted by poets and novelists contrast sharply with the sagacity and benevolence of writers on education in the period. In a famous 1808 lecture, for instance, Coleridge, attacking Lancaster's punishment practices, said that no boy who had suffered them had any need to 'stand in fear of Newgate or feel any horror at the thought of a slave ship'.[41] Richard Altick quotes John Clare, who said that a dull boy might be beaten '4 times for bad reading in 5 verses of Scripture'.[42] A poignant fictional example is supplied by the elderly man who tells the narrator of *Vanity Fair*, in the second paragraph of the second chapter, that his agitation at breakfast was due to his having 'dreamed last night that [he] was flogged by Dr. Raine', on which the narrator comments, 'Dr. Raine and his rod were as awful to him in his heart, then, at sixty-eight, as they had been at thirteen'.

No notion of poetic licence can blur the picture of sadistic brutalising of the young to which the disciplining of a gentle daydreamer at Lowood contributes. The very real need to keep groups of children in order cannot possibly account for all this gratuitous cruelty. Why did otherwise decent and sensible school superintendents tolerate the presence on their staff of teachers who were not only incompetent but vicious? How could an outwardly respectable institution such as the Woodhouse Grove School starve boys into submission in 1823, after they refused to eat porridge stirred with a ladle last seen in the swill tub?[43]

Part of the answer was given in Section II above: teaching was not a prestigious occupation, and many people in it were entirely unsuitable for taking charge of children. Some of them owed such positions as they had to influential persons, who would take offence at their dismissal. And then, the Wesleyan/Evangelical idea of curbing children's evil propensities and breaking the will of young sinners was still sufficiently alive to be invoked by teachers accused of undue harshness. Mr Brocklehurst in *Jane Eyre* is a caricature, certainly; but many of the book's 1847 readers will have found his sermonising about mortifying the flesh of children to save their souls only too recognisable.

A child bullied the way Helen Burns was would quite naturally fix her hopes on the hereafter; earthly existence holds little in the way of promise for her, as she tells Jane in the night she dies ('By dying young I shall escape great sufferings. I had not qualities or talents to make my way very well in the world: I should have been continually at fault', I.ix.81). Her only reward for her prodigious learning and her submissive temper is Miss Temple's recognition and affection; Helen is neither competitive nor ambitious.

By contrast, Jane Eyre is keen to advance in the school and relishes her promotion to higher classes and new, prestigious subjects. Her teachers' approval matters greatly to her, firing her ambition. Jane's zeal is stimulated by an ardent desire to please her instructors, 'especially such as I loved' (I.x.83–4). In these respects, she is a typical representative of those Brontë pupils who go on to become successful teachers: all Brontë educators who are seen to cope well in their jobs take pleasure in dispensing praise where praise is due and find it a powerful stimulant to learning. (The obverse is seen in the terrible pedagogue Hortense Moore: it is symptomatic that she takes all the credit for Caroline's progress and utters 'incessant reprimands' on her pupil's labours, however well executed; see *Shirley* I.vi.76–9.)

The Brontës would have found Robert Owen's objection to the application of praise as well as blame in education incomprehensible.[44] Both their novels and other records show that they thought personal warmth between preceptor and pupil a powerful inducement to the acquisition of knowledge. Charlotte Brontë, experienced teacher and governess, knew how important it was for an instructor to 'win her young charge';[45] and the withholding of spontaneous approbation would have made such conquests difficult, if not impossible.[46] Praise from their demanding task-masters William Crimsworth and M. Paul, a strictly rationed commodity at the best of times, is the most precious reward for the young women who are falling in love with them.[47]

Villette is the only Brontë novel to dwell on public distinction as a tangible incentive to academic endeavour. That is not surprising in view of the importance of public examinations in Francophone educational culture;[48] besides, such shows of academic achievement would not be appropriate in charitable institutions or in schools for the lower classes.[49] Examination-day at Madame Beck's school is a major event: the only concentrated academic work done there is crowded into the two preceding months. Even pupils who never knew 'the stirring of worthy emulation, or the quickening of honest shame' (Lucy Snowe's best allies, which she invests much thought and effort in fostering; see *Villette* IX.84) have no desire to disgrace themselves before an audience. The description of the 'two months of real application' contains much that a present-day preparer for inspectorial visitations recognises: the best pupils are groomed to shine and the slow ones pushed as far as possible, in the hope that at least they will not ruin the whole performance by evincing too shocking ineptitude. Individual interests are as irrelevant as the acquisition of real insights; what matters is that the institution should be able to put on a display impressive enough to safeguard its good reputation and hence its future: 'A showy demonstration – a telling exhibition – must be got up for public view, and all means were fair to this end' (XV.153).

What the pupils of Madame Beck's school feel about this sudden burst of 'close, hard study' Lucy does not say, but some interesting pages of *Villette* are devoted to Lucy's and M. Paul's anticipation of the big day. While the person to whom a successful examination matters most is of course Madame Beck, that lady's 'despotic kinsman' M. Paul refuses to let her examine her own pupils in her favourite subject geography ('which she [teaches] well', XV.153). Insisting on the limelight for himself, he is annoyed at having to share some of it with Lucy Snowe, the only person competent to take English. Their exchanges on the eve of the public examination express the desire of able teachers to perform well and be seen to do so. Lucy's pretended indifference convinces the reader as little as it does M. Paul, who reminds her of the 'passionate ardour for triumph' she had displayed in the amateur theatricals. She can afford to offer the English examination to M. Paul, knowing that he cannot possibly do it. His idea of omitting it altogether (to which Lucy assents, on condition that Madame Beck agrees) is not very realistic either – it is hard to imagine the astute businesswoman Madame Beck forgoing the opportunity to dazzle the good people of Labassecour with 'the lisping and hissing dentals of the Isles' produced *en masse* (XV.153). The examination is, as M. Paul recognises, an opportunity for the solitary stranger to 'become known' (XV.156), making her mark as a teacher in Villette; and establishing a reputation as an able instructor is essential for her. Anybody in Lucy's position who wanted to open her own school (Lucy's dream) would definitely require such a reputation.

The public examinations in Madame Beck's establishment were the prelude to prize-giving, another time-honoured and universal incentive to academic effort.[50] The Brontës were familiar with it from their own experience: Charlotte repeatedly won medals for achievement at Roe Head, and both she and Anne received book prizes (though Anne's was for good conduct, not academic progress).[51] All the accounts of Charlotte's studies at Roe Head stress her single-minded pursuit of learning and her remarkably quick mind.

Charlotte Brontë was, in other words, ambitious, and ambitiousness lives in symbiosis with recognition. At a school where her hard work was rapidly and visibly rewarded, her ambitions took root in the soil of education in a way that none of her siblings (or, for that matter, her school-friends) ever came near. It is only natural that she should have created the only Brontë heroines who crave outwardly acknowledged success, and that these aspirations are played out in the field of education. Jane Eyre does not try to conceal her ambition, and nor, despite her deferential attitude to her 'maître', does Frances Henri. Lucy Snowe's attempts in that line are so obviously instances of overmuch protestation, repeatedly undercut by glowing gratification, as to lend *Villette* a dimension of irony that is too seldom appreciated. Jane Eyre's reply to Rochester's praise of her work with Adèle – 'Sir, you have now given me my "cadeau;" I am obliged to you: it is the meed teachers most covet; praise of their pupils' progress' (I.xiii.121) – may sound excessively demure, but what it actually amounts to is the ambitious professional's satisfied acknowledgement of praise for her work.[52]

THE ISSUE OF ROTE-LEARNING

The only way in which tiny, near-sighted Charlotte Brontë could win admiring recognition among her teenage schoolfellows was by impressing them with her knowledge, including knowledge of books and poems they had barely heard of, let alone read. Mary Taylor's often-quoted account of Charlotte's abilities stresses her capacious memory: she would sometimes 'repeat a page or two' from literary works that were only just appearing on the horizon for the other girls.[53] It is easy to imagine their amazement and Charlotte's gratification at it.

No issue was more often raised in discussions of what and how children and young people should study than rote-learning. As in the matter of corporal punishment, there was a wide gulf between the wisdom disseminated by educationists and what actually went on in schoolrooms of all kinds. Time and again, decade by decade, writers on education spoke out against the practice of making children memorise 'facts', names, and chunks of text that meant little or nothing to them. It made no difference: 'repetitions' – parroting rote-learned material back at the teacher – still prevailed.

Before more is said about the overwhelming opposition to rote-learning among late-eighteenth-century and early-nineteenth-century writers on education, the case in its favour should be given a hearing. David Blair's *The Universal Preceptor* sums it up: 'To fill the storehouse of the memory is the rational business of education at a season of life [childhood] when the powers of reason have not acquired a useful degree of action'.[54] The idea was that when the 'powers of reason' began to manifest themselves in a meaningful way, the young person's mind should already be 'stored . . . with interesting ideas for contemplation and conversation'.[55] Thus no time would be lost: trained to reproduce the information-loaded paragraphs at the drop of a hat, the young learner would start to develop advanced insights the moment his or her intellect became capable of analysis and synthesis.

Rational as this policy might have seemed to some, the case against stocking the memory of children with as-yet-undigested information was made by a very large number of writers. The Edgeworths' opposition to the idea of the 'stored mind' is representative of the anti-rote-learning camp:

A number of facts are often stored in the mind, which lie there useless, because they cannot be found at the moment when they are wanted. It is not sufficient in education to store up knowledge; it is essential to arrange facts so that they shall be ready for use, as materials for the imagination, or the judgment, to select and combine. The power of retentive memory is exercised too much, the faculty of recollective memory is exercised too little, by the common modes of education.

Whilst children are reading the history of Kings, and battles, and victories, whilst they are learning tables of chronology and lessons of geography by rote, their inventive and their reasoning faculties are absolutely passive; nor are any of the facts which they learn in this manner associated with circumstances in real life.[56]

The point made by Maria Edgeworth, and many other opponents of rote-learning as a basic method of knowledge acquisition, was that items of information that were not understood did not amount to knowledge in the first place. Since they were essentially meaningless, the developing 'powers of reason' would not be able to connect with them. Therefore time spent memorising them was time wasted, quite apart from the danger of children's acquiring a distaste for any kind of schooling in the process.

The formulaic questions-and-answers books were especially vigorously attacked in this context, above all Richmal Mangnall's *Questions*.[57] Mangnall's excuse was that she had never intended her best-selling schoolbook to be used as a set of texts for rote-learning, but as a guide directing teachers and learners to the basic facts. Whatever Mangnall may have intended, however, her volume was indeed used as a kind of catechism, and it was not the only one of its kind. A chilling example of the sort of 'useful knowledge' young children were expected to ingest and regurgitate is provided by a book that appeared in 1830:

Q. What are yams?
A. A certain root used by the Americans for feeding their negroes.
. . .
Q. What is garlic?
A. A bulbous root of an offensive smell, and strong flavour, much eaten by the lower classes of the French, Spaniards, and Portuguese.[58]

The questioning of little Jane Eyre by Mr Brocklehurst at Gateshead adheres to this classic Q&A model, as every 1847 reader would recognise ('"They [the wicked] go to hell," was my ready and orthodox answer'; I.iv.32). An instance from a book called *Instruction for Children, in Familiar Dialogues on the Principles of the Christian Religion, for the Use of Private Families and Sunday Schools* indicates the kind of 'orthodox' answer that an inquisitor like Brocklehurst would expect:

T[EACHER]: What do you mean by hell?
C[HILD]: A place where the soul will be as miserable as the body would be if it were cast into fire.
. . .
T. Who will be so miserable as to be sent there?
C. All those that leave this world under God's anger.[59]

Of course, Brocklehurst's eschatological quizzing of young Jane also recalls the rote-learning of the catechism – an enduring phenomenon, as many people living today can testify, but one which caused some uneasiness in the early nineteenth century, not least among certain politicians.[60]

If there was so much considered and – at least to a present-day reader – persuasive opposition to 'repetitions' as a mainstay of education, why was it still going on, decade after decade? Once again, the main answer must be sought in the field of 'human resources'. First of all, rote-learning was a tremendous staff saver: the child did the actual work, and all the teacher needed to be able to do was to read the text repeated by the pupil, thus ensuring that he/she had got it right. Not only did the pupil not have to understand what he/she produced; the listener was not required to know anything about it either. Consequently, monitors and pupil-teachers were ideal for the job. Even among adult teachers of all descriptions, knowledge of a subject sometimes did not extend far beyond the simplest textbooks. In such a situation, the set questions and answers were an obvious solution for the teacher, enabling him or her to remain on firm ground. In other words, low teacher competence poorly remunerated kept costs to a minimum. In addition, one teacher could 'hear repetitions' from a large number of pupils at the same time. That was of course practical in schools with many pupils, where a high pupil/teacher ratio was an economic necessity. The din in such classrooms, with scores, even hundreds, of high-pitched young voices rising in a monotonous gabble – often enough containing different groups repeating different texts – must have been maddening as well as deafening.[61]

Approaching the issue of rote-learning from a present-day perspective is not easy in that the twentieth century loaded the dice so heavily against this educational method that its good points are hard to perceive and harder still to argue for. Some bold spirits in our own time venture to give public expression to their regret that children no longer learn poetry or songs by heart; but hardly anybody dares to make the point that introduces Mary Maurice's reflections on the uses and abuses of rote-learning:

To a certain extent, [rote-learning] is a valuable help in education, and in the study of a language nothing can supply its place; but to make every lesson one to be committed to memory is to waste precious time, and to overtask one faculty to the injury of the rest. Besides which, the easy acquisition of words is never a test of knowledge. Many governesses will subdivide the lessons for the day into so many portions to be committed to memory – grammar, geography, spelling, history, &c., wearying out the spirit of her pupil in order to save herself trouble; or it may be because she knows no better method of teaching. The innumerable small books which are provided to carry out this miserable system cannot be too strongly protested against; they seem to have been invented for the very purpose of preventing sound instruction.[62]

For anyone who wonders why the Brontës are not on record as rebels against rote-learning, it is important to remember that it did have advantages.

Maurice states the obvious point regarding language study, and anyone old enough to have learnt, say, the major rivers of their country or region by heart at school is likely to find such retained knowledge useful in later life. Besides, a capacious memory was generally held to be essential in itself; in James Jennings' words, it is the faculty on which 'most of our other mental processes depend . . . he who has not a ready memory . . . cannot have a large range of intellect'.[63]

Rote-learning is obviously a staple of the Lowood curriculum which neither the child Jane nor the adult narrator opposes. There is much 'repetition' (see, for instance, *Jane Eyre* I.v.44, 48 and 51), and Jane, 'being little accustomed to learn by heart', finds lessons long and hard at first (I.vi.53).[64] This is a point at which criticism of the pedagogical methods employed at Lowood could easily have been expressed or at least implied – but it is not. Later in the book, Jane's progress is described in a way that integrates rote-learning in an overall picture of favourable development:

I toiled hard, and my success was proportionate to my efforts; my memory, not naturally tenacious, improved with practice; exercise sharpened my wits; in a few weeks I was promoted to a higher class; in less than two months I was allowed to commence French and drawing. (I.viii.74)

The extent to which the child comes to accept, even relish, the setting that subjects her faculties to such rigorous training is stated in this chapter's final sentence: 'I would not now have exchanged Lowood with all its privations, for Gateshead and its daily luxuries' (I.viii.75).

The absence of articulated opposition to rote-learning is a notable factor where Charlotte Brontë's own schooling at Roe Head is concerned. One can easily imagine her dismayed at finding that what was required for a member of the senior class was the acquisition and reproduction of textbook passages, rather than the wide if 'unsystematic' knowledge she possessed – but neither shock nor disappointment at that state of affairs is on record anywhere. Charlotte caught up with the other senior girls in a matter of months, which says much not only about her determination and diligence but about her capacity for memorising as well. Whether congenital or 'improved by practice', like Jane Eyre's, her memory seems to have served her well, a circumstance which would naturally have inhibited any resentment at having to exercise it so strenuously. And then, of course, it enabled her to dazzle the other schoolgirls with her extraordinary stores of assimilated literature.

That was a kind of memorising that even opponents of soulless rote-learning found commendable. For centuries, it was accepted wisdom all over the Western world that children should learn the best poetry of the great masters by heart. Engraved on the memory, these nuggets of gold would serve as touchstones with regard to literary quality.[65] The idea may seem the epitome of old-fogeyism today, not least among people in the literary professions; but off the record a fair number of them agree.

This is not after all so surprising when one realises that one of the strongest attractions of literary studies was always the magic of words, and that learning by heart turns that magic into a personal possession. Charlotte Brontë's *Shirley* devotes a number of pages to recitations of texts – both poetry and prose – learnt by heart, and to the role played by such recitations in important emotional developments. On the evening when Robert Moore comes within an inch of yielding to the 'phrenzy' of love, Caroline Helstone says, 'When I meet with *real* poetry, I cannot rest till I have learned it by heart, and so made it partly mine' (I.vi.95). Another romantic milestone is passed in the much later chapter called 'The First Blue-Stocking', where Louis Moore and Shirley quote French literature to each other.

Significantly, one of the poems Shirley recites – prompted by Moore – is a piece of Bossuet that she was once made to learn 'as a punishment-lesson' (III.iv.492). Not an auspicious starting-point for a learning task, the 'punishment' nevertheless enthrals the teenage 'culprit' and makes her forget her decision to leave her uncle's house in high dudgeon. The inflicter of the punishment, Louis Moore, recalls that she 'never said a lesson with greater spirit' and gave him the unprecedented 'treat of hearing [his] native tongue spoken without accent by an English girl' (III.iv.492). A little later, Moore describes the process of learning literature by heart: 'I acquire deliberately both knowledge and liking: the acquisition grows into my brain, and the sentiment into my breast' (III.iv.493).

This kind of learning by heart is obviously a very long way away from the mechanical spouting of irrelevant 'facts' that blighted the early years of so many in early-nineteenth-century Britain. A frightful fictional example of the latter practice is supplied by Catherine Sinclair, whose Matilda 'must repeat the name of every captain of cavalry at the battle of Blenheim'.[66] It is hard to imagine such a task as anything but a punishment, irrespective of the reason why it was imposed.

In one of the Brontë novels, rote-learning does occur as a punishment and only as a punishment. The book is, not surprisingly, *Wuthering Heights*, and the two references to learning by heart are easily missed: they are briefly stated in contexts where the disciplining of young Catherine and Heathcliff is the central issue. Both instances occur in the sixth chapter, where the pair are adolescents:

[I]t was one of their chief amusements to run away to the moors in the morning and remain there all day, and the after punishment grew a mere thing to laugh at. The curate might set as many chapters as he pleased for Catherine to get by heart, and Joseph might thrash Heathcliff till his arm ached; they forgot everything the minute they were together again, at least the minute they had contrived some naughty plan of revenge[.] (I.vi.40)

'Cathy and I escaped from the wash-house to have a ramble at liberty, and getting a glimpse of the Grange lights, we thought we would just go and see whether the Lintons passed their Sunday evenings standing shivering in corners, while their father and mother sat eating and drinking, and singing and laughing, and burning their eyes out before the fire. Do you think they do? Or reading sermons, and being catechised by their man-servant, and set to learn a column of Scripture names, if they don't answer properly?' (I.vi.41)

In these passages, rote-learning comes across as one of several ways in which the adult world attempts to subjugate the young rebels, with little apparent success. It is interesting that the Scriptures are made to serve as an instrument of chastisement: the 'chapters' the curate sets Catherine will be chapters from the Bible, and the 'columns of Scripture names' smack of Old Testament genealogy and the sons of Jacob. Being made to learn pieces from Holy Writ thus forms part of a context of harassment and chicanery, on a par with being thrashed or kept hungry and cold.

The juxtaposition of rote-learning and corporal punishment was not unusual in early-nineteenth-century Britain, where the mechanical exercise of 'a faculty called Memory' was, in the words of one sardonic observer, apt to 'be acted-on through the muscular integument by appliance of birch-rods'.[67] Another ironical and more recent commentator describes the teaching of mathematics as a matter of pupils' learning unintelligible rules by heart and being flogged when they failed, on the principle 'of curing a disorder in a part which cannot be got at, by producing one in another which can'.[68]

Several commentators on women's education expressed concern that learning undigested fragments by heart was particularly prevalent in education for girls.[69] In 1845, the writer of an article on fashionable female education in *Fraser's Magazine* lamented:

Women learn nothing thoroughly; in their education the *reason of things* is altogether left out, they are taught by rote instead of rule. Their memories are quickened, their imaginations excited, their passions stimulated; but their understandings are left to slumber. . . . As they learn Lindley Murray 'by heart' and call it grammar, so they learn the art of playing 'by ear' and finger-craft, and think it music.[70]

THE PERFECT PEDAGOGUE: MISS TEMPLE OF LOWOOD

Lowood in *Jane Eyre* is not a fashionable establishment, and the schooling that Jane Eyre's understanding receives there – a schooling which includes rote-learning as a matter of course – is seen to set her up for life. From first to last, it is presided over by a woman who comes closer to being the ideal pedagogue than any other fictional Brontë character (or any teacher the Brontës ever knew, not even M. Heger excepted). Maria Temple is loved and respected by pupils and staff, who automatically fall silent and stand up when she enters. She is learned as well as accomplished, her fireside conversation with Helen Burns testifying both to the profundity of her knowledge (which includes the Classics) and to the enthusiasm with which she shares it with gifted pupils. The faults of which Helen Burns accuses herself are the subject of 'mild and rational' reproaches from Miss Temple; but, says Helen, 'if I do anything worthy of praise, she gives me my meed liberally' (I.vi.56). Miss Temple's teaching is of such a high quality that even Helen voluntarily moves out of her own dream world to be embraced by it. Many commentators on education over the centuries have defined the word 'educate' in terms of 'drawing out';[71] and Miss Temple, the model instructor, achieves that with Helen, the highly intelligent pupil whose worth no other mistress appreciates.

The worst educational establishment in the Brontë fiction is thus directed by the best teacher, but there is no real paradox here: while powerless to oppose the horrific physical régime to which Mr Brocklehurst and his accomplices on the Lowood staff subject the girls, the superintendent does what she can with the academic domain that is hers to control, training the pupils' minds, developing their skills and warming their hearts. In this portrait of the perfect pedagogue, Charlotte Brontë gathered the qualities that a good teacher should possess according to one of the Parsonage books, Wright's *Thoughts in Younger Life*: taking care to make learning a pleasure and not a mere task, she has a thorough acquaintance with the human mind, an extensive general knowledge, a commitment to encouraging early wisdom in her pupils and a tender and humane temper, neither too gentle nor too severe.[72] No wonder the loss of this beloved mentor makes 18-year-old Jane Eyre tire of Lowood in one afternoon.[73]

V

Originality and freedom

Introductory Remarks to Section V

To a Brontë reader influenced by the late-twentieth-century 'ideological turn' in literary studies, it may seem disappointing to be told that the Brontë sisters did not protest against prevailing notions in the sphere of education. Neither the records of their lives nor their works contain any radical challenges to received educational wisdom. This absence of 'progressive' attitudes cannot very well be ascribed to fear of going against public taste. As contemporary reviews show, the sisters' novels offended quite a few readers; and as Charlotte Brontë's correspondence and Anne Brontë's second preface to *The Tenant of Wildfell Hall* suggest, the authors were unaware that their works might upset some members of the reading public while they were writing and unrepentant when they found out.[1] If they did not express any marked deviations from the ideas and practices of contemporary educationists, it would hence seem likely that it was because there was nothing much in those ideas and practices that they found objectionable.

Disappointment along the lines outlined above is understandable, but there are two sources of comfort. First, as preceding sections have shown, there was much that was laudable in eighteenth- and nineteenth-century educational thinking. Second, there is an element of unbending courage, even audacity, in the Brontës' engagement with education in the wide sense of self-improvement. It comes out not in the content of views articulated in their writings but in the fearlessness with which they and their fictional heroines assert their right to express their opinions and values, and to mould their lives and works in accordance with them.

This concluding section begins with a look at ideas about docility, originality and genius in relation to the Brontës, with special attention to Charlotte Brontë's views on creativity and her role as her sisters' literary executrix. It then engages with the concepts of reason and feeling and the issue of personal freedom, ending with a consideration of the individual's responsibility for schooling and protecting her God-created self.

CHAPTER 14

Docility and originality

DOCILITY, ORIGINALITY AND GENIUS

Jane Eyre's recapitulation of the education of young Adèle – just under twenty years old at the ending of the narrative – has aroused some disapproval among Brontë critics. Part of that disapproval is associated with a word in the sentence that was already quoted once in this book, at the opening of Section III:

As she grew up, a sound English education corrected in a great measure her French defects; and when she left school, I found in her a pleasing and obliging companion: docile, good-tempered, and well-principled. (*Jane Eyre* III.xii.450)

A present-day reader will naturally read the word 'docile' as meaning 'submissive' and may take it to imply that Jane assumes power over, even oppresses, Adèle;[1] but that is not how 1847 readers would have understood it. Quite apart from the fact that the lady of the house would be in a position of some authority in relation to any junior member, especially a girl dependant, the primary meaning of 'docile' is not 'submissive' but 'teachable', and that is what it usually means in the fiction of Charlotte Brontë, as in much mid-nineteenth-century writing.[2]

One example of 'docility' used in this sense occurs in *The Complete Governess*: 'Every one who has had occasion to attend to [females] must have perceived, that in capacity they are no ways behind the other sex, and that they far exceed that sex both in diligence and in docility' (p. 2). Another is found in Thomas Arnold's comments on the uses and limitations of Mechanics' Institutes, which might at best '[help] to cherish a state of mind at once docile and inquiring'.[3] A fictional instance published 14 years after *Jane Eyre* testifies to the continued equation of 'docile' with 'willing and able to learn' in the second half of the nineteenth century: to ensure that young Eppie receives 'everything that was a good in Raveloe', Silas

Marner listens 'docilely, that he might come to understand better' to those who would enlighten him on that point.[4]

As long as one accepts that anyone who imparts instruction may be assumed to possess some 'good' that the recipient lacks, there is no reason to understand 'docile' as implying enforced meekness in the face of unwarranted peremptoriness. Being teachable – a word Jane Eyre uses both about Adèle (I.xii.108) and about her little servant in Morton (III.v.364) – simply means fulfilling the pupil's part of the bargain. Used of a person whose role calls for an ability to receive instruction, it is a term of unreserved approbation.

Nevertheless, there are more exalted qualities in the sphere of mental ability and artistic talent than docility. The highest of them is summed up in another word of particular relevance to the Brontës: originality.

When this characteristic is mentioned in Charlotte Brontë's novels, it usually manifests itself in connection with a relationship between a man and a young woman: she evinces it, he perceives it, and his recognition of her extraordinariness plays a vital part in his falling in love with her. To fastidious William Crimsworth, the ostentatious beauties of Mlle Reuter's school, and the far from unprepossessing proprietress herself, fade into insignificance beside the remarkable lace-mender Frances Henri; to Rochester's weary spirit and burdened mind, Jane Eyre's 'unusual' and 'perfectly new character' brings freshness and relief; steady and studious Louis Moore's love for Shirley was kindled when she was an unruly schoolgirl who doodled in his books and wrote imaginative compositions of a kind he had never seen before; and M. Paul, dictatorial, brilliant and eccentric, meets his match in the anything but conventional Lucy Snowe.

In the Brontë fiction, there is always an intrinsic connection between originality and intellectual/artistic capability in a woman. For instance, according to Frances Crimsworth Yorke Hunsden's Lucia, whose 'originality' he 'admired', was a stage artist ('you delighted in her talent whatever that was'; *The Professor* XXV.241). In the course of a memorable exchange between two men in *Shirley*, Robert Moore paints the picture of a woman worthy of true love, emphasising her mental qualities:

'Supposing, Yorke, she had been educated (no women were educated in those days); supposing she had possessed a thoughtful, original mind, a love of knowledge, a wish for information, which she took artless delight in receiving from your lips, and having measured out to her by your hand; supposing her conversation – when she sat at your side – was fertile, varied, imbued with a picturesque grace and genial interest, quiet-flowing but clear and bounteous . . .' (III.vii.540)

While the ideal woman would need to be educated and possess 'a love of knowledge', one observes that her readiness to be instructed by the man in her life adds to her charms: she is thus invested with both originality and docility. Similarly, even wary 'Mrs Graham' in *The Tenant of Wildfell Hall* accepts a suggested 'improvement' in her painting from Gilbert Markham, who is sufficiently knowledgeable about art to be 'delighted and surprised' by the 'freshness and freedom of handling' in her mature work (VII.64, V.44); and Gilbert's pleasure in recording her readiness to take his advice is evident (VII.64).

As these examples show, originality in a woman is presented as something that heightens her attractiveness rather than endangering masculine self-confidence. In other words, its unconventionality is anything but a threat to a man of (good) feeling. Other persons in the original woman's surroundings may, however, view her with suspicion and distaste. A particularly revealing example occurs in *Shirley*, where the eponymous heroine outrages the sensibilities of her prim-and-proper cousins:

> They had been educated faultlessly. All they did was well done. History, and the most solid books, had cultivated their minds. Principles and opinions they possessed which could not be mended. More exactly-regulated lives, feelings, manners, habits, it would have been difficult to find anywhere. They knew by heart a certain young-ladies'-school-room code of laws on language, demeanour, &c.; themselves never deviated from its curious little pragmatical provisions; and they regarded with secret, whispered horror, all deviations in others. The Abomination of Desolation was no mystery to them: they had discovered that unutterable Thing in the characteristic others call Originality. Quick were they to recognise the signs of this evil; and whenever they saw its trace – whether in look, word, or deed; whether they read it in the fresh, vigorous style of a book, or listened to it in interesting, unhackneyed, pure, expressive language – they shuddered – they recoiled: danger was above their heads – peril about their steps. What was this strange Thing? Being unintelligible, it must be bad. Let it be denounced and chained up. (III.iii.454)

Not content with this lengthy diatribe against the tyranny of mean spirits, the narrator lashes out again five chapters later:

> The Misses Sympson and the Misses Nunnely looked upon [Shirley], as quiet poultry might look on an egret, an ibis, or any other strange fowl. What made her sing so? *They* never sang so. Was it *proper* to sing with such expression, with such originality – so unlike a school-girl? Decidedly not: it was strange; it was unusual. What was *strange* must be *wrong*; what was *unusual* must be *improper*. Shirley was judged. (III.viii.545)

These two passages contain some of the most intense polemics in the Brontë fiction, forming an all-out onslaught on repressive conventionality in female education. Nevertheless, it should be noted that the conventionality attacked here is one of mode rather than substance. The originality which is the subject of the two *Shirley* passages has to do with expression, not with content. Shirley does not sing other songs than 'proper' young ladies; she just sings them differently. In regarding difference as a threat, especially when it comes accompanied by unusual personal advantages, the Misses Sympson and Nunnely do not deviate from exponents of envious mediocrity at any time.

Before looking at originality in the context of creativity rather than performance, the qualities associated with the concept should be reviewed. Deriving from the Latin for 'to rise', it primarily means 'beginning, first existence, fountain, source' (OED *origin*, 1 and 2). OED definitions under 'original' include 'that belonged at the beginning to the person or thing in question' (s.v. *original*; A1); 'not derivative or dependent' (4A); '[h]aving the quality of that which proceeds from oneself, or from the direct exercise of one's own faculties, without imitation of or dependence on others; such as has not been done or produced before; novel or fresh in character or style' (A5). As applying to a person, the definition under A5 runs, '[c]apable of original ideas or actions; given to the direct and independent exercise of the faculties in thinking or acting; that does things not known to have been done before; inventive, creative'.

Shirley's originality shows when she expresses herself in music (a ballad about love) in a way that 'proceeds from the direct exercise of [her] own faculties, without imitation of or dependence on others', to quote the OED. Her obverse is Blanche Ingram in *Jane Eyre*, who 'was not good . . . not original: she used to repeat sounding phrases from books; she never offered, nor had, an opinion of her own' (II.iii.185–6).[5]

The aspect of novelty is important in the context of originality and the Brontës, forming a bridge between freshness of expression and creative invention. Throughout the Brontë writings – correspondence and poetry as well as fiction, juvenile and adult – the opportunity to break through the confines of habit is presented as something to be sought for when lacking and resolutely grasped when supplied. Even if all that one can hope for is 'a new servitude', as in Jane Eyre's case (I.x.85), that is better than continuing to inhabit a milieu which does not offer the questing spirit any fresh nourishment. The extent to which the impulse to seek out new challenges is seen to drive women as well as men in the Brontë novels is striking.

Novelty is a dimension of the inventiveness that inspires original creations, 'things not known to have been done before' (OED s.v. *original,* A5b). Creativity plays significant roles in the Brontë fiction and is repeatedly brought up in Charlotte Brontë's letters. In all the mature Brontë writings, creative ability is seen to require a combination of talent and diligence. The importance of the latter was powerfully impressed on Charlotte Brontë by M. Heger's commentary on one of her *devoirs.* Reacting against his pupil's representation of natural inspiration acting on genius as a process devoid of conscious artistry laboriously acquired, Heger wrote:

> [L]e génie, sans l'étude et sans l'art, sans la connaissance de ce qui a été fait, c'est la force, sans le levier, c'est Démosthène sublime orateur, qui bégaie et se fair siffler –. c'est l'âme qui chante en-dedans, et qui n'a pr. exprimer ses chants intérieurs, qu'une voix rude et inculte . . . Certes [le] lapidaire ne fait pas le diamant, mais sans le lapidaire le plus beau diamant est un caillou.
>
> Poëte ou non étudiez donc la forme – Poëte vous serez plus puissant & vos œuvres vivront – Dans le cas contraire, vous ne ferez pas de poësie, mais vous en savourerez le mérite et les charmes –.[6]

Genius is a word with a special resonance in connection with the Brontës. It accompanies the Brontë scholar all over the research field, from the children's 'Genii' identities by way of Charlotte Brontë's exploration of the nature of genius in her Brussels *devoirs,* and the many references to the genius of the Bells in contemporary reviews, to the subtitle of Winifred Gérin's landmark biography, *Charlotte Brontë: The Evolution of Genius.*[7] It is not a very fashionable word in present-day literary studies, but its prominence in the Brontë domain compels the modern critic to contemplate its significance in appraisals of the creative abilities of the Brontës.

Although the definitions of 'genius' in a modern English reference dictionary are much the same as the ones in Samuel Johnson's *Dictionary* (published in 1755), it is natural to think of the word in relation to the Romantic linking of the genius and the prophet.[8] That is certainly the appropriate context in which to read Jane Eyre's panegyrics on genius. Inspired by the mention of Sir Walter Scott's *Marmion,* the narrator halts her tale to pay tribute to those who were truly great. Having regretted that readers in her own time no longer live in 'the golden age of modern literature' – that is, the age of the great Romantics – she exclaims:

But, courage! I will not pause either to accuse or repine. I know poetry is not dead, nor genius lost; nor has Mammon gained power over either, to bind or slay: they will both assert their existence, their presence, their liberty, and strength again one day. Powerful angels, safe in heaven! they smile when sordid souls triumph, and feeble ones weep over their destruction. Poetry destroyed? Genius banished? No! Mediocrity, no: do not let envy prompt you to the thought. No; they not only live, but reign, and redeem: and without their divine influence spread everywhere, you would be in hell – the hell of your own meanness. (*Jane Eyre* III.vi.370)

These are remarkable lines for several reasons, one of which is the investing of poetic genius with literally divine qualities. Its chief foe is mediocrity, a foe which has genius to thank for its salvation from itself. It is a bold image: assigning redemptive properties to the creations of the human spirit, albeit under the influence of a higher power, could be regarded as blasphemous. It is not the only passage in Charlotte Brontë's fiction to exhibit unorthodox thinking along these lines; Shirley's essay on Genius and Humanity in the chapter called 'The First Blue-Stocking' (III.iv.485–90) pursues a similar idea.

A *devoir* of Charlotte's written in 1843 had juxtaposed genius and mediocrity, too; but there the representation of mediocrity lacked the vehement condemnation unleashed on it in the *Jane Eyre* passage. In her draft of 'La Mort de Napoléon', Charlotte Brontë had observed that mediocrity cannot be forbidden to judge genius, but that its judgement will not always be 'juste'.[9] This piece, however, deals with political matters, not poetry; and although Charlotte took a lively interest in politics and its geniuses, she did not detach them from the terrestrial sphere.

Charlotte Brontë was not the only 1840s English writer to comment on the genius of Napoleon as well as that of sages from the realm of letters. Among the chief exemplars of hero status in Thomas Carlyle's *On Heroes, Hero-Worship, and the Heroic in History*, published in 1841, are Napoleon and Johann Wolfgang von Goethe. Charlotte had certainly heard of Carlyle's work and probably read it before April 1849.[10] (*Blackwood's* and *Fraser's* had ensured that she was acquainted with Goethe as well, years before venturing a couple of shrewd remarks on him in her correspondence.[11]) Carlyle's reflections on the originality of great men resemble Charlotte Brontë's ideas on individual truth and earnestness as the foundation of original creativity. Speaking of the great man's sincerity, Carlyle said:

At all moments the Flame-image glares in upon him; undeniable, there, there! – I wish you to take this as my primary definition of a Great Man. A little man may have this, it is competent to all men that God hath made: but a Great Man cannot be without it.

Such a man is what we call an *original* man; he comes to us at first hand. A messenger he, sent from the Infinite Unknown with tidings to us. We may call him Poet, Prophet, God; – in one way or other, we all feel that the words he utters are as no other man's words. Direct from the Inner Fact of things; – he lives, and has to live, in daily communication with that. (Page 73)

As her adoration of Wellington testifies, Charlotte Brontë was a hero-worshipper. Although she claimed that she did not 'quite fall in with [Carlyle's] hero-worship', she praised qualities in his work that were obviously germane to her own priorities, among them 'his manly love of truth' and 'honest recognition and fearless vindication of intrinsic greatness, of intellectual and moral worth'.[12] Carlyle was highly thought of by other women intellectuals of the mid-nineteenth century, too;[13] and even those who were irritated by his 'un-English' style agreed that he was 'an originalist of a very high order'.[14] To evince originality of that calibre was a mark of the greatest distinction.[15]

The opposite of original creativeness is what the eighteenth century had referred to as 'servile imitation'. In 1759, Edward Young's *Conjectures on Original Composition* stated the case for 'knowledge and genius' in terms that would also have seemed natural to men and women of letters a century later.[16] There was a difference between pre- and post-Romantics, though: if the former had looked down on 'mere imitation', their nineteenth-century successors saw additional reasons for being censorious. To the latter, imitators were not only tiresome wasters of time that would have been better spent reading the works of original geniuses; they betrayed the creative writer's duty to convey such original wisdom as would assist the wanderers through an unsettled age in their endeavour to find and hold on to truth. Charlotte Brontë's rueful condemnation of a novel by Alexander Harris, whom she respected as a writer on religion, is characteristic both of herself and of her time:

Reflective, truth-loving and even elevated as is Alexander Harris's mind – I should say he scarcely possesses the creative faculty in sufficient vigour to excel as a writer of fiction. He <u>creates</u> nothing – he only copies: his characters are portraits – servilely accurate . . . whatever is at all ideal is not original.[17]

In an earlier letter to the same recipient, Charlotte Brontë had stated, 'The first duty of an Author is . . . a faithful allegiance to Truth and Nature; his second, such a conscientious study of Art as shall enable him to interpret . . . the oracles delivered by those two great deities'.[18] Her comment on Harris' failure as a novelist pinpoints the difference between the non-fiction writer's and the 'Author's' obligations: it is the creative writer's duty to 'interpret oracles', establishing truths beyond mere accurate and thoughtful representation of what 'is'.[19] It is the credo of a conscious artist, schooled by years of studying the Romantic writers.

A QUESTION OF CREATIVITY: CHARLOTTE BRONTË AS HER
SISTERS' LITERARY EXECUTRIX

The preceding exploration of the concept of originality in conjunction with creativity and genius established a context in which to contemplate the question of how Charlotte Brontë fashioned the images of her sisters Emily and Anne for posterity. The issue is relevant to the present work in that the matter of education, in a wide sense, plays a significant role in it.

Charlotte Brontë has had a bad press in recent years, especially with regard to her contributions to her sisters' posthumous reputations. One of the accusations made against her is that she knowingly misrepresented Emily and Anne's works and personalities. Her motives for acting as 'mythographer' have been described as partly self-protective, partly actuated by a wish to defend Emily, whom she allegedly tried to protect in death as she had done in life.[20] The latter motive is prevented from appearing laudable by hints that Charlotte's actions only made Emily's legacy more inaccessible to those who would have appreciated her better than her sister.

There is no doubt that Charlotte tampered with some of her sisters' poems, going well beyond an editor's prerogative. She may have destroyed literary materials after their deaths, possibly including part of a second novel by Emily.[21] Nor can it be denied that she grossly misjudged Anne's gifts as a writer, especially as demonstrated in *The Tenant of Wildfell Hall* (see below). It is less immediately obvious that posterity is entitled to impute selfishness and disingenuousness to her in this connection.

The gravamen of the charges against Charlotte, as articulated by Lucasta Miller among others, is that she patronised and infantilised her sister Emily as part of an attempt to idealise her as an untutored, misunderstood genius. By allegedly underplaying her sisters' reading, she represented them as rural innocents and forestalled doubts as to the originality of their works (after all, what one has not read one cannot imitate).

The primary documents in the case are Charlotte's 'Biographical Notice of Ellis and Acton Bell', the editor's preface to the new edition of *Wuthering Heights* in 1850 and the prefatory note to 'Selections from Poems by Ellis Bell', all written towards the end of 1850.[22] These documents tell the reader that Emily and Anne were not 'learned' – 'they had no thought of filling their pitchers at the well-spring of other minds; they always wrote from the impulse of nature, the dictates of intuition, and from such stores of observation as their limited experience had enabled them to amass' (324). While this is a selective representation in the sense that all the Brontës were intellectually ambitious, had read a great deal and drew extensively on their reading in their fiction, it is hard to regard it as deliberately manipulative, especially as the third paragraph of the same text speaks of 'books and study' as providing the sisters with enjoyment and occupation (319).

In saying that her sisters were not 'learned', Charlotte Brontë was not suggesting that they were 'uneducated', a characterisation employed by Miller.[23] The word as used in the mid-nineteenth century evoked formal and systematic academic study of a scholastic nature.[24] In disclaiming such attainments for her sisters Charlotte was simply stating an obvious fact.[25] That Emily and Anne were great readers who made the most of every opportunity to acquire knowledge on matters that interested them is not contradicted by her evidence.[26] The image of filling pitchers at the well-spring of other minds is closely linked to the creative situation and amounts to claiming that her sisters' fiction, with input from 'nature' and 'intuition', was the result of 'the direct exercise of [their] own faculties, without imitation of or dependence on others' – that is to say, it was original.[27] No claim was more important to make before a public who had to be convinced that Charlotte Brontë had not written the works of Acton and Ellis Bell. As previous pages have shown, too, no quality was associated with greater merit.

In according Emily more of that quality than Anne (Anne 'wanted the power, the fire, the originality of her sister, but was well-endowed with quiet virtues of her own'; 324), Charlotte Brontë doubtless contributed to consigning her youngest sister to the relative obscurity where she spent over a century.[28] Charlotte's rejection of *The Tenant of Wildfell Hall* as hardly worth preserving must strike a latter-day reader of this powerful novel as appallingly misguided – although it should be borne in mind that she was writing to refute the idea that this was the work of a writer in whom 'a morbid love for the coarse, not to say the brutal' had produced a book offensive not only to public taste but to morality.[29] Besides, the idea of Acton's inferiority to the other Bells, Currer in particular, was a widely shared notion at the time: Charlotte may have helped to perpetuate it, but she did not create it.[30] Of course, she had personal reasons for disliking her sister's second novel. Its merciless portrayal of alcoholism caused her anguish, both because it brought Branwell's tragedy before her again and because she felt that the tale had done the teller harm. The annals of literary history contain errors of judgement committed for less excusable reasons.

The account of the autonomy of creativity in Charlotte's preface to the new edition of *Wuthering Heights* certainly comes across as an attempt to excuse Emily for not having been in control of, and hence not fully responsible for, her work. To a Brontë scholar convinced that a great deal of high-calibre intellectual labour went into the making of Emily's novel, Charlotte's suggestion that it was the product of a potent but uncivilised genius may well seem misleading. However, that scholar has access to several decades of massive research by people whose ingenuity and detective instincts have shaped their terrain, sometimes perhaps a trifle over-zealously. Creative writers confronted with Charlotte's description of the power of which the owner 'is not always master – something that at times strangely wills and works for itself' (327) are more apt to recognise what their colleague was talking about a century and a half ago.[31]

Charlotte Brontë took care to attach the most powerful valorising terms to her sisters' works and lives that she commanded and felt able to use with complete truthfulness ('original' and 'genius' of Emily, 'sincere' and 'honest' of Anne, 'genuinely good and truly great' of both). If posterity has been inappropriately influenced by words written by a bereaved woman struggling to convince a sceptical mid-nineteenth-century audience of the separate identities of the 'Bells', and of the indisputable strengths of the now-silent ones as she saw them, surely posterity should accept some if not most of the blame for it.

CHAPTER 15

Liberty and responsibility

In view of the lofty status of originality in the nineteenth century, it might have seemed natural to place it in opposition to docility, at the expense of the latter. The late twentieth century taught Humanities scholars to think in terms of binarisms and tensions between contradictory phenomena, and anybody schooled in that tradition would instinctively pose one concept against the other, studying the oscillations in value between the opposite poles.

There is of course nothing inherently wrong with this mental habit; it has helped Brontë critics uncover plenty of complexity and depth beneath apparently – and deceptively – simple representations in texts by and on the Brontës. It has, however, encouraged too great attentiveness to dichotomies and aporias and too little to reconciliations and resolutions. To stay with the docility concept for a moment, a person who is teachable under appropriate circumstances demonstrates that he/she has the sense to acknowledge another person's superior knowledge and skills. Such acknowledgement is evidence of sound judgement allied to modesty. That combination is a strength, not a weakness, and the Brontë fiction shows it to be a strength promoted by a good education. Caroline Helstone is thus misguided in being a docile pupil of Hortense Moore's, not realising, unschooled as she is owing to her uncle's neglect of her education, that her cousin's authority is spurious. Conversely, Mary Rivers' docility when receiving instruction in drawing from Jane Eyre is entirely rational: in this one field Jane knows more than she, and that insight transforms the professional teacher into a grateful pupil.

REASON AND FEELING

The word 'rational' points in the direction of another pair of concepts which appear to invite being set up as binary opposites in relation to the Brontës: reason and feeling, especially in the domain of love and marriage. From the letter in which 24-year-old Charlotte Brontë tells Ellen Nussey that she is 'not so utterly the slave of feeling but that [she] can <u>occasionally hear</u> [the voice of Reason]' to Lucy Snowe's groaning under the 'bitter sternness' of Reason (*Villette* XXI.229) and Paulina's remarks on the 'fruitless torture of feeling' (*Villette* XXVI.304), this sphere is described as a site of conflict between head and heart.[1]

The unarmed combat between Mrs Yorke and Caroline Helstone in *Shirley* (in ch. II.xii, 'An Evening Out') offers a particularly intriguing palette of views on sense and sensibility: accused of being a sentimental dreamer untaught by hard experience and deficient in common sense, Caroline stands up for herself in a way that belies the accusations. She cannot refute the insinuation that she is in love with her cousin Robert, or in justice deny it to herself, but she turns her defence into an onslaught on her enemy's position, charging her with ignorance of the facts, deliberate and unprovoked malice, conjecture on insufficient evidence and simple prejudice (Caroline cannot help being the parson's niece; *Shirley* II.xii.403–406). Her method, in other words, is rational and her speech carefully controlled ('[s]he had spoken in the clearest of tones, neither fast nor loud', 405).

Lucy Snowe and Jane Eyre are constantly beset by emotions, and both attempt to pit reason and common sense against feelings they judge to be dangerous. In attempting to check their feelings for M. Paul and Mr Rochester, they are sometimes actually seen to be wrong about the facts of the situation: M. Paul has no intention of marrying his niece and Rochester none of marrying Blanche Ingram. Even so, the two young women employ rational means to prevent themselves from emotional shipwreck, and their devices are seen to be of some assistance in this respect. Jane's two-portraits ploy (II.i.160–2) utilises her artistic competence to discipline her feelings, helping her not to break down under Rochester's campaign to bind her to him emotionally by means of jealousy – a campaign which founders on Jane's cold realisation that Blanche Ingram (a stranger to true feeling; II.iii.186) is not worth it.

Feeling and reason are hence not enemies; they are counterbalancing forces, dependent on each other for keeping the individual on course through life.[2] The more passionate his or her disposition, the more he or she needs to exercise the rational faculties.[3] Passion in the sense of a predisposition for uncontrolled anger is altogether reprehensible;[4] but 'the passions' in the sense of powerful emotions generally have their dangers, too.[5] Schooling them is no easy matter, as all Anne and Charlotte Brontë's protagonists demonstrate; but the reconciliation of genuine emotion and good sense is at least attainable in their fictional worlds.

In one of the most illuminating critical comments ever made on reason and feeling in the Brontë novels, Barbara Hardy draws up a distinction between Charlotte and Emily Brontë where the balance of reason and feeling is concerned. Having suggested that Charlotte found the 'radical segregation of extremes of feeling and reason' in *Wuthering Heights* 'uncongenial', Hardy comments:

Charlotte thrives on the polarities of violence and control, freedom and limit, passion and reason, but devises a moral structure which resolves conflict and makes extremes meet, in her strong, tormented, but morally civilized and triumphant characters, Jane Eyre, Robert Moore, and Lucy Snowe.[6]

THE EDUCATION OF HARETON EARNSHAW

The statement that feeling and reason are segregated in *Wuthering Heights* applies not only to the first-generation 'lovers' but to the power of love as manifested in one of its few at least intermittently appealing characters, Hareton Earnshaw. As that power has a bearing on education in more than one sense, a review of its operation in *Wuthering Heights* is not out of place here.

Hareton is, as several critics have pointed out over the years, a child begotten and born in love, whose early childhood was spent in the care of a nurse who was devoted to him. After Nelly is taken away from him by his egoistic aunt, the only persons he can turn to are Joseph and Heathcliff – of his father he is understandably frightened. Heathcliff assuming the role of master of the house, Hareton attaches himself to him. To anyone who reads *Wuthering Heights* in the light of mainstream child-rearing theory, it is fascinating to see how Hareton's early upbringing asserts itself despite the brutishness that descends on him in consequence of Heathcliff's example and deliberate neglect. While Charlotte Brontë said that Heathcliff's regard for Hareton is one of the two things that prevent him from being a complete monster, it must not be forgotten that this regard is partly a result of the child's, and in due course young man's, trusting loyalty.[7] It makes Heathcliff (who is of course also affected by Hareton's marked physical resemblance to the elder Catherine) powerless to corrupt the boy: the love that enveloped him in his early childhood inoculated him against the destruction of his good qualities. Well might Heathcliff starve college-educated Hindley's son of even the curate's tuition as a measure of revenge on the lad's father;[8] his project is killed by a love he could not eradicate, a love that, ironically, extends to himself until death. Reason has nothing to do with it, and Hareton refuses to listen to Cathy when she tries to tell him how he has been cheated of his birthright by Heathcliff.

Not until Cathy learns to respect Hareton's affection for and allegiance to Heathcliff can love grow between the two young people.[9] In the scene where Cathy teaches Hareton to read, thereby pulling him up into her world, that love is seen to flourish in the soil of education.[10] It demonstrates that young Cathy's previous scorn for her illiterate cousin (which upsets both Nelly and Lockwood, as it surely does most readers; II.x.220 and II.xvii.266–8) has been replaced by a desire on her part to bridge the gulf between them by her own efforts. Besides, the reading lesson integrates the ideas of authority and superiority (formally, Cathy still has the upper hand) into an atmosphere of genial playfulness that effectively neutralises the differences between teacher and pupil. Despite the emphasis on banter and kisses, the reader is aware that intellectual/aesthetic predilections are not immaterial in the relationship between the new lovers: the preceding chapter in the novel laid a foundation for the eradication of the educational divide in having the still recalcitrant Cathy acknowledge that Hareton's literary tastes are the same as hers (II.XVII.267).

FREEDOM OF THE SPIRIT

It would be hard to imagine a more complete contrast to this bright scene than Jane Eyre's lessons in 'Hindostanee' at the hands of St John Rivers. Here, too, the pupil is (without realising it at the time) being groomed for elevation to the role of the instructor's spouse; but every sign of pleasure in learning and mastery is absent. Striving to satisfy St John's stringent demands, Jane comes under 'a freezing spell':

I daily wished more to please him: but to do so, I felt daily more and more that I must disown half my nature, stifle half my faculties, wrest my tastes from their original bent, force myself to the adoption of pursuits for which I had no natural vocation. He wanted to train me to an elevation I could never reach: it racked me hourly to aspire to the standard he uplifted. (III.viii.398)

Being turned away from what is 'natural' and 'original' in her is bad enough; the worst effect of St John's influence is that Jane loses her 'liberty of mind' (III.viii.397). Dependent on his praise, afraid to rouse his displeasure, the free spirit Jane Eyre – who had wrested the reluctantly admiring 'You *are* original' from him when she confronted him with his passion for Miss Oliver (III.vi.375) – becomes a slave to the man who has assumed control of her. She explains the change by claiming that she 'knows no medium . . . between absolute submission and determined revolt' when faced with antagonistic characters (III.viii.400). The reader perceives that

Jane's subjugation is also connected with growing despair at the absence of news of Rochester, as well as with her characteristic hunger for affection and approval.

Jane's servitude under St John's tutelage is the preliminary to his insisting that she accompany him to India as his wife. Weakened by months of labour to satisfy him, she nearly gives in; but her appeal to God at the decisive moment brings on the 'mysterious summons' from Rochester. It causes an immediate reversal of roles: Jane gives the orders and St John complies ('[w]here there is energy to command well enough, obedience never fails'; III.ix.420).[11] Seeking guidance from God rather than man, Jane Eyre regains her lost freedom in an instant. It is like the release of a spring: the swiftness of this dramatic change signals the extent to which Jane's submission to St John has been a process of steadily accumulated strain. She was wrong to enter into that process and wrong to have remained docile towards the wrong teacher for so long. As the relevant pages from *Jane Eyre* show, choosing whom to be responsive to is no small part of an individual's responsibility for herself.

Looking back on her memories of being swayed by two very different men, Jane-the-narrator comments:

> I was almost as hard beset by [St John] now as I had been once before, in a different way, by another. I was a fool both times. To have yielded then would have been an error of principle; to have yielded now would have been an error of judgment. (III.ix.418)

This is 'cool language' with a vengeance, and it brings two vital concepts into play: principle and judgement.

In order to follow principle and exercise judgement, the individual must possess the freedom to do so according to his/her own lights. The hatred of oppression that is so characteristic of the Brontë fiction stems in large part from a contention that no outside agent should be allowed to determine a person's moral and spiritual path of learning: anybody who is to pursue that path to a satisfactory conclusion must be free from interference.[12] The only authority is God, who created individuals and invested them with responsibility for their selves, and whose guidance is mediated through conscience.[13] Resigning any part of one's freedom to another human being is the height of folly.[14] 'Liberty was the breath of Emily's nostrils', wrote Charlotte Brontë in the prefatory note to 'Selections from Poems by Ellis Bell', linking the concept to physical freedom on the moors.[15] Charlotte herself may have been able to settle for what she had Jane Eyre call 'liberty of mind'; but all over her writings that liberty is shown to be an absolute necessity.

One of the most enduring reasons for the appeal of the Brontë fiction is its portrayal of searching spirits facing hardships and overcoming them. The life-projects of the people concerned are pursuits of self-education, full of intellectual and moral endeavour, undertaken in recognition of the free individual's responsibility for the outcome. Although the Divine assistance they solicit in times of trouble is always seen to come to their aid, the task of honouring their obligations to themselves and others is never less than formidable: establishing and maintaining a just balance between true, natural feeling and original intuition on the one hand and reason, principle and judgement on the other entails immense and unremitting effort. Latter-day readers may not share the values and convictions that inform these books; but the struggle to uphold one's integrity and secure solid self-respect, sometimes against the most overwhelming odds, captivates one generation after the next, whether or not they articulate their fascination in those terms. The book that supplied the most-quoted sentence from the Brontë fiction ('Reader, I married him') also contains an equally brief statement whose urgency will outlast centuries: '*I* care for myself'.[16]

Notes

INTRODUCTION

1. Also by the present writer and from the same publisher; a paperback was issued in 2004.

2. Margaret Smith's three-volume edition of *The Letters of Charlotte Brontë with a selection of letters by family and friends* appeared from the Clarendon Press in 1995 (1829–1847), 2000 (1848–1851) and 2004 (1852–1855), respectively. A work of consummate and meticulous scholarship, it also liberated Brontë scholars from dependence on the tainted Shakespeare Head edition (Oxford: Blackwell, 1933, reissued in 1980), *The Brontës: Their Lives, Friendships and Correspondence*, by T. J. Wise and J. A. Symington. Juliet Barker's masterly biography *The Brontës* appeared from Weidenfeld & Nicolson (London) in 1994, an abundant, up-to-date and reliable source of biographical information on the entire family. (Its sole flaw – but a notable one in a work which relies so much on documentation pertaining to Charlotte Brontë – is the seemingly instinctive hostility to Charlotte that colours its interpretations of her actions and motives.) Christine Alexander's book *The Early Writings of Charlotte Brontë* (Oxford: Blackwell, 1983) and her edition of Charlotte Brontë's juvenilia (*An Edition of the Early Writings of Charlotte Brontë*, Oxford: Blackwell, 1987 and 1991) contributed masses of valuable information about the Brontës' early life. In 2003, Alexander and Smith brought out another immensely useful work, *The Oxford Companion to the Brontës* (Oxford University Press). (On Lucasta Miller's *The Brontë Myth* of 2001, see above pp. 206f.)

3. Peter Gordon and Denis Lawton, *Curriculum Change in the Nineteenth and Twentieth Centuries* (London: Hodder and Stoughton, 1978), p. 61.

4. The opening sentence in Robert Ulich's Preface to *Three Thousand Years of Educational Wisdom: Selections from Great Documents* (Cambridge, MA: Harvard University Press, 1947 and 1954), p. v. Other useful historical works that situate the British Isles in the context of Western education are Harry G. Good and James D. Teller, *A History of Western Education* (London: Macmillan, 1969; this is the third edition of a work that first appeared under Good's name only); Frederick M. Binder (ed.), *Education in the History of Western Civilization* (Toronto: Collier-Macmillan, 1970); E. S. Lawrence, *The Origins and Growth of Modern*

Education (Harmondsworth: Penguin, 1970); and James Bowen, *A History of Western Education*, vol. III ('The Modern West Europe and the New World'; London: Methuen, 1981).

5. Cf. Henry Dunn, *Principles of Teaching; or, the Normal School Manual: Containing Practical Suggestions on the Government and Instruction of Children* (London, 1839; this is the third, enlarged edition), p. 2: 'The great defect in most books of education, it has been well observed by an experienced teacher [Jacob Abbott], is, that "we are taught almost exclusively how to operate on the *individual*. We are continually meeting with remarks which sound very well by the fire-side, but which are totally inefficient and useless in school, from their being apparently based upon the supposition, that the teacher has but *one* pupil to attend to at a time".'

6. Two relatively recent landmark studies in this domain are Sally Shuttleworth's *Charlotte Brontë and Victorian Psychology* (Cambridge University Press, 1996) and Heather Glen's *Charlotte Brontë: The Imagination in History* (Oxford University Press, 2002).

7. In the introduction to the 2005 'Anniversary Edition' of *Myths of Power: A Marxist Study of the Brontës*, Terry Eagleton says that the Brontë sisters may in some ways 'be ranked among those strange oxymoron beasts, radical conservatives'; p. xiii (Basingstoke: Palgrave Macmillan, 2005; *Myths of Power* was first published in 1975).

8. Historians are sometimes good role models in this respect. One of the reasons for the success, among readers of the most dissimilar ideological persuasions, of Linda Colley's *Britons: Forging the Nation 1707–1837* (New Haven: Yale University Press, 1992) is the author's underlying enthusiasm for her period and its people, warts and all.

9. According to a character in a dialogue on 'Female Authorship' in *Fraser's Magazine* of April 1846, the great aim of education should be 'to put young people in the way of educating themselves; for, until they feel the necessity for self-culture, we can do little for them' (vol. XXXIII, 466). The local Yorkshire newspapers carried reports on the activities of, for instance, the 'Batley Literary and Mental Improvement Society' and the 'Gomersal Wesleyan Mental Improvement Society' (the supplement of the *Leeds Mercury* for 9 January 1847, 9).

10. See further pp. 149 and 159–60 above. Shuttleworth's characterisation of Charlotte Brontë's fiction is actually a far better description of *Wuthering Heights*: 'there is no overall moral vision against which to set the [novel's] achievements; no omniscient narrative voice in which we can place our trust' (*Charlotte Brontë*, pp. 246–7). On Charlotte, cf. G. M. Young in *Victorian England: Portrait of an Age* (Oxford University Press, 1936), p. 3; Young refers to her as a fanatic for the moral law, a fanatic who was also equipped with a greater 'aptitude and . . . capacity for rebellion' than anybody else except Harriet Martineau.

11. See, for instance, Penny Boumelha, *Charlotte Brontë* (New York and London: Harvester Wheatsheaf, 1990), pp. 19–26, 34–6, 44–6 and 63. An interesting recent development in this line is Richard A. Barney's concluding discussion

of the (first) proposal scene in *Jane Eyre* as an exponent of the 'paradigm of Eden'; see *Plots of Enlightenment: Education and the Novel in Eighteenth-Century England* (Stanford University Press, 1999), pp. 316–20.

12. On *Bildung*, *Erziehung* and *Entwicklung*, see, for instance, Franco Moretti, *The Way of the World: The Bildungsroman in European Culture* (London: Verso, 1987), pp. 15–17, and Barney, *Plots of Enlightenment*, pp. 30–1.

13. Moretti's outline of the classic *Bildungsroman* as proposing an exchange in which belongingness to a system 'that literally "takes care of everything"' is accepted at the expense of 'the possibility of directing one's life "to one's own risk and danger"' (p. 65 in *The Way of the World*) is diametrically opposed to fundamental principles in Charlotte Brontë's fiction, notably in *Villette*.

14. See, for instance, Bessie Rayner Belloc, *Remarks on the Education of Girls* (London, 1854), p. 4. Cf. E. S. Lawrence, *The Origins*, p. 15.

15. See the OED, 2 and 3 *s.v.* 'education'. The OED points out that the word is related to Latin 'educere', 'to lead forth'.

SECTION I EDUCATION AND SOCIETY

1. Briggs's *The Age of Improvement* was first published in 1959 and reissued by Longman in 2000.

2. See, for instance, Gertrude Himmelfarb, *Victorian Minds* (London: Weidenfeld and Nicolson, 1968), pp. 283–4.

3. *Courier* 23 August 1828 about W. Pinnock's *A Comprehensive Grammar of Modern Geography and History*, quoted in a publisher's blurb at the back of Pinnock's *A Comprehensive Grammar of the English Language* (1830), which Charlotte Brontë owned.

CHAPTER I THE EDUCATION OF THE PEOPLE

1. Commenting on the state of popular education in *The History of England during the Thirty Years' Peace 1816–1846* (London, 1850), vol. II, p. 712, Harriet Martineau wrote, 'While in no department of benevolent action has there been more energy and good-will than in extending Education, in none are we more behind the needs of the time'.

2. This passage is discussed in Marianne Thormählen, 'Where we are today: Issues resolved and issues outstanding', in R. J. Duckett (ed.), *The Brontës and Education: Papers Presented To The Brontë Society Weekend Conference September 2004* (Haworth: The Brontë Society, 2005), pp. 87–8.

3. See, for instance, John William Adamson, *English Education 1789–1902* (Cambridge University Press, 1930), pp. 24–5 and W. B. Stephens, *Education in Britain, 1750–1914* (Basingstoke: Macmillan, 1998), pp. 5–8. A comprehensive account is found in J. M. Goldstrom, *The Social Content of Education 1808–1870: A Study of the Working Class School Reader in England and Ireland* (Shannon: Irish University Press, 1972), ch. 1 ('The Religious Phase'). For a contemporary description, see Horace Mann's *Census of Great Britain, 1851*.

Education in Great Britain: Being the Official Report [and so on] (London, 1854), pp. 11–15. On earlier attempts to promote national education, see Alan Richardson, *Literature, Education, and Romanticism: Reading as Social Practice* (Cambridge University Press, 1994), pp. 86ff.

4. See further pp. 97ff. above.

5. It had been anticipated to some extent by the Revised Code of 1862; see John Hurt, *Education in Evolution: Church, State, Society and Popular Education 1800–1870* (London: Paladin, 1972; first published by Rupert Hart-Davis Ltd in 1971), pp. 69ff.

6. The quotation is from Martineau's *History*, vol. II, p. 712. By contrast, Martineau held up the example of 'various parts of the Continent' where 'the spectacle might be seen of children sitting on the same bench, Catholics, Protestants, and Jews, having their understandings opened, their consciences awakened, and their affections flowing out upon one another, with a prospect before them of co-operation in their future lives'; vol. II, p. 251. For a modern scholarly review of Continental developments in education in relation to behind-the-times England, see Pamela Horn, *Education in Rural England 1800–1914* (Dublin: Gill and Macmillan, 1978), pp. 47–51.

7. *Hansard* 17 August 1833. Cobbett was the Whig MP for Oldham and author of *Rural Rides*. (He was no favourite of Charlotte Brontë's; see Smith, *Letters* I, pp. 111 and 112n8.) For an account of the thwarted campaigns for state-supported popular education and the ambivalent attitudes of people usually thought of as 'progressive', see Andy Green, *Education and State Formation: The Rise of Education Systems in England, France and the USA* (Basingstoke: Macmillan, 1990), pp. 261ff.

8. See, for instance, W. E. Hickson, *Dutch and German Schools. An account of the present state of education in Holland, Belgium, and the German States, with a view to the practical steps which should be taken for improving and extending the means of popular instruction in Great Britain and Ireland* (London, 1840).

9. See Kay's *Recent Measures for the Promotion of Education in England*, pp. 24 and 31 in the 16th edition of 1839, on the superiority of Holland and the German states. For his remarks on Napoleon as deliverer, see *The Social Condition and Education of the People in England and Europe* (London, 1850), vol. I, p. 328.

10. Vol. XXXVIII (July 1835), 16.

11. See, for instance, vol. XXXVIII (July 1835), 16–24. A French expert on education in Prussia, Victor Cousin, was frequently referred to in *Blackwood's* columns as a critic of irreligiousness in French education at all levels; see, for example, vol. XXXV (February 1834), 248, and vol. XLV (February 1839), 286. (*Blackwood's* says less about the same Cousin's admiration for enlightened Prussian policies in the educational sphere. By contrast, *Fraser's* quotes Cousin on Prussia with respect in connection with the 1846–47 debates; see vol. XXXV, March 1847, 259. So does the *Leeds Intelligencer* of 10 October 1846, 4, whose brief comment on Cousin runs, 'we need not say who he is').

12. See W. F. Hook, *On the Means of Rendering More Efficient the Education of the People. A Letter to the Lord Bishop of St. David's* (1846), especially

pp. 40–1. While *Blackwood's* avoided commenting on the issue in 1846–47, beyond a cautious acknowledgement that education was indeed an area in which extensive government effort was required (vol. LX, Aug. 1846, 257, 'The late and the present ministry'), the other Tory periodical read by the Brontës, *Fraser's Magazine*, expressed a degree of agreement with the government and with Hook. Stopping short of declaring uncompromising support, *Fraser's* insisted that something had to be done and that voluntary efforts would never suffice. See vols XXXIV (Sept. 1846), 370–6 ('National education'), XXXV (March 1847), 253–69 and XXXVI (Aug. 1847), 169–81 (the latter two under the heading 'Education of the people'). (The September 1846 piece was approvingly quoted by the *Leeds Intelligencer* of 5 Sept. 1846 (6).)

13. 'On National Education', *Leeds Intelligencer* 27 March 1847, 5; pp. 186–7 in Dudley Green (ed.), *The Letters of the Reverend Patrick Brontë* (Stroud: Nonsuch, 2005). Margaret Smith points out that Charlotte Brontë must have written most of *Jane Eyre* by late March 1847; see, for instance, *Letters* I, p. 520n4. The history of Patrick Brontë's engagement with elementary education in his parish is told in fascinating detail by Michael Baumber in 'Patrick Brontë and the development of primary education in Haworth', *BST* 24, Pt 1 (April 1999), 66–81.

14. *The Letters of Edward Baines, Jun., to the Right Hon. Lord John Russell, Letter III* (pamphlet printed in London, 1847), p. 17. Though a Whig and a Methodist, and the son of a man whom the teenager Charlotte Brontë had declared she abhorred (Smith, *Letters* I, p. 136), Edward Baines Jr was – as Juliet Barker puts it – 'one of the Brontës' heroes' (*The Brontës*, p. 863n28). He was a stalwart of the Mechanics' Institutes movement, and his dedication to the mental improvement of the lower classes is seen all over his writings. Baines's pride in the educational achievements of northern England goes against the widely held view that the state of education was particularly dire in the North, but improvement does seem to have been swift in Yorkshire. An indication may be seen in Horace Mann's Census of 1851, where the City of York had the highest percentage of children in schools of all the measured districts; see *Census*, p. 34.

15. *The Social, Educational, and Religious State of the Manufacturing Districts in 1843* (Leeds, 1843), p. 29. See also Andy Green, *Education and State Formation*, pp. 274–6.

16. An anti-Hook pamphlet by fellow cleric and prominent participant in the debates on education, Richard Burgess, affords an idea of how heated arguments could become. Burgess maintained that the accounts of more favourable teacher-pupil ratios on the Continent were 'specious'; that separating secular schooling from religious instruction had rendered Continental educational schemes 'abortive', fostering unprincipled 'democrats and infidels'; and that, in any case, '[t]he intelligence of our English people is not to be measured by any . . . statistical rule; . . . we have a thousand ways of instructing our people which continental states know nothing of' (*A Letter to the Rev. W. F. Hook, D. D., Vicar of Leeds, on his proposed plan for the Education of the People*, London, 1846, p. 29). (Burgess' opposition to Hook was sufficiently well known for the

Leeds Intelligencer leader of 15 August 1846 to mention it; p. 4.) The point about a shortage of teachers was a sensitive one. The great advantage of the monitorial system practised in early-nineteenth-century Britain (see above p. 157) was that it extended basic literacy with minimal staff. Other countries that tried it rejected it as ineffective, concluding, according to Hickson, that '[t]here is but one secret in education – good teachers, and a sufficient number for the work' (*Dutch and German Schools*, p. 42).

17. *Leeds Mercury*, 13 March 1847, 4.
18. See, for instance, the *Leeds Intelligencer* for 17 April 1847, 4.
19. Including William Morgan of Bradford, whose support for the government scheme is repeatedly mentioned in the *Leeds Intelligencer*; see 27 March 1847, 6–7, and 3 April 1847, 5.
20. See Baumber, 'Patrick Brontë', for an account of the Sunday school at Haworth and neighbouring communities, especially pp. 66–9.
21. See, for instance, W. B. Stephens, *Education in Britain*, pp. 3–5, and John McLeish, *Evangelical Religion and Popular Education: A Modern Interpretation* (London: Methuen, 1969), pp. 58ff. (on Hannah More's Mendip schools). For a contemporary view, see Mann's *Census*, pp. 69–70.
22. This Act prescribed two hours of schooling a day for the working child, but implementation was erratic. See, for instance, John Lawson and Harold Silver, *A Social History of Education in England* (London: Methuen, 1973; I have used the 1978 reprint), pp. 273–4.
23. On Patrick Brontë's involvement with the Bradford Auxiliary Bible Society, see Juliet Barker, *The Brontës*, pp. 55 and 61. Taxes on paper and publications ('taxes on knowledge') were consecutively abolished in the mid-nineteenth century; see Nigel Cross, *The Common Writer: Life in Nineteenth Century Grub Street* (Cambridge University Press, 1985), p. 95.
24. See, for instance, McLeish, *Evangelical Religion*, pp. 46 and 56.
25. Quoted by Barker, *The Brontës*, pp. 183–4.
26. Cf. Hook, *On the Means*, p. 48: 'Many young men and women, who have no other day in the week for recreation and leisure . . . consecrate their little leisure on the Lord's Day to the training of little children in the way they ought to go. Each has a separate class, and becomes personally acquainted with the character of each member of the class'.
27. See, for instance, McLeish, *Evangelical Religion*, pp. 54–5.
28. Vol. XXXII (Sept. 1832), 343.
29. See Joyce Goodman, 'Undermining or building up a nation? Elizabeth Hamilton (1758–1816), national identities and an authoritative role for women educationists', *History of Education* 28.3 (1999), 279–96, and Gary Kelly, *Women, Writing, and Revolution, 1790–1827* (Oxford: Clarendon Press, 1993), pp. 282–91.
30. See Goodman, 'Undermining or building up the nation?', 289–91.
31. The relevant passages are mentioned in an insightful article by Paul Schacht, 'Jane Eyre and the history of self-respect', *Modern Language Quarterly* 52.4 (December 1991), 423–53 (438–9 and 441).

32. See Barker, *The Brontës*, pp. 2–3. John Lock and W. T. Dixon's *A Man of Sorrow: The Life, Letters and Times of the Rev. Patrick Brontë 1777–1861* (London: Nelson, 1965) may be more than a little fictionalised in places, but the underlying appraisal of Patrick Brontë's character seems sound; the first chapter outlines a family where means were scanty but hard work ensured respectability.

33. Among volumes now in the Brontë Parsonage Museum that bear witness to Patrick Brontë's interest in science are Sir Humphry Davy's classic *Elements of Chemical Philosophy* (London, 1812); the Zoological Society's *The Gardens and Menagerie of the Zoological Society*, vol. I (London, 1830); John Murray, *System of Materia Medica and Pharmacy* (Edinburgh, 1813); and *A System of Anatomy from Monro, Winslow, Innes, and the Latest Authors* (Edinburgh, 1784). (Thomas John Graham's *Modern Domestic Medicine* of 1826 has often been referred to as Patrick Brontë's medical bible, and with reason – it is full of his notes and a fascinating object of study in itself.)

34. A copy of Fresnoy's *Geography* is in the Brontë Parsonage Museum, inscribed with the names Hugh Brontë, P. Brontë and Walsh Bronte. *The Universal Preceptor; being an easy Grammar of Arts, Sciences, and General Knowledge* was written by the diligent educational author David Blair and published by the likewise diligent publisher of educational literature Richard Phillips; I have read the second edition of 1811. The authors of the two-volume *Systematic Education: or, Elementary Instruction in the Various Departments of Literature and Science, with Practical Rules for Studying Each Branch of Useful Knowledge*, William Shepherd, Jeremiah Joyce and Lant Carpenter, were Dissenter ministers (I used the third edition of 1822).

35. On the Classical subjects, see above pp. 121ff.

36. See, for instance, Richard D. Altick, 'Publishing', in Herbert F. Tucker (ed.), *A Companion to Victorian Literature & Culture* (Oxford: Blackwell, 1999), pp. 291 and 302, and Richardson, *Literature, Education, and Romanticism*, pp. 222–4. On working-class opposition to the kinds of reading with which the S.D.U.K. would supply the lower orders, see Brian Simon, *Studies in the History of Education 1780–1870* (London: Lawrence & Wishart, 1960), pp. 229–31.

37. On the connection between the two, see, for instance, Mabel Tylecote, *The Mechanics' Institutes of Lancashire and Yorkshire before 1851* (Manchester University Press, 1957), p. 32.

38. See Stephens, *Education in Britain*, p. 63.

39. According to J. W. Hudson, an early historian of the movement, quoted by Simon in *Studies in the History of Education*, p. 158.

40. See John Roach, *A History of Secondary Education in England, 1800–1870* (London: Longman, 1986), pp. 104, 114, 153 and 202.

41. See Stephens, *Education in Britain*, pp. 70–3.

42. *Leeds Intelligencer* 22 August 1846, 4.

43. For a summary on the position of women in the Mechanics' Institutes, see June Purvis, *A History of Women's Education in England* (Open University Press, 1991), pp. 98–9.

44. On the Brontës and the Keighley Mechanics' Institute, see Clifford Whone, 'Where the Brontës borrowed books: The Keighley Mechanics' Institute', *BST* 11.60 (1950), 344–58; Ian Dewhirst, 'The Rev. Patrick Brontë and the Keighley Mechanics' Institute', *BST* 14.5 (Pt 75, 1965), 35–7; Lock and Dixon, *A Man of Sorrow, passim*; Tom Winnifrith, *The Brontës and Their Background: Romance and Reality* (New York: Barnes & Noble, 1973), pp. 85–6 and 91–5; Barker, *The Brontës*, pp. 147–8 and 212–13; and Shuttleworth, *Charlotte Brontë*, pp. 23–7 (see also Shuttleworth's note on the Haworth Mechanics' Institute, p. 252n20).
45. See Smith, *Letters* I, pp. 214–15.
46. Timothy Claxton, *Hints to Mechanics, on Self-Education and Mutual Instruction* (London, 1839), 'A selection of exercises for popular institutions' annexed to the work itself (pp. 217–22). Claxton includes information about the Keighley Mechanics' Institute, stating the number of members as 119 and the number of library 'volumes' as 896 (p. 224).
47. See John van Wyhe, *Phrenology and the Origins of Victorian Scientific Naturalism* (Aldershot: Ashgate, 2004), p. 185.
48. Charlotte Brontë's connection with phrenology has been thoroughly examined by Sally Shuttleworth in *Charlotte Brontë*, pp. 57–70; see also pp. 162, 181 and 202. On phrenology in *The Tenant of Wildfell Hall*, see Marianne Thormählen, 'The villain of *Wildfell Hall*: aspects and prospects of Arthur Huntingdon', *Modern Language Review* 88.4 (Oct. 1993), 831–41 (834–6). Nicholas Dames's 'The clinical novel: Phrenology and *Villette*', *Novel: A Forum on Fiction* 29.3 (Spring 1996), 367–90, is orientated towards the 'gaze' concept. A more down-to-earth approach to phrenology in a Brontë context is found in Beth Torgerson's *Reading the Brontë Body: Disease, Desire, and the Constraints of Culture* (Basingstoke: Palgrave, 2005), pp. 77–81.
49. See van Wyhe, *Phrenology*, p. 128. Another excellent book on phrenology in the nineteenth century is Roger Cooter's standard work of 1984, *The Cultural Meaning of Popular Science: Phrenology and the Organization of Consent in Nineteenth-Century Britain* (Cambridge University Press).
50. van Wyhe, *Phrenology*, pp. 181 and 203.
51. *Ibid.*, pp. 129–30 and 140.
52. *Considerations on Phrenology, in connexion with an Intellectual, Moral, and Religious Education* (London, 1839), p. 23.
53. See, for instance, Mrs John Pugh, *Phrenology considered in a Religious Light; or, Thoughts and Readings Consequent on the Perusal of 'Combe's Constitution of Man'* (London, 1846), especially pp. 79–84, 105, 137 and 143. It seems likely that at least Anne Brontë knew Pugh's book; see Thormählen, 'The villain', 835–6.
54. *Remarks on National Education* (Edinburgh, 1847), p. 9; see also pp. 15ff. (Combe supported national education and did not believe it would need to be compulsory; p. 32.) See also *Lectures on Popular Education* (Edinburgh 1837, corrected and enlarged edition), p. 34: '[E]very thing in the world is regulated by laws instituted by the Creator'. Combe's *Lectures*, delivered in 1833, were reprinted in *Chambers's Journal* and thus gained a wide readership, which may

well have included the Brontës; in *Shirley*, this periodical is said be one that Caroline Helstone and William Farren would have enjoyed if it had existed in their day (III.ii.445).

55. In one of *Blackwood's* 'Noctes Ambrosianae', the 'Ettrick Shepherd' argues against phrenologists ('a peculiar people, jealous o' good works'), especially female ones who, he says, are mannish and immodest. A lady named 'Miss Gentle' objects: 'Phrenology is now quite epidemic, Mr Hogg, among our sex in Edinburgh'; vol. XX (July–Dec. 1827), 119 and 117. (A dog called 'Bronte' figures in this dialogue.)

56. On women and phrenology, see also Shuttleworth, *Charlotte Brontë*, p. 65.

57. See van Wyhe, *Phrenology*, pp. 180–6. On Combe's influence in the sphere of education, see Stephen Tomlinson, 'Phrenology, education and the politics of human nature: the thought and influence of George Combe', *History of Education* 26.1 (1997), 1–22, and N. W. Saffin, *Science, Religion & Education in Britain 1804–1904* (Kilmore, Vict.: Lowden, 1973), pp. 171–4. See also p. 131 above.

58. See, for instance, the Rev. C. [Charles] Mayo, *Memoir of Pestalozzi*, a lecture delivered at the Royal Institution, May 1826, 2nd ed. of 1828, pp. 21–2, and C. W. J. Higson (ed.), *Sources for the History of Education* (London: The Library Association, 1967), p. 80.

59. The word 'catechism' of course implied that the information contained in the book was adapted to learning by heart. On rote-learning in education, see above pp. 187ff.

60. *Essays on Practical Education* in two volumes, originally published in 1798; I have used the 1815 edition (published by Turner in London), where the pertinent references are on pp. iii and vii–viii in the Preface.

61. *Aids to developement [sic]; or, Mental and Moral Instruction Exemplified* (London, 1829), vol. I, p. 12.

62. See above p. 124 and below p. 258n11.

63. Cf. Lucy Snowe's answer to M. Paul when invited to acknowledge her ignorance: 'I am ignorant, monsieur, in the knowledge you ascribe to me, but I *sometimes*, not *always*, feel a knowledge of my own' (*Villette* XXX.355).

64. See Barker, *The Brontës*, pp. 128–9. Cf. above p. 91.

65. See above p. 191.

66. See above p. 166.

67. See Barney, *Plots of Enlightenment*, p. 29 on self versus system in the context of Romantic thinking. As epigraph for his idiosyncratic but lively and information-packed *Science, Religion & Education*, Saffin chose a Carlyle quotation, 'Few mortals, it is to be feared, are permanently blessed with that felicity of "having no system"'.

CHAPTER 2 THE IMPROVEMENT OF THE MIND

1. In a gesture towards the Chartists, on whose agenda education was a big item, Russell said that he tried to secure public peace without repression and saw education as conducive to that peace. Speech in the House of Commons 20 June

1839 on the Government Plan for promoting National Education, separately
printed, p. 20 (second edition, 1839). It was a view shared by many, among them
Sir James Kay-Shuttleworth and his American counterpart Horace Mann; see
Trygve R. Tholfsen's edition of *Sir James Kay-Shuttleworth on Popular Education* (New York: Teachers College Press, 1974), p. 33 (Tholfsen's introduction).

2. The two are, of course, Charlotte and Anne. Whether Branwell ever felt that
   obligation is difficult to tell. Emily's attitude to education is a complicated
   issue; see above pp. 149 and 159–60.
3. See Winifred Gérin, *Anne Brontë* (London: Nelson, 1959; I have used the 1976
   Allen Lane edition), p. 86.
4. M. A. Stodart's *Hints on Reading: Addressed to a Young Lady* of 1839, a work
   which advises against fiction and poetry (with the exception of Spenser's *Faerie
   Queene*) for girls, commends Watts's *Improvement* in the following terms:
   '[This] work I mention the more willingly on account of the well-known
   opinion of Dr. Johnson respecting it, viz. – that "no teacher of youth can be
   said to have fulfilled his duty, if he does not recommend this treatise to the
   perusal of his pupils"' (pp. 19–20 in Stodart's book.)
5. See, for instance, Alan Rauch, *Useful Knowledge: The Victorians, Morality,
   and the March of Intellect* (Durham: Duke University Press, 2001), p. 134.
   Incidentally, Rauch stresses the pedagogical functions of Charlotte Brontë's
   fiction; see especially pp. 131 and 163 ('she engages the reader in a . . . complex
   process of learning'; p. 163).
6. See Smith, *Letters* I, pp. 129–31. On this letter, see also pp. 89 and 95 above.
7. Watts's book was intended for readers of both sexes; see above p. 138. Other
   works with 'improvement' in their titles are Elizabeth ('Mrs John') Sandford,
   Female Improvement (London, 1836), as well as Priscilla Wakefield's *Mental
   Improvement: Or, the Beauties and Wonders of Nature and Art* (1794–97), available in an edition by Ann B. Shteir for Colleagues Press (East Lansing, 1995),
   and *Reflections on the Present Condition of the Female Sex, with Suggestions for
   Its Improvement* (the second edition publ. in London, 1817).
8. *Female Improvement*, vol. I, p. 183. On the distinction between reading and
   study, see above pp. 137ff.
9. *History*, vol. II, p. 596.
10. Martineau's and Henry George Atkinson's *Letters on the Laws of Man's Nature
    and Development* (London, 1851) contains Atkinson's two-page onslaught on
    Christianity on rational grounds (pp. 203–5) and the same author's dismissal
    of the Bible and religion as 'a romance'; 'Baron Munchausen [sic] is a tame
    affair to it' (p. 234). On Charlotte Brontë's reaction to this book, see Smith,
    Letters II, pp. 547, 561 and 574.
11. See Pauline Nestor's sensitive exploration of the contradictory forces in
    Charlotte Brontë's prose in *Charlotte Brontë* (Basingstoke: Macmillan, 1987),
    pp. 30–1, and Philip Davis' incisive remarks on Charlotte Brontë in relation
    to her sisters, and to Harriet Martineau's *Deerbrook*, in *The Victorians*, The
    Oxford English Literary History vol 8, 1830–1880 (Oxford University Press,
    2002), pp. 363–4.

12. Anne Brontë's designation of Helen's fateful mistake in her preface to the second edition of *The Tenant of Wildfell Hall*, p. 4 in the World's Classics edition.

13. The serious nature of Helen's error is explained in Marianne Thormählen, 'Aspects of Love in *The Tenant of Wildfell Hall*', in Julie Nash and Barbara A. Suess (eds), *New Approaches to the Literary Art of Anne Brontë* (Aldershot: Ashgate, 2001), pp. 153–71 (especially pp. 154–8).

14. As Birgitta Berglund points out, what Lucy Snowe celebrates as truth – her conviction that M. Paul will marry his ward – is in fact a delusion; see 'In defence of Madame Beck', *Brontë Studies* 30.3 (Nov. 2005), 185–211 (204). Carol Bock regards Lucy as 'a storytelling *interpretant*' rather than a truth-teller; see *Charlotte Brontë and the Storyteller's Audience* (Iowa City: University of Iowa Press, 1992), pp. 127–48.

15. See also the exchange between Caroline and Mrs Pryor in II.i.222. Having been told by Caroline that she 'always [likes] the truth', her as yet unacknowledged mother, another former self-deluder who paid a terrible price, expressed her approval, adding, 'adhere to that preference – never swerve thence'.

16. See Thormählen, *The Brontës and Religion*, pp. 259–60n41.

17. *Letters, 1848–1888*, ed. G. W. E. Russell (London and New York, 1901), vol. II, p. 359, quoted by Walter E. Houghton in *The Victorian Frame of Mind 1830–1870* (New Haven: Yale University Press, 1957), p. 13. It should be borne in mind that nineteenth-century melioristic optimism always coexisted with doubt about the validity and durability of progress. For instance, about 20 years before Mill wrote the quoted letter a writer well known to the Brontës expressed such concerns, Robert Southey in *Sir Thomas More: Colloquies on the Progress and Prospects of Society* (1829). For a review of Southey's misgivings about his age, see R. W. Harris, *Romanticism and the Social Order 1780–1830* (London: Blandford, 1969), pp. 271–3.

18. On the 'restless relativism' and subjectivity of the Victorians, see Robin Gilmour, *The Victorian Period: The Intellectual and Cultural Context of English Literature, 1830–1890* (London: Longman, 1993), ch. 1, especially pp. 30–1.

19. *The Victorian Frame of Mind*, p. 14.

20. *The Daughters of England: Their Position in Society, Character, and Responsibilities* (London, 1842 and 1845), p. 115. On Arnold, see Houghton, *The Victorian Frame of Mind*, p. 17n60.

21. This popular work of didactic fiction appeared in 1836 (London); the quoted passage is on p. 121.

22. *Remarks*, p. 12. The Sandford quotation is from *Female Improvement*, vol. II, pp. 192–3.

23. This is not, of course, to suggest that previous generations were not equally dedicated to truth; the entire eighteenth century reverberates with protestations of its importance both to right thinking and to right action. But the early-nineteenth-century combination of ethics and epistemology in this area interacts with a sense of the elusiveness and complexity of truth, an element

of unease that is not felt in such earlier writers on education as Locke, Fénelon and Rollin.

24. The authors of *Systematic Education* summarised the benefits of an allegiance to truth in the following terms: '[T]he love of truth should influence us in all our investigations. The question should always be, not is this speculation ingenious and brilliant, but is it solid and just: and if truth be our real object, and we pursue it with patient attention, and under the guidance of good sense, and judicious reflection and observation, we can scarcely fail to attain what will reward us for our labour, both in the culture of the understanding, and in the conduct of life' (p. 341).

25. See, for instance, F. D. Maurice's dedication of a revised edition of *The Kingdom of Christ* to Derwent Coleridge. (First published in 1837, Maurice's work bore the full title *The Kingdom of Christ, or Hints on the Principles, Ordinances, & Constitution of the Catholic Church. In Letters to a Member of the Society of Friends.*) In this connection one must remember that where the highest truth, God's truth, was concerned, it was impermissible for human beings to compromise. What may strike later ages as a deplorable absence of give-and-take should be seen in that context.

26. See Smith, *Letters* II, pp. 22–4; Smith's suggestion as to the likely content of Williams' letter (p. 24n5) seems well-founded. For a masterly analysis of truth as the central tenet in Charlotte Brontë's artistic creed, see Inga-Stina Ewbank, *Their Proper Sphere: A Study of the Brontë Sisters as Early-Victorian Female Novelists* (Cambridge, MA: Harvard University Press, 1966), pp. 161–5. See also Earl A. Knies, *The Art of Charlotte Brontë* (Athens: Ohio University Press, 1969), pp. 52–5.

CHAPTER 3 HOUSEHOLD EDUCATION VERSUS SCHOOL TRAINING

1. *Leeds Intelligencer* 4 December 1823, 1; quoted in Barker, *The Brontës*, p. 118.

2. See Lock and Dixon, *A Man of Sorrow*, ch. 1. Edward Chitham's *The Brontës' Irish Background* (Basingstoke: Macmillan, 1986) devotes a chapter to the young Patrick's teaching (pp. 77–91).

3. Juliet Barker's assumption that Tighe instructed Patrick Brontë in the Classics seems likely (see *The Brontës*, pp. 5–6); but according to Lock and Dixon his first and most important Classics tutor was the Presbyterian minister Andrew Harshaw (p. 7). Cf. Richard Wilson in *The Tenant of Wildfell Hall*, 'a retiring, studious young man, who was studying the classics with the vicar's assistance, preparing for college, with a view to enter the church' (I.18).

4. See, for instance, Richardson, *Literature, Education, and Romanticism*, p. 55.

5. According to Buckworth, young persons should be instructed by their parents even after reaching the '*years of maturity*'. See *A Series of Discourses, Containing a System of Doctrinal, Experimental, and Practical Religion, Particularly Calculated for the Use of Families*, p. 276; according to the inscription on the flyleaf of the Haworth copy, Patrick had owned it since 1811, when it first appeared.

John Locke's *Some Thoughts Concerning Education* indicates how familiar the arguments on both sides had been for over a century. Acknowledging that the school environment will make a boy 'bolder, and better able to bustle and shift amongst Boys of his own age', besides giving him the benefit of competition and emulation, Locke still preferred the home, deploring the hazarding of a boy's innocence and virtue 'for a little Greek and Latin'. See § 70, pp. 128–9 in John W. and Jean S. Yolton's edition of Locke's *Some Thoughts Concerning Education* (Oxford: Clarendon Press, 1989). On the opposition to school training among leading eighteenth-century educationists, see Nicholas Hans, *New Trends in Education in the Eighteenth Century* (London: Routledge and Kegan Paul, 1951), pp. 181–8.

6. At least, this order of priority was constantly asserted in printed works on education from all quarters; as ensuing chapters show, pious theory and worldly practice did not always agree.

7. Pages 10–11 in the 5th edition of 1839 (first published in 1833). On home education and the Brontës, see also Drew Lamonica, *'We Are Three Sisters': Self and Family in the Writing of the Brontës* (Columbia: University of Missouri Press, 2003), pp. 14–25 (Lamonica quotes Richmond's statement 'A good home is the best of schools', pp. 14–15).

8. Published in 1778, the book carries the subtitle, *or, Poems, Letters, and Essays, Moral, Elegiac, and Descriptive.* The quoted passage is on p. 160. Of course, Patrick Brontë had seen improvements in public and private education in his lifetime; but not even the schools he knew personally, such as the Wesleyan Woodhouse Grove school where he was examiner for the Classics (and met Maria Branwell) in 1812, were model institutions. Cf. p. 185.

9. For an excellent summary of Patrick Brontë's reasons for choosing Roe Head, see Barker, *The Brontës*, pp. 171–2.

10. Coreen Turner suggests that Patrick Brontë's 'understanding of the fragile nature of Branwell's character' was one reason why the boy was kept at home. See "'With what eagerness . . .'": The influence of Patrick Brontë on his children's education', Duckett (ed.), *The Brontës and Education: 2004 Conference*, p. 17.

11. 'Home-sickness' in Tom Winnifrith (ed.), *The Poems of Charlotte Brontë: A New Annotated and Enlarged Edition of the Shakespeare Head Brontë* (Oxford: Blackwell, 1984), p. 94. The school rebellions of the 1790s (see, for instance, Richardson, *Literature, Education, and Romanticism*, p. 82) were obviously known in Haworth Parsonage; see the young Charlotte Brontë's piece on a school mutiny in *Tales of the Islanders*, in Alexander's *An Edition*, vol. I, pp. 99–102.

12. On the education of Victor Crimsworth, see above pp. 45f. Cf. also Heather Glen, *Charlotte Brontë*, pp. 48–9. The pros and cons of a home education for girls are reviewed in John Todd's *The Daughter at School* (London, 1853), pp. 30ff., Todd coming down on the side of school because it offers standards, stimulus, professional teaching and incentives to grow up as a mature adult accustomed to living among other people.

CHAPTER 4 PARENTS AND CHILDREN

1. Mary Maurice's *Aids to Developement* is an instructive example; the model maternal teacher Mrs Eustace's little boy comments: 'I wish, mamma, every thing reminded me of God, as it does you; I should be much happier if that was the case' (vol. II, p. 158).

2. On Evangelical upbringing, see Doreen M. Rosman, *Evangelicals and Culture* (London: Croom Helm, 1984); pp. 98–9 in the 1992 Gregg revivals reprint. Cf. also Glen, *Charlotte Brontë*, p. 74, and p. 156 above.

3. *Letters on Education. With observations on religious and metaphysical subjects* (Dublin, 1790), Part I, p. 53 (Letter IX). On Rousseau, see also pp. 113–14 and 156–7 above. Mary Wollstonecraft devoted considerable space to the horrors of mendacity in *Thoughts on the Education of Daughters* of 1787; see pp. 13–15 and 21 in the facsimile edition from Thoemmes Press (Bristol, 1995).

4. *Essays on Practical Education*, vol. I, p. 243 in the 1815 edition of the Edgeworths' educational classic published by Hunter in London.

5. *Ibid.*, I.251. Macaulay had made the same point (I.54).

6. See, for instance, Edward Chitham's retelling of and speculations about the story in *A Life of Emily Brontë* (Oxford: Blackwell, 1987), pp. 27–9. (These are the questions and answers: Maria, asked about the best way of spending time, replied, 'laying it out in preparation for a happy eternity'; Elizabeth, asked about the best education for a woman, defined it as 'that which would make her rule her house well'; Charlotte, asked about the best book in the world, answered the Bible, with 'the Book of Nature' in second place; Branwell recommended that anyone who wished to know the difference between the intellects of men and women should consider the differences in their bodies; Emily, asked what to do with Branwell when he was naughty, replied, 'reason with him, and when he won't listen to reason, whip him' (an exact parallel to the sequence of events in the Appendix to Samuel Wilderspin's *On the Importance of Educating the Infant Poor [and so on]*, pp. 213ff. in the enlarged 2nd edition of 1824); and Anne, aged four, said that 'age and experience' were what a child like her wanted most. The quotations from Patrick Brontë's letter to Mrs Gaskell, dated 30 July 1855, were taken from Green's edition of Patrick Brontë's *Letters*, p. 239.)

7. Subsequent scholarly probing of their evidence has confirmed the essential truthfulness of Charlotte Brontë's father as well as of her husband.

8. See her *Reciprocal Duties of Parents and Children* of 1818, pp. 21–2 and 60–1. Incidentally, Taylor has a particularly interesting chapter on the problem of 'rustic' parents 'overtaken' by educated offspring (pp. 74–85) – a fairly frequent one in an era of swift middle-class expansion. The idea of parents respecting their children was nothing new; for instance, Locke had urged fathers to have 'a great reverence' for their sons, quoting the Latin adage '*Maxima debetur pueris reverentia*'; § 71, p. 133 in the Yoltons' edition of *Some Thoughts*.

9. The story of little George and his hatchet was familiar to nineteenth-century children from books such as *Abbott's Reader; A Series of Familiar Pieces, in Prose and Verse; Calculated to Exercise a Moral Influence on the Hearts and Lives of*

Young Persons. By the authors of *The Young Christian*; *The Corner-Stone*; *The Teacher*; *The Mother at Home*; *The Child at Home*; *&c.* (London, 1835; this is the second edition), pp. 161–2.

10. *Letters to a Young Lady, in which the duties and character of women are considered, [and so on]* (London, 1806), vol. I, p. 78. The quotation from Thomson's 'Spring', a commonplace in educational contexts at the time, is of course also present in *Agnes Grey* (I.9).

11. *A Series of Discourses*, p. 275. The word 'passionate' is interesting as a term of explicit censure; it is the quality Mrs Reed invites the child Jane Eyre to admit to, having had to back down from the accusation of deceitfulness (*Jane Eyre* I.iv.37).

12. See Susan Brooke, 'Anne Brontë at Blake Hall: An Episode of Courage and Insight', *BST* 13.68 (1958), 239–50 (241, 247).

13. Cf. Thormählen, *The Brontës and Religion*, pp. 168–9. See also Stevie Davies, *Emily Brontë* (1998, in the Northcote House and British Council series Writers and Their Work), pp. 54f. on the cruel child in Emily's 'Le Chat' *devoir*, and cf. *Shirley* III.iii.462, where Shirley says that schoolboys usually seem 'little ruffians' to her, 'who take an unnatural delight in killing and tormenting birds, and insects, and kittens, and whatever is weaker than themselves'. Laments over children's cruelty to helpless animals are not of course specific to the nineteenth century (or to Britain, or even to boys); for an earlier example, see Sarah Fielding's *The Governess: or, Little Female Academy*, 'The life of Miss Jenny Peace', pp. 31–2 in the 1749 edition issued in facsimile by Oxford University Press in 1968, with an introduction by Jill E. Grey (p. 130 in the OUP volume). In a different context, Miss Jenny says, 'Remember, if you abuse a Dog or Cat, because it is in your Power, you are like [a] cruel Monster' (pp. 73–4; pp. 171–2). Locke also deplored boys' cruelty to animals, '[f]or the custom of tormenting and killing of Beasts will, by degrees, harden their Minds even towards Men' (§ 116, p. 180 in the Yoltons' edition of *Some Thoughts*). On childish cruelty to animals in the context of Lockean – and Rousseauan – thought, see also Tess Cosslett, *Talking Animals in British Children's Fiction, 1786–1914* (Aldershot: Ashgate, 2006), pp. 21–3.

14. *An Inquiry concerning the Nature and Operations of the Human Mind, in which the Science of Phrenology, the Doctrine of Necessity, Punishment, and Education, are particularly considered* (1828). A 'Lecture delivered at the Mechanics' Institution, London', this publication may well have formed part of Mechanics' Institutes libraries available to the Brontës. (The publishers are stated as being 'Poole and Edwards' of Ave-Maria-Lane in London, 'Successors to Scatcherd and Letterman'; the names Poole and Scatcherd are of course intriguing in a Brontë context.)

15. A quotation from Louisa Hoare's *Friendly Advice, on the Management and Education of Children; addressed to Parents of the Middle and Labouring Classes of Society* (London, 1824), p. 21. Hoare's book is sometimes so close to *Agnes Grey* that one wonders whether the correspondences are quite coincidental; cf., for instance, Hoare's 'promise only what you mean to perform, and threaten

only what you [can] execute' (p. 31) with Agnes' 'I must be cautious to threaten and promise nothing that I could not perform' (III.25).

16. *Reciprocal Duties*, pp. 59–60.
17. *Ibid.*, p. 59. (See Daniel 6, verses 8 and 12.)
18. Hoare, *Friendly Advice*, p. 5; Hoare also exhorts parents to conceal any disagreements and refrain from interfering when the other parent disciplines a child, with realistic quotations such as 'Why can't you let the child alone? – come to mother, Johnny'.
19. See, for instance, Taylor, *Reciprocal Duties*, pp. 24–34.
20. *Ibid.*, p. 168.
21. Jeremiah Joyce, author of much educational literature, included lists of the duties of parents and children in *An Analysis of Paley's View of the Evidences of Christianity* in three parts, Part I pp. 27–9 in the 7th edition of 1826. Joyce's handbook was recommended at the back of Goldsmith's geography, which the Brontës owned; the importance of setting a good example is mentioned on p. 27. The fact that this book existed, and in many editions (it seems to have been first published in 1795), testifies to Paley's enduring prestige (see further p. 146 above).
22. In the Brontë Parsonage Museum copy of Hannah More's *Moral Sketches of Prevailing Opinions and Manners, Foreign and Domestic: with Reflections on Prayer* (London, 1819; this is the third edition), passages on 'CONSISTENCY, that infallible criterion of a highly-finished Christian character' are marked and underlined (pp. 126–8).
23. Elizabeth Hamilton, *Letters on the Elementary Principles of Education*, 7th (London, 1824), vol. I, pp. 57–8 and 95. Hamilton urges parents not to allow children to interrupt and be nuisances engrossing the mother's whole attention (p. 87). One of her examples of misguided indoctrination of children is interesting as an illustration of the evolution of the term 'democrat': the parents of a little boy who says '*I hate demotats!*' were wrong to teach the infant mind that it is acceptable to hate anyone (pp. 57–8).
24. Cf. Joyce's *Analysis* of Paley which states, 'Parents have no right over the lives of their children, or to sell them into slavery. They exceed their authority when they consult their own interest at the expense of their children's happiness' (p. 28 in the 1826 edn).
25. Cf. Eagleton, *Myths of Power*, p. 103.
26. See Lamonica, 'We Are Three Sisters', pp. 168–9. On the Yorke family, see also Pauline Nestor, *Female Friendships and Communities: Charlotte Brontë, George Eliot, Elizabeth Gaskell* (Oxford: Clarendon Press, 1985), pp. 123–4, and cf. Helene Moglen, *Charlotte Brontë: The Self Conceived* (New York: Norton, 1976), pp. 165–8.
27. Ten years earlier, in the fragmentary story 'Ashworth', Charlotte Brontë had briefly sketched a downright grim household, with warring parents and a son sent to Eton 'not that he might acquire an education, but that he might be out of [his father's] sight'. See Charlotte Brontë, *Unfinished Novels* (Stroud: Alan Sutton and the Brontë Society, 1993), pp. 19–20. The son in due course comes

to detest his own children. The pattern occurs in the juvenilia, too, where the Duke of Northangerland is not content with disowning his sons but actually orders their destruction.

28. Mary Summers points to this scene as a manifestation of household disharmony with an adverse effect on children's behaviour in *Anne Brontë Educating Parents* (Beverley: Highgate, 2003), p. 18.

29. *A Series of Discourses*, p. 259. Mrs William Parkes allowed that a wife's better judgement and principles might persuade her to oppose her husband's moral errors; see *Domestic Duties, or, Instructions to Young Married Ladies on the Management of Their Households [and so on]* (London, 1825), pp. 3–4.

30. Lee Talley suggests that Anne Brontë brought Methodist Evangelicalism to bear on the treatment of education in *The Tenant of Wildfell Hall*; see 'Anne Brontë's method of social protest in *The Tenant of Wildfell Hall*' in Nash and Suess (eds), *New Approaches*, pp. 127–51, especially pp. 137 and 140–5.

31. The same ground is gone over by two troubled fathers in Charlotte Brontë's 'Ashworth'; see p. 53 in Charlotte's *Unfinished Novels*.

32. *Reciprocal Duties*, p. 93.

33. *Letters*, I.154. Cf. Locke, *Some Thoughts*, § 70, p. 129 in the Yoltons' edition: having established that the 'Retirement and Bashfulness' in which girls are reared do not make them 'less knowing or less able Women', Locke suggests that boys would become as capable and virtuous as they if raised at home under good influences, 'for Courage and Steadiness . . . lie not in Roughness and ill Breeding. Vertue is harder to be got than a Knowledge of the World; and if lost in a Young Man, is seldom recovered'.

34. The literature on this subject is vast, and one reference must suffice here: Colley's chapter on 'Womanpower' in *Britons*, pp. 237–81, reviews the arguments in relation to the debaters (male and female, the latter including More, Wollstonecraft and, later, Ellis) who shaped the early-nineteenth-century climate of opinion.

35. Winifred Gérin's biography of Branwell Brontë draws a parallel between Victor Crimsworth and Branwell (and between Branwell's misfortunes and the educational tenets of 'Mrs Graham' in *The Tenant of Wildfell Hall*); see *Branwell Brontë* (London: Nelson, 1961), pp. 19–20 and 24. (Gérin believes that Branwell briefly attended a local grammar school while his sisters were at Cowan Bridge; see pp. 8–9 and 17–19.)

36. In his dispute with 'Mrs Graham', Gilbert Markham says, 'it is better to arm and strengthen your hero, than to disarm and enfeeble the foe' (III.30).

37. See Richardson, *Literature, Education, and Romanticism*, p. 82. It is interesting to find that Thomas Arnold, writing instructions on his sons' education in case of his premature death, told his brother-in-law to help Mary Arnold settle somewhere where the boys could attend a day school and be 'under [their mother's] care at other times'. See J. R. de S. Honey, *Tom Brown's Universe: The Development of the Victorian Public School* (London: Millington, 1977), p. 23.

CHAPTER 5 PROFESSIONAL EDUCATORS IN THE HOME

1. Where the Victorian period is concerned, Cecilia Wadsö Lecaros' *The Victorian Governess Novel* (Lund: Lund University Press, 2001) supersedes earlier work on governesses in fiction such as Katharine West's *Chapter of Governesses: A Study of the Governess in English Fiction 1800–1949* (London: Cohen & West, 1949). Lecaros is also highly informative on real-life governesses. On the situation of governesses in the nineteenth century, see Pamela Horn, 'The Victorian governess', *History of Education* 18.4 (1989), 333–44; Alice Renton, *Tyrant or Victim? A History of the British Governess* (London: Weidenfeld and Nicolson, 1991); and Kathryn Hughes, *The Victorian Governess* (London: Hambledon Press, 1993). A pioneering study of the governess' difficult social position was M. Jeanne Peterson, 'The Victorian Governess: Status Incongruence in Family and Society' in Martha Vicinus (ed.), *Suffer and Be Still: Women in the Victorian Age* (Bloomington: Indiana University Press, 1972). Mary Poovey's *Uneven Developments: The Ideological Work of Gender in Mid-Victorian England* (Chicago University Press, 1988) contains a feminist discussion of the position of the governess in relation to the wife/mother in the family she serves. (This discussion forms part of a frequently reprinted chapter called 'The anathematized race: The governess and *Jane Eyre*'.) Poovey has also contributed a short chapter called 'Jane Eyre and the Governess in Nineteenth-Century Britain' to Diane Long Hoeveler and Beth Lau (eds), *Approaches to Teaching Brontë's Jane Eyre* (New York: The Modern Language Association of America, 1993), pp. 43–8. Trev Broughton and Ruth Symes' (eds) *The Governess: An Anthology* (Phoenix Mill: Sutton, 1997) is a very enjoyable introduction to the subject, and Leonore Davidoff and Catherine Hall's *Family Fortunes: Men and Women of the English Middle Class, 1750–1850* (first published in 1987; I have used the revised Routledge reprint of 2002) is informative on governesses (as on many other things). R. A. Colby's chapter on 'Lucy Snowe and the good governess' in *Fiction with a Purpose: Major and Minor Nineteenth Century Novels* (Bloomington: Indiana University Press, 1967), pp. 178–212, situates *Villette* in the context of educational debates around 1850. With reference to the Brontës, see also Dara Rossman Regaignon, 'Instructive sufficiency: re-reading the governess through *Agnes Grey*', *Victorian Literature and Culture* 29.1 (2001), 85–108; James R. Simmons, Jr, 'Class, matriarchy, and power: contextualizing thes governess in *Agnes Grey*' in Nash and Suess (eds), *New Approaches*, pp. 25–43; and Cecilia Wadsö Lecaros, '"Lessons in the art of instruction": Education in Theory and Practice in Anne Brontë's *Agnes Grey*', *Nordic Journal of English Studies* I.1 (2002), 133–51.

2. Typically, Charlotte Brontë wrote disparagingly of her employer, Mrs White of Upperwood House, and her 'bad grammar and worse orthography' (Smith, *Letters* I, p. 253). The same tendency is seen in contemporaneous governess novels such as Lady Blessington's *The Governess* (1839); see Inga-Stina Ewbank, *Their Proper Sphere*, pp. 62–3.

3. 'The Brontës as governesses', *BST* 9 (1939), 217–35 (233).

4. See Winifred Gérin, *Anne Brontë*, p. 122.
5. 'Anne Brontë at Blake Hall', p. 243. The same point is made at greater length by Regaignon, 'Instructive sufficiency', pp. 85–6, 91–2, 94, 100–101.
6. See Smith, *Letters* I, pp. 191–4, 249 and 252–3.
7. *Ibid.*, p. 189.
8. See Barker, *The Brontës*, pp. 358–9 and Smith, *Letters* I, p. 258.
9. See also Muriel Spark's shrewd and amusing reflections on 'The Brontës as teachers', in *The Essence of the Brontës: A Compilation with Essays* (London & Chester Springs, PA: Peter Owen, 1993), pp. 13–20, and Tom Winnifrith, 'The Brontës were not very good teachers but had the right ideas', pp. 6–9 in Duckett (ed.), *The Brontës and Education: 2004 Conference*.
10. *Governess Life*, p. 31. Maurice mentions the military and the clergy as comparable examples.
11. *Ibid.*, pp. 32–4.
12. Mr and Mrs Armitage of High Royd were not yet 30 when they employed Miss Weeton in 1812 but already had several children, the eldest ('the bad sheep that infects the flock', according to Weeton) aged seven. See *Miss Weeton's Journal of a Governess*, Vol. I, 1807–1811 (Newton Abbot: David & Charles, 1969, a reprint of Oxford University Press's 1936 *Miss Weeton* with a new introduction by J. J. Bagley), pp. 57–9.
13. On female rivalries, see Lecaros, *The Victorian Governess Novel*, pp. 208–16.
14. See, for instance, Lecaros, *The Victorian Governess Novel*, pp. 156–61. A memorable fictional example occurs in Dickens' *Little Dorrit* (first published in 1857), ch. XXI, where the morbid Miss Wade complains of the 'artful devices' of the nurse whom she accuses of alienating the children's affections (pp. 665–6 in the 1994 Penguin edition).
15. Ch. VIII, p. 115 in the 1960 Everyman edition of Gaskell's *Life of Charlotte Brontë*.
16. See Smith, *Letters* I, p. 518 (on their letters to Anne, 'crammed with warm protestation of endless esteem and gratitude'), and *Letters* II, p. 152.
17. See, for instance, Elizabeth Langland, *Anne Brontë: The Other One* (Basingstoke: Macmillan, 1989), pp. 97ff.; Maria Frawley, *Anne Brontë* (New York: Twayne, 1996), p. 85; Drew Lamonica, *'We Are Three Sisters'*, pp. 120–2; James Simmons, 'Contextualising'; Regaignon, 'Instructive Sufficiency'; and Lecaros, '"Lessons"'. Introductions to *Agnes Grey* stress this aspect; in addition to Robert Inglesfield's introduction to the World's Classics edition, see Angeline Goreau's to the Penguin edition of *Agnes Grey* (first published in 1988).
18. The quoted passages are from pp. 51–2.
19. *'We Are Three Sisters'*, p. 122. A similar point is made by Mary Summers in 'Parents beware! Anne Brontë's message on education', in Duckett (ed.), *The Brontës and Education: 2004 Conference*, p. 53.
20. Few governesses in fact and fiction were as generously welcomed as Jane Eyre, as Jane herself points out (I.xi.96). On the arrival as an ingredient in governess tales, see Lecaros, *The Victorian Governess Novel*, pp. 81–94.

21. See, for instance, Glen, *Charlotte Brontë*, ch. 5, especially pp. 98–100, and Shuttleworth, *Charlotte Brontë*, pp. 161–2.
22. On the latter, see above pp. 131–2. Jerome Beaty connects Jane's discontent with Godwinian impulses; see *Misreading* Jane Eyre: *A Postformalist Paradigm* (Columbus: Ohio State University Press, 1996), pp. 78–80.
23. On the salaries of governesses and tutors, see above p. 58.
24. Cf. the governess bride's farewell to her charges in the anonymous *The Governess, or, Politics in Private Life*, which Charlotte's publishers Smith, Elder had brought out in 1836: 'Gertrude turned to fold in her arms, the darling objects of her past care and anxiety: her fortitude forsook her, and after tenderly embracing them, and pressing to her heart, again and again, their sweet mother, she was conducted . . . to her carriage, exhausted by . . . deep feeling' (p. 306). (The lady married an uncle in the family.) In the night when Jane Eyre escapes from Thornfield, her 'cool language' in respect of Adèle breaks down: she breathes a fond goodbye in the direction of the nursery ('Farewell, my darling Adèle!', III.i.320).
25. *The Victorian Governess Novel*, pp. 29–43.
26. This is the dimension which caused Elizabeth Rigby to criticise *Jane Eyre* for its 'pervading tone of ungodly discontent'; see her *Quarterly Review* review of December 1848, vol. 84, 153–85, easily available – albeit abridged – in Miriam Allott (ed.), *The Brontës: The Critical Heritage* (London and Boston: Routledge and Kegan Paul, 1974), pp. 105–12 (109). The quoted phrase was one of those that Charlotte Brontë repeated in *Shirley* (in the chapter called 'Mrs. Pryor', II.x.376).
27. See Lecaros, *The Victorian Governess Novel*, pp. 267–72. One example of the perverseness of Dickens' Miss Wade in *Little Dorrit* is her alienation of the affections of her fiancé, a nephew in the family where she works as a governess and someone the self-tormentor admits to loving.
28. See, for instance, Knies, *The Art of Charlotte Brontë*, p. 161; W. A. Craik, *The Brontë Novels* (London: Methuen, 1968; I have used the University Paperback edition of 1971), pp. 147–8; Robert Bernard Martin, *The Accents of Persuasion: Charlotte Brontë's Novels* (London: Faber & Faber, 1966), pp. 139–40; Tom Winnifrith, *The Brontës and Their Background*, p. 141; Inga-Stina Ewbank, *Their Proper Sphere*, pp. 185–6; and Valerie Grosvenor Myer, *Charlotte Brontë: Truculent Spirit* (London: Vision, 1987), p. 102.
29. For a lucid summary of the 'balancing' of masculine and feminine positions in *Shirley*, see Nestor, *Charlotte Brontë*, pp. 78–9. On the 'transgendering' of Louis Moore as a 'governess figure' and nurse, see Patricia Ingham, *The Language of Gender and Class: Transformation in the Victorian Novel* (London: Routledge, 1996), pp. 50–2. Janet Gezari brings out the erotic-seductive aspects of the relationship in *Charlotte Brontë and Defensive Conduct: The Author and the Body at Risk* (Philadelphia: University of Pennsylvania Press, 1992), pp. 119–20.
30. For instance, having snatched an engagement from the jaws of rejection, he tells Shirley, as an answer to her question 'Are we equal at last?', 'You are younger, frailer, feebler, more ignorant than I' (III.xiii.623).

31. G. H. Lewes' infamous review in the *Edinburgh Review* of January 1850 (XCI, 153–73) observed that Louis writes things that 'every one feels he would never have written at all' (p. 169 in Miriam Allott's *Critical Heritage* volume). While it may go against the grain to agree with anything in this piece that – understandably – caused Charlotte Brontë so much pain, it has to be admitted that Lewes made his point here.

32. Cf. Lecaros, *The Victorian Governess Novel*, pp. 238ff. At one point Shirley says to Louis, 'it is like a tutor to talk of the "satisfaction of teaching" – I suppose *you* think it the finest employment in the world. I don't – I reject it' (III.xiii.619).

33. Cf. Ewbank, *Their Proper Sphere*, pp. 199–200.

34. As Judith Williams has pointed out, 'Shirley is in love with Louis right from the beginning; she is never a "single" woman': *Perception and Expression in the Novels of Charlotte Brontë* (Ann Arbor: UMI Research Press, 1988), p. 75.

35. *Ibid.*, pp. 77–8. Several critics have said that Louis' ascendancy seems to diminish Shirley, 'usurping' her voice and place; see, for instance, Kate Lawson, 'The Dissenting Voice: *Shirley*'s Vision of Women and Christianity', *Studies in English Literature 1500–1900* 29 (1989), 729–43 (739–40), and Nestor, *Charlotte Brontë*, pp. 79–80. In her article 'Heroes and hero-worship in Charlotte Brontë's *Shirley*', *Nineteenth-Century Literature* 54.3 (Dec. 1999), 285–307, Pam Morris discusses Shirley's 'willing subordination' in the context of that 'assertive challenge to male authority that allows the novel's heroes – Helstone and Robert and Louis Moore – to demonstrate their power to command and subdue' (303).

36. See III.xiii.614: 'I am now a man of thirty: I have never been free since I was a boy of ten. I have such a thirst for freedom – such a deep passion to know her and call her mine – such a day-desire and night-longing to win her and possess her'.

37. 'Hints on the modern governess system', vol. XXX (November 1844), 578; the next page contains a spirited equal-work-equal-pay proposal ('if . . . they produce the same results, by what equity is the woman, because she is a woman, to receive lower wages than the man?'). *Fraser's* admitted that tutors would usually have a public-school education followed by university attendance, but did not accept that this warranted 'the immense disparity in the remuneration'. Branwell Brontë, who had no formal education, had a salary twice that of his sister Anne when they worked as tutor and governess in the same family; see Winnifrith, *The Brontës and Their Background*, pp. 174 and 260n59.

38. As so often, Juliet Barker's *The Brontës* is the best source of up-to-date summaries and well-informed guesses; see pp. 333–5 and 456–69.

39. *Ibid.*, p. 322; the account is found in a letter to his friend John Brown.

40. See Hughes, *The Victorian Governess*, pp. 184–7 and 196–7. On the curriculum at Queen's, see also Mary Maurice, *Governess Life: Its Trials, Duties, and Encouragements* (London, 1849), pp. 43–4. Hughes makes the important point that Queen's did not aim to create a new female professional class, but to ensure that governesses were better treated and paid as gentlewomen performing a valuable civilising service to society; see especially p. 186. Cf. also *The Governess, or, Politics in Private Life*: 'no lady [should] receive into her house any other

than a well educated and perfect gentlewoman'; if that were the invariable practice, '[t]he wretched race of low-born, ignorant, and vulgar governesses' would be returned to the shops and farms where they belonged (p. 310).

41. Hughes, *The Victorian Governess*, p. 181. Few governesses could even dream of the £150–200 p.a. suggested by Elizabeth Appleton in *Private Education; or, A Practical Plan for the Studies of Young Ladies* (2nd rev.ed., London 1816), p. 11, to say nothing of her idea of the governess' being able to retire on a competency at 40. But Appleton was a prescient observer: she regretted the perceptible growth in the number of governesses, partly because '[w]here the market is overstocked, the commodity loses value', p. 12.

42. From the early 1840s onwards, as Harriet Martineau wrote in her *History of England*, Vol. II, the 'position of this unfortunate class', 'one of the most suffering classes of society', was at least no longer neglected by that society, although only a few of 'the suffering multitude of female educators' would actually be recipients of practical aid; pp. 560–1. (See also pp. 713–14 on the desirability of 'professional requisites to obtain professional dues' for governesses.)

43. Smith, *Letters* II, p. 64; see also n. 4 on p. 67. Charlotte's ambivalent feelings about 'Ladies Colleges' at the time of *Villette*'s publication are articulated in a letter to Miss Wooler from London; see Smith, *Letters* III, p. 111 (and Smith's instructive note 4 on p. 112).

44. *Ibid.*, p. 65. On the formal training of governesses in relation to their labour market, see also Poovey, *Uneven Developments*, p. 151.

45. *Letters* II, p. 226; see also n. 3 on pp. 227–8.

46. Mrs Pryor's former employer had warned her of the danger of ending up in a lunatic asylum where, according to contemporary commentators (including Rigby in the *Quarterly Review*), governesses were over-represented. Pamela Horn has found this widespread notion untenable on the basis of available evidence ('The Victorian governess', p. 338).

47. See Barker, *The Brontës*, p. 150.

48. Mary Maurice was up in arms against this 'great foible of the present day', demanding rhetorically, 'was any one ever "finished"?' *Governess Life*, p. 75.

49. Anne Brontë made the modest narrator adopt free indirect discourse applied to the Murray girls' point of view in describing her small progress as it were from the outside: 'Miss Grey was a queer creature . . . but . . . they could be quite sure her approbation was sincere . . . it was better to keep her in tune, as when she was in a good humour she would talk to them, and be very agreeable and amusing sometimes, in her way, which was quite different from mama's, but still very well for a change' (*Agnes Grey* VII.69–70).

50. As Henry Dunn wrote, '[t]he great medium of all domestic culture, it can never be too frequently repeated, is FAMILY HAPPINESS. Where this is absent, no good can be effected at home' (*Principles of Teaching*, p. 231).

51. Smith, *Letters* I, p. 192.

52. On the duty of anyone who raises a child to bear his or her eternal welfare in mind, see Marianne Thormählen, 'Anne Brontë's *Sacred Harmony*: A discovery', *Brontë Studies* 30.2 (July 2005), 93–102 (99–100).

53. Among the most important qualifications in a governess, Mary Maurice listed readiness to work towards mutual understanding with parents; *Governess Life*, pp. 72–3. In *Agnes Grey*, Anne Brontë provided a fictional illustration of just how difficult that might be.

CHAPTER 6 SCHOOLS AND SCHOOLING

1. See, for instance, ch. VIII in *Villette*, where the weary directress of a Roman Catholic educational establishment finds a moment's rest listening to her children reciting English Protestant texts to their nursery-governess.
2. For some early instances, see Donald Hopewell, 'Cowan Bridge', *BST* Part XXXI (1921), 43–9; Edith M. Weir, 'Cowan Bridge: New light from old documents', *BST* Part LVI, vol. XI (1946), 16–28; and Dame Myra Curtis, 'Cowan Bridge school: An old prospectus re-examined', Part LXIII, vol. 12 (1953), 187–92 (Curtis shows that Weir was taken in by a parody, but Weir's materials are interesting in themselves). On the 1857 Cowan Bridge debate, see Sarah Fermi and Judith Smith, 'The real Miss Andrews: teacher, mother, abolitionist', *Brontë Studies* 25, Pt 2 (Oct. 2000), 136–46 (137–9), and Glen, *Charlotte Brontë*, pp. 66 and 80. On the school itself in the context of girls' education, see Gillian Avery, *The Best Type of Girl: A History of Girls' Independent Schools* (London: Andre Deutsch, 1991), pp. 48–51.
3. School staff read the girls' letters home, a common practice which was decried in a highly condemnatory article in *Fraser's Magazine* XXXI (June 1845), 'An inquiry into the state of girls' fashionable schools': 'Many schoolmistresses make a rule of reading every letter written and received: by such a plan the girls are left at their mercy' (704). The Cowan Bridge prospectus – after a sentence almost exactly paralleled in the one the Brontës drew up for their own prospective school – ended with the statement 'All letters and parcels will be inspected by the Governess' (i.e., the headmistress). That sentence does not occur in the Brontë sisters' own prospectus.
4. Barker, *The Brontës*, pp. 118–23 and 133–41.
5. For Barker's account of Roe Head, see *The Brontës*, pp. 170–5, 181–3 and 235–9.
6. For a readable account which also quotes liberally from Charlotte's Journal, see Rebecca Fraser, *Charlotte Brontë* (London: Methuen, 1988; I have used the 2003 Vintage edition), pp. 104–108 and 112–14. The following *cri de coeur* from the Roe Head Journal is especially poignant: 'am I to spend all the best part of my life in this wretched bondage, forcibly suppressing my rage at the idleness the apathy and the hyperbolical & most asinine stupidity of those fat-headed oafs and on compulsion assuming an air of kindness, patience and assiduity?' (Quoted from the Journal in the Brontë Parsonage Museum.)
7. See Esther Alice Chadwick, *In the Footsteps of the Brontës* (London: Pitman, 1914), pp. 122–37; Barker, *The Brontës*, pp. 235–7, 293–6 and 306–307; Chitham, *Life of Emily Brontë*, ch. 9 (pp. 100–21); and Katherine Frank, *Emily Brontë: A Chainless Soul* (London: Hamish Hamilton, 1990), pp. 118–26.

8. See Smith, *Letters* I, p. 182; Charlotte wrote to Ellen Nussey on 2 October 1838, expressing her fear that Emily 'will never stand' the work 'from six in the morning until near eleven at night'. (Charlotte's description may have been an exaggeration, as some scholars have pointed out.)

9. See pp. 79–94 in Janet Gezari's edition of *Emily Jane Brontë: The Complete Poems* (Harmondsworth: Penguin, 1992). One of these poems expresses the speaker's homesickness during a brief spell away from 'The noisy crowd', which seems an apt description of a class of pupils; see Gezari's comment on p. 254.

10. For descriptions of the Brontës' school project, see Fraser, *Charlotte Brontë*, pp. 203 and 207–11, and Barker, *The Brontës*, pp. 439–40. Anne was not as closely involved in the enterprise as Charlotte and Emily, but the prospect was welcome to her, and she spoke of the idea with her customary cautiousness and good sense in her 1841 diary paper. See Barker, *The Brontës*, pp. 359–60. For relevant passages in Charlotte's letters, see, especially, Smith, *Letters* I, pp. 255 and 258 (on what home meant to her), 260, 262, 266 (the school plan is 'our polar star & we look to it under all circumstances of despondency') and 268. Charlotte also wrote about the project to M. Heger, using almost exactly the same phrase – 'J'ai cependant mon projet', *Letters* I, p. 355 – as she gave to Frances Henri ('pourtant j'ai mon projet'; *The Professor* XVII.131).

11. *The Brontës*, pp. 439–40.

12. The history of Roe Head/Dewsbury Moor is one example of ups-and-downs; see, for instance, Winifred Gérin, *Charlotte Brontë: The Evolution of Genius* (Oxford: Oxford University Press, 1967; I have used the OUP paperback of 1991), pp. 173ff.

13. See Marianne Thormählen, '"Une saine éducation anglaise lui corrigea ses défauts français": L'École dans la fiction de Charlotte Brontë' in Guyonne Leduc (ed.), *L'Éducation des femmes en Europe et en Amérique du Nord de la Renaissance à 1848* (Paris: L'Harmattan, 1997), p. 484. Lord Morris made the same point in his 1997 Brontë lecture, 'The Brontës and Education, Education, Education', *BST* 22 (1997), 1–18 (7–8). See also p. 194 above.

14. Admittedly, the reader learns little about this school except that it is well appointed and flourishes under its diligent directress, who soon turns it into a pensionnat; see *Villette* XLII.493–4.

15. Rauch points out that Crimsworth's 'career as an educator places him in the very special position of connecting the aristocracy with the middle classes through knowledge'; *Useful Knowledge*, p. 139.

16. Cf. Smith, *Letters* I, p. 189: 'I am as yet "wanting a situation – like a housemaid out of place" – by the bye Ellen I've lately discovered that I've quite a talent for cleaning – sweeping up hearths dusting rooms – making beds &c so if everything else fails – I can turn my hand to that – if anybody will give me good wages, for little labour I won't be a cook – I hate cooking – I won't be a nursery-maid – nor a lady's maid far less a lady's companion . . . I will be nothing "but a house-maid"' (letter to Ellen Nussey, 15 April 1839). The

tone of the passage is humorous, but it does not come across as altogether nonsensical.

17. See Berglund, 'In defence of Madame Beck', 200. On the difference between teaching a pupil one only sees in a schoolroom and taking charge of a child in the home for most of his or her waking hours, see above p. 178.
18. See above pp. 11ff.
19. See p. 84.
20. Paulina's dismayed exclamation when she realises that Lucy Snowe is not a lady of leisure (*Villette* XXV.285).
21. Of course, such a teacher would also earn much more. In a letter to M. Heger, Charlotte Brontë said that she had been offered a post as head teacher ('première maîtresse') at a Manchester boarding school, with a £100 annual salary; see Smith, *Letters* I, p. 355.
22. *Governess Life*, p. 40.
23. See Hughes, *The Victorian Governess*, p. 186 on the 'amateur' status of the governess.
24. See, for instance, Lance G. E. Jones, *The Training of Teachers in England and Wales during the Nineteenth Century* (Bath: Chivers, 1933), chs I–IV. On the existing teacher-training institutions in 1846, see Hook, *On the Means*, pp. 62–5. Hook's proposals for teacher training were comparatively ambitious, involving at least two years of training. See Mann's *Census* on the situation in 1851, pp. 30–1. On teacher training in the British and Foreign School Society, see Henry Bryan Binns, *A Century of Education: Being the Centenary History of the British & Foreign School Society 1808–1908* (London: Dent, 1908), pp. 134–8 and 161–4.
25. See, for instance, *Blackwood's Edinburgh Magazine* XXX (August 1831), 306–307, where the interlocutor called 'Courtney' insists that the government should see to it that the educators of the people received careful training. It is clear from the context, however, that the training envisaged here is primarily a matter of morality ('the "terra firma" of sound principle'), not of pedagogy or instruction in subjects and skills. *Fraser's Magazine* was more insistent on teacher training in the latter respects, pointing out, in 1847, that 'the greater number of schoolmasters [in England] . . . never received any training at all', quoting Derwent Coleridge (son of S. T. Coleridge, Principal of St Mark's College Chelsea and a pioneer who put candidates for the teaching profession through three years of training) on the subject; see vol. XXXV (March 1847), 269.
26. See, for instance, Asher Tropp, *The School Teachers: The Growth of the Teaching Profession in England and Wales from 1800 to the Present Day* (London: Heinemann, 1957), pp. 5–25.
27. From *The School and the Teacher*, an educational periodical; quoted by Tropp, *The School Teachers*, p. 26.
28. A summary statement quoted in Lawson and Silver, *A Social History*, p. 288. While Harriet Martineau found 'the function of the Educator somewhat more respected than it used to be' in 1850, she admitted that there were 'still suburban

villages where the inhabitants [were] too genteel to admit persons engaged in education to their book-clubs', however ridiculous such prejudice would seem to 'the wiser majority of the middle class'; *History*, vol. II, p. 713.

29. Dunn, *Principles of Teaching*, p. 5.
30. Page 48. See also P. H. J. H. Gosden (ed.), *How They Were Taught: An Anthology of Contemporary Accounts of Learning and Teaching in England* (Oxford: Blackwell, 1969), p. 23, and Binns, *A Century*, p. 138.
31. See, for example, Mann's *Census*, pp. 35–7.
32. Here is a sample from vol. XXXII (September 1832): 'It is too late now to enquire . . . whether . . . New England, with its journals, its reading-rooms, its mechanics' institutions, its Reform processions and public meetings, is better than Old England, with its loyalty, its devotion, its charity, and its unobtrusive industry' (343). Tory to the core, Charlotte Brontë was still very much a creature of the 'reading-rooms' and 'mechanics' institutions' culture of self-improvement.
33. See above pp. 16–18.
34. See, for instance, Goldstrom, *The Social Content*, pp. 22–5. Goldstrom mentions Sarah Trimmer as an eminent representative of this status-quo-orientated view.
35. See above p. 170.
36. On class in the Brontë fiction, see also Eagleton's *Myths of Power*, a classic work of Brontë criticism which employs a very different approach from the one used in the present study.
37. See Tholfsen, *Sir James Kay-Shuttleworth*, pp. 4, 9 and 14.
38. This was a danger against which early-nineteenth-century writers on education sometimes warned their readers. See, for instance, Priscilla Wakefield, *Reflections*, p. 55.

SECTION III SUBJECTS AND SKILLS

1. On the docility concept, see above pp. 199ff.
2. On the concept 'a sound English education', see, for instance, Josephine Kamm, *Hope Deferred: Girls' Education in English History* (London: Methuen, 1965), p. 170, and Marjorie R. Theobald, 'The accomplished woman and the propriety of intellect: a new look at women's education in Britain and Australia, 1800–1850', *History of Education* 17.1 (1988), 21–35 (25).

CHAPTER 7 A SOUND ENGLISH EDUCATION

1. On needlework, placed after the accomplishments in this book, see above pp. 118ff.
2. Page 359 in *The Complete Governess: A Course of Mental Instruction for Ladies; with a Notice on the Principal Female Accomplishments. By an Experienced Teacher* (London, 1826).
3. 'Education, as treated by the Brontës', *BST* 6 (1925), 261–75 (272).

4. See W. A. C. Stewart and W. P. McCann, *The Educational Innovators: 1750–1880* (London: Macmillan, 1967), p. 87, and West, *Chapter of Governesses*, pp. 61 and 65. A socially ambitious girl in Mary Taylor's *Miss Miles, or a Tale of Yorkshire Life 60 Years Ago* augments her gentility by '[learning] the use of the globes and poonah painting'; p. 208 in the 1990 Oxford University Press edition, by Janet H. Murray, of a novel written by one of Charlotte Brontë's two best friends.

5. Page 119. According to Rex Walford, 'the Rev. J. Goldsmith' was a pseudonym – one of several – adopted by Sir Richard Phillips, publisher of a large number of schoolbooks; see *Geography in British Schools 1850–2000: Making a World of Difference* (London: Woburn Press, 2001), p. 23.

6. The main title of the book is *Geography for Youth: Or, a short and easy Method of Teaching and Learning Geography*. The full title is too extensive to reproduce, but one detail is noteworthy: '*To which is prefixed, A Method of Learning Geography without a Master, for the Use of such grown Persons as have neglected this useful Study in their Youth*'. The book was printed in Dublin (in 1795), and the Prunty family in Ireland may well have acquired it for self-educating purposes.

7. A footnote on p. 93.

8. Pages 79–80 in Goldsmith's book. Compared with some expressions of racism in contemporary schoolbooks, Goldsmith's remarks are fairly mild. See, for example, William Mavor's *Natural History for the Use of Schools, and of Young Persons in General*, a book that remained popular in the early nineteenth century and was one of a number of Longman schoolbooks recommended at the back of Goldsmith's book. Its second edition of 1801 calls 'the negroes of Africa' '[s]tupid, indolent, and often mischievous' while insisting that whiteness is 'not only the most beautiful but also the most expressive colour', which the Creator had originally bestowed on mankind (pp. 17–21). Mavor wrote a number of schoolbooks that were widely used; so did a fellow clergyman, David Blair, whose *The Universal Preceptor* (also recommended at the back of Goldsmith's geography) expressed a similarly low opinion of Africans (p. 104 in the second edition of 1811).

9. Page 92. Blair voiced a similar view on pp. 104–109 in *The Universal Preceptor*, blaming the 'barbarous state' of Africans on the slave trade in a manner that does not spare the 'civilised' Europeans. Several writers known to the Brontës proclaimed the moral superiority of the suffering slave to his tormentors. Cowper is the best-known example; another is Legh Richmond, part of whose literary fame rested on his 'Negro servant'.

10. From the Preface of Thomas Salmon's *A New Geographical and Historical Grammar: Wherein the Geographical Part is Truly Modern; and the Present State of the Several Kingdoms of the World is so interpreted, As to render the Study of Geography both Entertaining and Instructive* (Edinburgh, 1771), p. vii. In the *Oxford Companion to the Brontës*, Christine Alexander and Margaret Smith rightly point out that Salmon's maps of Africa were 'even cruder' than the 'Anglocentric' representations in Goldsmith's book (p. 207); but it should be

observed that the idea of the brotherhood of man is present in these books as well. The fact that Salmon's book preceded both the American and the French Revolutions serves as a reminder that much eighteenth-century benevolence rested on this persuasion.

11. *Essays on Practical Education*, vol. I, p. 453 in the 1815 edition. It might be pointed out that Hester Chapone warned her young niece that she would be 'shocked at the injustice and cruelty' of the European conquerors of America; Letter X, 'On reading history', p. 133 in the 1821 Edinburgh edition of Chapone's *Letters on the Improvement of the Mind*.

12. Porny's real name was Antoine Pyron du Martre; see Higson, *Sources*, p. 45.

13. Page 104 in the 12th edition of 1810. Besides its linguistically orientated components, the book contains a short introduction to French poetry and prosody. It was a well known but not universally admired book; see, for instance, Appleton, *Private Education*, pp. 141, 143, 150, and 152 in the 2nd revised edition of 1816.

14. At the back of W. Pinnock's *A Comprehensive Grammar of the English Language* of 1830, of which Charlotte Brontë owned a copy, the same author's *A Comprehensive Grammar of Geography and History* was advertised along with lavish praise from reviewers, who found the mixture of 'dry' geography and entertaining history particularly successful.

15. Page 108 in the Edinburgh edition of 1821.

16. See, for instance, Ellis' *The Daughters of England*, p. 110, and Thornley's *The True End of Education and the Means Adapted to It: In a series of letters to a lady entering on the duties of her profession as private governess* (Edinburgh, 1846), pp. 53ff.

17. Philip Collins supplies an exhaustive and judicious analysis of this undertaking in *Dickens and Education* (London: Macmillan, 1965), pp. 60–9.

18. 'Chronology' was commonly thought of as a branch of history; Mrs Chapone's book on the subject, *Letter on Chronology*, published before the turn of the century, was still read well into the nineteenth.

19. *The Women of England, Their Social Duties, and Domestic Habits*, p. 336 in the third edition of 1839 (London). The 'ingenious' and 'commendable' devices seem hopelessly complicated to a present-day reader: by making certain vowels and diphthongs correspond to figures, pupils were supposed to learn to memorise dates. See, for example, pp. 261–2 in Blair's *Universal Preceptor* (1811 edition).

20. On rote-learning as a pedagogical device, see above pp. 187ff.

21. Still, this kind of 'history' does of course tend to be what we remember through life. For a large part of the twentieth century, too, Alfred and the burnt cakes were probably one of the few scraps of 'history' known to most British people. Cf. Dylan Thomas' schoolboy poem 'A Lifebelt': 'I'm clear that Alfred burnt the cakes / But when?' (the lifebelt in question being 'Ten-Six-Six').

22. In *A Legacy for Young Ladies* (London, 1826), p. 51. Her distinction between the sexes is relevant to the Brontës as children; it was Branwell who delighted in military campaigns and whose 'first book' was *My Battell Book*, written when he was nine.

23. *A Legacy*, p. 132. A generation later Mary Maurice pointed to the ability of good biographies to instruct readers about general social developments by 'entering . . . into the domestic conditions of those who . . . took a leading part in society'; see *Governess Life*, p. 95.

24. The reign of Charles I was a popular topic in history studies, partly thanks to David Hume's eloquent treatment of it in his *History of England*; see vol. III, chs L-LIX in the Dolby edition of 1824, especially pp. 285–90 on the King's execution and character. Hume, whose *History* Charlotte Brontë recommended to Ellen Nussey in her suggestions-for-further-reading letter of 1834 (pp. 129–31 in Smith, *Letters* I), stressed the King's courage and dignity and the grief of his shocked subjects after his murder. (In a story written at about the same time as the letter to Ellen, Charlotte had called Hume 'the most celebrated of the historians above alluded to'; see vol. II of Alexander's *An Edition*, p. 361.) There were a number of references to Charles I in *Blackwood's* during the Brontës' youth, and French writers, including Bossuet and Rollin, frequently mentioned his human virtues.

25. See, for instance, her remarks on Louis Philippe in a letter to W. S. Williams (28 February 1848), p. 35 in Smith, *Letters* II.

26. The phrase is borrowed from Fannie Ratchford's adaptation of a line from a poem of Charlotte's for her classic study of the Brontë juvenilia, *The Brontës' Web of Childhood* (New York: Columbia University Press, 1941). As children, the Brontë siblings wrote numerous 'histories'; see, for instance, Alexander, *The Early Writings* and Glen, *Charlotte Brontë*, *passim*.

27. On this expression and its significance in early-nineteenth-century intellectual life, see A. Dwight Culler, *The Victorian Mirror of History* (New Haven: Yale University Press, 1985), pp. 39ff.

28. On Wellington's envisaged future fame, see the end of Charlotte's Brussels *devoir* 'La Mort de Napoléon' in Sue Lonoff's critical edition of Charlotte and Emily Brontë's *The Belgian Essays* (New Haven: Yale University Press, 1996), p. 281. Harriet Martineau has described Charlotte's tearful gratitude for Martineau's 'doing justice' to Wellington in her *History of the Thirty Years' Peace*; see Gérin, *Charlotte Brontë*, p. 458, and Martineau's *History*, vol. I, p. 495. (On general hero-worship of Wellington, see Houghton, *The Victorian Frame of Mind*, pp. 309–10.) For the origin of Charlotte's idolatry, see Alexander, *The Early Writings*, p. 24, and Richard Offor, 'The Brontës – their relation to the history and politics of their time', *BST* 10.4, pt 53 (1943), 150–60 (152–3). The consistent pro-Wellington stance of *Blackwood's* will have been an extra bonus on the part of that journal in Charlotte's eyes; for an example germane to the feelings expressed in her 'Mort de Napoléon', see vol. XXXII (July 1832), 75: 'an exulting posterity will point to his career as uniting that of *both* of the greatest men of antiquity [Caesar and Cato]'. See also *Shirley* III.viii.554–5. On Charlotte Brontë's idolising of Wellington in that novel, and what her treatment of him says about her politics, see Philip Rogers, 'Tory Brontë: *Shirley* and the "MAN"', *Nineteenth-Century Literature* 58.2 (Sept. 2003), 141–75. Glen takes a different view of Wellington in *Shirley*; see *Charlotte Brontë*, pp. 175–6.

29. See Alexander, *The Early Writings*, p. 64. Charlotte's juvenilia repeatedly refer to Napoleon, too. In a story called 'The Enfant' of 1829, Napoleon is kind to a man with the depressing name of Hanghimself, and the 'Journal of a Frenchman' combines a fascination with Napoleon with idolatry of Wellington; see Alexander, *An Edition*, vol. I, pp. 34–6 and 222–3. There is more on Napoleon in the second volume of 1991; see 'The Green Dwarf', pp. 139–43. Napoleon also figures in poetry by both Branwell ('Ode to Napoleon') and Charlotte ('Napoleon', a translation of a poem by Henri Auguste Barbier); see Victor A. Neufeldt's edition of *The Works of Patrick Branwell Brontë*, vol. I (New York and London: Garland, 1997), pp. 58–60, and pp. 233–4 in Winnifrith's edition of *The Poems of Charlotte Brontë*.

30. See, for instance, Canto 3, stanzas 36ff. of *Childe Harold's Pilgrimage*. The copy of *Childe Harold* in the Brontë Parsonage Museum (a tiny book, allegedly printed in Paris in 1827) carries the signature 'P. B. Brontë, 1835'.

31. See Lonoff's commentary, pp. 308–309 in *The Belgian Essays*, and pp. 416–17 in Juliet Barker's *The Brontës*.

32. Smith, *Letters* II, pp. 35–6 (28 February 1848). It is interesting to note that Emily Shirreff suggested Southey's *Life of Nelson*, also recommended to Ellen by Charlotte in the 1834 letter, as a corrective against any excessively pro-Napoleonic views acquired via Thiers; see Shirreff's *Intellectual Education, and its influence on the character and happiness of women* (London, 1858), pp. 374–5. In 1845, *Fraser's* warned potential Thiers readers of the danger of developing Bonapartist sympathies, calling Thiers's *Histoire du Consulat et de l'Empire* 'the production of a brilliant Buonapartist partisan' (vol. XXXI, May 1845, 520).

33. *Geography for Youth*, pp. 73 and 79n. Lenglet du Fresnoy's schoolbooks seem to have been extremely popular; for instance, Higson records a 31st edition of his *Geography for Children* in 1829 (*Sources*, p. 135).

34. *Historical and Miscellaneous Questions, for the Use of Young People; with a Selection of British, and General Biography [and so on]*, 10th edition (London, 1813), p. 112 (Charlotte's copy in the Brontë Parsonage Museum). Blair's *Universal Preceptor*, published in 1811, is also strategically polite to Napoleonic France – it 'bids fair to form a fifth great monarchy [after the Assyrian monarchy and the Persian, Macedonian and Roman-German empires], or at least to govern the ancient continent' (p. 266).

35. *Hints on Reading*, p. 26. Stodart quotes William Paley who had said, with reference to Gibbon, 'It is easy . . . to parry an argument, but who can withstand a sneer?'

36. That was the year when the Mechanics' Library at Keighley acquired its Gibbon. See Alexander, *The Early Writings*, pp. 23–4 and 261n49. On another reference for the name Zenobia, see Glen, *Charlotte Brontë*, pp. 15–16n32. In addition, the masterpiece of the French eighteenth-century dramatist Prosper Jolyot de Crébillon, *Tragédie de Rhadamiste et de Zénobie* (1711), might be relevant.

37. Smith, *Letters* I, p. 130; on the Universal History, see p. 131n13.

38. Pages 128–9 and 137, from Letter X 'On reading history', in the 1821 Edinburgh edition. See also Gérin, *Charlotte Brontë*, p. 65, and Barker, *The Brontës*, pp. 219–20. Patrick Brontë owned a copy of Hume's *History of England*.
39. *Letters*, Part I, p. 81. Macaulay's *Letters* were widely read and praised, by, among others, the Edgeworths in *Practical Education* (vol. I, p. 331 in the edition quoted above).
40. Vol. I, pp. 264–5 in the third edition of 1822.
41. A footnote in Henry Brougham's *Practical Observations Upon The Education Of The People* proclaimed that 'this popular work' should never be published without notes 'to warn the reader of the author's partiality' and 'careless and fanciful narrative'; p. 2 in the 15th edition of 1825.
42. *Private Education*, p. 74 in the second edition of 1816.
43. Page 83 in the 8th edition of 1828 (Edinburgh).
44. *Advice to Governesses* (London, 1827), p. 122.
45. Over 30 years before the new edition of 1847, Appleton had criticised 'the learned doctor's' use of words which children did not understand; *Private Education*, p. 243 in the 2nd edn. Another popular spelling book was Lindley Murray's *An English Spelling-book; with Reading Lessons Adapted to the Capacities of Children [and so on]*, which appeared in many editions.
46. Cf. the following warning against overloading sentences: 'When an author tells me of his hero's courage in the day of battle, the expression is precise, and I understand it fully: but if, from the desire of multiplying words, he should praise his courage and fortitude . . . my idea begins to waver. He means to express one quality more strongly, but he is in truth expressing two: courage resists danger, fortitude supports pain'. As a result, 'my conception of the object [becomes] indistinct'. Page 283 in the copy acquired by Charlotte Brontë, either at Roe Head or shortly afterwards (the 13th edition of 1818), now in the Brontë Parsonage Museum. (The appendix also contains a useful section on figures of speech, with examples from the classics of English literature.)
47. The subtitle runs *With Exercises; Written in a Familiar Style, Accompanied with Questions for Examination, and Notes Critical and Explanatory*. These exercises and questions are a distinctive feature of Pinnock's book, which otherwise resembles its predecessor Murray in many respects. Charlotte Brontë's signature is on the fly-leaf of the Haworth Parsonage copy of the 1830 edition of Pinnock's grammar. On the point in time when she came to possess Murray's and Pinnock's grammars, see Barker, *The Brontës*, p. 869n14.
48. As Sue Lonoff points out in the introduction to the *Belgian Essays*, Margot Peters' *Charlotte Brontë: Style in the Novel* (Madison: The University of Wisconsin Press, 1973) devotes more space to discussions of Charlotte's language than other studies; see Lonoff, pp. lxxi and 387n165. There is room for more research on style and the Brontës, however.
49. On the aural element in Heger's teaching, see Lonoff, *The Belgian Essays*, pp. xxxix–xl, and Edward Chitham, *The Birth of* Wuthering Heights: *Emily Brontë at Work* (Basingstoke: Macmillan, 1998), p. 58. On Heger's pedagogy, see above pp. 164ff.

50. See, for instance, Gérin, *Charlotte Brontë*, p. 57.
51. Pencil strokes in the margins of Charlotte's copy accompany the central definitions and probably indicate passages to be learnt by heart.
52. See Barker, *The Brontës*, pp. 129 and 859n58. Barker points out that the shortcomings of the Brontë girls (similar remarks were made about Maria and Elizabeth on admission) should not be regarded as evidence of failure on Patrick Brontë's part to educate his children properly. Practically all Cowan Bridge girls were described in those terms, probably so as to reflect subsequent credit on the school for remedying their deficiencies (p. 128).
53. See Alexander, *The Early Writings*, pp. 19–20, Barker, *The Brontës*, p. 221, and Chitham, *Birth of* Wuthering Heights, p. 24.
54. Inspectors of schools documented the incompetence of some schoolmistresses in terms of how many spelling mistakes they made (17 in 23 lines is one 'disgraceful' example); see Gosden, ed., *How They Were Taught*, p. 23.
55. Efforts were made to make the subject as palatable as possible to children: Mrs Marcet's *Mary's Grammar*, published in 1835 and hence too late to be of any benefit to the Brontës as young learners, cheerfully admits that grammar is a 'dry study' (Preface) and then tackles all the morphological categories in dialogue form, interspersed with little stories. It is a charming book of its kind, by one of the most productive and successful authors of educational literature for schools and homes. On Marcet, see also pp. 95 and 162.
56. See *The True End of Education*, pp. 160 and 180. The model father Mr Stanley in Hannah More's *Coelebs in Search of a Wife* (first published in 1809) teaches his overly vivacious daughter Phoebe 'a tincture of mathematics', as '[a] habit of computing steadies the mind, and subdues the soarings of imagination'; ch. XXXIX, p. 203 in the 1995 edition published by Thoemmes Press (Bristol), with an introduction by Mary Waldron.
57. *Governess Life*, pp. 76–7.
58. See, for instance, Wakefield, *Reflections*, p. 92.
59. That Charlotte Brontë was aware of the desirability of mathematical correctness is seen in the story 'Mina Laury' of 1838, whose heroine displays 'a most businesslike sharpness and strictness' when balancing her books, detecting '[t]he slightest fault'; p. 34 in the 1995 Penguin edition of *Mina Laury*.
60. *Private Education*, p. 114.
61. The answers are 898,250,400 minutes and 48,000 sparrows. The much-marked volume, an edition published in Dublin in 1789, includes instructions in bookkeeping and a chapter on the 'Dignity of trade'. One noteworthy aspect of Voster's book is its eulogies on commerce and its defence of tradesmen's gentleman status, which agree well with the valorisation of businessmen in *The Professor* and *Shirley*.
62. The Haworth prospectus is reproduced in many books about the Brontës; see, for instance, Gérin, *Charlotte Brontë*, p. 273.
63. See XIX.198, XXVII.313 and XXX.351.
64. Of course, not all men were, or are, keen on science either. Birkbeck Hill ceased teaching the natural sciences at Bruce Castle School largely because he

found himself unable to inspire his boys with enthusiasm for the technicalities of chemistry, having 'very little taste that way' himself (he taught Latin and French). See Stewart and McCann, *The Educational Innovators*, p. 120.

65. Jerom Murch's *Mrs. Barbauld and Her Contemporaries: Sketches of Some Eminent Literary and Scientific Englishwomen* (London, 1877) describes the recognition won by Somerville as 'universal [and] of the highest kind', pointing out that successive governments (first Peel, then Russell) granted her a munificent pension (pp. 159–60).

66. The fifth, revised and enlarged edition of 1817 makes up some 700 pages altogether. According to David Layton, *Science for the People: The origins of the school science curriculum in England* (London: Allen and Unwin, 1973), the work sold more than 150,000 copies in America alone (p. 31).

67. *A Legacy*, p. 51.

68. Cf. Sally Shuttleworth, Gavin Dawson and Richard Noakes, 'Women, science and culture: science in the nineteenth-century periodical', *Women: A Cultural Review* 12.1 (2001): 'To maintain that nineteenth-century women, whether as writers or readers, lived largely in cultural isolation from the world of science, is to perpetuate one of the most misleading myths of the Victorian age' (70). Schools, however, did not teach much in the way of science in the first half of the nineteenth century; see Layton, *Science for the People*, pp. 23ff.; Jane Mattisson, *Knowledge and Survival in the Novels of Thomas Hardy* (Lund Studies in English 101, 2002), pp. 85–90; and James F. Donnelly, 'The "humanist" critique of the place of science in the curriculum in the nineteenth century, and its continuing legacy', *History of Education* 31.6 (2002), 535–55.

69. Lynn Barber's *The Heyday of Natural History: 1820–1870* (London: Jonathan Cape, 1980) supplies the following definition of 'natural history': 'the study of the *three* Kingdoms of Nature, animal, vegetable, and mineral, [which means that it] included geology, as much as botany and zoology' (p. 27). As Lynn L. Merrill's splendid apologia for the study of natural history as a vital component in Victorian culture explains, the most important difference between this subject and science does not reside in subject matter but in approach. Natural-history enthusiasts studied concrete objects in all their manifestations, mindful of their aesthetic properties; scientists pursued theories. See *The Romance of Victorian Natural History* (Oxford University Press, 1989), pp. 14 and 81–2.

70. One of the books owned by Patrick Brontë was *The Gardens and Menagerie of the Zoological Society Delineated [and so on]* (1830). There are some slight pencil sketches, possibly by Anne Brontë, on the inside back cover.

71. The British fondness for birds that has struck so many foreigners has a long history. Sections on birds take up much space in eighteenth- and nineteenth-century natural-history books. For example, William Mavor's *Natural History* states that 'BIRDS [are] the most beautiful and most innocent tribes of the creation. To contemplate the lustre of their plumage, and listen to their notes of love; to study their propensities, and their pursuits; will provide an exhaustless fund of rational entertainment' and serve to remind humans of the importance of their own domestic duties (pp. 333–4 in the second edition of 1801).

72. On White, see Merrill, *The Romance*, pp. 22–3, and Barber, *The Heyday*, pp. 41–
    4. The 2004 paperback *The Illustrated History of Selborne* from Thames &
    Hudson, compiled by Ronald Davidson-Houston and beautifully illustrated
    by colour plates from the British Library, recently made 'this most captivating
    of books' (as the blurb says) available to present-day readers.

73. See Barber, *The Heyday*, pp. 13–15, and Merrill, *The Romance*, pp. 10 and 25–6.

74. One of these works was Priscilla Wakefield's *An Introduction to Botany, in a
    Series of Familiar Letters*, which ran into many editions (the ninth appeared
    in 1823) and was repeatedly recommended in works on the education of girls.
    Another was Madame de Genlis' three-volume work, translated by Eliza P.
    Reid, called *Historical and Literary Botany* (short title; published in 1826).
    Incidentally, Blanche Ingram reels off botanical terminology to demonstrate
    her superior knowledge of this subject (*Jane Eyre*, II.ii.172–3).

75. On Charles Kingsley's endeavour to assert the manliness of natural-history
    study, see Francis O'Gorman, '"More interesting than all the books, save one":
    Charles Kingsley's construction of natural history', pp. 146–61 in Juliet John
    and Alice Jenkins (eds), *Rethinking Victorian Culture* (Basingstoke: Macmillan,
    2000). (Merrill discusses Kingsley on pp. 215–35 in *The Romance*.) On women
    and Victorian natural history, see also Barber, *The Heyday*, pp. 37 and 125–38.

76. See Barber, *The Heyday*, pp. 21–4, and Merrill, *The Romance*, pp. 42–3. Barber's
    chapter on the geologist Hugh Miller and his attempts, a few years before
    Darwin, to reconcile geology and Genesis makes fascinating reading (pp. 225–
    38).

CHAPTER 8 RELIGION AND EDUCATION

1. In an 1847 report, an Inspector of Schools named Joseph Fletcher insisted
   that '[t]he "classics" of the poor in a Protestant country must ever . . . be
   the Scriptures'; quoted in Anne Digby and Peter Searby, *Children, School and
   Society in Nineteenth-Century England* (London and Basingstoke: Macmillan,
   1981), p. 76. One example of the way in which the Bible might frame a lesson
   is that an obvious approach to the natural history of the bear would be by
   way of Elijah's bears that killed the naughty children; see J. M. Goldstrom,
   'The content of education and the socialization of the working-class child
   1830–1860' in Phillip McCann (ed.), *Popular Education and Socialization in
   the Nineteenth Century* (London: Methuen, 1977), p. 100. See also J. L. Hammond and Barbara Hammond, *The Age of the Chartists 1832–1854: A Study of
   Discontents* (London: Longmans, 1930), pp. 168–216 in the 1967 Kelley reprint
   ('Economic Classics', New York). For Hammond references to the Bible as a
   schoolbook, see pp. 173–4 and 212.

2. In addition to works mentioned above, the following have been especially
   helpful in tracing the sectarian disputes in English education: C. Birchenough,
   *History of Elementary Education in England and Wales from 1800 to the Present
   Day* (London: W. B. Clive, 1914); Bruno Dressler, *Geschichte der englischen*

Erziehung: Versuch einer ersten kritischen Gesamtdarstellung der Entwicklung der englischen Erziehung (Leipzig: Teubner, 1928); and Mary Sturt, *The Education of the People: A History of Primary Education in England and Wales in the Nineteenth Century* (London: Routledge and Kegan Paul, 1967).

3. See Birchenough, *History of Elementary Education*, pp. 78–9.
4. Conversely, Patrick Brontë's letter to the *Leeds Intelligencer* includes a collocation of 'divine knowledge' and 'useful science' which does not seem to have caused the writer any qualms whatsoever; see p. 187 in Green's edition of *The Letters of Patrick Brontë*.
5. *On the Means*, p. 40. See also p. 13 above.
6. *On the Means*, pp. 10, 44 and 69. Hook expressed great dissatisfaction with the quality and extent of actual religious instruction in schools; see pp. 41–6.
7. Page 73 in the copy in the Brontë Parsonage Museum. The book's subtitle is *A Modern Tale; in which are interwoven some cursory remarks on Religion and Politics*; it was published by Baldwin, Cradock and Joy in London, 1818. Both the subtitle and the epigraph, Horace's *utile dulci* lines, state the writer's desire to instruct and entertain at the same time.
8. For examples, see Elizabeth Sandford, *Female Improvement*, vol. I, p. 198, and Catherine Sinclair, *Modern Accomplishments*, p. 106.
9. Vol. XXXI (April 1832), 585.
10. John Venn [son], ed. by Henry Venn [grandson], *The Life and a Selection from the Letters of the Late Rev. Henry Venn, M.A.* (London, 1834), p. 422. On Henry Venn and the reverence in which he was held in Patrick Brontë's home, see Thormählen, *The Brontës and Religion*, pp. 16 and 22.
11. Hester Chapone's dissatisfaction with the available religious literature in the context of the teaching of the young comes out in a passage in *Letters on the Improvement of the Mind* where she tells the recipient, her young niece, that while '*religion* is the most important of all [her] pursuits, there are not many *books* on that subject' which Chapone can recommend (p. 108). Mary Wollstonecraft also felt that '[b]ooks of theology are not calculated for young persons; religion is best taught by example'; *Thoughts*, p. 53. (Incidentally, Wollstonecraft advised against teaching a child to read by the Bible; 'so sacred a book' should not be associated with the arduousness of a task (pp. 53–4).) Similar reservations against devotional literature were articulated in the nineteenth century; see Kate Flint, *The Woman Reader 1837–1914* (Oxford: Clarendon Press, 1993), p. 80.
12. On Cyril Hall as a model clergyman, see Thormählen, *The Brontës and Religion*, pp. 201–203. In an account of a cleric whom both Patrick Brontë and his friend the author admired, William Morgan described how John Crosse used to catechise children in a way they relished, flocking around him; see *The Parish Priest: Pourtrayed in the Life, Character, and Ministry, of the Rev. John Crosse, A.M.* (London, 1841), p. 92.
13. *Moral Sketches of Prevailing Opinions and Manners, Foreign and Domestic: with Reflections on Prayer*, third edition (London, 1819), p. 119.

14. Twenty-one-year-old Anne set herself the task of studying it systematically; see Maria Frawley, 'Contextualizing Anne Brontë's Bible', in Julie Nash and Barbara A. Suess, *New Approaches*, pp. 1–13.
15. Quoted by Gérin, *Charlotte Brontë*, p. 75.

CHAPTER 9 THE ACCOMPLISHMENTS

1. *Blackwood's Edinburgh Magazine* vol. XXXV (February 1834), 245.
2. *Reflections*, pp. 92–3 in the 2nd edition of 1817.
3. *The Complete Governess*, p. 2.
4. *Female Improvement* vol. II, pp. 9–10.
5. *Blackwood's* vol. XXII (July 1827), 'Noctes Ambrosianae', p. 117. The phrase 'strictures on female education' of course recalls Hannah More, whose *Strictures on the Modern System of Female Education with a View to the Principles and Conduct of Women of Rank and Fortune* (1799) became widely read, going through thirteen editions; see, for instance, Lynne Agress, *The Feminine Irony: Women on Women in Early-Nineteenth-Century English Literature* (Rutherford: Associated University Presses, 1978), p. 60. More's warnings against the current over-emphasis on accomplishments (the 'phrenzy of accomplishments', the 'contagion' of which the middle classes have caught; p. 69) resounds through much contemporaneous courtesy literature.
6. As Jane Sellars says, Bessie 'puts Jane through her paces'; 'Art and the artist as heroine in the novels of Charlotte, Emily and Anne Brontë', *BST* 20.2 (1990), 57–76 (63). Cf. p. I.iii.25, where the same skills are said to have been acquired by school-educated girls in the home that was Bessie's former workplace.
7. It is a little surprising that Rick Rylance does not mention this statement of Bessie's in his '"Getting on": ideology, personality and the Brontë characters' in Heather Glen (ed.), *The Cambridge Companion to the Brontës* (Cambridge University Press, 2002), pp. 148–69. For a discussion of *Jane Eyre* and class that diverges from the perspectives examined in the present book, see Susan Fraiman, *Unbecoming Women: British Women Writers and the Novel of Development* (New York: Columbia University Press, 1993), pp. 88–120 (and notes on pp. 161–6).
8. *Practical Education* II, pp. 194–5 in the 1815 edition.
9. See, for instance, Parkes, *Domestic Duties*, pp. 367–70. Parkes was careful to point out that the accomplished woman's ability to amuse not only her husband and friends but also herself made it imperative for a married woman to keep practising her music and drawing ('the more sedentary resources . . . she possesses by which her time may be innocently and cheerfully occupied, the less will she suffer from any occasional privations of society or even of health'; p. 369).
10. See, for instance, Barker, *The Brontës*, pp. 150, 212 and 394–5. On Emily and music, see Edward Chitham, *Life of Emily Brontë*, p. 56; Stevie Davies, *Emily Brontë*, Writers and Their Work, pp. 39–44; and Robert K. Wallace, 'Emily

Brontë and music: Haworth, Brussels and Beethoven', *BST* 18.92 (1982), 136–41. Wallace has devoted an entire monograph to Emily's interest in Beethoven, *Emily Brontë and Beethoven: Romantic Equilibrium in Fiction and Music* (Athens and London: University of Georgia Press, 1986). Akiko Higuchi recently published an inventory, with contextualising comments, called *The Brontës' World of Music: Music in the Seven Novels by the Three Brontë Sisters* (Tokyo: Yushodo Press, 2005).

11. From the Preface of the 1844 *Musical Library* volumes. The aim of the work, according to the Preface, was to collect 'music by the best masters, ancient and modern; the ancient in a state adapted to the improved condition of musical instruments' and the modern ones 'the best that the continent of Europe and our own country could supply'.

12. *The Art of the Brontës* was published by Cambridge University Press in 1995. A catalogue more than an academic monograph, it nonetheless contains all the information on the Brontës as artists that Brontë readers could wish for. An early account of all the Brontës' love of art was supplied by the brother of Branwell's best friend; see Francis A. Leyland, *The Brontë Family with Special Reference to Patrick Branwell Brontë*, recently reissued with a new introduction by Charles Lemon (London: Routledge/Thoemmes, 1997), pp. 126–7. (The work first appeared in 1886.) A recent article by Christine Alexander affords insights into art as an accomplishment at Roe Head; see 'Charlotte Brontë, her school friends, and the Roe Head album', *Brontë Studies* 29 (March 2004), 1–16.

13. *Art of the Brontës*, pp. 9–35.

14. Patrick Brontë bought a cottage piano for his children in 1833 or 1834, when they were all in their teens; see Barker, *The Brontës*, p. 212. As Alexander and Sellars point out, Thomas Bewick's *A History of British Birds* – a favourite of young Jane Eyre's – was the Brontë children's first copy-book (*Art of the Brontës*, p. 22); and artistic representations of Byron and his poetry were 'the greatest single influence on the subject and style of the Brontës' drawings' (*ibid.*, p. 17).

15. *The Complete Governess*, pp. 472–3.

16. See Hermione Lee, 'Emblems and enigmas in "Jane Eyre"', *English* 30 (Autumn 1981), 233–55 (241–2); Ian M. Emberson, 'The shadow of her thoughts: pictures as symbols in the novels of Charlotte Brontë', *The Brontë Novels: 150 Years of Literary Dominance*, ed. Bob Duckett (Haworth: The Brontë Society, 1998), pp. 57–78 (67–76); and Alison Byerly, *Realism, Representation, and the Arts in Nineteenth-Century Literature* (Cambridge University Press, 1997), pp. 93–5.

17. See Alexander and Sellars, *Art of the Brontës*, pp. 42ff.

18. See Paul Oppé's long essay on art in G. M. Young (ed.), *Early Victorian Britain 1830–1865*, vol. II (London: Oxford University Press, 1934), pp. 101ff.

19. Oppé states that English art from 1830 to 1865 was characterised by 'the complete dominance of subject over treatment and of the intellectual and moral elements over the sensory and aesthetic' (p. 140).

20. For an attempted rehabilitation of Gilbert Markham, see Thormählen, 'Aspects of love', pp. 164–8. That Anne Brontë endowed him with artistic/aesthetic understanding is a significant circumstance not dwelt on in Antonia Losano's otherwise admirable article 'The professionalization of the woman artist in Anne Brontë's *The Tenant of Wildfell Hall*, *Nineteenth-Century Literature* 58.1 (June 2003), 1–41. (Losano rightly attacks previous critics' simple symbolic-biographical comments on Anne Brontë's own art and on artworks in her fiction, situating Anne Brontë's novel in the context of the shift from amateurism to professionalism in mid-nineteenth-century women's art.)

21. *Thoughts*, p. 26.

22. In fact, *Agnes Grey* also contains a meretricious musician and a worthy artist. The latter is Agnes' sister Mary, who contributes to the household income by selling her artwork (I.7–8), like Helen in *The Tenant of Wildfell Hall* – a way of supporting themselves that was sometimes recommended to women above the working-class level in society. See, for instance, Priscilla Wakefield's *Reflections*, pp. 98–9 in the second edition of 1817.

23. Rochester expressly compares Bertha to Blanche: 'I found her a fine woman, in the style of Blanche Ingram; tall, dark, and majestic' (III.i.305). See Martin, *The Accents of Persuasion*, p. 102.

24. On the significance of the concept 'original' in the Brontë context, see above pp. 200ff.

25. On conscience and Divine guidance in *Jane Eyre*, see Thormählen, *The Brontës and Religion*, pp. 69–70, 79–80 and 164–6.

26. As Byerly points out, Blanche's musical performances display mere 'technical facility', a sign of her 'shallow exhibitionism'; *Realism*, pp. 97–8.

27. On Latin and Greek in the education of both sexes, see above pp. 121ff.

28. *The Women of England*, p. 335.

29. *A Legacy*, pp. 46–9.

30. See Elizabeth Sandford, *Female Improvement*, vol. I, p. 172, and Sarah Ellis, *The Young Ladies' Reader; or, Extracts from Modern Authors* (London, 1845), p. 3.

31. See Lecaros, *The Victorian Governess Novel*, pp. 65 and 71–4.

32. In *The Daughters of England*, Sarah Ellis pointed out that even lower-class women could now, thanks to improved communications, expect to go abroad at some time in their lives (p. 91).

33. Hickson praises the good Belgian private schools and recommends 'the English traveller at Brussels' to visit 'the institution of M. Vandermaelen'; p. 13 in *Dutch and German Schools*.

34. See Enid L. Duthie, *The Foreign Vision of Charlotte Brontë* (London: Macmillan, 1975), pp. 23–4.

35. Most of her errors concern prepositions; indeed, Emily's first efforts show that she had a firmer grasp of concord than Charlotte. (It is tempting to speculate that Charlotte was aware of her own potential weakness in that quarter and that that awareness comes out in Shirley's reply to Louis Moore's suggestion that she, being out of practice, could not now write French as well as she

used to: "'Oh! no. I should make strange work of my concords now", *Shirley* III.iv.485.) On Emily's Brussels *devoirs*, see also Chitham, *Life of Emily Brontë*, pp. 143–8.

36. At 14 Charlotte Brontë will not, for instance, have needed to write 'elle, french for, she'; her letter in French to Ellen Nussey of 18 October 1832 is full of mistakes, but it is inconceivable that its writer was still a beginner in 1831. Charlotte's 'Journal of a Frenchman' of 1830 contains a number of sentences in execrable French, but it is the French of an early learner who has got to the stage of being able to piece simple sentences together. For some examples, see Alexander, *An Edition*, vol. I (1987), pp. 372 and 374 (Alexander has corrected the worst howlers in the running text, on pp. 221–3 and 252, but provided Charlotte's original French at the back of the book).

37. Reprinted on p. 153 in Lonoff's volume.

38. The copy of this book that is in the Brontë Parsonage Museum, published in 1806, has plenty of notes on its covers, including snippets of verse in pencil and lists of fictitious names, many with literary associations.

39. See, for instance, Elaine Showalter, 'Charlotte Brontë's use of French', *Research Studies* 42 (1974), 225–34, and pp. 179–98 in Duthie, *Foreign Vision*.

40. See pp. 15 and 21–2 in Lonoff's volume. (Lonoff's entry on Chénier in Alexander and Smith's *Oxford Companion to the Brontës* suggests that 'the narrator' of *Shirley* is somewhat sceptical about the poem, but the sceptical attitude is clearly Hortense's.) See also p. 142 above.

41. See, for instance, Lonoff, p. lvii in the *Belgian Essays* volume.

42. Even the strait-laced M. A. Stodart accepts Lamartine and, somewhat reluctantly, Chateaubriand; see *Hints on Reading*, pp. 95 and 72. Elizabeth Appleton, no controversialist either, recommends Bernardin's *Paul et Virginie*; see *Private Education*, p. 147.

43. On Rousseau, see *Villette* XXXIV.392 and XXXVIII.442; on Sand, see Smith, *Letters* II, 485. It has been suggested that Charlotte read Sand in the early 1840s; see Duthie, *Foreign Vision*, pp. 16–18, and Patricia Thomson, *George Sand and the Victorians: Her Influence and Reputation in Nineteenth-Century England* (New York: Columbia University Press, 1977), pp. 61–79.

44. See above pp. 158 and 182.

45. The name of the 'evil fairy' in *Villette*, Mme Walravens, should perhaps be mentioned in this context, too. See also the reference to Rousseau in *Shirley* II.i.228. On the possibility of viewing *Shirley* as at least in part an appropriation of Rousseau's *La Nouvelle Héloïse*, see Harriet Björk, *The Language of Truth: Charlotte Brontë, the Woman Question, and the Novel* (Lund: Gleerup, 1974), pp. 123–5, and Elizabeth Gargano, 'The education of Brontë's new *Nouvelle Heloïse* in *Shirley*', *Studies in English Literature 1500–1900* 44.4 (Autumn 2004), 779–803. In view of the scepticism Charlotte Brontë clearly felt against Rousseau, Tom Winnifrith and Edward Chitham's designation of *Jane Eyre* as 'the prime example of Rousseauesque belief in the innocence and spiritual insight of the child' is not unproblematic; see *Charlotte and Emily Brontë: Literary Lives* (Basingstoke: Macmillan, 1989), p. 57. In Charlotte's 1840 letter

to Hartley Coleridge she says that Rousseau often writes like an old woman; see Smith, *Letters* I, p. 241. Her disgust with Rousseau is paralleled in F. D. Maurice's Dedication, to Hartley Coleridge's brother Derwent, of *The Kingdom of Christ*, p. 8 in the Everyman's Library edition of 1906: S. T. Coleridge's 'manly denunciation' in *Aids to Reflection* 'of the sentimental school must be painful to many in our day [*The Kingdom of Christ* was first published in 1837] who have practically adopted the Rousseau cant, though they have changed a little the words that express it'. (A review of Southey's edition of *The Pilgrim's Progress*, with a *Life of John Bunyan*, in *Fraser's Magazine* quotes Samuel Taylor Coleridge as having been less than complimentary about Rousseau's 'constitutional melancholy'; vol. III, February–July 1831, 62.) Richmal Mangnall said of Rousseau that he 'experienced many vicissitudes in life, chiefly owing to his want of steadiness'; p. 326 in Charlotte Brontë's copy of the *Questions*. On Mary Wollstonecraft's rejection of Rousseau and his idea that the education of women would make them less subservient to men (which would be against the natural order of things), see Renton, *Tyrant or Victim?*, pp. 31 and 39–40.

46. See Thormählen, 'Anne Brontë's *Sacred Harmony*', 96–8. To the best of my belief nobody had noticed these jottings before. Brontë Parsonage Museum staff authenticated the handwriting as Anne's.

47. See, for instance, Lecaros, *The Victorian Governess Novel*, p. 65. Maria Young in Harriet Martineau's *Deerbrook* of 1839 studies German on her own with a dictionary and a grammar; see p. 37.

48. *Female Improvement*, vol. I, p. 173.

49. *Ibid.*, vol. I, p. 174. In *Deerbrook*, Martineau has Miss Young read Schiller's *Thirty Years' War*, adding, 'Every one has something to say about German literature; those who do not understand it asking whether it is not very mystical, and wild, and obscure; and those who do understand it saying that it is not so at all' (p. 37). The idea that German literature possessed 'mystical' characteristics was not new in the 1830s; defending such domestic classics as Locke's *Essay concerning Human Understanding* and Bishop Butler's *Analogy*, Hannah More had said that they supplied better reading than 'so much English Sentiment, French Philosophy, Italian Love-Songs, and fantastic German imagery and magic wonders' (*Strictures*, p. 183).

50. On the importance of German education and scholarship in early-nineteenth-century Britain, including their impact on Thomas Arnold, Julius Hare and Carlyle, see W. H. G. Armytage, *The German Influence on English Education* (London: Routledge and Kegan Paul, 1969).

51. See Smith, *Letters* I, pp. 284, 319, 322 and 324. As a curiosity, the 'Phrenological estimate of the talents and dispositions of a Lady' – that is, Charlotte Brontë in 1851 – by the phrenologist Dr Browne, whom Charlotte consulted together with George Smith, might be quoted in connection with her German: 'This Lady possesses a fine organ of language and can if she has done her talents justice by exercise express her sentiments with clearness precision and force – sufficiently eloquent but not verbose. In learning a language she would investigate its spirit and structure. The character of the German

language would be well adapted to such an organization'. Smith, *Letters* II, pp. 658–9.

52. *Female Improvement*, vol. I, p. 173.

53. See Edward Chitham, *A Life of Anne Brontë* (Oxford: Blackwell, 1991), p. 105.

54. The complete title is *Deutsches Lesebuch; Or, Lessons in German Literature, Being a Choice Collection of Amusing and Instructive Pieces in Prose and Verse, selected from the Writings of the Most Celebrated German Authors. Divided into Four Parts with Interlinear, Literal, and Free Translations.* On the fly-leaf of the Haworth copy, the following note appears: Anne Brontë / Thorp Green / March 7th / 1844.

55. For example, the German text, set in black-letter type, above the English 'As Henry the Fourth was travelling through a small town, several deputies came to meet him' runs, 'Als Heinrich der Vierte reiste durch eine kleine Stadt, verschiedene Abgeordnete kamen entgegen ihm' (p. 54).

56. See Chitham, *Life of Emily Brontë*, pp. 148–9, as well as Stevie Davies, *Emily Brontë: Heretic* (London: The Women's Press, 1994), pp. 47–53, and Davies' *Emily Brontë*, Writers and Their Work, pp. 48–9.

57. See Chitham, *Birth of* Wuthering Heights, pp. 17–26.

58. See Allott, *The Critical Heritage*, p. 32.

59. See John Hewish, *Emily Brontë: A Critical and Biographical Study* (London: Macmillan, 1969), pp. 125–8.

60. The short article was written by B. Gilbert and P. C. Cross and appeared in volume 15 (1970), 412–16.

61. As Mark M. Hennelly Jr has pointed out, the collocation of the names 'Moor' and 'Moor House' is noteworthy; see '*Jane Eyre*'s reading lesson', *Journal of English Literary History* 51.4 (Winter 1984), 693–717 (698).

62. See, for instance, Elizabeth Sandford, *Female Improvement*, vol. I, p. 174.

63. For Barrett, see *Blackwood's*, vol. LVI (1844), 635; the reference to Schiller in Sewell's *Margaret Percival* (London, 1847) is in volume I, p. 13; and the Edgeworth quotation comes from *Practical Education*, vol. II, p. 289 in the 1815 edition.

64. On the last-mentioned issue, see John Sutherland, *Is Heathcliff a Murderer? Great Puzzles in Nineteenth-Century Literature* (Oxford University Press, World's Classics, 1996), pp. 53–8. Of course, the Brontës' juvenilia contain scenes of great violence and brutality, too, and their reading habits were anything but squeamish, as the examples of Byron and James Hogg alone confirm.

65. Charlotte owned volume I of Schiller's *Säm[m]tliche Werke* in the Cotta edition of 1838. The volume includes some of his best-known poems, including 'Des Mädchens Klage', 'Die Bürgschaft', 'Das Lied von der Glocke' and 'An die Freude'; it also contains a poem praising the patriotic courage and humanity of Wilhelm Tell. The element of Continental Romanticism, French and German, in the works of the Brontës requires further analysis and synthetisation. So does the significance of Carlyle in that context – but detailed intertextual investigations fall outside the scope of this study. In addition to Duthie's *Foreign Vision*, Mary (Mrs Humphry) Ward's introductions to the Haworth edition of the Brontës remain one of the best places to go for basic information;

abbreviated versions are easily accessible in Allott's *Critical Heritage* volume (pp. 448–60). Barry Qualls's *The Secular Pilgrims of Victorian Fiction: The Novel as Book of Life* (Cambridge University Press, 1982) is another natural port of call, especially as regards Carlyle. Stevie Davies' work on Emily Brontë also repeatedly raises these topics.

66. Smith, *Letters* I, p. 268.
67. See Smith, *Letters* I, p. 269n4. There are references to Italian in Charlotte Brontë's juvenilia: Marion, Marchioness of Douro, had numerous Italian books to will away (vol. II of Alexander's *An Edition*, p. 318), and Zamorna's wife Mary uses an Italian expression ('a diretto pianto') in vol. III, p. 18. *Lives of Victorian Literary Figures: The Brownings, the Brontës and the Rossettis by their contemporaries*, ed. by Marianna Kambani (London: Pickering & Chatto, 2004), states that 'Miss Wooler was a woman of unusual brains and accomplishments, especially a fine Italian scholar' (p. 404). See also Gérin, *Anne Brontë*, p. 85.
68. See Appleton's *Private Education*, p. 138; Stodart, *Hints on Reading*, p. 115; and Ellis, *Daughters of England*, p. 91.
69. See the quotation from Patrick Brontë's *The Maid of Killarney*, p. 110 above.
70. See Rozsika Parker, *The Subversive Stitch: Embroidery and the Making of the Feminine* (London: The Women's Press, 1984), pp. 149–50, and Sally Hesketh, 'Needlework in the lives and novels of the Brontë Sisters', *BST* 22 (1997), 72–85 (81–2). Hesketh's article is a thorough and knowledgeable inventory of relevant passages from both biographical records and fictional texts, emphasising the moral dimensions of various kinds of sewing in the context of the nineteenth-century woman's life.
71. III.v.505–506 (the chapter called 'Phoebe'). See Parker, *The Subversive Stitch*, for a discussion of this scene which takes the interplay of femininity and masculinity into account.
72. *Ibid.*, pp. 168 and 151.
73. As Hesketh points out, patterns of Queen Victoria's spaniel were very popular (79).
74. *The True End of Education*, p. 219. On embroidered spaniels and other kinds of ornaments made by women, see Mrs C. S. Peel, 'Homes and habits', in G. M. Young's *Early Victorian England*, vol. I, pp. 77–151 (98), and Thad Logan, *The Victorian Parlour* (Cambridge University Press, 2001), pp. 164–70.
75. See Ellis' *The Daughters of England*, p. 80. A detail observed by Priscilla Wakefield in her 1817 (2nd edn) *Reflections on the Present Condition of the Female Sex* is striking in this context: Wakefield says that most designs for needlework were made by men, not women, and finds this state of affairs disgraceful (p. 102). In *Art of the Brontës*, Alexander and Sellars reproduce some patterns for collars and cuffs discovered in Charlotte's desk (pp. 265–7); Hesketh believes them to be 'original designs' ('Needlework', 75).

CHAPTER 10 MALE AND FEMALE EDUCATION

1. For example, Barbauld's *Legacy* states that the only real difference between men and women when it comes to acquiring knowledge and cultivating taste is 'that a woman is excused from all professional knowledge' (p. 42).

2. Christopher Stray emphasises the class-marker function of the Classics-orientated curriculum in *Classics Transformed: Schools, Universities, and Society in England, 1830–1960* (Oxford: Clarendon Press, 1998); see, for instance, pp. 21–2. See also John Chandos, *Boys Together: English Public Schools 1800–1864* (Oxford University Press, 1985), pp. 32–3, and Honey, *Tom Brown's Universe*, pp. 126–38. For a fictional example of Latin as a class-marker, see *David Copperfield*, ch. XVII, where Uriah Heep turns down David's offer of teaching him Latin because '[l]earning ain't for [him]' – he is 'much too umble to accept it' (p. 247 in the 1997 World's Classics edition by Nina Burgis, with an introduction and notes by Andrew Sanders).

3. Those opponents included women; for instance, M. A. Stodart thought that Mary Wollstonecraft and Mary Astell had been wrong in claiming the mental equality of the sexes. While women's affections are stronger than men's, according to Stodart, their intellect is weaker (and so are their appetites!). See *Female Writers: Thoughts on Their Proper Sphere, and on Their Powers of Usefulness* (London, 1842), pp. 14–17.

4. *Household Education* (London, 1849), pp. 240–1. See also Mary Maurice, *Governess Life*, p. 80 on the benefits of studying languages on the basis of a sound knowledge of Latin. The father of the model bride Lucilla in More's *Coelebs*, Mr Stanley, is said to have taught her Latin because she showed a natural aptitude for it (ch. XXXIV; pp. 201–203 in the 1995 Thoemmes edition).

5. See Sandford, *Female Improvement*, vol. I, pp. 192–6, and vol. II, pp. 169–72. The presence of such opinions in a middle-of-the-road writer like Sandford indicates that they were not confined to blue-stocking circles.

6. Emma Jane Worboise's *Thornycroft Hall* (1866; known to Brontëans for its defence of W. Carus Wilson) offers a fictional example. The girl narrator has brought her Latin grammar and Valpy's *Delectus* to her new home with a view to continuing her studies in them; but her 'aunt's indignation was almost uncontrollable; she pushed away the books with a look of utter contempt, remarking that though Latin might be a credit to a man, it was a disgrace to a woman' (p. 28). Cf. Patrick Brontë's fictional character Dr O'Leary in *The Maid of Killarney* of 1818: '[L]ovely, delicate, and sprightly woman, is not formed by nature, to pore over the musty pages of Grecian and Roman literature, or to plod through the windings of Mathematical Problems . . .'. However, O'Leary – with whose views the narrator often signals agreement – goes on to say, 'I do not say this of all women. For some have shone brightly, even in the learned world' (pp. 115–16). Contemplated in this context, the Classical ambitions of George Eliot's Dorothea do not appear entirely unrealistic; see *Middlemarch*, ch. 7. On Dorothea and the Classics, see Linda K. Robertson, *The Power of Knowledge: George Eliot and Education* (New York etc.: Peter Lang, 1997), pp. 140–1.

7. On Branwell Brontë's Classical attainments, see Barker, *The Brontës*, pp. 147, 166, 319–20, 332 and 335–6.

8. Cf. the compilation of Classical set texts at Woodhouse Grove school in 1822, a decade after Patrick Brontë's examinership in the Classics there, in J. T. Slugg, *Woodhouse Grove School: Memorials and Reminiscences* (London, 1885), p. 137.

9. A suggestion made by Barker and Chitham; see the latter's *Birth of* Wuthering Heights, p. 18.

10. *Ibid.*, ch. 2 ('Learning's Golden Mine'), pp. 17–32.

11. The authors of *Systematic Education* advised students of Valpy's *Delectus* (a 'most useful book') to approach it in the following manner: *Delectus* 'contains in its first pages a number of easy sentences, through which the student will, by the help of his dictionary and grammar, proceed with profit and pleasure' (p. 28). This appears to have been exactly what Anne did. *Systematic Education* addresses the would-be autodidact, whereas most writers on education agreed that the best place to study the Classics was a school, whatever drawbacks school life might entail. Not least in view of that circumstance, it is noteworthy that Dickens equipped Florence Dombey with the ability to advance far enough in the Latin exercise-books which were such a torment to young Paul for her to be able to tutor him (IV.xii, pp. 177–8 in the 1982 World's Classics edition of *Dombey and Son*, edited by Alan Horsman with an introduction and notes by Dennis Walder).

12. *The Brontës*, p. 920n89. On Anne and Latin, see also Gérin, *Anne Brontë*, p. 86.

13. See, for instance, Gérin, *Charlotte Brontë*, pp. 342–3.

14. Lonoff refers to Charlotte's 'longing for the classical training she lacked' as an established fact; p. 354 in the *Belgian Essays*. In a thesis called '"The fire and the chandelier were not sufficient company for me": Women of intellect in the novels of Charlotte Brontë' (Texas Tech University, 1996), Lisa L. Cox claims that Charlotte Brontë's 'novels constitute a protest against the limits that gendered education puts on women' (p. 88).

15. The full title is *Bibliotheca Classica; or, A Classical Dictionary, containing a full account of all the proper names mentioned in antient authors: with tables of coins, weights, and measures, in use among the Greeks and Romans: to which is now prefixed a chronological table*. The Brontës' copy was the third, enlarged edition of 1797.

16. See George Eliot's *The Mill on the Floss*, the first chapter ('Tom's "First Half"') of Book Second ('School-Time'). Chitham has compared the Tulliver siblings to Emily and Branwell Brontë; see p. 21 in *Birth of* Wuthering Heights.

17. Published in 1821, this was one of the many schoolbooks brought out by the indefatigable Sir Richard Phillips.

18. The relevant sentence runs (Cathy is speaking to Hareton): '. . . I came upon a secret stock [of books] in your room . . . some Latin and Greek, and some tales and poetry; all old friends – I brought the last here'. I read it as meaning that Cathy brought 'the last', i.e. the 'tales and poetry', to the Heights but that 'all' are 'old friends' of hers, the Classical works included.

19. On the situation of the woman writer in a male-dominated marketplace, see Cross, *The Common Writer*, ch. 5 (pp. 164–203).

20. The OED defines 'learned' under '2. Of a person' as 'deeply-read, erudite', supplying an example from Scott, 'That dreaded phenomenon, a learned lady'. Mrs Blimber in *Dombey and Son* 'was not learned herself, but she pretended to be, and that did quite as well' (IV.xi.152 in the World's Classics edition).

Miss Blimber is regarded by young Paul 'as a kind of learned Guy Faux' (IV.xii.173). Incidentally, Charlotte Brontë will have been aware of *Dombey and Son* even if she did not read the actual instalments as they appeared in 1846–47; the Supplement of the *Leeds Mercury* for 16 January 1847 reprinted a passage on Dr Blimber's school, the one where Miss Blimber is said to dig up dead languages 'like a Ghoule' (p. 12; Dickens' name is not mentioned, only the title of the work). (The relevant passage is found on pp. 151–2 in the World's Classics edition of *Dombey and Son*.)

21. See above p. 51 on governesses and boys.
22. The quotation is from Beatrice Steuart Erskine, *Anna Jameson: Letters and Friendships (1812–1860)* (London: T. Fisher Unwin, 1915), p. 211. Among female contemporaries of the Brontës who had learnt the Classics from their fathers was Florence Nightingale; see Deborah Graham, *The Victorian Girl* (London: Croom Helm, 1982), p. 128. Mary Ann Evans had to rely on other resources, including Locke's System of Classical Instruction; see Gordon S. Haight, *George Eliot: A Biography* (Oxford: Clarendon Press, 1968), p. 25 *et passim*. It might be added that the anonymous translator of Strauss's *Das Leben Jesu* was warmly praised for 'his' generosity in translating Greek quotations that had not been translated in the original German text (John Stores Smith's *Social Aspects*, presented by the author to Charlotte Brontë in 1850, was also published by Eliot's John Chapman; Smith's book reprints extracts from extremely favourable reviews of *The Life of Jesus, Critically Examined*). Elizabeth Barrett Browning was a Greek scholar; see, for instance, Alice Falk, 'Lady's Greek without the accents: Aurora Leigh and authority', *Studies in Browning and His Circle* 19 (1991), 84–92, and Jennifer Wallace, 'Elizabeth Barrett Browning: knowing Greek', *Essays in Criticism* L.4 (Oct. 2000), 329–53.
23. The Brontës, of course, knew it well; see, for instance, Charlotte Brontë's letter to Ellen Nussey of 29 May 1843 (Smith, *Letters* I, 320). On Defoe's opposition to the domination of the Classics, see D. P. Leinster-Mackay, *The Educational World of Daniel Defoe* (University of Victoria, English Literary Studies, 1981), pp. 73–4 and 82.
24. See Stray, *Classics Transformed*, pp. 17–19.
25. Cf. the following statement by J. S. Hodgson in 1839: '[A]ll the abler men who have written upon education, have condemned the system of teaching, in schools, Latin and Greek; that no reason can be given for the continuance of it; but that it is persisted in, entirely because certain influential individuals conceive their interest and reputation to be involved in it'; *Considerations on Phrenology*, p. 148. (Hodgson himself is an advocate of the Classics, though, resorting to the classic argument that they train and refine the mind.) On the Classics and science, see also Saffin, *Science, Religion and Education*, pp. 177–200.
26. *Lectures on Popular Education*, pp. 24–7. Among the people Combe mentions as being of the same mind are Locke, Gibbon, Adam Smith and Thomas Moore on Byron; p. 33.
27. *Ibid.*, p. 32.

28. Vol. XXXIX (January 1836), 100. Just over a decade later, *Fraser's* felt obliged to defend the conventional Classical education; see vol. XXXVI (Sept. 1847), 276–81. One problem for those who wanted to preserve the traditional curriculum was that the Classics were often poorly taught, even at the most prestigious schools; on Eton, see H. C. Maxwell Lyte, *A History of Eton College: 1440–1875* (London: Macmillan, 1875), pp. 364–7 and 405–11.

29. R[ichard] L[awrence] Archer, *Secondary Education in the Nineteenth Century* (London: Cass, 1966), p. 105.

30. On the ironic dimension in these observations, see Björk, *The Language of Truth*, p. 81.

31. The chapter on the virtuous woman is in Proverbs 31.

32. See Malcolm Seaborne, *The English School: Its Architecture and Organization 1370–1870* (London: Routledge & Kegan Paul, 1971), p. 97.

33. See Stewart/McCann, *The Educational Innovators*, p. 113. Thomas Day's well-known story of the moral and physical rehabilitation of a spoilt child, *Sandford and Merton* (1783–89), stressed physical strength and hardihood; see p. 25 in Stewart/McCann's book.

34. See Adamson, *English Education*, pp. 157–8, and Stewart and McCann, *The Educational Innovators*, p. 71.

35. Lady Fitz-Patrick in Sinclair's *Modern Accomplishments* offers a fictional example; see p. 110.

36. His article appeared in *Macmillan's Magazine* X.413–15; I have quoted from the reprint in Digby and Searby, *Children, School and Society*, p. 206. Maclaren did not think cricket and football suitable for girls, 'and there are excellent reasons against leap-frog'. Whatever has been said about the playing-fields of Eton, competitive games were only gradually accepted by beaks and heads in boys' public schools. Thomas Arnold was not over-enthusiastic about sports, being familiar with Aristotle's contention that too much activity of that kind can brutalise a person. See J. A. Mangan, *Athleticism in the Victorian and Edwardian Public School: The Emergence and Consolidation of an Educational Ideology* (Cambridge University Press, 1981), pp. 16–17, and Terence Copley, *Black Tom: Arnold of Rugby The Myth and the Man* (London and New York: Continuum, 2002), p. 150. (The Aristotle reference is to *Politics*, VIII:3–35.)

37. Charlotte herself spent less time outdoors than her sisters, and at Roe Head she did not join in the other girls' games, but her long walks at home in Haworth belie the impression of a small fragile person forever buried in books. On Madame Beck's school as a place where pupils' health was well taken care of, see above p. 63.

38. *The Mothers of England: Their Influence & Responsibility* (London, 1843), p. 329. See also Wakefield, *Reflections*, pp. 23–5, and M. A. Stodart, *Principles of Education practically considered, with an especial reference to the present state of female education in England* (London, 1844), p. 245.

39. *Remarks*, p. 6. In 1849, Mary Maurice's *Governess Life* urged governesses to take care of their own health and ensure plenty of ventilation and open-air exercise, insisting that 'Coomb's [sic] Physiology is a work which should be

studied by all who are employed in education' (pp. 109–10). Andrew Combe's contribution to improved health was praised by Harriet Martineau in her *History of England*, vol. II, p. 710; according to Martineau, his influence had spread throughout Great Britain and the USA by 1850.

40. What secures M. Vandenhuten's help is William Crimsworth's rescuing of his son from drowning – a feat William manages to pull off thanks to the physical education he had received at Eton (XXI.182).

41. A somewhat convoluted, Marxist-theoretically inspired account of William Crimsworth's professional fortunes (which neglects his wife's essential role in the Crimsworth wealth-creation project) is provided by Jennifer Ruth in 'Between labor and capital: Charlotte Brontë's professional professor', *Victorian Studies* 45.2 (Winter 2003), 279–303. On Frances' initiative and capabilities, see Rauch, *Useful Knowledge*, p. 140.

CHAPTER II BEYOND THE SCHOOLROOM: READING
AND THE BRONTËS

1. On the enduring ideal of refined leisure in the nineteenth century, see Margaret Dalziel, *Popular Fiction 100 Years Ago: An Unexplored Tract of Literary History* (London: Cohen & West, 1957), pp. 155–6.

2. See Davidoff and Hall, *Family Fortunes*, pp. 162–7 in the revised Routledge edition of 2002. Cowper was often recommended to young readers; see, for instance, Jane West's *Letters to a Young Lady*, vol. I, pp. 454–6, and William Mavor's *Classical English Poetry, for the use of schools, and young persons in general* (London, 1823; this is the 10th edition). Of course, Cowper was also a favourite of Jane Austen's. F. D. Maurice regarded Cowper's works as embodying truths that every human being had a right to share; see David Young, *F. D. Maurice and Unitarianism* (Oxford: Clarendon Press, 1992), p. 114. The many references to Cowper in mid-nineteenth-century periodicals – not least *Fraser's* – and schoolbooks bear witness to his enduring popularity.

3. See, for instance, *Shirley* II.i.226–8 and Anne Brontë's poem 'To Cowper'.

4. See Wheeler's 'Literary and Biblical Allusion in "The Professor"', *BST* 17, pt 86 (1976), 46. The *Cambridge Companion to the Brontës*, edited by Heather Glen (2002), helpfully summarises the current state of knowledge of where and how the sisters obtained reading matter; see, for instance, the contributions by the editor herself, Juliet Barker and Carol Bock, pp. 23–4, 30 and 45. Barker's *The Brontës* considers the evidence at some length; see especially pp. 145–50. The new *Oxford Companion to the Brontës* supplies excellent summary presentations of books owned and read by the Brontës, and Heather Glen's *Charlotte Brontë* contains much valuable information about Charlotte Brontë's reading. So does the considerably earlier *The Brontës and Their Background* by Tom Winnifrith (the chapter called 'The Brontës and their books', pp. 84–109). Anne Hiebert Alton supplies a useful review of 'Books in the novels of Charlotte Brontë' in *BST* 21, Pt 7 (1996), 265–74.

5. Smith, *Letters* II, p. 167.

6. *Ibid.*, p. 197 (5 April 1849).
7. See above p. 24.
8. Page 19 in the 1821 edition.
9. *Ibid.*, p. 27. On mid- and late-nineteenth-century developments as regards reading and study, see Kelly J. Mays, 'The disease of reading and Victorian periodicals', in John O. Jordan and Robert L. Patten (eds), *Literature in the Marketplace: Nineteenth-century British Publishing and Reading Practices* (Cambridge University Press, 1995), pp. 165–94, especially p. 181, and Flint, *The Woman Reader, passim.*
10. *Female Improvement*, vol. I, pp. 183 and 187. Incidentally, the superiority of study to mere reading is expressed by an unlikely Dickens character; Uriah Heep responds to David Copperfield's enquiries about his legal studies by the deprecatory 'my reading is hardly to be called study' (ch. XVII, p. 247 in the World's Classics edition of *David Copperfield*).
11. *The Improvement of the Mind*, Preface, p. vii.
12. *Female Improvement*, vol. I, p. 192.
13. For an excellent analytical account of the relevant developments, see Davidoff and Hall, *Family Fortunes*, pp. 180–92 in the revised Routledge edition of 2002. Björk's informative chapter 'The female sphere' places Charlotte Brontë in the context of women's conduct literature; see *The Language of Truth*, pp. 34–56.
14. Vol. XXXII (July 1832), 65.
15. *Social Aspects* (London, 1850), p. 170. Smith gave Charlotte Brontë a copy of his book which she acknowledged in two letters, the second somewhat tactlessly describing the book as marking the author's 'important progress' since he wrote his biography of Mirabeau (Smith, *Letters* II, pp. 428–9; the first letter to J. S. Smith is on pp. 352–3).
16. Anon., *Woman's Worth: or, Hints to Raise the Female Character* (London, 1844), p. 11. '[T]here is no better way of teaching how to live than in teaching how to die', says this writer, urging readers to base all teaching on religion; Agnes Grey's words to Rosalie look like a deliberate reversal: 'The end of Religion is not to teach us how to die, but how to live' (XXIII.186; the sentence is unrelated to anything said by Lady Ashby). On the uneasy relationship between the accomplishments and the domesticity ideal, see also Theobald, 'The accomplished woman', 21–35.
17. *Household Education* (London, 1849), pp. 240–41. For a consideration of Martineau's view of women's housekeeping proclivities, see Deirdre David, *Intellectual Women and Victorian Patriarchy: Harriet Martineau, Elizabeth Barrett Browning, George Eliot* (Ithaca: Cornell University Press, 1987), p. 55. Cf. Ann Taylor's *Reciprocal Duties*, p. 98: 'The *Kitchen*, no less than the *parlour* and the *nursery*, partake the happy effects of the superintendance [sic] of an *intelligent* mistress.' On p. 97, Taylor had asserted that '*reading* . . . must assuredly rank amongst the most indispensable qualifications of a female'. On Martineau's *Household Education* as an 'answer' to Hannah More's *Strictures*, see Linda H. Peterson, 'Harriet Martineau's *Household Education*: Revising the feminine tradition' in Patrick Scott and Pauline Fletcher (eds), *Culture and Education in*

Victorian England (Lewisburg: Bucknell University Press, 1990), pp. 183–94, especially p. 185.

18. The Brontë–Southey correspondence is on pp. 165–70 in Smith, *Letters* I.

19. As Joan Burstyn points out, Charlotte admits that virtue resides in denying oneself the luxury of reading for relaxation; see *Victorian Education and the Ideal of Womanhood* (London: Croom Helm, 1980), p. 106. Deirdre David calls Southey's advice '[o]ne of the more chilling denigrations of female ambition delivered to a woman in the nineteenth century'; see *Intellectual Women*, p. vii. – Ten years after Southey wrote to her, Charlotte Brontë will have read another letter from a famous male writer to an aspiring poet. Quoting the *New York Times*, the *Leeds Intelligencer* of 27 March 1847 reprinted Thomas Carlyle's recommendations to a hopeful young man, the gist of which is that literature cannot be the business of a man's life, and it ought not to be: 'a man was not sent into this world to make verses'; he should speak manfully, read a few good books carefully, and lead an active and well-ordered life. The *Leeds Intelligencer* exhorts all young would-be poets to 'Read and profit!' (7).

20. With reference to *Jane Eyre*, Micael M. Clarke rightly observes that 'Brontë . . . asserts the worth of women's work'; see 'Brontë's *Jane Eyre* and the Grimms' Cinderella', *Studies in English Literature 1500–1900* (Autumn 2000), 695–710 (705).

21. Cf. Barbauld's recommendation in *A Legacy*: '[O]f all reading, what most ought to engage your attention are works of sentiment and morals'; p. 52.

22. See above p. 210.

23. See above pp. 116f.

24. The scene has been analysed by previous scholars. See, for instance, Margaret J. Arnold, '*Coriolanus* transformed: Charlotte Brontë's use of Shakespeare in *Shirley*', in Marianne Novy (ed.), *Women's Revisions of Shakespeare* (Chicago and Urbana: University of Illinois Press, 1991), pp. 76–88, and Paul Edmondson, 'Shakespeare and the Brontës', *Brontë Studies* 29.3 (November 2004), 189–91. In a careful discussion in *Desire and Domestic Fiction: A Political History of the Novel* (Oxford University Press, 1987), Nancy Armstrong argues that the reading of *Coriolanus* in *Shirley* shows how Shakespeare is successfully appropriated for early-nineteenth-century concerns (pp. 214–19). Conversely, Kenneth Brewer maintains that the *Coriolanus* scene represents the attempt to use literature for didactic purposes as a failure; 'Lost in a book: Aesthetic absorption 1820–1880', diss., Stanford University June 1998, pp. 11–12. Cf. also Gezari, *Charlotte Brontë*, pp. 108–13; Philip Rogers, 'Tory Brontë', 147; and Christopher Lane, *Hatred & Civility: The Antisocial Life in Victorian England* (New York: Columbia University Press, 2004), pp. 97–8 and 103.

25. This poem was Chénier's most popular work and a favourite on both sides of the Channel in the early nineteenth century; see Francis Scarfe, *André Chénier: His Life and Work 1762–1794* (Oxford: Clarendon Press, 1965), p. 326.

26. Cf. pp. 455–6 in Jane West's *Letters to a Young Lady*: '[t]he innocence of his life, and the amiable tenor of his writings, seem to justify the resplendent

vision of hope which depictures [sic] him as awakening from his long night of wretchedness at the rapturous sound of "Well done, good and faithful servant, enter thou into the joy of thy Lord!"'

27. See 'Tradition and the individual talent', especially the conclusion of the second section. (Copyright policies at Faber and Faber preclude quotation.)

28. See Ellis' *The Daughters of England*, p. 162, and pp. 54–5 in Stodart's *Hints on Reading*.

29. The gift of the same work to 'Mrs Graham' is preceded by that otherwise strait-laced lady's having expressed an interest in it (*The Tenant of Wildfell Hall* VIII. 69–70).

30. On this passage, see also above pp. 203–4.

31. *Letters on the Improvement of the Mind*, pp. 114–15. Cf. *Advice to Governesses*, pp. 100–102.

32. *Female Writers*, p. 133. Novel-writing was even more dangerous for a woman than novel-reading, according to Stodart; see pp. 134ff.

33. Pages 60–1; but Flora submits to her father's approval where reading matter is concerned.

34. The point is stressed by Laraine Fergenson in 'Using collaborative learning to teach the themes of education, ignorance, and dispossession in *Wuthering Heights*' in Sue Lonoff and Terri A. Hasseler (eds), *Approaches to Teaching Emily Brontë's* Wuthering Heights (New York: Modern Language Association of America, 2006), pp. 171–2.

35. See Richard D. Altick, *The English Common Reader: A Social History of the Mass Reading Public, 1800–1900* (Columbus: Ohio State University Press, 1957; I have used the 1998 edition), pp. 262–4. Cheap freshly printed literary works would, from approximately 1830 onwards, be classics unrestricted by copyright and published in inexpensive series for general readers; see Altick, *Writers, Readers, and Occasions: Selected Essays on Victorian Literature and Life* (Columbus: Ohio State University Press, 1989), pp. 176ff. Other sources of relevant information are John Sutherland's *Victorian Novelists and Publishers* (London: Athlone Press, 1976), Richardson, *Literature, Education, and Romanticism*, especially pp. 185–7, and Alexis Weedon, *Victorian Publishing: The Economics of Book Production for a Mass Market, 1836–1916* (Aldershot: Ashgate, 2003). Flint's *The Woman Reader* is highly informative on many aspects of women's reading in the nineteenth century. For a very helpful compilation of texts on books and readers in the period, see pp. 261–305 in Francis O'Gorman (ed.), *The Victorian Novel* (Oxford: Blackwell, 2002), one of Blackwell's Guides to Criticism. A short but information-packed introduction to the subject is provided by Peter L. Shillingsburg in 'Book Publishing and the Victorian Literary Marketplace', pp. 29–38 in William Baker and Kenneth Womack (eds), *A Companion to the Victorian Novel* (Westport, CN: Greenwood Press, 2002).

36. Vol. II, ch. xi, pp. 208–209.

37. *The Young Ladies' Reader; or, Extracts from Modern Authors, adapted for educational or family use [and so on]* (London, 1845), p. 16.

38. See Smith, *Letters* I, pp. 129–32.

39. For a classic example, see Catharine Macaulay's *Letters on Education* of 1790. Ellen does seem to have been a Hortensia to Charlotte's Macaulay.
40. Stodart quotes Scott as having called Baillie 'the first poetic genius of the day'; see *Female Writers*, pp. 96–7. Among the large (for such a short book) amount of interesting material in Jerom Murch's *Mrs. Barbauld and Her Contemporaries* of 1877 is the moving story of Baillie's rise and fall, both of which, according to Murch, left her sweet personality unchanged.
41. On Wollstonecraft and her reputation, see Birgitta Berglund, *Woman's Whole Existence: The House as an Image in the Novels of Ann Radcliffe, Mary Wollstonecraft and Jane Austen* (Lund: Lund University Press, 1993), pp. 83–6. When writers like Elizabeth Sandford and Stodart, and somewhat later Bessie Rayner Belloc, mention Wollstonecraft, it is the ardent feminist they are interested in, not the 'scarlet woman'.
42. *The Poetry of Life* (1835), vol. II, pp. 96–9. Some schoolbooks printed after the great Byron scandal still recommended him, including Mavor's *Classical English Poetry*.
43. For instance, the *Outline of the Plan of Education to be Pursued in the Bristol College* of 1830 put in references to Butler and Paley as a means of guaranteeing the religious soundness of the new venture, pp. 22–3; and Lord John Russell's Speech in the House of Commons, on 20 June 1839, on the Government Plan for Promoting National Education referred to Paley's *Evidences of Christianity* as 'a book, which any person might be glad to read' (p. 9 in the 2nd edn of 1839). The schoolbook author Jeremiah Joyce's guide to Paley was mentioned above (*An Analysis*). The same Joyce was one of the co-authors of *Systematic Education*, where Paley's notions of virtue are attacked (pp. 378 and 414) but Butler's and Watts's works recommended without qualifications (pp. 416, 452 and 456). Among those who disapproved of Paley's moral philosophy was F. D. Maurice; see Robert O. Preyer, 'From Romantic to Victorian: The Germano-Coleridgian novels of John Sterling and F. D. Maurice', *Victorian Literature and Culture* 20 (1992), 141–60 (155). On Butler and Paley, cf. also Glen, *Charlotte Brontë*, p. 278.
44. *The Brontës*, p. 148. Barker points out that the Ponden Hall library, which she agrees the sisters probably used (many earlier scholars had regarded it as a major source of Brontë reading matter), was dominated by literature from the eighteenth century. It might be added that the major eighteenth-century authors were comparatively well represented in the modest collection of books in the Parsonage itself. On the relationship between the eighteenth and nineteenth centuries in a more general sense, see the introduction to Francis O'Gorman and Katherine Turner (eds), *The Victorians and the Eighteenth Century: Reassessing the Tradition* (Aldershot: Ashgate, 2004), pp. 1–13.
45. Erasmus Darwin's list of recommended literature in *A Plan for the Conduct of Female Education in Boarding Schools* of 1797 is strikingly liberal. Although he included Paley's *Evidences* and cautiously stated that '[b]ooks of controversial divinity are not recommended to Ladies' (p. 126), he had no qualms about recommending Nonconformist writers, Frances Burney's novels,

'M. Wolstencroft's' *Stories from Life* and Madame de Genlis' educational literature in translation (despite the Roman Catholic faith of the writer and her well-known adultery, both of which made her deeply suspect in the eyes of many subsequent compilers of suitable reading matter for young women).

46. See *The Common Reader*, pp. 151ff. in the 1998 edition.
47. *Ibid.*, p. 151.
48. Cf. Todd, *The Daughter at School*, ch. XI, in which the author tells his young audience not to read the Bible 'here and there a chapter', but passage by passage 'in a continuous course' and with complete attention (pp. 193–214).
49. Branwell's letters to the Editor of *Blackwood's*, and to Wordsworth, are cases in point; see Smith, *Letters* I, pp. 160–2, and Barker, *The Brontës*, pp. 232–4.
50. On Charlotte Brontë and *Blackwood's*, see Christine Alexander, 'Readers and writers: *Blackwood's* and the Brontës', *The Gaskell Society Journal* 8 (1994), 54–69, and Bock, *Charlotte Brontë*, pp. 11–16. A recent article by the latter traces the Brontës' involvement with *Fraser's Magazine*; see Carol A. Bock, 'Authorship, the Brontës, and *Fraser's Magazine*: "Coming forward" as an author in early Victorian England', *Victorian Literature and Culture* 29 (2001), 241–66.
51. See *Charlotte Brontë*, pp. 105ff.
52. Smith, *Letters* I, p. 160; the letter is dated 10 January 1837 and the writer was 19 years old.
53. On Jane Eyre, Helen Burns and *Rasselas*, see Bock, *Charlotte Brontë*, pp. 79–80. On books and reading generally in *Jane Eyre*, see also Carla L. Peterson, *The Determined Reader: Gender and Culture in the Novel from Napoleon to Victoria* (New Brunswick: Rutgers University Press, 1987), pp. 82–112; Valentine Cunningham, *In the Reading Gaol: Postmodernity, Texts, and History* (Oxford: Blackwell, 1994), pp. 341–62; and Cheryl A. Wilson, 'Female Reading Communities in *Jane Eyre*', *Brontë Studies* 30 (July 2005), 131–9.
54. Cf. the following well-known quotation from Elizabeth Barrett Browning's *Aurora Leigh* (published in 1856 but written about ten years earlier and hence contemporaneous with the first Brontë novels), I.700ff.: 'It is rather when / We gloriously forget ourselves and plunge / Soul-forward, headlong, into a book's profound, / Impassioned for its beauty and salt of truth – /'Tis then we get the right good from a book'.
55. On reading aloud, see Flint, *The Woman Reader*, pp. 100–102.
56. *Reflections*, pp. 93–4.
57. See, for instance, Parkes, *Domestic Duties*, pp. 381–3. Parkes points out that while families should feel free to enjoy light literature together in this way, ambitious works that seem 'heavy and tedious' when tackled on one's own may be made much more accessible by being read aloud by an able reader (p. 382; Parkes mentions *Paradise Lost* in this connection).
58. On Edgar Linton's withdrawal into the realm of books, and on reading in *Wuthering Heights*, see Robert McKibben, 'The image of the book in *Wuthering Heights*', *Nineteenth-Century Fiction* XV.2 (1960), 159–69.
59. The passages from *Shirley* quoted above serve as examples, as does the scene in *Jane Eyre* where Miss Temple and Helen Burns dazzle young Jane – 'they spoke

of books: how many they had read! What stores of knowledge they possessed!'
(I.viii.73).

60. According to Yukari Oda, these experiences caused Emily to lose not only
interest in education itself, but also faith in its benefits – a loss of faith reflected
in the scarcity of educational allusions in *Wuthering Heights*. See '*Wuthering
Heights*: Education as an intermediary factor', Duckett (ed.), *The Brontës and
Education: 2004 Conference*, 41–52, especially pp. 42 and 51. Young Catherine
Earnshaw certainly rejects edifying literature with vehemence (I.iii.17). Cf.
Stevie Davies, *Emily Brontë* (Writers and Their Work), p. 103, and Linda H.
Peterson's introduction to *Emily Brontë Wuthering Heights*, Case Studies in
Contemporary Criticism (Boston and New York: Bedford/St Martin's, 2003),
pp. 9–10. See also pp. 159–60 above.

SECTION IV STRATEGIES AND METHODS

1. See Collins, *Dickens and Education*, p. 137.
2. See *Education as History: Interpreting Nineteenth- and Twentieth-Century Education* (London: Methuen, 1983), pp. 18ff.
3. Unlike these three, Jane Eyre's village school in Morton is not a boarding
school; but the narrator/instructor leaves the reader in no doubt that it is a
tremendous success.

CHAPTER 12 PEDAGOGICAL PURPOSES AND PRINCIPLES

1. This opening sentence of Herbart's *Science of Education* is quoted and commented on in Edward J. Power, *Main Currents in the History of Education* (New
York: McGraw-Hill, 1962), p. 402.
2. Cf. Charlotte's letter to W. S. Williams of 1 March 1848, Smith, *Letters* II, p. 59:
'Lewes is nobly right when he says that Intellect is <u>not</u> the highest faculty of
man, though it may be the most brilliant; when he declares that the <u>moral</u>
nature of his kind is more sacred than the <u>intellectual</u> nature; when he prefers
"goodness, lovingness and quiet self-sacrifice to all the talents in the world."'
3. Hazelwood, an innovative school created by Thomas Wright Hill and his sons,
was an institution geared to training future leaders by promoting responsible
behaviour, encouraging individual achievement and offering a wide-ranging
curriculum that included natural science; see, for instance, W. A. C. Stewart,
Progressives and Radicals in Education 1750–1970 (London: Macmillan, 1972),
pp. 54–67. Under the management of Dr Charles Mayo, Cheam School –
famous from the days of William Gilpin – became the foremost Pestalozzian
school in England and was also remarkable for its instruction in the sciences;
see Stewart and McCann, *The Educational Innovators*, pp. 169–78.
4. See, for instance, Dunn, *Principles of Teaching*, p. 15.
5. Catharine Macaulay's *Letters on Education* and the Edgeworths' *Practical Education* illustrate this ambivalence towards Rousseau. So does Henry Home,
Lord Kames's *Loose Hints upon Education, Chiefly Concerning the Culture*

of the Heart (London and Edinburgh, 1781; there were many subsequent editions).

6. On Evangelical education in connection with the Brontës, see Thormählen, *The Brontës and Religion*, pp. 20–2, and Glen, *Charlotte Brontë*, pp. 68–82. The connection between the Evangelical idea of original sin and the Augustinian tradition of the child's depravity is brought out by Richardson in *Literature, Education, and Romanticism*; see especially pp. 14 and 17. Locke had also opposed the idea of original sin; see, for instance, Bowen, *A History*, p. 176.

7. Richard Lovell Edgeworth was one of them; his attempt to educate his son according to the *Émile* ideal was a much-regretted failure.

8. On Pestalozzi, see Kate Silber, *Pestalozzi: The Man and His Work* (London: Routledge and Kegan Paul, 1960; there was a fourth edition in 1976), as well as Adamson, *English Education* and Stewart and McCann, *The Educational Innovators, passim,* and E. S. Lawrence, *The Origins*, pp. 188ff. (ch. 19). Hugh M. Pollard discusses Pestalozzi in England in *Pioneers of Popular Education 1760–1850* (London: Murray, 1956), pp. 171ff., and Geoffrey Howson deals with Pestalozzi's impact on the teaching of arithmetic in *A History of Mathematics Education in England* (Cambridge University Press, 1982), pp. 107–10. Pestalozzi's influential conception of the object lesson is succinctly explained in Mattisson, *Knowledge and Survival*, pp. 61–2. (Mattisson's section on nineteenth-century educational theory and practice is an excellent summary; pp. 58–62.)

9. See Pollard, *Pioneers*, pp. 182–6, and Stewart and McCann, *The Educational Innovators*, pp. 169–78.

10. Brontë scholarship usually represents Charlotte Brontë's personal acquaintance with Kay-Shuttleworth, from 1850 onwards, as something of a burden for her. In view of Kay-Shuttleworth's work to promote national education, he must have been a hero to Patrick Brontë, who understandably encouraged the acquaintance. On Charlotte Brontë and Sir James Kay-Shuttleworth, see Gérin, *Charlotte Brontë*, pp. 419–28, Baumber, 'Patrick Brontë', 79, and David Warwick, 'Squire and "She authors": Sir James Kay-Shuttleworth, Charlotte Brontë and Elizabeth Gaskell', *Brontë Studies* 23, Pt 2 (Oct. 1998), 159–69. Dickens read Kay-Shuttleworth but found him heavy going; see Collins, *Dickens and Education*, p. 18.

11. On Andrew Bell the man, see J. M. D. Meiklejohn, *An Old Educational Reformer: Dr. Andrew Bell* (Edinburgh and London, 1881), p. 120.

12. On practices in Bell's and Lancaster's monitorial schools, see, for instance, Gosden, *How They Were Taught*, pp. 1–8, and Lawson and Silver, *A Social History*, pp. 241–6. Although the shortcomings of the monitorial system were obvious to most participants in the educational debate in the 1840s, shortage of resources meant that it was still being practised; for a grim description of the outcome, see Hook, *On the Means*, p. 18.

13. The OED describes a monitor as a 'senior pupil in a school . . . who has special duties assigned to him, esp. that of keeping order, and who may occasionally . . . act as a teacher to a junior class'; *s.v.* 'monitor', 2. The duties assigned to the

monitors at Lowood are obviously practical rather than educational, as is natural in that Lowood is not a monitorial school but a boarding-school for (broadly speaking) middle-class girls; see *Jane Eyre* I.v.44 and I.v.47.

14. While scales and numbers must be borne in mind in a comparison of Pestalozzi and Bell as educationists, Pestalozzi's ideas were also implemented, and held to be successful, in large classes. Even Edward Baines Jr admitted that 'the methods of communicating elementary knowledge in the schools of Prussia', which relied greatly on 'the system of Pestalozzi', were 'admirable', but hastened to add that they were also known, and spreading fast, in England; see Baines's ninth *Letter* to Russell, p. 81 in the 7th edition (the first appeared in 1846) of Baines's *Letters to the Right Honourable Lord John Russell [and so on] on State Education* (London, 1847).

15. *Woman, in her social and domestic character* (London, 1831), p. 168. The Thomson lines are of course also alluded to by the as yet untried Agnes Grey (I.9–10).

16. A rationale for this transformation is suggested in Marianne Thormählen, 'The lunatic and the devil's disciple: The "lovers" in *Wuthering Heights*', *The Review of English Studies* 48 (1997), 183–97.

17. See p. 267n60.

18. Robert Barnard, *Emily Brontë* (The British Library, 2000, in the Writers' Lives series), p. 27. Barnard accounts for Emily's willingness to go to Brussels by pointing out that the trip would 'stimulate and exercise her mental and creative powers', 'always a dominant imperative with her' (p. 50).

19. The notion, advanced in Sandra M. Gilbert and Susan Gubar's *The Madwoman in the Attic: The Woman Writer and the Nineteenth-Century Literary Imagination* (New Haven and London: Yale University Press, 1979), p. 275, that 'education for Emily Brontë is almost always fearful, even agonizing', possibly '[reflecting] the Brontës' own traumatic experiences at the Clergy Daughters School and elsewhere', is not entirely easy to understand. By contrast, Muriel Spark's speculations about Emily's ambivalence towards sustained rational effort raise important questions; see *The Essence of the Brontës*, pp. 233–7.

20. The over-all significance of education in *Wuthering Heights* has recently been skilfully brought out by Laraine Fergenson in her contribution to Lonoff and Hasseler's *Approaches to Teaching* Wuthering Heights, pp. 167–74.

21. Naturally enough, Rousseau's insistence that young children should not be made to undergo any formal tuition struck eighteenth- and nineteenth-century commentators as peculiar; see, for instance, p. 5 in Kames's *Loose Hints*: 'Rousseau advances a strange opinion, that children are incapable of instruction before the age of twelve'.

22. See Thormählen, *The Brontës and Religion*, p. 245n1.

23. From the Preface of the 1813 edition in Haworth Parsonage (n.p.).

24. From the Preface of the 1810 copy of Porny's *Grammatical Exercises* in the Brontë Parsonage Museum (n.p.).

25. Lord John Russell quoting Fénelon in his Speech on the Government Plan for Promoting National Education, separately printed, p. 10.

26. *Governess Life*, p. 85.

27. Abbott was an American, and the 1833 Boston edition of his book presents him as 'Late Principal of the Mt. Vernon Female School, Boston, MA'. The full title of Abbott's book is *The Teacher, or Moral Influences Employed in the Instruction and Government of the Young: Intended Chiefly to Assist Young Teachers in Organizing and Conducting Their Schools*. In 1834 a new edition appeared in London, from Seeley & Co., revised by Charles Mayo. The relevant passage from *The Teacher* is on p. 77 in the revised edition.

28. Stewart and McCann, *The Educational Innovators*, pp. 61 and 71–2.

29. Dressler, *Geschichte der englischen Erziehung*, p. 262 (my translation).

30. See, for instance, Abbott, *The Teacher*, pp. 58ff. in the revised edition.

31. *Ibid.*, p. 29 in the revised edition. As any experienced teacher knows, the co-operation of *all* is rarely realisable.

32. On Fröbel in Britain, with an emphasis on post-1850s developments, see Evelyn Mary Lawrence (ed.), *Friedrich Froebel and English Education* (London: Routledge and Kegan Paul, 1953). See also Rosemary O'Day, 'Women and education in nineteenth-century England', in Joan Bellamy, Anne Laurence and Gill Perry (eds), *Women, Scholarship and Criticism: Gender and Knowledge c. 1790–1900* (Manchester University Press, 2000), p. 98. Cf. the 'father' of modern pedagogy, John Amos Comenius, who wrote the first version of his *School of Infancy* in 1630 (in Czech): '. . . tell [the children] that learning is not labor, but that amusement with books and pen is sweeter than honey. And [so] that of this amusement children may have a foretaste, they can be given chalk. With it they may draw on slate or paper, angles, squares, circles, little stars, horses, trees. It is unimportant whether or not these are likenesses, provided they delight the mind'. *The School of Infancy*, ed. Ernest M. Eller (Chapel Hill: University of North Carolina Press, 1956), p. 120. On Comenius and his importance to subsequent educationists, in Britain and elsewhere, see E. S. Lawrence, *The Origins*, pp. 95ff. (ch. 8).

33. 'In all successful teaching the *interest* of the child must be sustained', stated the Preface of Henry Dunn and John Thomas Crossley's first reader 'for the Use of Schools and Families', *Daily Lesson Book* I (London, 1840), p. 4.

34. Vol. I, pp. 486–7 in the 1815 edition.

35. Henry Dunn and John Thomas Crossley, *Daily Lesson Book for the Use of Schools and Families* III (London, n.d. [1840]), preface, p. 3. The poetical pieces include a liberal selection from Cowper, some Wordsworth and such famous passages from Shakespeare as Portia's lines on 'the quality of mercy'.

36. *Female Writers*, p. 150.

37. For instance, Stodart worried that the mingling of truth and fiction in Mrs Sherwood's work 'may foster female vanity'; *Female Writers*, p. 153. I have not found any reference to *The Fairchild Family* in the writings of the Brontës, though the book is sometimes mentioned in the Brontë literature as a terrifying bearer of Evangelical notions of upbringing (for instance by Glen in *Charlotte Brontë*, pp. 69 and 80n61).

38. For example, Stodart disapproved of the 'Socinian tenets' (Barbauld was a Dissenter) in Barbauld's *Hymns in Prose for Children* (*Principles of Education*,

p. 76n.) and regretted the absence of religious sentiment in Edgeworth (*Hints on Reading*, p. 49).

39. See further pp. 187ff.

40. On Marcet, see also pp. 95 and 246n55. Marcet was obviously a good businesswoman, too; she taught Maria Edgeworth – belatedly – the importance of retaining and exercising one's copyright. See Erskine, *Anna Jameson*, p. 256.

41. 'Mrs Marcet', p. 389 in Martineau's *Biographical Sketches* (London, 1869). On Jane Haldiman Marcet in the context of early-nineteenth-century education and economics, see J. R. Shackleton, 'Jane Marcet and Harriet Martineau: pioneers of economics education' in *History of Education* 19.4 (1990), 283–97 (285–90).

42. Novelty is seen as something desirable and invigorating elsewhere in *Jane Eyre*, too. '[C]hange, stimulus' is what Jane desires when she is '[gasping] for liberty' after Miss Temple's departure (I.x.85), and her first meeting with Mr Rochester excites her partly because it is something 'new' and 'active'; 'I was weary of an existence all passive' (I.xii.115). Cf. *The Professor* XXV.229: William Crimsworth appreciates that his wife cannot lead a 'quiescent and inactive' life.

43. According to Charlotte Brontë's Roe Head Journal, the girls who came up to her and asked perfectly reasonable questions were 'dolts' who made her want to 'vomit'. (In Murray's and Pinnock's grammars, the section on nouns follows immediately after the one on articles, so it was natural for Charlotte's pupils to want clarification on that distinction.)

44. See Hewish, *Emily Brontë*, p. 47; as Hewish observes, the story 'seems true to the character of the woman who wrote "The Cat"'.

45. See, for instance, West, *Chapter of Governesses*, p. 71.

46. See Smith, *Letters* I, p. 253. Cf. the observations on Mrs Gaskell's children in *Letters* III, pp. 47–8, 156 and 183.

47. See Chitham, *Life of Anne Brontë*, pp. 52–3 and 56.

48. Charlotte's exasperated comment, on 24 August 1838 in a letter to Ellen Nussey, on her work at Dewsbury Moor (the Misses Wooler's new school after Roe Head); Smith, *Letters* I, p. 180. A poem written about a year earlier, 'The Teacher's Monologue', speaks about homesick reveries during a brief interlude from the 'yoke' and the 'long task' in 'this strange, coarse world around' – a dismal description of the teacher's plight. See Winnifrith's edition of *The Poems of Charlotte Brontë*, pp. 51–2.

49. Cf. Maria Young's statement in Harriet Martineau's *Deerbrook* of 1839 that teaching has its good points, but that they are as nothing compared to the 'sublime delights of education' (vol. I, p. 40).

50. Page 147 in the Everyman edition of 1960 (ch. XI).

51. See Chapter XI in Gaskell's *Life of Charlotte Brontë*, pp. 145ff. in the 1960 Everyman edition.

52. Subtitled *Some Reminiscences of the Real Monsieur and Madame Heger* (London: T. C. & E. C. Jack, 1914).

53. *Charlotte Brontë's Promised Land: The Pensionnat Heger and Other Brontë Places in Brussels*, published by The Brontë Society in 2000, and *The Pensionnat*

Revisited: More Light Shed on the Brussels of the Brontës, privately printed in 2003. These booklets focus on places rather than people, but offer interesting sidelights on activities as well.

54. 'The education of Charlotte Brontë: A pedagogical case study', *Pedagogy: Critical Approaches to Teaching Literature, Language, Composition, and Culture* 1.3 (2001), 457–77. Barker's *The Brontës* summarises the available evidence with acumen and efficiency; see pp. 383–6 and 412–15. The Brussels chapter in Duthie's *The Foreign Vision of Charlotte Brontë* is also helpful; see especially pp. 38–41, 44–8, 53–4 and 59–60. Rebecca Fraser's article 'Monsieur Heger: Critic or catalyst in the life of Charlotte Brontë?', *Brontë Studies* 28.3 (Nov. 2003), 185–94, is an engaging review of Heger's significance in Charlotte Brontë's development. Cf. also Lawrence J. Dessner, *The Homely Web of Truth: A Study of Charlotte Brontë's Novels* (The Hague: Mouton, 1975), pp. 16–18.

55. Gaskell must surely have realised the truth; see, for instance, Gérin, *Charlotte Brontë*, pp. 571–2 and Fraser, *Charlotte Brontë*, 'Epilogue', p. 489 in the 2003 Vintage edition. In the Penguin edition of Gaskell's *Life*, the editor Alan Shelston says that Gaskell knew about Charlotte's feelings for Heger (p. 30 in the 1985 edition).

56. Jane Carlyle's remarks on the reliability of Elizabeth Gaskell state a different case: 'I am the readier to believe the poor woman [Lady Scott, the former Mrs Lydia Robinson] innocent or at least nothing like so bad as M*rs* G has painted her; because I have had the evidence of my own senses that M*rs* G speaks too fast, and nothing she narrates is to be wholly relied on[.] The novel writer tendency to dramatise everything, the desire to *ingratiate* herself as a popular Lioness, and (I think) a natural deficiency of *precision* both in her thoughts and feelings make her *I have found* a person rather dangerous to associate with'. Letter to George Lillie Craik of 4 May 1857, *Jane Carlyle Newly Selected Letters*, ed. Kenneth J. Fielding and David R. Sorensen (Aldershot: Ashgate, 2004), p. 225 (emphases in the original).

57. See Lonoff, *The Belgian Essays*, pp. lxiii and 357. Inga-Stina Ewbank's discussion of the stylistic/rhetorical weaknesses of *The Professor* remains authoritative; see *Their Proper Sphere*, pp. 178–80.

58. *The Secret*, p. 167; see also p. 177. Macdonald regards this as an expression of direct adherence to Rousseau.

59. Cf., for instance, Mary Maurice on the necessity of maintaining a sense of the 'awfulness' of the task: a teacher should never say, '"these are my plans, my way of teaching – see how my pupils advance". When once this spirit creeps into the mind, the teacher is spoiled, because she lacks humility'. *Governess Life*, p. 123; see also p. 70.

60. *The Secret*, p. 175.

61. Quoted from p. 323 in the 1998 World's Classics edition of *Wuthering Heights*. See further pp. 206ff. above.

62. The sisters' different responses have often been described by scholars; see, for instance, pp. xxx–xxxiii in Lonoff's edition of the Brussels essays and p. 384 in Barker's *The Brontës*.

63. Gaskell, *Life*, ch. XI, p. 152 in the Everyman edition. Her 1843 *devoir* on Charles-Hubert Millevoye's 'La Chute des Feuilles' suggests that she came to appreciate the method; see Lonoff, *The Belgian Essays*, pp. 240ff.

64. The *locus classicus* is Quintilian's 'Ut magistrorum officium est docere, sic, disciplinorum, praebere se docilis: alioqui neutrum sine altero sufficiet'. Quoted by Charles Rollin in his *Traité des études*, vol. IV in the 1838 edition (original date of publication 1726–31), p. 376n. (in 'Deuxième partie', ch. V, 'Du devoir des écoliers').

65. Mary Maurice, for instance, having said that reading good authors with older pupils is a way of forming their minds, stated that essay-writing excites 'mental activity' and added, '[a]ll affectation in writing should be discouraged, *and mere imitation of others*' (*Governess Life*, p. 96; emphasis added).

66. Macdonald, *The Secret*, p. 221. Any modern writer who ever started writing a piece of creative prose immediately after ingesting a hefty chunk of Joyce, Mann or Proust will understand this prescription.

67. See especially p. 467 in 'The education of Charlotte Brontë'.

68. On Charlotte's Roe Head distinctions, see Barker, *The Brontës*, p. 174 (Barker's chapter on Roe Head is aptly headed 'Emulation rewarded').

69. IV.238 in the 1838 edition. Rollin's *Traité des études* went through a number of editions in the eighteenth and nineteenth centuries and was well known in the British Isles; for instance, Higson records copies of the revised 1845 edition in two of the institutional libraries she examined (*Sources*, items B887 and C1241).

70. In her article on Charlotte Brontë's education, Lonoff says that Heger's methods were 'a century ahead of those then prevalent in England' (465), and in the essay volume she points out that Lawrence Dessner saw a striking similarity between Heger's literary instruction and the approach of the New Critics (p. xlvi). Macdonald claims that Heger 'followed Rousseau faithfully' (*The Secret*, p. 217), but in the Belgian-essay volume Lonoff says that Rousseau was not in Heger's agenda (p. lx).

71. *Traité des études*, IV.242 in the 1838 edition.

72. Lonoff, *The Belgian Essays*, p. xxviii.

73. *Traité des études*, IV.250. As so often, Quintilian is the original source for Rollin.

74. Part of a title in *Traité* (vol. I): *De la Manière d'enseigner et d'étudier les Belles-Lettres, par rapport à l'esprit et au cœur*. This was translated into English as *The method of teaching and studying the belles lettres* in the 1730s, a work which appears to have been widely disseminated in Britain; see Higson, *Sources*, items B888 and B889.

75. The story is told in *The Secret*, pp. 216–17.

76. *Ibid.*, p. 216; on p. 218, Macdonald states her opinion that '[t]he Teacher of genius is born and not made'. Earlier in her book Macdonald had italicised the following testimonial to Heger: *'he was before all things a born teacher, and one who saw the world as his class-room, and his fellow-creatures in the light of pupils'* (p. 132).

CHAPTER 13 SCHOOLROOM PRACTICES

1. On Agnes' impossible job, see Frawley, *Anne Brontë*, p. 95. Frawley's book is intended as an introduction to Anne Brontë and serves this purpose very well while also containing much good and independent criticism. The chapter on *Agnes Grey* is a case in point.

2. As Henry Dunn advised fledgling teachers, 'Bear in mind . . . that the first step you have to take, in moral as well as intellectual education, is, TO ESTABLISH YOUR AUTHORITY. There never was a more absurd notion than that which is becoming popular in some quarters, that children may be governed without authority . . . Do not listen to this mischievous trash for a moment' (*Principles of Teaching*, p. 25). Dunn emphasised that '*children naturally love order*' (p. 43, Dunn's italics).

3. See Frawley's *Anne Brontë*, pp. 111–16. On the role of the governess in *Agnes Grey*, see above pp. 51f.

4. The French word 'adresse' has a wide range of connotations, including 'savoir-faire' and '(diplomatic) adroitness'. Cf. Rollin, p. IV.276 in *Traité*: 'Il faut bien de la tête, bien de l'adresse à un maître, pour tenir en main et conduire les rênes de tant d'esprits d'un caractère tout différent'. One shrewd trick which William learns is one that many teachers of large classes in lecture halls have adopted: 'I had found that in entering with aplomb and mounting the estrade with emphasis consisted the grand secret of ensuring immediate silence' (XIV.108).

5. See, above all, her letters to W. S. Williams in May–June 1848; Smith, *Letters* II, pp. 63–6, 72–4, 226–7. See above pp. 59–60.

6. See Barker, *The Brontës*, p. 128.

7. See, for instance, Gérin, *Charlotte Brontë*, p. 57.

8. Ch. XI in Gaskell's *Life*; p. 150 in the 1960 Everyman edition.

9. On Jane's professional good sense with Adèle, see Margaret Hulmes, 'The Brontë heroines as disciplinarians', in Duckett (ed.), *The Brontës and Education: 2004 Conference*, p. 34.

10. Pages 106–107 in Sinclair's 1836 tale. The reasons for Miss Porson's high opinion of conversation as an educational device resemble those advanced by Isaac Watts in *The Improvement of the Mind*. Cf. also the mode of conveying knowledge by 'a series of Instructive Conversations' in Wakefield's *Mental Improvement*.

11. The word 'desultory' used of knowledge acquisition had specific connotations in the methodically minded nineteenth century (especially among Evangelicals and utilitarians), designating the opposite of the 'systematic' mindset described above (pp. 22–3). See Altick, *The Common Reader*, p. 132.

12. A point also noted by Simmons, 'Contextualising', p. 38.

13. On physical force in *Agnes Grey*, see also Simmons, 'Contextualising', p. 37.

14. See, for instance, Mary Maurice's *Governess Life*, pp. 89ff. The repetition of individual words as a component in the tuition of young children has a long history. It was, for instance, a feature of Comenius' infant-school programme; see *Bowen's History*, p. 87.

15. '[A] clear reflection of Charlotte's own attitudes', in Hulmes's words; 'The Brontë heroines', p. 38.
16. See above p. 60.
17. Smith, *Letters* II, pp. 64–5.
18. See Smith, *Letters* II, p. 64; Charlotte herself underlined the words 'instruct' and 'educate'.
19. On the debate on domestic versus school education, see pp. 33ff. above.
20. 'Biographical Notice of Ellis and Acton Bell'; *Wuthering Heights*, p. 322.
21. See above p. 168.
22. See *Villette* XXVII.311 and XXXIII.380–1.
23. 'The education', 459; see also the following pages.
24. See Lecaros, '"Lessons"', 137, 143–4 and 147–8, and Simmons, 'Contextualising', pp. 36ff.
25. See, for instance, Rollin, *Traité*, pp. IV.268 and 274–5. Miss Patty Lockit in Sarah Fielding's *The Governess* knows that her best hope of being happy at school involves 'always [loving those] who are so good as to instruct me' (p. 113 in the Oxford University Press facsimile edition of 1968 of *The Governess or, Little Female Academy*, with an introduction by Jill E. Grey). On 'the discipline of love' in Romantic thought, see Richardson, *Literature, Education, and Romanticism*, pp. 62–3. Henry Dunn's 1839 *Principles of Teaching* urged the new teacher to remember that '*the affections of your pupils must be secured . . . [i]f they do not love you, they will repel all your attempts to do them good*' (p. 147). This is not a phenomenon that belongs to the past only; asked a couple of years ago what parents could do to help teachers succeed with their children, a very experienced primary-school teacher replied without hesitation, 'Letting them love us'.
26. Rousseau disapproved of Locke's 'great maxim' of reasoning with children, finding it meaningless and even counter-productive; see, for instance, Bowen, *A History*, p. 186.
27. Cf. p. 158 above. Bettina L. Knapp ascribes (imperfect) knowledge of Rousseau's approach to education to Mrs Bloomfield; see 'Anne Brontë's *Agnes Grey*: The feminist; "I must stand alone"', in Nash and Suess, *New Approaches*, p. 66.
28. *Letters on Education*, p. 62. The Edgeworths followed suit: 'the language of blows need seldom be used to reasonable creatures', *Practical Education*, vol. I, p. 323 in the 1815 edition. In a noble passage on the purpose of punishment in general, Maria Edgeworth wrote that 'the partial evil of punishment is . . . to be tolerated by the wise and humane legislator, only so far as it is proved to be necessary for the general good' (I.288–9). Naturally, Pestalozzi and Fröbel were also against corporal punishment. Rollin, in the early eighteenth century, only allowed the use of 'la verge et le fouet' on rare occasions and for serious transgressions – otherwise these instruments held 'quelque chose d'indécent' (*Traité*, p. IV. 255).
29. See Stewart and McCann, *The Educational Innovators*, p. 230. An 1845 H. M. Inspector's report states that 145 out of 163 schools asked whether they used corporal punishment replied in the affirmative; see Gosden, *How They Were*

Taught, pp. 18–20. The same report distinguishes between girls' and boys' schools in this respect, claiming that a mistress who cannot run a school for girls without a rod 'may well doubt whether she is fitted for that particular situation', p. 20.

30. See, for instance, Michael McCrum, *Thomas Arnold Head Master* (Oxford University Press, 1989), pp. 73–7. The boy in the March case – who later turned out to have been innocent – was punished for mendacity, a reason for Arnold's 'incontinent fury' in that he had an 'almost pathological hatred of lying' (p. 76). On flogging at Eton in the days of Dr Keate's Provostship (1809–34), see Lyte, *A History of Eton College*, pp. 372–5.

31. See Donald K. Jones, 'Socialization and social science: Manchester Model Secular School 1854–1861', in Phillip McCann (ed.), *Popular Education and Socialization in the Nineteenth Century* (London: Methuen, 1977), pp. 127–8. See also Silver, *Education as History*, p. 26.

32. See the chapter on rewards and punishments in Stewart and McCann, *The Educational Innovators*, pp. 219–41, and p. 331 on Ellis.

33. *Dutch and German Schools*, p. 61.

34. *On the Importance*, p. 140. Similarly, Dunn was not prepared to say that the teacher can always dispense with corporal punishment, carefully problematising the issue; see *Principles of Teaching*, pp. 136–8.

35. See Stewart and McCann, *The Educational Innovators*, p. 229.

36. Pages 68–9 (Letter XI). Rollin referred to public disgrace ('honte publique') as a remedy of last resort; *Traité*, p. IV. 262.

37. It was not of course unusual for schools known to the Brontës to inflict both kinds of punishment; see, for instance, Barker, *The Brontës*, on Woodhouse Grove, p. 125. One wonders whether Barker is not somewhat too complimentary towards Woodhouse Grove ('a model of its kind'); cf. the porridge incident mentioned below and the following account from a boy who was there from 1812 to 1818, at a time when Patrick Brontë was associated with the school: 'I was thrashed every day. I have no doubt that I generally deserved it; but it was too much – it did no good . . .' Clifford W. Towlson (ed.), *Woodhouse Grove School 1812–1962: A Hundred and Fifty Years of Memories and Recollections* (Leeds, 1962, printed by Maney), p. 19.

38. See Gérin, *Anne Brontë*, p. 132.

39. Edward Chitham, *Life of Anne Brontë*, p. 60.

40. See, for example, Sturt, *The Education of the People*, p. 25, Stewart and McCann, *The Educational Innovators*, p. 229 and Joyce Taylor, *Joseph Lancaster The Poor Child's Friend: Educating the Poor in the Early Nineteenth Century* (Kent: The Campanile Press, 1996), p. 11. (Taylor, however, admits that there is a sly reference to Lancaster's flogging boys in the *Ingoldsby Legends* by R. H. Barham (p. 92).)

41. See Richard Holmes, *Coleridge: Darker Reflections* (London: HarperCollins, 1998), pp. 130–1.

42. *The Common Reader*, p. 150; Altick is referring to Edmund Blunden's 1931 edition of *Sketches in the Life of John Clare*, p. 51.

43. The harrowing story is told in Towlson, *Woodhouse Grove School*, pp. 23–5. It is also mentioned in Barker, *The Brontës*, pp. 857–8n44.
44. See Stewart and McCann, *The Educational Innovators*, pp. 71–2. Exalting some pupils before others was a practice decried by other educationists as well. For instance, George Combe disapproved of the kind of prize-giving and place-taking that elicits self-love and vanity in pupils just because they happen to have done better than the others. Encouraging pupils and making use of their pleasure in learning for its own sake were greatly preferable. See the Postscript to the second edition of Combe's *Lectures on Popular Education*, pp. 111–16.
45. See Smith, *Letters* II, p. 64.
46. Cf. Dunn in *Principles of Teaching*: 'The *judicious use of praise*, is another powerful means of gaining the affections of children. An encouraging smile, a gentle pressure of the hand, a word of commendation, will sometimes do wonders in the way of winning young hearts' (p. 35). It should be pointed out, however, that a number of educationists worried that children might become over-dependent on praise. See, for instance, Elizabeth Mayo, *Practical Remarks on Infant Education* (London, 1837), p. 30.
47. The 'Master and Pupil' poem in *The Professor* speaks of the pupil's learning to read her master's approval (he 'begrudged and stinted praise') in his face, claiming that this was her 'best meed' (XXIII. 202–205; pp. 235–9 in Winnifrith's edition of *The Poems of Charlotte Brontë*).
48. Cf., for instance, Rollin's *Traité*, pp. IV. 325–47.
49. Admitting that annual examinations have their uses in a parochial school, John Sandford emphasised that they 'should be conducted with as little parade as possible, and so as actually to test the knowledge of the children', by someone other than the master and on unprepared subjects; *Parochialia; or, Church, School, and Parish [and so on]* (London, 1845), p. 183. (Sandford did not oppose prize-giving, as long as recipients really deserved their distinctions.)
50. Cf., for instance, Rollin's *Traité*, p. IV. 292: 'La distribution des prix qui se fait à la fin de l'année avec solennité est un des moyens les plus efficaces pour exciter et entretenir l'émulation dont je parle'.
51. See, for instance, Barker, *The Brontës*, pp. 174 and 237.
52. See Hulmes, 'The Brontë heroines', p. 34.
53. See Barker, *The Brontës*, p. 173.
54. Page iv in the Preface to the 2nd edition of *The Universal Preceptor* (1811).
55. *Ibid.*, pp. vi–vii.
56. *Practical Education* I, pp. 444–5 in the 1815 edition. Much earlier, Isaac Watts had opposed the same idea; see E. S. Lawrence, *The Origins*, p. 143.
57. On this mainstay of education, well known to the Brontës, see above p. 88. On the connection between the Brontë family and Mangnall's Crofton Hall, see Barker, *The Brontës*, pp. 117–18, and Chris Butcher, 'Richmal Mangnall and the Brontë Connection', *Brontë Studies* 29 (Nov. 2004), 229–36. Cf. Flint, *The Woman Reader*, pp. 39 and 193.

58. *The Child's Guide to Knowledge, Being a Collection of Useful and Familiar Questions and Answers, ON EVERYDAY SUBJECTS, ADAPTED FOR YOUNG PERSONS, And arranged in the simplest and easiest language*, 'by a Lady' [Mrs Fanny Ward], pp. 73 and 77 in the enlarged third edition of 1830.

59. The copy I read, published in Whitby, carried no date but seems to have appeared around 1820; the quoted snippet of interrogation appears on p. 4. Subsequent responses have the child proclaim that the way to be saved goes by repentance and believing in Jesus Christ, and that two of several reasons for not telling lies are that 'God may strike us dead' and that '[a]ll liars shall have their portion in the lake of fire'; see pp. 13 and 25.

60. In 1839, for instance, in connection with the Government Plan for Promoting National Education, both Russell and Lansdowne spoke out against the practice of making children learn the catechism by heart without (and that was of course the important point) understanding it. Their speeches, on 20 June 1839 (Russell to the Commons) and 5 July (Lansdowne to the Lords) were separately printed; see pages 10 and 29 respectively.

61. Frances Power Cobbe's account of the noise in the expensive but ineffectual girls' school she attended is a classic in the history of female education in the early nineteenth century. See *Life of Frances Power Cobbe, as told by herself* (London: Swan Sonnenschein & Co., 1904), p. 61. On distracting noise in monitorial schools, see Horn, *Education in Rural England*, pp. 44–5.

62. *Governess Life*, p. 87.

63. *An Inquiry*, p. 38.

64. For an example of the use of the word 'repetitions' from Charlotte Brontë's letters, see Smith, *Letters* I, p. 145.

65. For two nineteenth-century examples, see *Les Ornemens [sic] de la mémoire, ou Les Traits brillans des poètes français les plus célèbres*, the fifth edition of which was published in Paris in 1835, and H. Courthope Bowen's *Studies in English for the Use of Modern Schools: Prose and Poetry to be Learnt by Heart* (London, 1876). In the eighteenth century, Kames included a selection of prose tales and poetry of an edifying nature 'to be got by Heart for improving the Memory' at the end of his *Loose Hints* (pp. 311–48).

66. *Modern Accomplishments*, p. 111.

67. Carlyle's *Sartor Resartus: The Life and Opinions of Herr Teufelsdröckh in Three Books*, ch. III ('Pedagogy'), p. 75 in P. C. Parr's 1913 Clarendon Press edition.

68. Howson, *A History*, p. 89.

69. See Adamson, *English Education*, p. 282, and Kamm, *Hope Deferred*, pp. 168–9.

70. 'An inquiry into the state of girls' fashionable schools', *Fraser's* vol. XXXI (June 1845), 707.

71. See above p. 4.

72. On this book, see p. 35 above.

73. '[S]chool-rules, school-duties, school-habits and notions, and voices, and faces, and phrases, and costumes, and preferences, and antipathies: such was what I

knew of existence. And now I felt that it was not enough: I tired of the routine of eight years in one afternoon' (*Jane Eyre* I.x.85).

SECTION V ORIGINALITY AND FREEDOM

1. The extent to which the Brontë novels shocked contemporary readers has often been exaggerated; for a balanced view, see Kathleen Tillotson, *Novels of the Eighteen-Forties* (Oxford: Clarendon Press, 1954), pp. 54–64 and 258–60 (the latter on *Jane Eyre*).

CHAPTER 14 DOCILITY AND ORIGINALITY

1. Shuttleworth goes so far as to say that this sentence aligns Jane, in her relationship with Adèle, with Mrs Reed; see *Charlotte Brontë*, p. 181. Laura Morgan Green finds Jane's concluding words about Adèle 'chilling'; see *Educating Women: Cultural Conflict and Victorian Literature* (Athens: Ohio University Press, 2001), pp. 42–3. See also Boumelha, *Charlotte Brontë*, p. 70, and Fraiman, *Unbecoming Women*, p. 109.
2. The OED 1 definition *s.v.* 'docile' reads 'Apt to be taught; ready and willing to receive instruction; teachable', supplying an 1845 quotation from Sarah Austin: 'His docile and intelligent pupil'. For instance, Mary Rivers is 'docile' when taught drawing by Jane Eyre (III.iv.350–1); Justine Marie in *Villette* is said to be 'docile and amiable' if not very bright (XLI.490); and Caroline Helstone is a 'docile' pupil (*Shirley* I.vi.76). (In a few other passages from *Shirley*, however, 'docile' does suggest subjugation; see I.vii.100 and III.viii.560.) When Jane begins to teach Adèle, she finds the child 'disinclined to apply' but 'sufficiently docile' (I.xi.103).
3. T. W. Bamford (ed.), *Thomas Arnold on Education: A Selection from his Writings* (Cambridge University Press, 1970), p. 63.
4. Ch. XIV of George Eliot's *Silas Marner*, p. 129 in the World's Classics edition of 1996, edited by Terence Cave.
5. Cf. above pp. 109–10.
6. Quoted from Lonoff, *The Belgian Essays*, p. 249. On the opposite page, Lonoff translates: 'Genius, without study and without art, without the knowledge of what has been done, is force without the lever; it is Demosthenes, a sublime orator, who stammers and gets himself hissed; it is the soul that sings within and which, to express its inner songs, has only a rude and uncultivated voice. . . Certainly the lapidary does not make the diamond, but without the lapidary the most beautiful diamond is a pebble. Poet or not, then, study form. If a poet you will be more powerful & your works will live. If not, you will not create poetry, but you will savor its merit and its charms.' The later essay on 'Athens saved by poetry' is also relevant; see pp. 334ff. in Lonoff and Duthie, *Foreign Vision*, pp. 209–10.
7. For a thorough discussion of 'genius' in the Brussels essays and the role of the concept in Charlotte Brontë's development, see Lonoff, *The Belgian Essays*,

pp. l–lv and lxxi. Barker deals with the relevant essays at some length, too; see *The Brontës*, pp. 414–18. See also Shuttleworth, *Charlotte Brontë*, p. 65.

8. Houghton provides a lucid summary of the after-effects of the Romantic idea of the genius as truth oracle in *The Victorian Frame of Mind*, pp. 152–4; see also pp. 306–307.

9. See Lonoff, *The Belgian Essays*, pp. 270–3.

10. See Smith, *Letters* II, p. 202, and Pam Morris, 'Heroes', 291. Carlyle devoted most of his chapter on 'The hero as man of letters' to Johnson, Rousseau and Burns (all of whom failed, in his view, to attain Goethe's stature), because 'the general state of knowledge about Goethe' in Britain was so poor; p. 255. (Carlyle was less than enthusiastic about Rousseau, thinking him a 'sadly *contracted* hero' warped by '*Egoism*'; but at least he was 'heartily *in earnest*', pp. 299–300 (emphases in the original).)

11. See Smith, *Letters* II, pp. 251 and 254.

12. *Ibid.*, p. 202.

13. For example Harriet Martineau, Margaret Fuller, Elizabeth Barrett and Marian Evans.

14. The *Monthly Review* 155 (May 1841), quoted in D. J. Trela and Rodger L. Tarr, *The Critical Response to Thomas Carlyle's Major Works* (Westport, CN: Greenwood Press, 1997), p. 97. Charlotte Brontë was one of the many who found Carlyle's 'Germanisms' annoying; see Smith, *Letters* II, p. 74.

15. Handbook wisdom has it that originality only became a virtue as a result of the Romantic upheaval in literature and culture, but the eighteenth century had also eulogised originality and genius. See, for instance, Francis Gallaway, *Reason, Rule, and Revolt in English Classicism* (Lexington: University of Kentucky Press, 1966), pp. 218–25. Incidentally, Charlotte Brontë's copy of Mangnall's *Questions*, published in 1813, praises William Cowper as an 'original genius' (p. 223), and La Fontaine's miscellaneous works are said to 'possess the merit of originality'.

16. See Gallaway, *Reason, Rule, and Revolt*, pp. 221–2. An 1846 dialogue on 'Female authorship' in *Fraser's* stressed that no writer should ever imitate, but stick to his or her own style (vol. XXXIII, April 1846, 462).

17. Smith, *Letters* II, p. 197.

18. Smith, *Letters* II, p. 98. Cf. Tillotson, *Novels*, p. 288.

19. Cf. *Villette* XXI.234: 'I had great pleasure in reading a few books, but not many: preferring always those in whose style or sentiment the writer's individual nature was plainly stamped; flagging inevitably over characterless books, however clever and meritorious'.

20. See especially Chapter 7 ('Interpreting Emily') in Lucasta Miller's *The Brontë Myth* (London: Vintage, 2001), pp. 170–99. Cf. also Barker, *The Brontës*, pp. 654–7. (Barker's hostile attitude to Charlotte shows in such expressions as 'her peculiar gift for reinventing the past where her sisters were concerned' (p. 598), employed when describing a period of desperate grief.) Charlotte's role in shaping the image of Emily had of course been remarked on before; see, for instance, Lyn Pykett's *Emily Brontë* (Basingstoke: Macmillan, 1989),

pp. 2–17. (A volume in the Macmillan series on women writers, Pykett's forthright and humane book is an excellent introduction to Emily.)

21. It should, however, be pointed out that one of the leading Brontë biographers, Edward Chitham, disagrees with the often-repeated hypothesis that Charlotte destroyed early and Gondal work by Emily and Anne, saying that there is 'absolutely no evidence for this'; see Chitham's extremely useful *A Brontë Family Chronology* (Basingstoke: Palgrave Macmillan, 2003), p. 213. Robert Barnard, another Brontë veteran whose instincts command respect, believes that Emily herself destroyed both the second novel and the Gondal writings because 'she wanted to be remembered only by work in which she could feel a total confidence and pride' (*Emily Brontë*, p. 93).

22. Reprinted in the World's Classics edition of *Wuthering Heights*, to which quotations in the present discussion refer. These three texts are also reprinted in Smith, *Letters* II, Appendix II, pp. 742–53. Smith draws attention to some inaccuracies in the texts in n. 1 on p. 474 in the same volume, after the letter to Williams where Charlotte states the purpose of the 'Biographical Notice' as '[giving] a just idea of their identity' (p. 474). Smith corrects the errors while justly characterising this document as 'illuminating and irreplaceable'.

23. See *The Brontë Myth*, p. 192.

24. See above pp. 128–9.

25. By the time she wrote this text Charlotte Brontë had come to know at least one 'learned' woman personally, namely Harriet Martineau, whose prodigious intellectual capabilities could have made even a Brontë feel inferior with regard to education.

26. Nor would Charlotte Brontë regard 'learning' as the highest good in an educational context. Cf. Johnson's *Dictionary of the English Language*, in which the following quotation from Locke is used to make an important distinction: 'Till a man can judge whether they be truths or no, his understanding is but little improved: and thus men of much reading are greatly *learned*, but may be little knowing' (*s.v.* 'learned').

27. The last quotation is from the OED definition quoted above.

28. In respect of Anne, Miller is both fair and eloquent; see pp. 156–8 in *The Brontë Myth*. For a fresh and thought-provoking presentation of Anne Brontë as 'the most successful author in the Brontë family' at the time of her death, see Bock, 'Authorship', 252–3.

29. The quotation is from the *Spectator* review of 8 July 1848 (XXI, 662–3) and appears on p. 250 in Allott's *Critical Heritage* volume.

30. For instance, the *Literary World* reviewer of *The Tenant of Wildfell Hall* described it as 'infinitely inferior' to *Jane Eyre* (12 August 1848); see p. 259 in *The Critical Heritage*. (Incidentally, this reviewer believed all the 'Bell' novels to have been written by the same (woman) writer, to whom he/she repeatedly ascribed 'genius'.)

31. Cf. Lucy Snowe's discourse on the intractable tyrant 'the Creative Impulse', *Villette* XXX.356–7, and Smith, *Letters* II, p. 10 (the letter to G. H. Lewes of 12 January 1848). To the extent that Charlotte Brontë's representations of her

sisters downplayed their serious artistry and deliberate deskwork, she dealt with their professional concerns as she did with her own. Even in letters to people she knew and trusted, she was reticent about the workshop aspects of her writing. A point made by Tillotson (*Novels*, pp. 89–90) is relevant here: when Charlotte Brontë wrote her preface to *Wuthering Heights*, she had experienced London society and realised that the Yorkshire people depicted in Emily's book must seem 'alien', and hence in need of an apologia, to cultured Southerners.

CHAPTER 15 LIBERTY AND RESPONSIBILITY

1. See Smith, *Letters* I, p. 218; Charlotte tells her friend that she expects to remain single.
2. Cf. *Jane Eyre* II.vi.237, where Jane juxtaposes feeling and judgement in relation to the Reed sisters, concluding that the presence of one quality without the other makes a person unbearable.
3. The following lines in Hannah More's *Moral Sketches* are underlined in the Haworth copy: 'Judgment is so far from being a cooler of zeal, as some suppose, that it increases its effects by directing its movements; and a warm heart will always produce more extensive, because more lasting good, when conducted by a cool head' (pp. 124–5).
4. Cf. Smith, *Letters* I, p. 253. Of her employer Mrs White, 25-year-old Charlotte Brontë wrote, 'If any little thing goes wrong she does not scruple to give way to anger in a very coarse unladylike manner – though in justice no blame could be attached where she ascribed it all – I think passion is the true test of vulgarity or refinement'.
5. One of Patrick Brontë's *Cottage Poems* (Halifax, 1811), 'Epistle to the Rev. J– B–', refers to the passions as '[t]hese imps of hell!' (p. 9). F. D. Maurice's novel hero Eustace Conway speaks of 'those great enemies of knowledge – the passions'; *Eustace Conway, or, The Brother and Sister* (London, 1834), vol. I, p. 162.
6. *Forms of Feeling in Victorian Fiction* (Athens: Ohio University Press, 1985), p. 103. See also David Lodge's classic analysis of elemental imagery in *Jane Eyre*, 'Fire and Eyre: Charlotte Brontë's war of earthly elements' in *Language of Fiction: Essays in Criticism and Verbal Analysis of the English Novel* (London: Routledge and Kegan Paul, 1966), pp. 114–43.
7. Page 327 in *Wuthering Heights* (from 'Editor's Preface'). The other characteristic that redeems Heathcliff from utter monstrosity in Charlotte's eyes is 'his half-implied esteem for Nelly Dean'.
8. See, for instance, Sue Lonoff, 'Broadening minds with the Brontës', *Brontë Studies* 28.3 (Nov. 2003), 198.
9. See Thormählen, *The Brontës and Religion*, pp. 138 and 140–1.
10. As Stevie Davies says, 'Love and education retrieve him'; *Emily Brontë: Heretic* (London: The Women's Press, 1994), p. 121.
11. See Thormählen, *The Brontës and Religion*, pp. 69–70 and 79–80. In Thomas Vargish's characteristically succinct words, '[p]rayers are answered with a

promptness and consistency worthy of attentive omnipotence' in *Jane Eyre*; *The Providential Aesthetic in Victorian Fiction* (Charlottesville: University Press of Virginia, 1985), p. 60.

12. Cf. Mr Weston's satisfaction at having his own parish because there is 'nobody to interfere with [him]' (*Agnes Grey* XXIV.191). See also Smith, *Letters* I, p. 317, where Charlotte Brontë expresses her relief, to Branwell, at not being 'interfered with' in Brussels.

13. See Thormählen, *The Brontës and Religion*, pp. 164–7.

14. Cf. the Rev. H. Highton's sermon on the death of Dr Thomas Arnold, preached in the Church of St Matthew, Rugby, on Sunday, June 19th, 1842: 'Another great distinguishing point in his character, and one which he also pressed constantly on others as of the very greatest importance, was *individual independence of mind*. A belief and a conviction, founded merely on the belief and convictions of other men . . . was no belief at all of our own. It was merely the belief of other men, not of ourselves. The spirit of despotism, and any claim to exclusive privileges, we know he abandoned in all things, but most of all, despotism and claims of exclusive authority in matters of the mind and spirit. Oppression of all kinds is *atrocious*, but *spiritual* tyranny is *devilish*' (separately printed by Hatchard *et al.*, pp. 7–8).

15. Page 329 in the World's Classics edition of *Wuthering Heights*.

16. *Jane Eyre* III.i.317.

Select bibliography

Names of publishers are not supplied in respect of works published before 1900. The place of publication is London unless otherwise stated. Extremely long titles (in the primary sources) have been abbreviated. The letters '**BPM**' at the end of an entry on a primary source signify that the relevant volume is in the collection of books once owned by the Brontës in the Brontë Parsonage Museum. For the editions of the Brontë novels that were used in this book, see Abbreviations and editions.

PRIMARY SOURCES

Abbott, Jacob, *The Teacher, or, Moral Influences Employed in the Instruction and Government of the Young; Intended Chiefly to Assist Young Teachers in Organizing and Conducting Their Schools*, Boston, 1833.

Anon., *Advice to Governesses*, 1827.

— *The Complete Governess: A Course of Mental Instruction for Ladies; with a Notice on the Principal Female Accomplishments*, 1826.

— *The Governess, or, Politics in Private Life*, 1836.

— *Woman's Worth: or, Hints to Raise the Female Character*, 1844.

Appleton, Elizabeth, *Private Education; or, A Practical Plan for the Studies of Young Ladies*, 2nd revised edn, 1816.

Baines, Edward Jr, *Letters to the Right Honourable Lord John Russell [and so on] on State Education*, 7th edn, 1847.

Barbauld, Anna Laetitia, *A Legacy for Young Ladies*, 1826.

Belloc, Bessie Rayner, *Remarks on the Education of Girls*, 1854.

Blair, David, *The Universal Preceptor; being an easy Grammar of Arts, Sciences, and General Knowledge*, 2nd edn, 1811.

Brontë, Anne, *The Poems of Anne Brontë: A New Text and Commentary*, ed. Edward Chitham, Macmillan, 1979.

Brontë, Charlotte, *An Edition of the Early Writings of Charlotte Brontë*, 3 vols, ed. Christine Alexander, Oxford: Basil Blackwell/Shakespeare Head Press, 1987 and 1991.

— *The Poems of Charlotte Brontë*, ed. Tom Winnifrith, Oxford: Basil Blackwell/Shakespeare Head Press, 1984.

Brontë, Emily, *Emily Jane Brontë: The Complete Poems*, ed. Janet Gezari, Harmondsworth: Penguin, 1992.

Brontë, Patrick, *The Maid of Killarney; or, Albion and Flora*, 1818.

— *The Letters of the Reverend Patrick Brontë*, ed. Dudley Green, Stroud: Nonsuch, 2005.

Broughton, Trev, and Ruth Symes (eds), *The Governess: An Anthology*, Phoenix Mill: Sutton, 1997.

Buckworth, John, *A Series of Discourses, Containing a System of Doctrinal, Experimental, and Practical Religion, Particularly Calculated for the Use of Families*, Leeds, 1811. **BPM**.

Carlyle, Thomas, *On Heroes, Hero-Worship, and the Heroic in History*, 1841.

Carpenter, Lant, Jeremiah Joyce and William Shepherd, *Systematic Education: or, Elementary Instruction in the Various Departments of Literature and Science, with Practical Rules for Studying Each Branch of Useful Knowledge*, 3rd edn, 1822.

Chapone, (Mrs) Hester, *Letters on the Improvement of the Mind*, first publ. in 1773; the edn used for the present study appeared in Edinburgh in 1821.

Claxton, Timothy, *Hints to Mechanics, on Self-Education and Mutual Instruction*, 1839.

Combe, George, *Lectures on Popular Education*, corrected and enlarged edn, Edinburgh, 1837.

Dunn, Henry, *Principles of Teaching; or, the Normal School Manual: Containing Practical Suggestions on the Government and Instruction of Children*, 3rd enlarged edn, 1839.

Edgeworth, Maria, and Richard Lovell Edgeworth, *Essays on Practical Education*, 1798. Published in many editions; the one used for this book appeared in 1815 (2 vols).

Ellis, Sarah, *The Daughters of England: Their Position in Society, Character, and Responsibilities*, 1842 and 1845.

— *The Women of England, Their Social Duties, and Domestic Habits*, 3rd edn, 1839.

Fresnoy, Abbé Lenglet du, *Geography for Youth: Or, a short and easy Method of Teaching and Learning Geography [and so on]*, Dublin, 1795. **BPM**.

Gaskell, Elizabeth, *The Life of Charlotte Brontë*, 1857. Many editions have appeared over the years; the one used for this book is the 1960 reprint of the Everyman edn.

Goldsmith, the Rev. J. [pseud. for Sir Richard Phillips?], *A Grammar of General Geography*, new and corrected edn, 1823. **BPM**.

Gosden, P. H. J. H. (ed.), *How They Were Taught: An Anthology of Contemporary Accounts of Learning and Teaching in England*, Oxford: Blackwell, 1969.

Hamilton, Elizabeth, *Letters on the Elementary Principles of Education*, 7th edn, 1824.

Hickson, W. E., *Dutch and German Schools. An account of the present state of education in Holland, Belgium, and the German states [and so on]*, 1840.

Higson, C. W. J. (ed.), *Sources for the History of Education*, The Library Association, 1967.

Hoare, Louisa, *Friendly Advice, on the Management and Education of Children; addressed to Parents of the Middle and Labouring Classes of Society*, 1824.

Hodgson, J. S., *Considerations on Phrenology, in connexion with an Intellectual, Moral, and Religious Education*, 1839.

Home, Henry, Lord Kames, *Loose Hints upon Education, Chiefly Concerning the Culture of the Heart*, 1781.

Hook, Walter Farquhar, *On the Means of Rendering More Efficient the Education of the People. A Letter to the Lord Bishop of St. David's*, 1846.

Irving, David, *The Elements of English Composition*, 8th edn, Edinburgh, 1828.

Jennings, James, *An Inquiry concerning the Nature and Operations of the Human Mind, in which the Science of Phrenology, the Doctrine of Necessity, Punishment, and Education, are particularly considered*, 1828.

Johnson, Benjamin, *A Grammar of Classical Literature*, 1821.

Lempriere, John, *Bibliotheca Classica; or, A Classical Dictionary, containing a full account of all the proper names mentioned in antient authors [and so on]*, 3rd edn, 1797. **BPM**.

Lonoff, Sue (ed.), *The Belgian Essays Charlotte and Emily Brontë: A Critical Edition*, New Haven: Yale University Press, 1996.

Lyons, J. C., *The Science of Phrenology, as applicable to Education, Friendship, Love, Courtship, and Matrimony, Etc.*, 1846.

Macaulay, Catharine (later Graham), *Letters on Education. With observations on religious and metaphysical subjects*, Dublin, 1790.

Mangnall, Richmal, *Historical and Miscellaneous Questions, for the Use of Young People; with a Selection of British, and General Biography [and so on]*, 10th edn, 1813. **BPM**.

Mann, Horace, *Census of Great Britain, 1851. Education in Great Britain: Being the Official Report [and so on]*, 1854.

Martineau, Harriet, *Deerbrook*, 1839.

— *The History of England during the Thirty Years' Peace 1816–1846*, 2 vols, 1849 and 1850.

— *Household Education*, 1849.

Maurice, Mary, *Aids to Developement; or, Mental and Moral Instruction Exemplified*, 2 vols, 1829.

— *Governess Life: Its Trials, Duties, and Encouragements*, 1849.

More, Hannah, *Coelebs in Search of a Wife*, 1809; 1995 ed. by Thoemmes Press, Bristol, with an introduction by Mary Waldron.

— *Moral Sketches of Prevailing Opinions and Manners, Foreign and Domestic: with Reflections on Prayer*, 3rd edn, 1819. **BPM**.

— *Strictures on the Modern System of Female Education with a View to the Principles and Conduct of Women of Rank and Fortune*, 1799.

Murray, Lindley. *English Grammar, adapted to the Different Classes of Learners*, 13th edn, 1818. **BPM**.

Parkes, Mrs William, *Domestic Duties, or, Instructions to Young Married Ladies on the Management of Their Households [and so on]*, 1825.

Pinnock, W. *A Comprehensive Grammar of the English Language: With Exercises; Written in a Familiar Style, Accompanied with Questions for Examination, and Notes Critical and Explanatory*, 1830. **BPM**.

'Porny, Mr' (Antoine Pyron du Martre), *Grammatical Exercises, English and French*, 12th edn, 1810. **BPM**.

Rabenhorst Pocket Dictionary of the German and English Languages, 5th edn, 1843. **BPM**.

Richmond, Legh, *Domestic Portraiture [and so on]*, 5th edn, 1839.

Rollin, Charles, *Traité des études*, 1726–1731; the edition used for this study was published in Paris in 1838.

Rowbotham, John, *Deutsches Lesebuch; Or, Lessons in German Literature [and so on]*, 1837. **BPM**.

Salmon, Thomas, *A New Geographical and Historical Grammar: Wherein the Geographical Part is Truly Modern [and so on]*, Edinburgh, 1771. **BPM**.

Sandford, Elizabeth ('Mrs John'), *Female Improvement*, 2 vols, 1836.

Sinclair, Catherine, *Modern Accomplishments, or The March of the Intellect*, 1836.

Smith, Margaret (ed.), *The Letters of Charlotte Brontë with a Selection of Letters by Family and Friends*, Oxford: Clarendon Press. Vol. I, *1829–1847*, 1995; vol. II, *1848–1851*, 2000; vol. III, *1852–1855*, 2004.

Stodart, M. A., *Female Writers: Thoughts on Their Proper Sphere, and on Their Powers of Usefulness*, 1842.

— *Hints on Reading: Addressed to a Young Lady*, 1839.

Taylor, (Mrs) Ann, *Reciprocal Duties of Parents and Children*, 1818.

Tholfsen, Trygve R. (ed.), *Sir James Kay-Shuttleworth on Popular Education*, New York: Teachers College Press, 1974.

Thornley, Margaret, *The True End of Education and the Means Adapted to It: In a series of letters to a lady entering on the duties of her profession as private governess*, Edinburgh, 1846.

Tocquot, J. F., *A New and Easy Guide to the Pronunciation and Spelling of the French Language*, 1806. **BPM**.

Voster, Elias, *Arithmetic in Whole and Broken Numbers [and so on]*, Dublin, 1789. **BPM**.

Wakefield, Priscilla, *Reflections on the Present Condition of the Female Sex, with Suggestions for Its Improvement*, 2nd edn, 1817.

Watts, Isaac, *The Improvement of the Mind*, 1741. The edition used for this study was published in 1821.

West, (Mrs) Jane, *Letters to a Young Lady, in which the duties and character of women are considered [and so on]*, 1806.

Wilderspin, Samuel, *On the Importance of Educating the Infant Poor [and so on]*, 2nd edn, 1824.

Wollstonecraft, Mary, *Thoughts on the Education of Daughters*, 1787; 1995 facsimile edn from Thoemmes, Bristol.

Wright, George, *Thoughts in Younger Life on Interesting Subjects; or, Poems, Letters, and Essays, Moral, Elegiac, and Descriptive*, 1778. **BPM**.

Yolton, John W. and Jean S. (eds), *John Locke: Some Thoughts Concerning Education*, Oxford: Clarendon Press, 1989; first publ. in 1693.

SECONDARY SOURCES

Adamson, John William, *English Education 1789–1902*, Cambridge University Press, 1930.
Alexander, Christine, *The Early Writings of Charlotte Brontë*, Oxford: Blackwell, 1983.
Alexander, Christine, and Jane Sellars, *The Art of the Brontës*, Cambridge University Press, 1995.
Alexander, Christine, and Margaret Smith (eds), *The Oxford Companion to the Brontës*, Oxford University Press, 2003.
Allott, Miriam (ed.), *The Brontës: The Critical Heritage*, Routledge and Kegan Paul, 1974.
Altick, Richard D., *The English Common Reader: A Social History of the Mass Reading Public, 1800–1900*, Columbus: Ohio State University Press, 1957; the 1998 edition was used for this book.
Barber, Lynn, *The Heyday of Natural History: 1820–1870*, Jonathan Cape, 1980.
Barker, Juliet, *The Brontës*, Weidenfeld & Nicolson, 1994.
Barnard, Robert, *Emily Brontë*, The British Library Writers' Lives series, 2000.
Barney, Richard A., *Plots of Enlightenment: Education and the Novel in Eighteenth-Century England*, Stanford University Press, 1999.
Baumber, Michael, 'Patrick Brontë and the development of primary education in Haworth', *BST* 24, Pt 1 (April 1999), 66–81.
Berglund, Birgitta, 'In defence of Madame Beck', *Brontë Studies* 30.3 (Nov. 2005), 185–211.
Binns, Henry Bryan, *A Century of Education: Being the Centenary History of the British & Foreign School Society 1808–1908*, Dent, 1908.
Birchenough, C., *History of Elementary Education in England and Wales from 1800 to the Present Day*, W. B. Clive, 1914.
Björk, Harriet, *The Language of Truth: Charlotte Brontë, the Woman Question, and the Novel*, Lund: Gleerup, 1974.
Bock, Carol, *Charlotte Brontë and the Storyteller's Audience*, Iowa City: University of Iowa Press, 1992.
Boumelha, Penny, *Charlotte Brontë*, Harvester Wheatsheaf, 1990.
Bowen, James, *A History of Western Education*, vol. III, 'The modern West Europe and the New World', Methuen, 1981.
Briggs, Asa, *The Age of Improvement 1783–1867*, 1959; the edition used for this study appeared from Longman in 2000 (Harlow).
Brooke, Susan, 'Anne Brontë at Blake Hall: An episode of courage and insight', *BST* 13.68 (1958), 239–50.
Burstyn, Joan, *Victorian Education and the Ideal of Womanhood*, Croom Helm, 1980.

Byerly, Alison, *Realism, Representation, and the Arts in Nineteenth-Century Literature*, Cambridge University Press, 1997.

Chadwick, Esther Alice, *In the Footsteps of the Brontës*, Pitman, 1914.

Chitham, Edward, *The Birth of* Wuthering Heights: *Emily Brontë at Work*, Basingstoke: Macmillan, 1998.

— *A Brontë Family Chronology*. Basingstoke: Palgrave, 2003.

— *A Life of Anne Brontë*, Oxford: Blackwell, 1991.

— *A Life of Emily Brontë*, Oxford: Blackwell, 1987.

Colley, Linda, *Britons: Forging the Nation 1707–1837*, New Haven: Yale University Press, 1992.

Collins, Philip, *Dickens and Education*, Macmillan, 1965.

Craik, W. A., *The Brontë Novels*, Methuen, 1968.

Davidoff, Leonore, and Catherine Hall, *Family Fortunes: Men and Women of the English Middle Class, 1750–1850*, 1987; the revised Routledge reprint of 2002 was used for this study.

Davies, Stevie, *Emily Brontë*, Northcote House and British Council, Writers and Their Work series, 1998.

Digby, Anne, and Peter Searby, *Children, School and Society in Nineteenth-Century England*, Basingstoke: Macmillan, 1981.

Duckett, R. J. (ed.), *The Brontës and Education: Papers Presented to the Brontë Society Weekend September 2004*, Haworth: The Brontë Society, 2005.

Duthie, Enid L., *The Foreign Vision of Charlotte Brontë*, Macmillan, 1975.

Eagleton, Terry, *Myths of Power: A Marxist Study of the Brontës*, Basingstoke: Macmillan, 1975, reissued by Palgrave in 2005.

Ewbank, Inga-Stina, *Their Proper Sphere: A Study of the Brontë Sisters as Early-Victorian Female Novelists*, Cambridge/MA.: Harvard University Press, 1966.

Fergenson, Laraine, 'Using collaborative learning to teach the themes of education, ignorance, and dispossession in *Wuthering Heights*', in Sue Lonoff and Terri A. Hasseler, *Approaches to Teaching Emily Brontë's* Wuthering Heights, New York: The Modern Language Association of America, 2006, 167–74.

Flint, Kate, *The Woman Reader 1837–1914*, Oxford: Clarendon Press, 1993.

Fraser, Rebecca, *Charlotte Brontë*, Methuen, 1988.

Frawley, Maria, *Anne Brontë*, New York: Twayne, 1996.

Gérin, Winifred, *Charlotte Brontë: The Evolution of Genius*, Oxford University Press, 1967.

— *Anne Brontë*, Nelson, 1959; the Allen Lane paperback of 1976 was used for this study.

Glen, Heather, *Charlotte Brontë: The Imagination in History*, Oxford University Press, 2002.

Glen, Heather (ed.), *The Cambridge Companion to the Brontës*, Cambridge University Press, 2002.

Goldstrom, J. M., *The Social Content of Education 1808–1870: A Study of the Working Class School Reader in England and Ireland*, Shannon: Irish University Press, 1972.

Green, Andy, *Education and State Formation: The Rise of Education Systems in England, France and the USA*, Basingstoke: Macmillan, 1990.

Hadow, Sir William Henry, 'Education, as treated by the Brontës', *BST* 6 (1925), 261–75.

Hammond, J. L., and Barbara Hammond, *The Age of the Chartists 1832–1854: A Study of Discontents*, Longman, 1930; repr. in 1967 by Reprints of Economic Classics, New York: Kelley.

Hardy, Barbara, *Forms of Feeling in Victorian Fiction*, Athens: Ohio University Press, 1985.

Hesketh, Sally, 'Needlework in the lives and novels of the Brontë sisters', *BST* 22 (1997), 72–85.

Hewish, John, *Emily Brontë: A Critical and Biographical Study*, Macmillan, 1969.

Horn, Pamela, *Education in Rural England 1800–1914*, Dublin: Gill and Macmillan, 1978.

— 'The Victorian governess', *History of Education* 18.4 (1989), 333–44.

Houghton, Walter E., *The Victorian Frame of Mind 1830–1870*, New Haven: Yale University Press, 1957.

Hughes, Kathryn, *The Victorian Governess*, Hambledon Press, 1993.

Kamm, Josephine, *Hope Deferred: Girls' Education in English History*, Methuen, 1965.

Knies, Earl A., *The Art of Charlotte Brontë*, Athens: Ohio University Press, 1969.

Lamonica, Drew, *'We Are Three Sisters': Self and Family in the Writing of the Brontës*, Columbia: University of Missouri Press, 2003.

Langland, Elizabeth, *Anne Brontë: The Other One*, Basingstoke: Macmillan, 1989.

Lawrence, E. S., *The Origins and Growth of Modern Education*, Harmondsworth: Penguin, 1970.

Lawson, John and Harold Silver, *A Social History of Education in England*, Methuen, 1973.

Layton, David, *Science for the People: The Origins of the School Science Curriculum in England*, Allen and Unwin, 1973.

Lecaros, Cecilia Wadsö, *The Victorian Governess Novel*, Lund University Press, 2001.

Lock, John, and W. T. Dixon, *A Man of Sorrow: The Life, Letters and Times of the Rev. Patrick Brontë*, Nelson, 1965.

Lonoff, Sue, 'The Education of Charlotte Brontë: A pedagogical case study', *Pedagogy: Critical Approaches to Teaching Literature, Language, Composition, and Culture* 1.3 (2001), 457–77.

Losano, Antonia, 'The professionalization of the woman artist in Anne Brontë's *The Tenant of Wildfell Hall*', *Nineteenth-Century Literature* 58.1 (June 2003), 1–41.

Macdonald, Frederika, *The Secret of Charlotte Brontë: Some Reminiscences of the Real Monsieur and Madame Heger*, T. C. & E. C. Jack, 1914.

McKibben, Robert, 'The image of the book in *Wuthering Heights*', *Nineteenth-Century Fiction* 15.2 (1960), 159–69.

McLeish, John, *Evangelical Religion and Popular Education: A Modern Interpretation*, Methuen, 1969.

Martin, Robert Bernard, *The Accents of Persuasion: Charlotte Brontë's Novels*, Faber & Faber, 1966.

Mattisson, Jane, *Knowledge and Survival in the Novels of Thomas Hardy*, Lund Studies in English No. 101, Lund, 2002.

Merrill, Lynn L., *The Romance of Victorian Natural History*, Oxford University Press, 1989.

Miller, Lucasta, *The Brontë Myth*, Jonathan Cape, 2001, and Vintage, 2002.

Morris, Pam, 'Heroes and hero-worship in Charlotte Brontë's *Shirley*', *Nineteenth-Century Literature* 54.3 (Dec. 1999), 285–307.

Murch, Jerom, *Mrs. Barbauld and Her Contemporaries: Sketches of Some Eminent Literary and Scientific Englishwomen*, London, 1877.

Myer, Valerie Grosvenor, *Charlotte Brontë: Truculent Spirit*, Vision, 1987.

Nash, Julie, and Barbara A. Suess (eds), *New Approaches to the Literary Art of Anne Brontë*, Aldershot: Ashgate, 2001.

Nestor, Pauline, *Charlotte Brontë*, Basingstoke: Macmillan, 1987.

Parker, Rozsika, *The Subversive Stitch: Embroidery and the Making of the Feminine*, The Women's Press, 1984.

Poovey, Mary, *Uneven Developments: The Ideological Work of Gender in Mid-Victorian England*, Chicago University Press, 1988.

Pykett, Lyn, *Emily Brontë*, Basingstoke: Macmillan, 1989.

Rauch, Alan, *Useful Knowledge: The Victorians, Morality, and the March of Intellect*, Durham: Duke University Press, 2001.

Richardson, Alan, *Literature, Education, and Romanticism: Reading as Social Practice*, Cambridge University Press, 1994.

Rogers, Philip, 'Tory Brontë: *Shirley* and the "MAN"', *Nineteenth-Century Literature* 58.2 (Sept. 2003), 141–75.

Saffin, N. W., *Science, Religion & Education in Britain 1804–1904*, Kilmore, Vict.: Lowden, 1973.

Shuttleworth, Sally, *Charlotte Brontë and Victorian Psychology*, Cambridge University Press, 1996.

Silver, Harold, *Education as History: Interpreting Nineteenth- and Twentieth-Century Education*, Methuen, 1983.

Spark, Muriel, *The Essence of the Brontës: A Compilation with Essays*, Peter Owen, 1993.

Stephens, W. B., *Education in Britain, 1750–1914*, Basingstoke: Macmillan, 1998.

Stewart, W. A. C., *Progressives and Radicals in Education 1750–1970*, Macmillan, 1972.

Stewart, W. A. C. and W. P. McCann, *The Educational Innovators: 1750–1880*, Macmillan, 1967.

Stray, Christopher, *Classics Transformed: Schools, Universities, and Society in England, 1830–1960*, Oxford: Clarendon Press, 1998.

Sturt, Mary, *The Education of the People: A History of Primary Education in England and Wales in the Nineteenth Century*, Routledge and Kegan Paul, 1967.

Theobald, Marjorie, 'The accomplished woman and the propriety of intellect: a new look at women's education in Britain and Australia, 1800–1850', *History of Education* 17.1 (1988), 21–35.

Thormählen, Marianne, *The Brontës and Religion*, Cambridge University Press, 1999.

— 'The lunatic and the Devil's disciple: The "lovers" in *Wuthering Heights*', *The Review of English Studies* 48 (May 1997), 183–97.

— '"Une saine éducation anglaise lui corrigea ses défauts français": L'école dans la fiction de Charlotte Brontë', in Guyonne Leduc (ed.), *L'Éducation des femmes en Europe et en Amérique du Nord de la renaissance à 1848*, Paris: L'Harmattan, 1997.

— 'The villain of *Wildfell Hall*: Aspects and prospects of Arthur Huntingdon', *Modern Language Review* 88.4 (Oct. 1993), 831–41.

Tillotson, Kathleen, *Novels of the Eighteen-Forties*, Oxford: Clarendon Press, 1954.

Tropp, Asher, *The School Teachers: The Growth of the Teaching Profession in England and Wales from 1800 to the Present Day*, Heinemann, 1957.

van Wyhe, John, *Phrenology and the Origins of Victorian Scientific Naturalism*, Aldershot: Ashgate, 2004.

Williams, Judith, *Perception and Expression in the Novels of Charlotte Brontë*, Ann Arbor: UMI Research Press, 1988.

Wilson, Lady Barbara, 'The Brontës as governesses', *BST* 9 (1939), 217–35.

Winnifrith, Tom, *The Brontës and Their Background. Romance and Reality*, Macmillan, 1973.

Young, G. M. (ed.), *Early Victorian Britain 1830–1865*, 2 vols, Oxford University Press, 1934.

Index

Hammond, Barbara: 248n
Hammond, J. L.: 248n
Handel (Händel), Georg Friedrich: 105
Hans, Nicholas: 227n
Hardy, Barbara: 211
Hare, Julius: 254n
Harris, Alexander: 205; Charlotte Brontë on
     205
Harris, R. W.: 225n
Harshaw, Andrew: 226n
Hasseler, Terri A. (ed.): 264n
Haydn, Joseph: 105
Hazelwood: 267n; *see also* Hill
Heger, Constantin: 6, 23, 87, 91, 112, 113, 116,
     126, 160, 164–9, 174, 180, 194, 203, 238n,
     239n
Hemans, Felicia: 145
Hennelly, Mark M., Jr: 255n
Herbart, Johann Friedrich: 155
Hesketh, Sally: 120, 256n
Hewish, John: 255n, 271n
Hickson, W. E.: 183, 218n, 220n, 252n
Highton, Rev. H.: 283n
Higson, C. W. J.: 223n, 242n, 244n, 273n
Higuchi, Akiko: 251n
Hill, George Birkbeck Norman: 246n; Hill,
     Thomas Wright 267n; Hill family at
     Hazelwood 132, 155
Himmelfarb, Gertrude: 217n
history: as subject 25, 84–90; in Charlotte
     Brontë's fiction 84, 85, 86
Hoare, Louisa: 229n, 230n
Hodgson, J. S.: 21, 22, 259n
Hoeveler, Diane Long (ed.): 232n
Hoffmann, E. T. A.: 113, 114, 116
Hogg, James: 103, 223n, 255n
Holmes, Richard: 276n
Home, Henry, Lord Kames, *see* Kames
Homer, *Iliad*: 124
Honey, J. R. de S.: 231n, 257n
Hook, Walter Farquhar: 13, 98, 218n, 220n, 239n,
     268n
Hopewell, Donald: 237n
Horace: 124, 249n
Horn, Pamela: 218n, 232n, 236n, 278n
Horsman, Alan (ed.): 258n
Houghton, Walter E.: 28, 225n, 243n, 280n
Howson, Geoffrey: 193, 268n
Hudson, J. W.: 221n
Hughes, Kathryn: 232n, 235n, 236n, 239n
Hulmes, Margaret: 274n, 275n, 277n
human-interest angle in the study of history:
     86
Hume, David: 89, 156, 243n
Hurt, John: 218n

'imitation', the concept: 205
imitation as a mode of learning: 166–7
Ingham family at Blake Hall: 40, 184
Ingham, Patricia: 234n
Inglesfield, Robert: 233n
Instruction for Children (Q&A schoolbook): 189
irreligiousness among the lower orders: 139
Irving, David: 90
Italian language: standing of 118; Charlotte
     Brontë and 117–18; *see also* accomplishments

Jenkins, Alice (ed.): 248n
Jennings, James: 40, 191
John, Juliet (ed.): 248n
Johnson, Benjamin: 126–7
Johnson, Samuel: 25, 145, 146, 224n, 280n;
     Rasselas 147; *Dictionary* 203, 281n
Jones, Donald K.: 276n
Jones, Lance G. E.: 239n
Jordan, John O. (ed.): 262n
Joyce, Jeremiah: 221n, 230n, 265n

Kambani, Marianna (ed.): 256n
Kames, Henry Home, Lord: 156, 267n, 269n,
     278n
Kamm, Josephine: 240n, 278n
Kay, Joseph: 12, 14, 218n
Kay-Shuttleworth, James: 12, 14, 74, 154, 157,
     224n; acquaintance with Charlotte Brontë
     268n
Kelly, Gary: 220n
kindness in boys, emphasis on: 43
Kingsley, Charles: 134, 248n
Knapp, Bettina L.: 275n
Knies, Earl A.: 226n, 234n

La Fontaine, Jean de: 280n
Lamartine, Alphonse Marie Louis de: 113
Lamonica, Drew: 52, 227n, 230n, 233n
Lancaster, Joseph: 70, 157, 183, 184
Lane, Christopher: 263n
Langland, Elizabeth: 233n
Lansdowne, Henry, 3rd Marquis of: 278n
Lau, Beth (ed.): 232n
Laurence, Anne (ed.): 270n
Lawrence, D. H.: 3
Lawrence, E. S.: 215n, 217n, 268n, 270n, 277n
Lawrence, Evelyn Mary (ed.): 270n
Lawson, John: 220n, 239n, 268n
Lawson, Kate: 235n
Lawton, Denis: 215n
Layton, David: 247n
'learned', the concept: 128, 258n; as applied to
     Anne and Emily Brontë 206, 207
learning by heart, *see* rote-learning